# HANI
A Life Too Short

*For Isabella, Lola and Sinead*
*and*
*Nadia, Qaim and Zorina*

# A LIFE TOO SHORT

## JANET SMITH & BEAUREGARD TROMP

Jonathan Ball Publishers
JOHANNESBURG • CAPE TOWN

All rights reserved.
No part of this publication may be reproduced or transmitted,
in any form or by any means, without prior permission
from the publisher or copyright holder.

© Janet Smith & Beauregard Tromp, 2009
© Photographic copyright holders for the pictures in the photo section
are credited with each caption.

First edition published in trade paperback in 2009 by
JONATHAN BALL PUBLISHERS (PTY) LTD
PO Box 33977
Jeppestown 2043

Reprinted twice in 2009 and once in 2010.

Printed in paperback in 2010.
Reprinted twice in 2012.

Second trade paperback edition published in 2023.
ISBN: 978-1-77619-237-3

DISCLAIMER

*The authors have made every effort to contact all those interviewees
whose interviews are used in this volume, to secure permission for
the use of their interviews. Any oversight is regretted.*

Edited by Alfred LeMaitre
Cover design by Sean Robertson
Front cover photograph by Greg Marinovich /
South Photos / Africa Media Online
Text design by Triple M Design, Johannesburg
Set in 11/16pt Minion Pro

# CONTENTS

| | | |
|---|---|---:|
| | Acknowledgements | vii |
| | Introduction | ix |
| Chapter 1 | The Roots of a Man | 1 |
| Chapter 2 | Fort Hare | 20 |
| Chapter 3 | Flight into Exile | 39 |
| Chapter 4 | The USSR | 59 |
| Chapter 5 | Kongwa | 68 |
| Chapter 6 | Wankie | 83 |
| Chapter 7 | The Memorandum | 106 |
| Chapter 8 | Lesotho | 126 |
| Chapter 9 | Kabwe | 152 |
| Chapter 10 | Angola | 170 |
| Chapter 11 | Coming Home | 209 |
| Chapter 12 | The Assassination | 231 |
| Chapter 13 | Anne Duthie | 276 |
| | Postscript | 290 |
| | Epilogue 2023 | 296 |
| | Appendices | 331 |
| | Notes on Sources | 352 |
| | Index | 364 |

# ACKNOWLEDGEMENTS

*The authors would like to thank:*

James April
Bonile Bam
Esther Barsel
George Bizos
Jennifer Bruce
Luli Callinicos
Comrade J
Diane de Beer
Antoine de Ras
Ayanda Dlodlo
Anne Duthie
Mark Gevisser
Andile Haneae
Aluta Hani
Cleopatra Hani
Nolusapho Hani

The extended Hani family
Bantu Holomisa
Johannesburg Central Library
Ronnie Kasrils
Alf Kumalo
Steve Lawrence
Joyce Leeson
Rachael Lerutla
Rashid Lombard
Hermanus Loots
The people of Lower Sabalele,
    Cofimvaba
Ben Magubane
Mac Maharaj
Thami Mali
Buti Manamela

Ike Maphoto
Emmanuel Maphatsoe
Pule Matakoane
Zakes Molotsi
Ruth Mompati
Livingstone Mqotsi
Mavuso Msimang
Linda Mti
Mothobi Mutloatse, who asked us to undertake this project in the first place
Mbulelo Mzamane
Phyllis Naidoo
Sukhthi Naidoo
Gasson Ndlovu
Castro Ngobese
Marwanqana Nondala
Alban Nyimbana
Blade Nzimande
Mahalele Qolombeni
Vino Reddy and the Gandhi-Luthuli Documentation Centre, University of KwaZulu-Natal
Patrick Ricketts
Albie Sachs
Mujahied Safodien
Christa Scholtz
Sechaba Setsubi (otherwise known as Comrade Charles)
Archie Sibeko (Zola Zembe)
Max Sisulu
Sparks

Sipho Tshabalala
University of Fort Hare, ANC archives
University of the Witwatersrand archives
Charles Villa-Vicencio

*As well as*

Moegsien Williams, editor of *The Star*, without whose unwavering support and belief the book would never have happened.
Jovial Rantao, deputy editor of *The Star* and editor of the *Sunday Independent*
Kevin Ritchie
Cecilia Russell
Our patient family and friends – Ricky is die beste! – and colleagues, who not only kept on asking when the book would be finished, but knew it eventually would
Our editor Alfred LeMaitre
Our designer Kevin Shenton
Jeremy Boraine and Francine Blum of Jonathan Ball Publishers who supported us throughout the publishing process
Our agent Monica Seeber

# INTRODUCTION

It was late November 2007, and the rivalry between Thabo Mbeki and Jacob Zuma dominated the headlines after months of brazen animosity. The two were about to face off at the ANC's 52nd national conference, to be held at the University of Limpopo in Polokwane, and neither man could afford to lose. The meeting became the nastiest dust-up in ANC history since the historic conference at Morogoro, Tanzania, in 1969. For the first time in nearly 40 years, the ANC was challenged from within by clashing egos and, to a lesser extent, ideology. Mbeki, not so much an ideologue as a man with a formidable ego, could not escape the fact that his name had been a key factor at both meetings.

But another name was consistently evoked in the run-up to Polokwane, just as it had also been, very prominently, at Morogoro. That name was Chris Hani. And the reason his name kept coming up in 2007 was because the ideals of the assassinated SACP leader and former MK commander so readily transcended the savage fights being managed between Luthuli House and the Union Buildings. Quite simply, Hani believed that liberation should free the poor from hunger and landlessness. He cherished nonracialism. He rejected personal power. Surely these had always constituted the shared vision of the movement?

So, as preparations for the conference in Limpopo heated up, the faithful kept asking: what would Hani have done? He had only once attempted to challenge for high office within the party – the position of deputy president. That had been at the first conference back home in 1991 after FW de Klerk had unbanned the liberation movements a year earlier. But both Hani and Thabo Mbeki, his rival for that post, were persuaded to step back in favour of the revered Robben Islander and confidant of Nelson Mandela, Walter Sisulu.

At that time, the ANC was determined to present a united front. The same had been true at Morogoro in 1969, when a controversial document drafted by Hani and others had criticised corruption within the leadership. This had created deep distress within the liberation movement, and it was only the intervention of then ANC president OR Tambo that had saved Hani's political future and restored some order.

The gloves were off by the time Polokwane rolled around. No Hani. No OR. No niceties. But certainly many parallels. Indeed, what would Hani have done, where would he have been, had he not been murdered by Polish right-winger Janusz Walus on 10 April 1993? At Polokwane, an otherwise ordinary town in the thornveld on the Great North Road to Zimbabwe, it was do or die. Would Hani, who has been committed to lore as perhaps South Africa's only quintessentially romantic guerrilla fighter, be properly honoured as what some within the ANC called 'a living link' between the rough times of 1969 and 2007?

Watching events unfold in the run-up to Polokwane, we were struck by how little was known about Hani. Paging through archived interviews with the then avowed communist, the same facts always seemed to come up – his love of the classics, his personal charm and his revolutionary fervour. There was little insight into the fabric and texture of the man who died too soon. So as journalists at *The Star* we started a journey, aimed at coinciding with the 15th anniversary of his murder, that would give the newspaper's readers a deeper understanding of his life and ideology.

As we found out more about his life, we discovered that the events we were witnessing firsthand as the ANC shuddered before Polokwane – and afterwards, when Thabo Mbeki resigned and the ANC split when the Congress of the People was launched – were in no way unique. And Hani, always prescient, had noted in 1969 what he called 'the rot,' and warned vociferously against it again before he died.

CHAPTER 1

# THE ROOTS OF A MAN

*I have been half in love with easeful death ... now more than ever seems it rich to die, to cease upon the midnight with no pain.*

– JOHN KEATS, 'ODE TO A NIGHTINGALE'

The *impepho* smoulders, the scent roughly serene as it disperses high above the gathering, inviting the ancestors to the sacred reunion. The fragrance is unmistakable, dancing down into the valley below with the swing of the sand road from the homestead pitched high on the hill. If there's enough strength in it, it might even reach the graves on the other side of the rise where Mary, a peasant, and Gilbert, a worker, lie together for eternity.

Up on that hill, the scent of the traditional herb, the spirit contact, is pure and intoxicating. It's at its most intense inside the heavy stone walls of Nolusapho Hani's kraal. For the duration of the ceremony, the goats that usually occupy the kraal have been moved to the adjoining harvested vegetable garden, and the tilled soil is littered with lambs.

The kraal is a place where only the grandfathers, fathers and sons of the family are permitted. Men take precedence over women here. They're leading their brother out of one world and into another. It's the way it has always been done: with the blood of a beast, the pride of a man is distinguished. Soon, only the crimson skin of the slaughtered ox lies sprawled in the centre.

The grandmothers, mothers and daughters, excluded for generations from the gathering of men, nestle outside the walls, bare legs poking out beneath orange skirts, necks festooned with beads, their laughter tight, lovely and low. They embrace the children bounding in and out of the convivial circle, the youngest jumping over rocks like young frogs in the brisk August sunshine.

The Hani family spear – symbolising sorrow and joy, life and death, the pulsing contradictions of blood – has been used a lot of late. The children admire it even as they keep their distance. Two brothers – the eldest, Mbuyiselo Victor, and the youngest, Christopher Nkosana – have died. Their parents, Mary and Gilbert, died within six years of each other, after the murder of their middle son, Martin Tembisile. Mary – who had spent her life working for her family – couldn't survive an ailment of the heart.

The night before the Washing of the Spades, under an opulent spill of stars, the children of the extended Hani family had raced around, from the verandahs to the secrecy of the dark vegetable garden, joyful at the adventure of a night-time game.

The ceremony is all about blood, the Hani family preparing to pay their last respects and send Victor on his final journey, an act that would take place early the next morning. They had been arriving for days, by bus from as far away as Stellenbosch and by bakkie from as close as Queenstown. By Friday night, there were 60 or 70 people at Nolusapho Hani's household. Her husband Victor had been dead for 11 months, and the time had come at last for him to go home.

The slaughter was to commence at 6 am, although the men assemble closer to eight, to exchange greetings in the ripening morning breeze before turning their attention to the task at hand. Nolusapho's herd, usually quiet at this hour, is led out of the kraal with low grunts and bellows, and agitated clunks of the hooves. In Sabalele, a bank balance is visible for all to see, bleating and stamping in front of a homestead. Soon, only one animal remains, the sacrificial ox, marked days before.

Now the men move into the kraal, most with their backs close to the stacked wall. It is time. The one designated to kill the ox steps forward.

There is a defiant hush. Carefully, carefully, a quick, deadly thrust to the nape of the neck to draw out the beast's power. The spear remains inside the flesh as the animal flails wildly, weakening, consternation in its eyes, excitement in the faces of the men. The horns search blindly for a perpetrator. The five-metre radius, hemmed in by the imposing walls of the kraal, quickly becomes a very small space. Quick steps left, then right, a dance in tune with the out-of-step animal.

Slower. Meeker. Its power is waning. The men move back. As the ox grinds its hooves into the floor, clouds of dust billow up from beneath it. Then, with a rhythmical baulking, surely its last, the animal thuds heavily, awkwardly, to the ground. A knife, and the throat is slit.

Expert hands go to work, taking the animal apart. Head, innards, rump, ribs. All quickly disseminated and briefly dunked in a bucket of water. Skewers of thick wire are thrust through blocks of meat, which are randomly tossed onto glowing coals.

The greybeards and ambling boys convene on the low wooden benches along the walls, each with knife in hand. They gather around the fire, some with jeans peeping underneath overalls they will soon outgrow.

The meat emerges sealed in black burn, and tender. Those on the benches eat first, thrusting their hands into the presented bowls. By the time the sun has dropped behind the rim of hills surrounding the homestead, all the meat has been consumed.

'Today we eat only meat. All day, meat,' says one young man serving. Those sharing in the peace after the slaughter, the time to celebrate, would have thought a lot about Dushe, the name by which they knew Victor Hani, brother of Sabalele's greatest son Martin Tembisile, later known as Chris Hani. Now both were gone. Victor had died almost a year before, on 29 September 2007. Their younger brother Christopher Nkosana had died in Cofimvaba hospital in February 2004 after a short illness. Chris Hani had been shot dead, many hours away, on 10 April 1993.

Today the family will guide the older brother home in the company of their ancestors. But they are saddened that there was never such a farewell for Chris in his village of Sabalele. For his family there, his death was an ending without the proper farewells. His remains are not in this soil, though they belong there, they say.

\* \* \*

After Queenstown, the lonely road stretches out ahead. We've been listening to Hugh Masekela's *African Breeze*, the trumpeter's warmest tide of love music for his country. As Masekela eases his belly fire of a voice into the live version of 'Coal Train', the blur of the Cofimvaba wilderness shifts from the margins of poverty into uncompromising beauty. It is difficult to stay away from this place.

This was not the first time we had made the journey, from Johannesburg via East London, through the defeated little university town of Alice. Skirting the midway trade of Queenstown, and all the way down the great highway to St Marks, Chris Hani's birthplace rolled away in the misty hinterland of heavenly sighs that the people still call Transkei.

The first time we went there was months before the 15th anniversary of Hani's assassination. We had set up interviews with those who knew Hani as a child, for a series of stories for *The Star*. The villagers still refer to him as Martin or Tembisile, never as Chris. By the time he had adopted his *nom de guerre*, choosing the name of his younger brother, Sabalele was a talisman for the battles that were to come.

We were searching for something else when we went to Sabalele for the first time: an understanding of one of the world's great revolutionary heroes, of one of the most revered individuals within a proudly collectivist movement. So we had to start in the hills of his childhood, to try to find a man who could have occupied the highest office.

The last time Hani returned to Sabalele was in 1993, just three weeks before his death, and his arrival immersed the villagers in honour. Everyone who hoped they might still mean something to him had gathered in Gilbert and Mary's three-roomed homestead. The people realised that absence, of an especially momentous 30 years, could have made him forget, but still they waited. Among them were his oldest friends,

Marwanqana Nondala and Mahelele Qolombeni, their smiles chased into the pattern of age on their faces, and his primary school principal, Alban Nyimbana.

Hani was without peer. He remembered everyone by name, and the memory of that momentary sensation – that they might indeed have meant something to such an important man – still brings a flash of emotion for the people of his past. Everyone we met who had known Hani reflected on this quality: his compassionate interludes with people, his understanding of how human detail matters.

When the villagers had last seen Hani, in 1962, he was 20 years old, a Fort Hare graduate in classical and legal studies and a socialist intrigued by the possibilities of overthrowing pain and injustice. He was tall, thickset and handsome, with a ready joke and a renowned facility for jovial banter. At that time, he was involved with the bright Judy Thunyiswa, a schoolgirl in Alice when they met. He was on his way to do his articles at the law firm of Schaeffer and Schaeffer in Cape Town, where his father Gilbert lived.

The next thing the people of Sabalele heard, Hani had vanished, like so many others. And he was gone for the next three decades. So was his father, banished to Lesotho. Mary Hani – who remained illiterate – was left to a peculiar suffering, sporadically harassed by the police and invested with a longing that would not recede.

When Hani, by then a father of four, returned home in 1993, he would have opened the back door of his father's house and walked straight into the dining room. Perhaps he would have gone to the window with its view of the plot marked out where he had been born in 1942. His embrace of his old life, shown by his warmth on his return, allowed the villagers to admire him more intimately.

The way they lined up established something of an ad hoc guard of honour for the former Umkhonto we Sizwe (MK) chief of staff and general secretary of the South African Communist Party (SACP). At that moment, it seemed as if it was the beginning again, the birth of a new relationship between the village and the man. His consciousness had been raised there. He had always talked about it, thought about it, been driven by it.

In an interview, he spoke warmly of his village, but inherent in every line was his eternal reason for doing what he did: the poverty hurt. He wanted it to be different. He wanted poor people to experience the dignity and honour they deserved. He wanted the kind of freedom that would reach, and gain meaning, into the next generation and the next. But for now, it hurt.

'Many of the people I knew as a youth were there to welcome me,' Hani told academic and historian Charles Villa-Vicencio in an interview for the 1991 book *The Spirit of Hope*:

The older folk were proud to receive a child home ... I also met some of my school friends and realised how little had changed.

Women were still walking five kilometres to fetch water, carrying it on their heads back to their meagre homes. People were still walking 15 kilometres to the nearest store to buy soap or sugar. A few people had radio, no-one had television and the problems of illiteracy were as sharp as they were when I was a child. I was revisiting my life of 40 years earlier. It was a strange and fearful experience.

I visited the church, the priest, talked with the nuns and remembered how I used to enjoy getting up early on Sunday mornings to perform my duties as an altar boy. They listened to my stories from the past and attended the ceremony later that day to welcome me home. There was no concern that I was a communist, and I found myself as much at home among the religious community of Cofimvaba as I had before I left that place in the early fifties.

Hani was very busy after he returned home. Everybody wanted to speak to him, especially Nelson Mandela. The ANC's Jessie Duarte said in a *Frontline* interview for American television:

Madiba really loved Chris Hani. Chris was one of the people who saw him at least once a week. He was able to talk to Madiba about a great number of things. They had a vision about youth cadet colleges.

Chris's politics fascinated Madiba. Chris, as a man, fascinated him, and he often described Chris as one of the valuable jewels the ANC had in its fold.

On the morning that Chris was killed, he [Madiba] was at his house in the Transkei, and I phoned him. When I spoke to him, he was shocked. He was very worried, and decided that he would go to see Chris's family immediately. That was his reaction. That he would drive from where he was to see Chris's family.

It was who he was. His first concern was to make sure that the immediate family was okay. He was very saddened by it. It was a loss that he knew could not be replaced.

In 1993, the people of Sabalele would have been content knowing there would be a next time, and a time after that, to see Hani again, to talk through what mattered. Their only desire was that he would be among them again. When he died, the necessity to complete his journey was immense. There had been no Washing of the Spades for Hani. Nothing could happen without the consent of his widow, Limpho Hani, and she decided to lay him to rest in South Park Cemetery, Boksburg, a short drive from where they lived and where he died.

\* \* \*

On our third visit to Sabalele, we met Cleopatra Thunyiswa Hani. At first, Hani's eldest daughter, now 43, was reluctant to untangle the story of her parents, or herself. We had had long conversations on the phone – she had moved from the village to King William's Town – and she spoke a lot about the difficult divides in her life.

Cleo Hani is afraid of what Phakamisa, the township where she now lives, represents, and what damage it could do to her son, Aluta. At the time of the 15-year anniversary, he was also nearly 15, born a mere three months after his grandfather's assassination. The boy has an enigmatic relationship with the man he does not know. Had Hani lived, perhaps Aluta would not have had to exist in such poverty.

People sometimes speak of a son born to Hani, but Cleo dismisses this.

'People play as if they knew Tembisile. But they don't know Tembisile. He was a very loving man. He would have told us if he had a son.'

This is one of the many mysteries. When Hani died, a few used the ever-changing narrative of his last years to claim they were his closest confidants. Those who were indeed close to him as comrades, even his bodyguards or drivers, have raged about those who have made claims upon friendship, which Hani could neither deny nor affirm, to hoist themselves up. When did these friendships bloom? Everybody shrugs. A friendship with Hani, say those who believe they know, was not only based on military convictions or on what Indian writer Rabindranath Tagore called 'giving and taking, meeting and uniting'. It was about the inside of a man's heart.

There are letters written by Hani – for example, to Durban lawyer Phyllis Naidoo – that offer tenderness, an insight into his private life which reflects something more than acquaintance. He trusted Naidoo enough to ask her to write his biography, but he died before they were able to spend the hours she needed to talk his life through with him.

The late Steve Tshwete was certainly a close friend. His official MK bodyguards in exile say Hani and Pallo Jordan would joke and laugh together: they, too, had a rapport and a strong bond. In a speech at the launch of the Chris Hani Institute at the Parktonian Hotel in April 2003, Jordan spoke memorably about a comrade who was caught in social, political and religious cross-currents:

I remember once teasing him – because we regularly ribbed each other – 'The line of work that really would have suited you is that of a village priest.' To which he responded, in all seriousness – 'Laddie, it's in this job that I feel I am truly doing the Lord's work!'

Some might say that was blasphemous, but if a God exists, I think he/she knows how to count them! If indeed Comrade Chris was performing God's work, it was because he had read and taken to heart the eleventh of Karl Marx's Theses on Feuerbach: 'Philosophers have only described the world in different ways; the point however is to change it.'

Every year, around the anniversary of Chris Hani's murder, promises are made by government and those who claim to be comrades. Cleo Hani couldn't care less about that, and she holds no grudges. The Hanis of Sabalele – and, indeed, the whole community – have had to get on with it by themselves.

Gradually, the conversation ebbed and flowed between the hopes Cleo has for herself and her son, and her reminiscences of a father she seldom saw and who she knew even less. Beauty is evident in her face; she's a lot like her father. But she has a great responsibility to Chris Hani's grandson, and it is not easy being the mother of a teenager.

On the day of the Washing of the Spades, she rested her hand gently on the boy's shoulder, an unconscious token of love. His eyes stared abstractly, but Aluta was meditating on what was being said. Her words were stern, yet not loud enough for anyone to hear. He had to be reprimanded for forgetting to bring the goats and cattle home from the hills. In any case, everybody knew what he had done.

In a place like Sabalele, people who really know what happened hardly say a word. Those who have no idea of the truth are the ones who can't stop talking. So this was Aluta's saving grace; this was his shield.

On the day of the Washing of the Spades, he had been allowed into the Hani kraal, where the rest of the older boys and men had gathered to pay their respects to Dushe. Aluta Martin Tembisile Thunyiswa Hani was now a young adult. So there was some excitement for him about this occasion. The novelty of filial acceptance and anticipation. The blood of a beast had been spilt. There was laughter among the teenage boys gathered in one corner. Aluta, smaller than most of them, timidly joined in. The sleeves of his grey overall were folded at the wrist, the hems of the trousers bunched over his shoes.

He knew that the moment his mother arrived, there would be words about his indiscretion over forgetting to return the livestock to the kraal. His great-aunt, Nolusapho Hani – his guardian while his mother was in King William's Town – had already punished him. She had taken away his treasured bicycle, given to him by his mother on a trip home from

Phakamisa. In Sabalele, beatings and rebukes are used to discipline children. But it goes further. Here, a child is made to understand that possessions are a luxury. Especially a bicycle. Here, they take away the things you prize most.

\* \* \*

Far away, in South Park cemetery, on 10 April 2008, two Hanis sat together, wedged between COSATU general secretary Zwelinzima Vavi and the SACP's Blade Nzimande – the representatives of the workers and oppressed. They kept company with Tokyo Sexwale, the former Robben Island prisoner turned tycoon, who had become the face of black business since resigning as Gauteng Premier.

Hani's memorial, discreet at first, had to be redone after it was vandalised in 1995. Today, it is a huge red marble stone with the flags of the ANC and SACP adorning either side. Buried alongside him is respected comrade Thomas Nkobi, former treasurer-general of the ANC.

On the day of the 15-year anniversary, a contingent of supporters arrived at the cemetery toyi-toyiing and chanting liberation songs. They were a mere whisper of the tens of thousands who had gathered at South Park cemetery in unmitigated anger and grief for Hani's burial in 1993.

The trio of Vavi, Nzimande and Sexwale spent the afternoon trading verbal exchanges from the podium, to the amusement of the buoyant crowd. The two Hanis – Limpho, elegant in a black suit and oversized sunglasses, and her doting daughter, Lindiwe – smiled dutifully.

Limpho Hani had not been back to Sabalele for 15 years although her daughters had, taken there by Limpho's father, Ntathi Sekamane. The Hanis in that small village in the Transkei believed she would come. She just hadn't done it yet, and this perplexed us. No one would say what they really believed was the reason for her absence. No one would go on record, and Limpho Hani herself declined to be interviewed.

\* \* \*

Back in Sabalele when we were doing our research, we had wanted to experience Hani's environment so we could get an understanding of where he grew up and how this affected his early life. We wondered whether this had not also been a preoccupation of his widow. It had, for instance, taken him two hours to get to school every day and to church on Sundays, and another two hours back. So we took the walk he took, through a wintry landscape that he must have known well. While we walked, we encountered an old man, who was ready for us well before we reached him.

He waited for us on his morning stroll to the hamlet of Zigudu, a few minutes' walk ahead, his silence interrupted by our conversation. Zigudu houses the mission station where Hani had first discovered the nature of the soul, displaying wisdom unusual for a child.

Voices and laughter travel here. You can hear echoes as gentle as the brush of a skirt on the ground, or as strong as the rumble of drums and the wail of hymns from a funeral service over the next hill and the hill after that.

The old man saw us coming – unmistakably out of place – from some distance. So when he began the conversation he wanted to have, but in Xhosa, his head was tilted back, the warm surprise shyly rehearsed for strangers.

We didn't understand his opening remarks, even though his curiosity was so obvious. His white hair and beard, threadbare grey jacket, navy trousers and herder's stick were nondescript, so for a moment the three of us stood there, waiting. The road to Zigudu is a route of necessary patience, every turn a deceit when you think you've almost reached your destination. The road's only obligation is to the river that twists alongside it. In the distance are the lime-green and pink huts that stand out like drawing-pins on the hills. Black and white plovers pick at the wealth of the land, the tapping of their beaks applause for the harvest, before they bounce off the waves of grass.

'I don't speak English,' the old man said, and then tried. 'Where ... you going? Why you don't use a car? Why are you walking?' We explained our need to walk, to slow things down and understand the walk that Hani took every day of his childhood. We were looking for answers to our questions about Hani, and we hoped that we might understand more, doing things this way.

'You like to walk?' the old man exclaimed, excited, before jumping full-tilt into a caricature of a man running, his arms and legs pumping in an exaggerated fashion as he stayed rooted to the spot. His soft smile at our laughter indicated an appreciation for his joke. We were strangers no more after that meeting on the road to Zigudu.

For Hani, the road would have simply been the road, the time it would take to get from here to there, and nothing more. There would surely have been fewer and fewer pauses to take in the majesty, no lingering to marvel. But we could imagine how thoughtful Hani might have been on those walks.

Hani's two daughters with his wife Limpho had more in their beauty of their mother. Nomakhwezi died before her 21st birthday, in a loss which magnified her mother's apparently well-kept pain. A miracle baby born after her mother fell pregnant again following an earlier, brutal miscarriage in detention, Nomakhwezi was just 15 when she heard the four fatal shots that ripped into her father on a weekend he had set aside for them to be together. When their father was killed, her younger sister Lindiwe was away with her mother, and her older sister Neo was in Cape Town.

Cleo, the oldest sister, has her father's face – soft, handsome, with a distinctive swell to the jawline. You don't expect the resemblance to be so immediate, but it's clearly an identity written into her bones. Her son Aluta is cast completely in his mother's image. Cleo was pregnant when she received the news that her father's life had been taken. All that remains for her now is their likeness.

Hani's mother once revealed why Hani's slightly raised top lip was so distinctive. He was a thumb-sucker until he was almost 10, but only in the dignity of privacy. His mother said she remembered him in his most solitary childhood moments, always with his thumb in his mouth, often reading, often thinking.

Cleo insists on her right to be as like her father as would ever have been possible. She spontaneously reveals how she loves books, how contented she is across a chessboard, or enjoying time with no more than the radio for company. But was she simply believing the hype?

Hani was the boy of books in Sabalele. His teachers and principals at Zigudu and Sabalele Primary were roused by his complexity and his acumen. Some, like his old primary-school headmaster, Alban Nyimbana, said they have yet to meet another child quite like Chris – and he was a child in 1956. The key to this insight, this pulsing energy so remarkable for his time and circumstances, was revealed later.

His aunt, his father's sister, who stayed in Zondi, Soweto, was the first person to become a teacher in his family, and she apparently taught Hani to read, write and count before he entered Sub A. 'She was a source of tremendous influence to all of us,' Hani recalled in an interview with historian and OR Tambo biographer Luli Callinicos:

This girl, coming from that sort of area, studying to become a teacher. She taught me a few necessary rhymes and began to open up a new world even before I got to school. A world of knowing how to write the alphabet, how to count, in other words, not only literacy but numeracy.

Because of that background, when I went to school I was in a better position than most boys in the village, and I remember how the principal got encouraged, how I would read a story and actually memorise that story and without looking at the book, I would recite it word for word.

Hani's old friend, Mahelele Qolombeni, smiles as he remembers 'a very sweet person'. He's relieved to be able to talk about long ago:

Normally when we came back from school, we had to look after the cattle and sheep, and we'd ride donkeys. We used to play soccer together and he was quite good at stick fighting. He was so good that some of us were quite scared of him, but he was very humble. What was important to him was school. He wasn't very interested in girls. He'd just look at them and watch the other boys chasing.

Alban Nyimbana, now 77, strides over the tumble of hills like a man 50 years younger. He's handsome, debonair and witty. He's got no time for Christians, but at his age he feels the world has lost faith in the empirical. He wishes he could talk of such things with Hani, who was way ahead of the other children when they met. 'He was too advanced,' says Nyimbana, himself a talented young man in his twenties when he was appointed to head Sabalele Primary – before he had ever taught in a classroom.

'We were highly excited when, at the end of Standard 5, [Hani] topped the whole circuit of 37 schools. He used to walk daily down this road.' Nyimbana indicates a parched avenue of rutted sand. Every year when the anniversary of Hani's assassination comes around, there is talk of fixing the road that runs through Sabalele. At least it's been graded, making it more passable for the occasional car or Toyota Hilux bakkie – far more effective and sturdy, and now as numerous as taxis in these parts.

'They were always a big crowd of children, and I was also there,' says Nyimbana. 'While we walked, we used to talk about his future.' The school, built in the shadow of a colonial bell-stand engraved in 1907, was a 40-minute walk from the rondavels on Hani's hill.

But there was another place that meant even more to the boy: the Roman Catholic mission church and school in tranquil Zigudu, where, even today, there is no electricity and no running water. As an altar boy there, Hani met German priest Peter Graeff, who, with his conviction that the church belonged to black people, made a significant impression on the young Chris. He was mesmerised by the world of the priests, and developed a lifelong affinity for Latin.

The church was a symbol of perseverance. The priests would travel on horseback to the most inaccessible parts of Sabalele, preaching the gospel, encouraging children to go to school, praying for the sick and offering advice. They were nurses, teachers, social workers and fathers where there were so few.

'Many of the males were away working on the mines, some in Cape Town and others on the sugar plantations in Natal,' Hani told Charles Villa-Vicencio:

Many of us grew up under the supervision of our mothers, combining schoolwork with working in the fields and tending the livestock. I was a thoughtful boy and often asked questions about the suffering of our people, finding a measure of childhood relief in the message of the church which told us that there would be a better world in the hereafter. At the same time, I admired the selflessness of the priests that worked among us. They lived alone, frugal and puritan in their lifestyle, visiting the sick and ministering to the poor. I learnt to admire the discipline of the mission. I was inspired and challenged by the example of the priests. To be a priest seemed to me a natural development.

Although Hani's parents had been baptised at the height of missionary activity in the eastern Cape in the 1920s, neither thought of themselves as Christian. He said he never saw them going to church. Instead, Gilbert and Mary Hani, and many of the other villagers, practised African traditional religion. Gilbert Hani could see no purpose in Christianity; it was said that the priests were running stokvels from behind the safety of the stained-glass windows, and when this was discovered by among others, Gilbert himself, the men in cassocks lashed out at the communists. Or so the rumours went.

So there was no choice for Hani. He never became Father Martin. But when he joined the Communist Party, in 1960, he was still a devout member of the church. Hani later told Villa-Vicencio:

The Party and the church were for me complementary institutions. I saw positively no contradiction between them, [but] as time passed, I began to view the church as indifferent to the socioeconomic improvement of black people, even though I was sure that the Bible demanded the opposite.

The Party and the ANC were, at the time, emphasising the need for the suffering of the poor to be redressed, and by 1962 my enthusiasm for religion was on the decline. The dichotomy between the promises of a good life after death and insufficient concern for the suffering of the present age began to take its toll on my thinking. During that same year I joined MK inside the country and my involvement in the church no longer seemed very important to me. In brief, I came to the conclusion that the political organisations to which I belonged were doing far more than the church to eradicate the suffering of the people.

In this ethical context I, in turn, began to question the existence of God. 'If there is a God,' I asked, 'what is this God doing about the suffering of people?' But that was and to a certain extent still is for me a personal, private concern.

I am an atheist but I see religion as a philosophy, like other secular or materialist philosophies, engaged in the important task of grappling and seeking to unveil the mysteries of the universe. Perhaps I understand religion better than I did when I was most at home within it.

\* \* \*

In 1955, the ANC and its allies were gathering notes from the oppressed world of its membership and its sympathisers. The movement faced growing repression from the new apartheid state consolidated by Prime Minister DF Malan, who had retired the year before. On 25-26 June 1955, the Congress of the People was held in Kliptown, outside Johannesburg. Word spread around the country that a Freedom Charter was being compiled. There were those who rebelled against it, particularly those who refused to relinquish their Africanist identity – whether they were middle class or peasants – and embrace its nonracial sentiment. And there were those who saw an opportunity to try and divide the Congress movement if they spoke against it. But the champions of the nascent struggle insisted that those who were committed to the ANC should know it, speak it, live it, and sign up to it. Pieces of paper were distributed both well before and during the Congress of the People among the crowds gathered on Kliptown's dirt square. Each person was given an opportunity to say what they felt should be contained in the charter. Some needs were simple. One man wrote that he wanted a warm coat so that he would no longer be cold in winter.

\* \* \*

By the time we return to Nolusapho's hut, people have already reported to her on the two strangers they met along the road to Zigudu. The men are still gathered in the kraal. The women are dishing up huge enamel plates full of food. Some attending the gathering are now walking around with cups of *nqomboti* (traditional beer). Covered with a lid wrapped in sack cloth, the metre-high plastic drum of beer stands in the centre of the hut, the sand mixed with goat droppings keeping the base in place. Culturally, traditional beer has no place at a ceremony like this. 'This is the good thing about democracy,' jokes Nolusapho from a reed mat where her bed would normally be.

Inside the Hani rondavel, old women line the walls, their bare legs and feet stretched out in front of them under their layers of patterned skirts. It's difficult to see through the choke of haze inside the rondavel, smoke coming off the pan of red coals in the centre. Even the bright blue kitchen cabinets, where Cleo is dishing up plates of food, are obscured along the back wall.

She's been up since 3am, making tea for the visitors. It's a quiet duty at that time of the morning. The sky is intense and dark. Members of the Hani family have come from far and wide and now lie sleeping on the floors in half-built rooms in the house next door. Limpho, Neo and Lindiwe are not among them. 'They have not come yet,' is the constant refrain of Nolusapho, her effervescent smile momentarily fading. She still hopes. Cleo has not yet had a chance to build a relationship with her sisters or Limpho, and has never felt the need to seek them out. Instead, this gathering makes her think about her mother, Judy Thunyiswa. She misses Judy, who died quietly in Johannesburg, just as all her family members had done before her. They simply went to sleep and never woke up.

Judy and Martin, both serious young scholars, had met in Alice, a picturesque town some 300 kilometres from Sabalele. Alice measured its revenue in school terms: blazers and textbooks, apples, gumballs and liquorice. Judy attended the girls' school, St Matthews. Martin went to Lovedale. Theirs was a meeting of hearts and minds that lasted until the mid-1960s, when Cleo was born. Their daughter is not certain about what drew them closer as the years went on. Was it operational? Was it love?

Her mother was an activist, especially once she left Middledrif, the village of her girlhood. Her parents, both teachers in that area, had not wanted her to be with Hani. They were educated people. He was the son of peasants, his mother was illiterate. Her prospects – she was a burgeoning intellectual – were so much better than that. But the young lovers found it difficult to stay away from each other, even after Chris went into exile.

Cleo wonders what it would have been like if her parents had been there, this night. People must understand, she told us, they were young. The time wasn't right. As she stirs the tea, she wonders about her son, sleeping in the old Hani house, further down, up another hill, above the graves of Gilbert and Mary, where Chris, they say, should be buried.

By Sabalele standards, the house is luxurious; as you walk in, a huge dining room table with soft high-back chairs dominates the room. Chris bought these for his parents. And the massive dressing table in the adjoining room would have embarrassed Mary Hani, caught unawares after a lifetime of head-down self-sacrifice to ensure her children's survival and, later, even their prosperity. From the dining room window, gaping down at the dip before Nolusapho's home, mounds of jagged rock remain as a reminder of where they started. In Xhosa tradition, a home is never destroyed, but rather naturally returns to where it came from, battered, beaten and finally absorbed into the earth.

Now, the concrete verges protect the old Hani home, which stands empty, under a film of dust. Aluta occasionally comes up here to wander through empty rooms that tell of another time. Aluta had done more than just not collect the herd that day when his bicycle was taken away from him. Life in the village of his ancestors, where Hanis have lived for generations, sometimes feels like it's standing still. But the evils of city life will not leave Sabalele untainted.

Still, Cleo would persist with him here, in this rural enclave, far away from Phakamisa township where, just recently, a woman was gang-raped and stabbed 38 times. Cleo doesn't want him anywhere near that kind of violence. She doesn't want Aluta to endure the same life she had, being shunted from one place to the next, always trailing her mother as Judy went in search of greener pastures, from time to time just a taxi ride away from Chris.

Cleo claims she had clandestine meetings with her father. In Lesotho, she says, she would challenge him on his renowned morning run, trying to stay ahead of him but never succeeding. Or, sharing a meal, the two exchanging little more than knowing glances, the playful Chris 'stealing' a potato from her plate, Cleo stealing one right back.

For all the good, wholesome memories she has of growing up, there are at least as many bad ones. In Sabalele, Aluta could have a better chance. Here, boys can become good men. Like his grandfather. Like his uncle, Victor, whose life will be celebrated today.

In a picture on the wall closest to the door, Jesus, with golden locks and eyes like blue ice, clutches a strawberry heart, the rays of his goodness shimmering through his robes. He's making the sign of peace, his index and middle fingers raised together in benediction. It's not a curiosity. Nolusapho Hani is a churchgoer. Her toddler granddaughter, Khensani Hani – who lies curled up under a blanket next to her grandmother after hours of play in the shadows on the silent hills behind the house – goes with her to church down that same Zigudu road every Sunday.

Animal horns, carefully nailed to the underside of the thatch, are the artefacts of the ancestors. An ornate gilt clock ticks soundlessly under the hum of voices, a chorus about long ago and today. The corruption. The criminalisation of the youth. There should be conscription. There should be more white people in charge. If only Chris had lived. Everything would have been better. It was the promise of his birth.

CHAPTER 2

# FORT HARE

We lost Cleo Hani somewhere between a rash of phone-call shops – their minders huddling under zinc overhangs on a cold morning – and the open road home. Phakamisa is an extension of the sprawling townships closest to Queenstown. But we could not find her house. We kept on driving past, seeing other names on signboards until eventually a woman in a gold BMW took pity on us, spoke to Cleo on the cellphone and then drove in front of us to take us right to her door, a mere five minutes from where we had given up.

It was something that seemed to happen to us quite often, as if there is a need to be searching for something in the Transkei. In a sense, there is no mystery to the landscape – but only if you know it. And in the case of the Hani household in Sabalele, there simply are no directions. The best you're likely to get are descriptions full of misunderstandings, and a veil of adjectives. There are no streets, no roads, no names. Just rondavels, and concrete bus stops. Cows strolling wistfully across the sandy tracks, barkless dogs and sheep calling to lambs out of line.

Begin the trip by taking the main tar road out of Queenstown through a landscape of gorges where the light is tremulous with expectation.

Drive until you get to the pointer for Cofimvaba. You'll probably miss it the first time; it's a mere consolation for those who insist on signs. Turn left, or you'll be on your way to Cathcart – if you're lucky. Otherwise, you'll be lost in the sadness of the heavenly Amatola Mountains.

Drive down a solitary path. Look out for the post office at St Marks and turn right. Pass the church and the white swans, the custodians of the dam. After crossing numerous bridges, past dozens of ruined automobile chassis, buildings buried in reeds and the indignity of lonely long-drops in the open grass, you'll have to ask. Some of the people living here speak Xhosa, some Afrikaans. Only a few speak English. Eventually, up a hill, left at the grey hut with the blue roof, keep going along the verge and park before you ram into a huddle of rocks.

The first time we went to Sabalele, the villagers, living mostly without lights and none with running water, were still virulently pro-ANC. The party had won 82.6 percent of the vote in the 2004 election. Major General Bantu Holomisa, who gave Hani protective and political cover in Umtata after Hani's return home in 1990, took just under 10 percent for his United Democratic Movement. The PAC got 2.19 percent. The tattered liberal conscience of the Democratic Alliance scored just over 3 percent. No contest, really.

It would have been a small ballot. Most of the people living in the villages are under 20, most of them children, and there's a negligible spike in people in their 40s. HIV and migrant labour rip the middle out – the mothers and fathers of the babies. It seems strange that statistics say there are so few old people because, as you drive, many seem to glide past on the road like ghosts, the women swaddled in blankets, multiple layers of skirts and scarves, the men startlingly fit. Cleo Hani says there are many over the age of 90. They just walk and walk, for hours, usually alone but sometimes in pairs or sometimes with old dogs, equally slow, equally determined.

The anniversary of Hani's murder always means the same thing for Sabalele: about a month or two before, shiny 4x4s arrive outside Nolusapho Hani's rondavel, and representatives of councils, municipalities and the province discuss 'an occasion' to mark 10 April. Much hand-shaking and back-slapping takes place, while the villagers stand around watching the knot of ambitious middle managers in open-necked shirts who keep tucking their fingers into their belts to tug up their trousers.

To mark 15 years, the new clinic would be completed and opened. A beast would be slaughtered and a ribbon cut. The last time there was this much fanfare here was when a water project named for Hani was opened by President Thabo Mbeki 10 years after the assassination.

When we first met Nolusapho Hani – in widow's weeds, her severe black scarf tight around her forehead – we were struck by her remarkable yet mysterious presence. It was as if she could not shed her smile, as if her smiles were her only expression, but also unmistakably disconnected from much of her conversation.

There's been so much sadness. The past drifts with disappointment. Her wit, a stream of consciousness preoccupied with nostalgia, allows Nolusapho to speak and laugh confidently about falling in love 50 years before, when she was a graceful little girl. Her crush was on her neighbour, Victor Hani, who revealed his charm during those rambling hours on the road to school with his younger brothers, Tembisile and Christopher.

But Nolusapho's age has also hardened her to the less idyllic life, the betrayals in the everyday political world, the cynical meaning in the completion of the new clinic. Like a conjuring trick, it had finally emerged out of the neglect of Sabalele in 2008, its flat brown facebrick and sombre, bureaucratic squareness rammed against the soft horizon of colourful one-roomed huts. As we walked back down the hill to her hut after the obligatory tour of the clinic's two rooms, Nolusapho said it was simply too small – and what's the use? It isn't open every day. How will the infirm or pregnant women get up the hill? It is at the very top. With another smile, elusive in its meaning, Nolusapho noted, 'When Tembisile died, there were lots of promises from government. We're waiting.'

It was late when we left Sabalele that first day. Night dropped like a hood over the village, and suddenly everything around us was pitilessly dark. We were certain that if a lost cow stepped into the road, we could lose control of the hired car. Once in the thickly lined avenue of rich silver trees that lead to the sign for Cofimvaba, there are a few other cars, but only every now and then.

You need patience on the main route back to Queenstown. Every few kilometres, a figure with a Stop sign, like a ghostly ferryman, steps out into the delicate dust of headlights to call you to a halt. Then, it could be a 15-minute wait, sometimes longer, before cars can move again, down a single carriageway, squeezed against orange traffic cones. No one seems to know why. No one asks.

\* \* \*

Back in Johannesburg, Sauer Street has four lanes of morning mayhem. Number 54 Sauer Street is Luthuli House, the national headquarters of the African National Congress (ANC). Hundreds of taxis squall acrimoniously around it throughout the day, thousands of pedestrians darting among the minibuses. Inside Luthuli House there was a creeping sense of emergency in the months before the 15th anniversary of Hani's death. The question, to put it plainly, was, how to honour Hani? There was already an annual Chris Hani memorial lecture, where party intellectuals – the Mbekis, Pallo Jordan and others – had paid homage. There was a Chris Hani Institute in humble COSATU House at the base of the Queen Elizabeth Bridge, although it consisted of not much more than two librarians, a few books and posters, a box of business cards and a fax machine.

The biggest hospital in the southern hemisphere is situated at the teeming gateway to Soweto, where Hani had been a fugitive on and off, directing and accelerating sabotage, during the 1970s and 1980s. The hospital has been called Chris Hani-Baragwanath for many years, to the consternation of even progressive lobbyists, who insisted they could name a dozen worthy doctors who had served the ANC in the camps in Angola and elsewhere who were surely more deserving of the title.

The municipality in which Cofimvaba lies was also renamed to honour its fallen hero. And the municipality in Alice has a Chris Hani Drive – a narrow strip of tar, flanked by poverty. So it goes on. Yet these bureaucratic honours have never seemed quite enough.

Hani's face is ubiquitous in salvaged revolutionary posters and old photographs in offices and corridors all over Luthuli House, and in COSATU House, headquarters of the Congress of South African Trade Unions, where there are photocopies of photocopies of pictures of Hani.

In December 2007, during the midsummer of the ANC's discontent, its top delegates gathered to spit vitriol in Polokwane, and Hani was recharged for that event, too, with the SACP, the Young Communist League (YCL), the South African Students Congress (SASCO), the MK Military Veterans Association (MKMVA), the ANC Youth League (ANCYL), everybody, wanting a piece of his monument.

Zwelinzima Vavi, the general secretary of COSATU, is succinct about Hani's influence: 'Our future is written in the blood of Chris Hani'. So we struggle to understand why Sabalele remains on the periphery of the collective conscience while it was always at the forefront of Hani's imagination.

* * *

In the waning dark, the huts of Sabalele emerge dreamlike in the first light to lift off the mountains. A knot of cattle, already adrift from the early morning herd, are startled by people walking along the main track over the series of bridges where not much more than the memory of a river washes below. Kraals marked out in rocks punctuate the rough green scrub. From a distance, these are the crop circles of gentle hills, but those who take the road to Qamata Station – the only road in Sabalele – know the terrain to be compassionate only to stray dogs and goats.

Qamata was not much more than a cheerless platform on the way to Queenstown and Stutterheim in 1956, when 14-year-old Chris Hani boarded the train for Lovedale College in Alice. The station in Alice was more substantial, a place of frequent arrivals and departures, the back and forth that keeps a small town from death. It had benches polished to a dark sheen, a large, elegant clock and six decorative doors to six offices. A wide platform on one side overlooked two sets of tracks bordered by thick flowering bushes, loud with the cries of birds deep inside the foliage.

Today, derelict Alice station is a battered ruin of the pretty postcard. In each of the six offices live a different group of homeless people. These days, only freight trains roll through. No one gets off there anymore.

In Hani's days at Lovedale, the fields of the Presbyterian mission known as the 'African Eton' were indeed lovely, but the school was racist and forbidding. Yet there was no other direction for a boy whose yearning to learn had exceeded the education of Zigudu Primary, where he had completed two years in one. He did the same thing at nearby Cala Secondary, and then it was clear that the schools of the village sprawl had lost their power over the remarkable teenager.

Hani left for Lovedale a couple of days before the first assembly, sharing a quiet meal with his mother and his brothers before they left to walk together to the station. They got up early, around 2am, to allow enough time for a journey on foot. Hani lit the stove with wood chopped the day before. Mary Hani made sweet black tea and prepared slices of bread for their breakfast, cut from hot round loaves blackened on the fire. A couple more slices were packed for the journey.

At 15, Hani was not yet as tall as he would become, although he already had a distinctive way of walking, as if on tiptoes. To his mother, he was an exceptional boy, a good son. Once they had had breakfast, Mary, Tembisile, Victor and Christopher shared the load: a trunk with bedding, a plastic bucket with cutlery inside, a worn-out suitcase for his clothes and a basket of homely provisions – bread, a wedge of butter or margarine, a bottle of cooldrink, a couple of apples, some hard-boiled eggs, washing powder and soap. It was a bumpy trail, kilometres long, but they stayed together, speaking occasionally, otherwise in silence.

In January in Cofimvaba, the air was warm enough. In July, it was icy, but Hani still had to take the early-morning train, which arrived around 5.30am, to reach Queenstown in time to meet the Stutterheim engine at a siding. That second train took him right into Alice, stopping a 15-minute walk away from the sacred University College of Fort Hare, not far from Lovedale. Only the fragile flow of the Tyume River separates the two institutions.

When Hani walked out of Alice station, he would have passed the men in pleated trousers leaning against their cars with their arms folded. The bonnets and hubcaps of the cars would have been polished to a gleam. The taxi drivers liked to joke around with each other to pass the time, but they had to be discreet. White people, especially those staying at the Alice Hotel over the road from the tracks, might complain. It might be some time before the men got a fare, and the five-minute drives to Lovedale were hardly worth the trouble. But those students with money could still hire the spacious luxury of a private car to ferry them to the white gates of the school.

The couple of shillings' fare was too much for Hani, though, so he, like most of the other boys, would likely have hired a donkey cart, which would trundle past the general dealers' stores, where the boys were allowed to shop twice a week – if they had a few pounds. Luxuries were rare, and treats like this were for the rich boys, the children of African gentry from places like Grahamstown. Hani got a little pocket money during sheep-shearing season when his mother sold hides and wool. After some months, his father managed to buy his mother a sewing machine, and that brought in a small extra income.

Despite the ubiquity of parental sacrifice, life at Lovedale was a communal torture. The 5.30am daily ablutions were particularly hard. After making their beds, the boys took their towels to the outdoor bathroom to wash in icy water – even on the cruellest days of winter. If it was raining, they still had to shower under the open skies. Toilets were also outside, and a long walk away. There was no way to flush, and the bourgeois boys found this quite a misery.

Boys like Hani found life behind the wooden school gates miserable for other reasons. The approach – up a sunlit avenue of benevolent old oaks, past the flower gardens and neat outbuildings, across the road from a lonely stone church – was not unpleasant. Less encouraging were the cold grey bricks and black window glazing of the schoolhouse and the raw steel beds and rough straw mattresses in the dormitories.

After the July school holidays, Hani plotted his position on Qamata Station platform more carefully. At the first sign of the train's headlamps, he would get ready to bundle his possessions onto the train ahead of the young intellectuals from Fort Hare. He wanted to get on board quickly, to get a good seat in the political enclave. Outside, in the brisk winter wind, he would pull his Lovedale blazer tighter around him, and blow on his hands for warmth. Once in the train, though, the ambience changed entirely. Depending on where you sat, and whose circles you could enter, the conversation in some second-class compartments was all politics. These were hothouses, thick with the excitement of rebellion, the conspirators inside them as ardent as prophets.

Transkei was in deep pain. In the late 1950s, the new apartheid prime minister, HF Verwoerd, cowed the region with government's most hollow insult. In his legislative debut, Verwoerd had decided Transkei would be South Africa's model of separate development, an idea embodied in the Promotion of Bantu Self-Government Act 46 of 1959. Blacks would be permitted to work in the land of their birth, but they would ultimately lose their citizenship to that of their allotted 'homeland' (later termed 'bantustan').

In Hani's case, he and his family would be relegated to Transkei, under the rule of Kaiser Matanzima. If urban protest was inevitable, so too was peasant insurrection, albeit for different reasons. The battle was led by the brilliant communist journalist, Govan Mbeki, who was based in Port Elizabeth. Mbeki's paper, *New Age*, raged underground as it revealed the heroism of the Congress movement against the forces of capital.

Copies of *New Age* would have been well-thumbed on Hani's school train. It was in those rumbling coaches, and in the barely lit corners of dormitories and under trees, that the young men would discuss national and world events. There was solidarity in disappointment and anger when a firebomb devastated the *New Age* offices in 1958 in an act of state sabotage. Filing cabinets crammed with years of records were obliterated.

In 1956, there was no more absorbing issue in South Africa than the arrest on 5 December of 156 black and white ANC members and supporters. It would take another four years for the state to fail to prove that the trialists' association with the Freedom Charter – the loudest voice yet of the marginalised majority – was treasonous. Even the white media instructed its readership to examine the trial closely: the National Party (NP) government had surely got it horribly wrong.

*New Age* trumpeted the 1957 Alexandra Bus Boycott, which saw thousands of township residents refuse to board Johannesburg's municipal transport service. A symbol of apartheid civic planning, Alexandra was just too far for black workers who had to travel up to 20 kilometres to work and 20 kilometres back. A crippling ticket price increase incensed them.

The paper also delivered the remarkable exposé by journalists Ruth First and Joe Gqabi – and later Henry Nxumalo of *Drum* magazine – of the Bethal farm labour scandal, which ultimately led to the Potato Boycott of 1957. The tragedy of workers in the eastern Transvaal being lured into virtual slavery on farms was covered widely in the conventional media after *New Age* fearlessly broke the story. Mbeki's paper was careful to tell the inside story of how the labourer-turned-revolutionary Gert Sibande led tens of thousands of ordinary black people around the country to boycott the Bethal potato crops, which had been sown in blood.

The investigation held the Lovedale students in thrall, and the militant Gqabi was a beacon for young recruits like Hani. During the Pondo peasants' revolt of 1960, Gqabi adapted the skills of a journalist, infiltrating others' lives, and becoming intimate with their hopelessness. That revolt was brutally put down by the oppressors, who executed 16 people and drove many more into silence. Gqabi, like Hani, never saw the dawn of freedom, the victim of an assassin's bullet.

In 1957, before Hani was recruited into the ANC by Lovedale head prefect Simon Kekana – chair of the Youth League at Lovedale and the local agent for *New Age* – he was drawn by the intellectualism of the influential Unity Movement and its outspoken youth wing, the Society of Young Africa (SOYA). The movement despised capital, and elevated that above white racism as the reason for black oppression. Yet he was troubled by their lack of action to counter the hardships of the people. He found it impossible to accept that wars against injustice could succeed if they remained only in the mind, and so the overt activism of the ANC took hold.

There was a necessary rite of passage for the 16-year-old recruit, to prove his discipline. His orders came from Kekana one evening. He had to locate and carry a heavy suitcase – containing the clothes of an enemy agent – to an appointed place, and burn it. For the teenage Hani, in an accelerated phase of conscientisation, this was his first taste of underground work. The rural uprisings that were stirring, especially in Pondoland, and the incendiary writings of Govan Mbeki assisted his decision to join the still-legal ANC and, clandestinely, the SACP.

For the bright young men of Lovedale and neighbouring Fort Hare, there were other battles ahead. The university was to become a Xhosa-only institution, by order of the state's Extension of University Education Act 45 of 1959. As time went on, Hani and the train intelligentsia held even more defiant, fundamental debates. A recalcitrant new organisation, the Pan Africanist Congress (PAC), led by Robert Sobukwe, announced its breakaway from the ANC in April 1959. Immediately, the rebels of the Congress movement began to turn the novelty of their presence at schools and universities into a powerful, undermining force. Within ten years, though, the PAC would be all but shattered, its membership disenchanted, its policies derided on the continent. But in 1959, it was undoubtedly a threat. It, too, concentrated its recruitment on the workers and the poor.

\* \* \*

Chris Hani at 15 would have been acutely conscious of rural poverty. Unrelenting drought and years of harm had ravished the fields of the peasants. The forced removal of families from arable land had left many destitute, reliant on the humble comforts of others. Those enterprising enough to have built up a reasonably sized herd had often been driven into stock culling because of overgrazing. A desperate few took advantage of the corrupt authorities and paid bribes to keep their cattle and sheep. But there was no way out of impossibly high taxes.

The only advantage afforded to Hani by the state was the Bhunga bursary, the United Transkei Territories General Council scholarship, which made it possible for him to go to Lovedale as an exemplary pupil. His father, Gilbert, with his sparse Standard 6 missionary education, was still one of the most educated people in the villages.

When the boy was by himself, fetching water from three, or even six, kilometres away, or milking the cows, or alone with his schoolbooks in the outhouse with the door hinged with a wire coathanger, he would consider the struggles of his parents, symbolic of so many others.

Like most men from Sabalele, Gilbert Hani had spent his sons' childhood away from home, disconnected from their boyhood rituals. But there was no choice. There was no other way of making money, but through migrant labour, to try to put a gifted child like Chris into the kind of elite education that might permit escape.

The papers of Phyllis Naidoo reveal that Gilbert Hani earned a scant 16 shillings per week as a migrant construction worker and, later, as a hawker plying an illegal trade, but this meant he had to live far away, in a hostel in Langa, Cape Town. Chris later joined him there when he started articles at the law firm of Schaeffer and Schaeffer after completing his BA at Fort Hare.

Much later, Chris would talk about what he had witnessed while growing up. It hurt him, 30 years on – the impetus for the ideology that remained with him until his death. He told Luli Callinicos:

Now I had seen the lot of black workers, extreme forms of exploitation. Slave wages, no trade union rights, and for me the appeal of socialism was extremely great. Workers create wealth, but in the final analysis, they get nothing. They get peanuts in order to survive and continue working for the capitalists.

So it was that simple approach, that simple understanding which was a product of my own observation in addition to theory. I didn't get involved with the workers' struggle out of theory alone.

It was out there, somewhere between Qamata and Alice, that Chris first considered socialism. When Callinicos asked him why he wasn't satisfied with being a member of the ANC at that time, and wanted to join the communists, his reply was frank:

I belonged to a world, in terms of my background, which suffered I think the worst extremes of apartheid. A poor rural area where the majority of working people spent their time in the compounds, in the hostels, away from their families. A rural area where there were no clinics and probably the nearest hospital was 50 kilometres away. Generally a life of poverty, with the basic things unavailable. So I never faltered in my belief in socialism. For me, that belief is strong because that is still the life of the majority of the people with whom I share a common background.

The inherent cruelty and dispossession intended by the Bantu Self-Government Act of 1959, which established the 'homelands', undoubtedly had an impact on Hani's political growth. Uprisings such as that at Witzieshoek in March 1950 – when police killed 14 peasants, arresting and detaining many more and, eventually, banishing the community's Chief Mopeli – affected him deeply.

His own father suffered the pain of banishment – first, bizarrely, to his own village but not his own home, and, finally, to Lesotho. And there were many others, like Chief William Sekhukhune, who was banished to Zululand in 1960 for his refusal to sell out his community to bantustan authorities, even upon military blockade, and eventually died of starvation.

\* \* \*

At Lovedale, Hani had only one pair of shoes, and one jacket, and he later told Phyllis Naidoo how it troubled him at first that some of the other children at Lovedale were better clothed. 'But I had accepted the fact that this was not important for me. What was important was to get my education.'

The administration at Lovedale had a certain vision of order and civilisation between the races. Hani and the other boys were allowed to be there only if they could live, without reproach, in the two worlds it harboured. Naidoo's papers and the oral testimony of students reveal how the paternalistic headmaster, Jack Benyon, forbade political activity and songs about Albert Luthuli and the Congolese martyr, Patrice Lumumba, particularly after a dormitory protest over the poor quality of the food served to the most disadvantaged students in the school dining room.

Lovedale – with its daily prayers and church services on Sundays – was a significant education in repression for Hani. The only students who ate reasonably well were those from well-off families, and – especially at Diwali and Eid – the Indian and Muslim boys. Some Indian students fetched weekly provisions parcels from home at the post office on their trips into Alice, and their bottles of atchar were quickly shared.

Meal times served to entrench poverty. The echo of hymns left a peculiar timbre once the dining hall fell silent after grace. Only manners, money and race mattered around the wooden tables. The white teachers sat separated from the black teachers on a slightly raised platform. Hani, whose family could barely afford his absence from the village, sat at one of the tables in the back where meat was served occasionally with pap or samp and beans or vegetables. Those who could afford to pay higher fees would eat meat up to three times a week, while the boys from wealthy homes had meat every day, butter with their bread and milk with their porridge.

The college routine was intense, with no respite even on Friday evenings when Hani would have to soak his clothes in washing powder in the plastic bucket he had brought from home. Washing and drying occupied Saturdays.

\* \* \*

By 1957, Hani was in the thick of it, while his later political rival, Thabo Mbeki, was the ANCYL secretary at Lovedale. Their Xhosa teacher, Mac Makalima, is quoted by Mark Gevisser, in his biography of Thabo Mbeki, as saying he remembered Hani vividly as a student leader and hothead, whose militant idols were Oliver Tambo, Nelson Mandela, Walter Sisulu and Anton Lembede.

By the end of 1958, Hani was ready to leave Lovedale, with English, Xhosa, Latin, History, Mathematics and Hygiene as his final subjects. (Afrikaans was not yet compulsory.) Papers lodged in the ANC archives at Fort Hare show that on 6 October, the 16-year-old Hani wrote in a neat handwriting to the university registrar: 'I beg to apply to be admitted as one of your students in the degree course. I am a candidate for the Senior Certificate at Lovedale.'

On 28 October, he filled in an application form for admission and was given the number 557/7679 for future dealings with the university. His application notes that his guardian was Gilbert Hani, a labourer at 79 Special Quarters in Langa, that he was a Roman Catholic – later he would say he was Presbyterian – and his vocation was Law. Two photographs had to be provided for Fort Hare's security network. One was attached to the student file, the other was for the library. Until 1959, the university had asked applicants only for a first name and surname, but when Hani filled it in, it also required a pass number. His was 2879218 and his father, as his guardian, filled in his number of 2231891. A necessary certificate of attainment and character was signed by Lovedale principal Benyon, and on 5 February 1959, Fort Hare admitted him, enclosing a railways concession certificate in the envelope with the letter.

The first instalment of fees of 27 pounds 10 shillings had to be paid in advance. As Hani's bursary application was refused and the fees were 90 pounds in total, Gilbert Hani had to pay off five instalments of 13 pounds each.

His son would join the prestigious alumni of Fort Hare, who comprised some of the continent's most illustrious graduates, including Nelson Mandela, Oliver Tambo, Govan Mbeki, Robert Sobukwe, Robert Mugabe, Quett Masire, Kaiser Matanzima and Mangosuthu Buthelezi.

Hani worked hard at university, in an undoubted act of redemption for his father. In his application for second year, dated 30 December 1959, he lists his first-year results: three second-class passes in English, Latin and Xhosa, and a third-class pass in Classics.

In 1991, two years before his death, Hani told an interviewer that he still longed to get a teacher's diploma and to study anthropology and sociology. He also had a dream at that time of getting a piece of land and growing vegetables and flowers. 'I have a passion for the soil. I wouldn't mind some land just to grow something and to feel the soil. I want to watch plants grow,' he said.

But in 1958, all he wanted was his BA, and the chance to exceed the expectations of his birth, so he requested financial help and chose from a list of scholarships advertised in the college handbook. Hani first stated on his form that the minimum amount of assistance he needed towards his fees would be the equivalent of R50. Then he deleted that, signing the deletion, possibly feeling compromised by his obvious poverty.

It seems that he never managed to pay his full debt to the registrar. In a letter to the Secretary for Bantu Education, Accounts Branch, Pretoria, found among Naidoo's papers and dated 22 July 1964 – a time when Hani was in Moscow, training to be a guerrilla fighter – the registrar suggested the magistrate at St Marks might be able to assist in tracing the debtor and his relatives. According to the registrar's records, the home address given by MT Hani was c/o Mr ES Puttergill, PO St Marks. The letter related to loans from the Department of Bantu Education for his second and third years. In second year, he got 50 pounds, and in 1961, his third year, 100 pounds.

By third year, he had passed English, Latin, Roman Dutch Law, Philosophy, Public Administration and Principles of Criminal Law, although his marks were not as exemplary as Hani would have liked. His June 1960 Progress and Proficiency Report is marked 'fairly good' with marks of 40, 49, 50 and 50. That the highest mark was 50 was a disappointment for Hani, whose clandestine political work had by then taken a destructive toll on his academic life. The warden noted that Hani's conduct and health were good.

Although quite tall, Hani looked young for his age in oversized trousers and the same brown sports jacket he wore for years. Although he was the youngest of the student leadership at Fort Hare, his influence was immense, recruiting students and workers, sloganeering, distributing banned leaflets and taking anti-republican instructions from Govan Mbeki's tireless Eastern Cape Command through a network of underground cells dubbed the 'Force Publique'.

Then came the order: 10 outstanding comrades were to be chosen to be quietly taken out of the country for training for six months. Hani refused. The enemy and the struggle, he said, are here, and he bolstered his ideological conversion to communism by seriously studying Marxism and reading trade union periodicals. Ideologues like Ray Alexander and Jimmy La Guma became his intellectual arbiters. Hani was determined to understand the theory that the national and the class struggle should be aligned, using a non-sectarian approach.

Govan Mbeki, who had been fired from teaching, infiltrated Fort Hare to investigate the problems on campus for *New Age*, and established political relationships with some of the students, including Hani. Mbeki recalled his protégé as being 'intolerant of anything that smacked of relationships with the government of the day. So the young Hani was part of the group who were committed to struggle against Afrikaner nationalism.'

The students asked Mbeki for help in organising underground structures, and it was around this time that he recruited Hani into the SACP. (The old Communist Party of South Africa had been dissolved and reconstituted as the South African Communist Party in 1953.) Hani was among a group of volunteers who, in turn, organised others at high schools, partly in the name of the SACP. Mbeki's memory was that Hani 'was amongst the leading cadres' for transforming scholars and students into Congressites, and later, aspirant soldiers for the people's army.

\* \* \*

The year 1960 was hell for the ANC. Horror had unfolded at Sharpeville and Langa on 21 March, when massacres left more than 70 dead and close to 200 wounded. South Africa was soon to be a defiantly white republic: Verwoerd and his government were diplomatically isolated by the Western democracies, but he showed no remorse, and simply quit the Commonwealth.

Although Tanzania celebrated its independence in 1961, and Chief Albert Luthuli was awarded the Nobel Peace Prize, the new year brought increased terror for black South Africans, who had gradually and inexorably become disenfranchised from their birthright.

The ANC, banned by Verwoerd in 1960, could no longer stand by as the human rights of its members were undermined through torture and detention without trial. More and more demanded a shift in the ANC's consciousness, calling on the Congress movement to take up arms. Passive resistance had become a disturbing *non sequitur* for young prodigies like Hani. He was among the first volunteers for the ANC's fledgling armed wing, Umkhonto we Sizwe (MK), formed on 16 December 1961. Yet not everyone in the leadership was comfortable with the subtext of necessary violence. Hani explained later:

The Party itself had debated and I think the Party as a whole endorsed MK, but it was ... a period of serious questioning and introspection and soul-searching on the part of the ANC, the Communist Party. It was the uncertainty about moving from non-violence to armed struggle without the existence of objective and subjective factors. Our people knew nothing about military struggle. The last wars that we fought were fought towards the end of the 19th century.

People had been deskilled in terms of understanding war. They were not even allowed to keep spears in their own houses.

But the launch of MK, at a secret venue in Johannesburg, couldn't have happened at a more critical juncture in the life of the party, its 50-year quest for peace ignored by the regime. Immediately, the legend of the first high command, led by Nelson Mandela out of Liliesleaf Farm, was born. 'Umkhonto we Sizwe will be at the front line of the people's defence. It will be the fighting arm of the people against the government and its policies of race oppression,' read the MK manifesto. 'It will be the striking force of the people for liberty, for rights and for their final liberation.'

At the Rivonia Trial, MK commander-in-chief Mandela asked the court:

What were we, the leaders of our people, to do? Were we to give in to the [state's] show of force and the implied threat against future action? Or were we to fight it? And, if so, how?

We had no doubt that we had to continue the fight. Anything else would have been abject surrender. Our problem was not whether to fight, but how to continue the fight.

At its birth, MK was determinedly nonracial. Mandela explained it in the broadest political context to the Pretoria Supreme Court: because the ANC stood for nonracial democracy, the armed wing 'shrank from any action which might drive the races further apart'.

The commander was clear: the ANC leadership had always prevailed upon black South Africans not to use violence. But this had achieved nothing. '[This meant] that our followers were beginning to lose confidence in this policy and were developing disturbing ideas about terrorism.' Oliver Tambo saw MK as becoming a classic revolutionary army, 'politically conscious ... conscious of its popular origin, unwavering in its democratic functions'.

For Hani, MK's military code resonated on a most profound level. The code stated: 'Umkhonto is a people's army fighting a people's war. It consists of the sons and daughters of the most oppressed, the most exploited sections of our people. For these reasons we claim with pride and truth: Umkhonto is the spear of the nation.'

MK's first sabotage action took place on the day the organisation was launched. Engineer Denis Goldberg, who had become a technical adviser to MK, had made two bombs. The timing device on one failed to work correctly, and the other was never detonated as the saboteur was betrayed. The police were waiting for him at the appointed place, and arrested him as he set the bomb.

\* \* \*

Gilbert Hani managed to put together enough money, on lay-by, to get his son a gown and mortarboard, a suit and new shoes for his graduation at Rhodes University in Grahamstown, where Fort Hare traditionally held its final ceremony. But Gilbert and Mary Hani were not allowed to show their pride in their son, as they were prohibited from attending the white university's celebration. At the end of the graduation ceremony, the audience broke into 'Die Stem', and, immediately afterwards, the Fort Hare students crushed the echo of their oppression with 'Nkosi Sikelel' iAfrika'. Hani's voice would have been among the loudest.

CHAPTER 3

# FLIGHT INTO EXILE

The young father holding the child on his lap sat quietly, staring straight ahead. The men of the Northern Rhodesia Police (NRP), in their distinctive khaki shorts, black and white socks and epaulettes, seemed determined as they boarded the train. Furtive glances were cast between the passengers. Muted words. Slowly the policemen went about their business, politely asking some of the young men aboard the train to accompany them.

As the train slowly rattled along the narrow-gauge tracks, through the dark Northern Rhodesian landscape, many of those on the 300-kilometre journey to Lusaka, the capital of the British protectorate, had nodded off or were slouched wearily in their seats. Occasionally a child's cry broke the monotony. But the young men dotted about the carriage had hardly moved during the journey, carefully noting every moment, every tension-filled stop along the way. And now, everybody was paying attention.

The police were looking for something. Someone. They were targeting the young foreigners, whose lighter skins had attracted the casual attention of their fellow travellers, even though they were scattered throughout the carriages, even though they seemed unrelated, and even though they had hardly exchanged a glance for hours. Others had taken more than a passing interest, and now made eye contact with the NRP men to direct their attention to the fairer passengers. Each sat or stood quietly in his place.

One by the one the group moving through the carriage grew. The young father seemed blissfully unaware as he sat with the child. Inside his mind was his real name: Martin Tembisile Hani. But here he had to be anonymous.

\* \* \*

Langa station. Early morning. People crammed into too few carriages at peak hour. Inside, the few seats went to the older women who would spend the rest of the day on their feet in factories or on their hands and knees polishing and cleaning in the middle-class suburban homes at the foot of Table Mountain. Feet shuffled in order not to trample others. Young men were propped up together where they stood. In winter especially, the passengers would strike up a popular Xhosa refrain, the throng immediately ordered as the baritones came in on time to counter the falsettos.

After the crinkle-cut iron sheets of Langa, tenement buildings announced the Coloured townships and the gradual movement through grey and then white areas towards the arms of that blue-grey mountain. This was another country, another world.

The screech of brakes signalled Cape Town station. Black people of all shades poured onto the platform, the bustling mass determined as they made their way towards the exits. Their counterparts travelling at the head of the train in the Blankes Alleenlik (whites only) carriage would be spared this jostling as they walked through their specially marked exits, into Adderley Street, past the Groote Kerk, around the bend past Parliament, and into Wale Street.

At a desk in the law offices of Schaeffer and Schaeffer, in softly carpeted offices lined with heavy, dark wood cabinets and row upon row of leather-bound books, a young Fort Hare graduate was clerking his way to a career in the legal fraternity. But it was not enough for Hani. Few things were.

In 1962, at the age of 21, he got to meet his father. *Really* meet the man who had only occasionally visited during those hard childhood years in Sabalele. They shared a room in the married-quarters hostel in the native township of Langa. Here, some things came easier for father and son, in spite of the press of people, living like pilchards in a Lucky Star tin, saving every last cent for the trip home to Transkei.

\* \* \*

Against all odds, the ANC was quite well organised in Cape Town. A Committee of Seven had been established to coordinate activities across the peninsula. But the birth of the PAC had given rise to new challenges. The PAC's drive for full-scale mass activity was gaining momentum, especially among the youth in the townships. Its March 1960 march to Cape Town (led by Philip Kgosana) had been a visible success, culminating in a three-week stay-away. Particular support for the PAC came from within the men's hostels in Langa, and the township seemed to be overwhelmingly supportive of Robert Sobukwe's party. Efforts by the ANC to drum up support often led to violent clashes between rivals.

But Cape Town had been tough on a personal level, too, for Gilbert Hani, a slight, bespectacled man who worked as a hawker by day. He and his good friend, Archie Sibeko, were accused of murdering a police officer in the township, and endured more than two weeks in solitary confinement before they were eventually cleared.

Gilbert Hani immersed himself in the political landscape, rising to be elected chairperson of the Langa Residents Association. Of course, that led to attention from the authorities. Ultimately, he would find himself banned and banished from the Cape Peninsula and ordered to move to Sabalele, though not to his home. The Bantu Commissioner was to decide where Hani senior would live, and the decision to ban him to his village was successfully overturned on appeal, but paramount chief Kaiser Matanzima intervened. Matanzima detested Gilbert Hani for challenging him on the question of an independent bantustan, so he ensured that Hani senior was given a mere 72 hours to find a job in Cape Town. Or else.

Meanwhile, it was natural for Chris Hani to carry on where he had left off at Fort Hare, as a young man whose devotion to justice was embedded in his being. He received the necessary support and understanding from his father and, particularly, his uncle Milton Hani, who lived in Kayamnandi township, outside Stellenbosch. Still under the mentorship of Govan Mbeki, the ANC leader in the Cape Province, Hani quickly found himself embroiled in trade union and political activity.

He became a frequent visitor to the offices of the Food and Canning Workers Union in Plein Street, just a few blocks from his workplace at the law firm. Here, activists like Oscar Mpetha, Elizabeth Mafikeng, Ray Alexander and Jack Simons – who all became legends of the struggle – went about the business of organising workers. Only a year before, when Hani had joined the Communist Party at Fort Hare, he had encountered the writings of Alexander in trade union periodicals, and was in awe.

Hani's ferocious appetite for reading also took him to the offices of *New Age*, also in Plein Street, where Brian Bunting was editor. Among the many people Hani encountered there was the young Cape Town activist James April, who became a comrade during the Wankie campaign.

By 1962, the state's repressive machinery had begun to harass and imprison many of the liberation movement's leading lights, and it also sought to stymie the influence of the labour movement. Hani immersed himself in organising workers, volunteering at the Roeland Street offices of the South African Congress of Trade Unions (SACTU), which had not yet been banned. When his union work allowed him time, he would also commit to the work of the ANC and SACP.

\* \* \*

The shifting support and frustrations in Langa were a microcosm of the larger problems facing the ANC. Early in 1962, the commander-in-chief of the newly formed MK, Nelson Rolihlahla Mandela, paid a visit to Cape Town as part of his countrywide tour to inform the regions of the way forward. Meeting at the Athlone home of traditional healer Gayika Tshawe, members of the regional committee were enthralled as the well-built orator with the deep, authoritative manner informed them of the need to take up arms. This was to be the M-Plan.

A regional MK command was formed, the leadership of which included Looksmart Ngudle, Elijah Losa, Mountain Qumbela and Felinyaniso Njamela. They, in turn, set up 11 units in key places such as Nyanga West, Nyanga East, Langa, Retreat, Maitland, Cape Town central and Kraaifontein. This scattering would ensure that detection of one unit would not bring the entire operation tumbling down.

With little support, and functioning with some autonomy, the regional command lit a fire from the flame. Engineer Denis Goldberg hired a farm just outside Mamre, about 50 kilometres from Cape Town, to conduct training courses. He was joined by lawyer Albie Sachs, activist Wolfie Kodesh, and Second World War veterans Harold Strachan, Jack Hodgson and Ben Turok. Elias Motsoaledi travelled from Johannesburg to teach the group how to make gunpowder. Some of the knowledge for making homemade bombs came straight from books, and involved readily available ingredients. In preparation for the training, Goldberg bought a big bottle of glycerine from a chemist in Adderley Street, causing the pharmacist to blurt out: 'Are you making a bomb?'

The first group selected for training consisted of 36 recruits, carefully chosen from the 11 units. Three of those in the training party – Mncedi Nontshatsha (Alfred Sharp), Mzwakhe Kondleka (James Masimini) and Charles Buqa (Sishuba) – later took part in the battles of Wankie and Sipolilo.

Bordered by a river on one side and an orchard on the other, the Mamre farm was a secluded spot. The volunteers spent days receiving weapons training, learning how to make explosive devices and even discovering how to steal or repair a car, in case they needed to escape in a hurry. At night, Goldberg or Ngudle would read to the men from great revolutionary works, or favourites like Jean-Paul Sartre's *The Wall* and Che Guevara's *Guerrilla Warfare*. Whereas Guevara's book dealt with the practicalities of waging the most clandestine operations in the most unpredictable terrain, Sartre's book was set against the backdrop of the Spanish Civil War when Franco's forces had successfully taken Madrid. The title refers to the wall against which captured prisoners were made to stand as they faced the firing squad. A crucial point in the story is when a prisoner facing execution gives his captors a false address to find a wanted comrade. By pure chance the comrade then moves to that self-same address, leading to his eventual capture and execution. The informer is spared.

The owner of the Mamre farm was away in Johannesburg and had not informed his workers of the arrangement with Goldberg so the workers' suspicions were aroused when they noticed the training group, and they summoned the police. The authorities staged a spectacular raid in which policemen and soldiers were dropped from helicopters. Sachs was left to try and convince the CID detectives that he and the others were training the young men for work as motor mechanics. The engines on display certainly lent credence to his claims. But the detectives were not so easily misled. Why were white men teaching natives? Anyway, they knew Sachs and Goldberg were 'political'. The entire group had to go to Mamre police station for further questioning.

Thirty-four, 35, 36. The CID director finished counting. The three dozen men and their captors had to cross the river on a tree trunk. As they made their way over the makeshift bridge, they warned a comrade popularly known as Mrabalala that he had best try to escape, as the police would surely detect his previous run-ins with the law. As he crossed the river, so the legend goes, Mrabalala slipped down into the quiet stream below, leaving only his nose protruding above the water. Once they had reached the other side, the CID detective insisted there were originally 36 men, but eventually accepted Sachs's assurance that there were only 35.

Perhaps not experienced in dealing with 'terrorists', the police proceeded to question the men without searching the area. Mrabalala, who had safely been left behind, took advantage of this lapse, quickly making his way from his hiding place on the banks of the river to gather up all the weapons and other incriminating material and hide them close to the water. Confident of his comrades' return, he even took the trouble to cook a meal for them.

Bang on time for the dinner bell, at 7.30pm, the men were brought back to their temporary home. Mrabalala watched from a safe distance. A belated police search yielded nothing. And the men who had been captives only minutes before broke out in freedom songs. Although the raid revealed nothing sinister, it's not at all surprising that the police remained utterly convinced that something dangerous was brewing. The men were to report to Mamre police station the next day and were ordered to vacate the farm. The owner was contacted in Johannesburg, and he quickly concurred with the police.

Although the men were released, it is likely that the incident caused the security police to sit up and take notice of the activities in the Cape. Many of the trainees made use of the skills they learned at the camp, taking part in acts of sabotage, cutting telephone lines and hurling petrol bombs at symbols of the apartheid regime.

\* \* \*

In the same year as the Mamre incident, Hani was elected to the highly secretive seven-man regional committee of the western Cape, where he served with the likes of Losa, Ngudle, Bernard Huna, Zoli Malindi, Zola Skweyiya and the chairperson, Archie Sibeko. The members of the committee were drawn from different branches, and, fearing infiltration or discovery, branch committees were unaware of the composition of the main command.

Hani's work as an activist had by now overtaken his ambitions within the legal profession. A lover of sport, he also organised youth teams in soccer, rugby and cricket. These also served as fronts for him to deliver the message of the ANC to the next generation. When it came to mobilising the proletariat, Hani got his hands dirty. The regime had to understand that black South Africans were debilitated by the suffering and humiliation they and their children experienced on a daily basis, Hani said. If the apartheid government did not want to sit down and negotiate, then the people would fight. And the fight started by a few would inspire and lift the spirits of a demoralised people.

A typical operation saw Hani and a small team creep out of Langa at night, navigating in silence the footpaths that led out of the township, using only hand signals to communicate. One of the group would act as a lookout while another produced a thick coil of rope. The group would throw the rope over the telephone line running alongside the road and pull the line down. Another favourite method of sabotage was to cut a small piece out of the line running alongside the telephone pole. It would take the authorities at least a day to replace the entire pole.

An ANC cell working on a construction site at the Bellville quarry, 25 kilometres from Cape Town, became the source of supply for dynamite that would be used in numerous acts of sabotage against symbols of state oppression.

With unrest steadily growing in the black townships of Cape Town, the authorities summoned Kaiser Matanzima from Transkei to calm the angry masses. A public meeting was held in Langa. As people sat down and the events got under way, the hall erupted in a flurry of gunshots. Police successfully whisked Matanzima away from the unseen gunmen. Later it was revealed that ANC members had strung firecrackers through and under the seats in the venue, setting them off moments before Matanzima was to speak.

Faced with an increasingly agitated population and risky acts of sabotage, Pretoria introduced a 90-day detention law, allowing the state to detain suspects without having to bring their captive before a magistrate. Suspects could be held indefinitely as the police would later re-arrest them for a further 90 days once they had completed their first three months in detention.

In Cape Town, the regional committee swung into action. Sibeko and Hani, together with comrades Faldon Mzonke and James Tyeku, had arranged to print leaflets at the home of a member of the Coloured People's Organisation. Using a Roneo machine, they printed 25 reams of leaflets decrying the repressive new law, and used the moment to deliver revolutionary propaganda about the reasons for the ANC's armed struggle. Certainly incendiary, the leaflets were designed to incite controlled rebellion.

The material was loaded into the boot of Tyeku's Ford while Mzonke made his way to work. On their way to Nyanga East, the group picked up Sibeko. But the trio were stopped at a police roadblock at one of the two entrances to the township. A Studebaker that had been following the group unnoticed for much of the journey now pulled in front of them. A search of the Ford left little doubt as to the group's activities. Hani and Sibeko were led away at gunpoint by Spyker van Wyk of the Security Branch, who had earned his nickname, Spyker ('nail'), for his elongated physical form and unpleasant demeanour. He and other members of the Security Branch had become familiar faces at trade union meetings.

As he led them to the waiting police van, Van Wyk warned the activists that he was 'not taking any nonsense' from them. Sibeko warned the younger, less experienced Hani not to let anything slip to the police. He would not, Hani assured him.

The first stop was Phillipi police station, where they were separated, with Sibeko taken to Athlone police station, where he spent the weekend. On Monday morning they were reunited at Wynberg Magistrate's Court, where they were formally charged under the Suppression of Communism Act and for furthering the aims of a banned organisation.

With the case postponed for a month and bail refused, the operatives were taken, manacled, to their homes, which were searched. Nothing was found. The next stop was the SACTU office in Roeland Street, where the typewriters were checked against the leaflets. Again, nothing.

Taken to Roeland Street Prison, Hani, Sibeko and Tyeku were stripped naked, finally being reunited with their clothing after a thorough search.

Only their pounds were declared and written down, the coins shared between corrupt wardens and prisoners assisting with the processing. New prisoners were separated by the internal prison 'government' – men who had been there before and had been rewarded for their years inside with prison gang ranks, which many carried tattooed across their bodies. At night the 'court' would sit. The prisoners' own system of magistrates, prosecutors, defence attorneys and policemen would be in attendance. At their mercy, a man's fate during his time in prison would be decided: whether he would be granted an opportunity to join a gang or be 'used'. But political prisoners were different. They were fighting against the forces of oppression. They were not criminals and would not be drawn into this macabre theatre, the court decided.

The ANC comrades spent the next 30 days in isolation cells, the movement ensuring they got food, books and newspapers. There was time for reflection, but there was frustration at the failure to do proper reconnaissance, for printing the leaflets at an untested contact and, mostly, for putting Hani in this position. When Sibeko had approached Gilbert Hani to get the young articled clerk involved in the movement's activities, it was in order to use Chris's advanced education to articulate the aims of the struggle. Hani could also be invaluable in harvesting support from urbanised Africans, especially those living in Ndabeni, who moved around freely with special blue exemption papers. He was supposed to write the literature, not print and distribute it, Sibeko remonstrated with himself. Either way, it was done.

At their next court appearance, the three were surprised to find Mzonke with them in the dock. Immediately, suspicion fell on Hani. As the youngest and most inexperienced member of the group, it seemed more likely that the police had got him to give more than his name and address during interrogation. But the 'usual' liberation movement lawyer, Sam Khan, allayed their suspicions by pointing out that Hani, Mzonke and Tyeku's fingerprints had all been found on the leaflets. It had been fairly easy to pinpoint Mzonke as he was missing a finger on one hand.

The group was sentenced to 18 months in prison with hard labour.

Bail was set at 125 pounds – a fortune at the time. But the power of the collective prevailed: contributions from factory and farm workers, sidewalk salesmen, community entertainers and vendors ultimately helped generate the funds to pay bail and contribute towards legal fees. Bail was extended while the propagandists considered leave to appeal. However, the magistrate failed to impose the same strict bail conditions as before, which had had the group reporting to a police station daily and being confined to the Wynberg district. This temporary lapse allowed Hani to travel to Lobatse, just inside the border with the British protectorate of Bechuanaland (Botswana).

\* \* \*

Across the country, the police were becomingly increasingly vigilant. Roadblocks were frequently set up, seemingly at random. Still, there were loopholes. Africans travelling in second class on a train from Cape Town to Johannesburg were perhaps less likely to arouse suspicion than those travelling in the 'cattle carriages' of third class. As Hani and the rest of the ANC western Cape leadership made their way north, they spent most of their time in the second-class carriage. When the conductor approached, the group scrambled up to their bunks and under blankets to avoid being noticed.

Once in Johannesburg, the group was collected by men driving kombis. They were taken to the Bechuanaland border, where they were to cross on foot illegally. They were to make their way to a house that, over time, became a way station for hundreds of courageous young men and women escaping into exile. The middle-aged man who greeted the group as they arrived was most familiar to Sibeko. He was Fish Keitsing, and the two had been among the 156 accused who stepped into the dock in 1956 during the Treason Trial. Now, the ANC's first underground conference since its banning in 1960 was about to kick off at Keitsing's house. This would be the last time for more than 30 years that the leaders of the liberation movement in exile and inside the country would convene in this way.

A monumental decision had to be made. For many of the regional representatives, this was the first time they had heard of the ANC's desire to pursue an armed struggle. So much of the discussion at Lobatse focused on how to implement this strategy and set up an underground network. Throughout these discussions, Hani and the rest of the regional leadership took a back seat, and let Govan Mbeki carry the flag for the Cape.

The conference re-energised the men from the Cape and made the prospect of a lengthy jail term fade into obscurity. Upon their return to Cape Town, however, a shock awaited Hani and Sibeko. The police were on their trail again. Their lawyers had apparently forgotten to seek leave to appeal, leaving police convinced that the two had skipped bail. Frantic negotiations eventually saw the men granted condonation of late appeal, but with the reimposition of strict bail conditions. By this time, Albie Sachs had become involved in the case. He was convinced the group would be set free on appeal. But the ANC and SACP regional committee decided that, should the appeal fail, the four convicted men should go into exile. Despite Sachs's protestations, politics now took over.

Policy at the time dictated that all cadres sent into exile should be unmarried, and Hani was the only one without a family of his own. However, the length of time to which the men had been sentenced, and the time they would spend away from their families, would be just as damaging. In February 1963, when their sentences were confirmed, the four split into pairs and went into hiding until a group could be assembled for the arduous journey into exile. Hani and Sibeko went into hiding together.

White sympathisers played an important part in protecting the fugitives. In one instance, activist Bernard Gottschalk drove the two to the home of another ANC supporter, Jack Tarshish, who owned a garment factory. His flat in Rondebosch became their refuge for a while, with Tarshish instructing the two to maintain total silence while he was away and not to open the door for anyone. Hani and Sibeko were determined to follow his instructions to the letter, and Sibeko recalled how once, during their stay, Tarshish, a narcoleptic, fell asleep standing at his front door. Although he was clearly visible to the fugitives through the peephole, there was nothing they could do but wait for him to wake up by himself. Finally, and to their great relief, Denis Goldberg's wife, Esmé, arrived and ushered Tarshish into his flat.

Holed up in that apartment, the risk of discovery ever-present, Hani and Sibeko kept their spirits up by discussing the way forward, what life would be like in exile, what to do should they get separated, and how to carry on the fight underground. They had to wait for instructions, and each visitor brought the hope that a move was imminent. But then it became clear that Tarshish's flat was becoming too exposed.

The routes to freedom were still at an experimental stage. Joe Modise, a streetwise fighter from Alexandra township in Johannesburg, had been appointed as the commander of the fledgling MK, and he had already left the country to set up communications channels and stops along the journey that would eventually lead to Tanganyika. A first group had departed from Transkei, and, slowly, more and more activists were starting to come in from the Cape and the Transvaal. Although planning was as meticulous as possible, the success of underground escape routes depended on the vigilance and dedication of individuals.

Many of those early flights into exile took cadres through Zeerust, a town effectively under the ANC's control after 1957, when the chief of the Bafarutse encouraged his people not to carry passes. Those arriving here from around the country were taken by bus and then left, seemingly in the middle of nowhere. A white handkerchief was a key sign to identify the contact person who would guide them the rest of the way. That man was almost always Simon Senna, a devotee of the liberation movement whose interventions ensured that hundreds of cadres were supported on those first steps along the narrow footpaths into Bechuanaland.

From the Cape, the first group to attempt the route into exile for training included Looksmart Ngudle. The group's first destination was Krugersdorp, and their story was that they were on their way to play a soccer match in Johannesburg. This become a popular cover for those fleeing the country in groups. But, upon arriving in Krugersdorp, there was no sign of their contact, a man known as Patrick Mthembu. So the small group decided to make their own way to the far-off Soweto home of Walter Sisulu, who was under house arrest at the time. It being a Sunday, the group used the cover provided by the throngs of soccer supporters at a nearby field to relay a message through Sisulu's son, Zwelakhe. Accommodation was secured at the home of a sympathiser. Ultimately, the group managed to escape and make it across the border to safety – and an entirely false sense of freedom.

As a result of these problems, the leadership had decided to send Sibeko ahead to ensure everything ran according to plan for the second group. As a representative at the drawing-up of the Freedom Charter in 1955, Sibeko's rudimentary knowledge of Johannesburg would be invaluable to the group, many of whom had never left the Cape Province.

Thus, in May, a huddle of young men, neatly dressed in blazers and slacks, each carrying a suitcase, assembled at Cape Town station. There were no parades and no fiery speeches; no band, no gushing parents, sobbing mothers or excited children. No one gave these soldiers a send-off. Instead, as the train rumbled across the Karoo and the young men settled into their second-class seats, thoughts of Cape Town provided comfort amid the uncertainty ahead.

When the men alighted at Krugersdorp station, the contact again failed to show. Sibeko quickly led the men away from the station to buses that would take them to Soweto. Here, the group was split up and taken to various homes where Sibeko had arranged safe haven. Hani spent more than a week in White City, Jabavu, with a family sympathetic to the struggle.

His charges safe and with time to contemplate the way forward, Sibeko was livid. Where was the contact? He made his way to Mthembu's house, where he found the man relaxing. Mthembu was nonplussed by Sibeko's sudden appearance, and insisted he had sent someone to the station who said the group had not been there. Mthembu argued with Sibeko, but it made no difference. The group still had to leave the country, and Mthembu's help was crucial. As the weeks passed, Sibeko visited

Mthembu daily while the group anxiously waited for word that final arrangements had been made.

Finally, the day arrived for the group to leave the cover of Soweto. By then, their number had swelled to 40 men, and two kombis were needed for the journey to the border. Word had been sent from the leadership that a nucleus of cadres was to be sent for training. The regions had responded, and soon Soweto had become a little crowded with would-be combatants. Those who had arrived at about the same time as Hani from other parts of South Africa were holed up in one hideout. Among the men joining the Cape Town group was Mark Shope, a prominent trade unionist who had done the trip before and would be the leader.

There was silence as the convoy made its way northwest to the border, the landscape remarkable to the young men, most of whom had never been more than 100 kilometres beyond their place of birth. A guide known as 'Pilot' appeared to take them over the border. Confidently keeping a steady pace ahead of his younger comrades, he took them deep into the shadows, hours later announcing they were in Bechuanaland. The journey had started at sunset. When dawn broke, the group was in another country.

Those going into exile would not forget Fish Keitsing's words as he guided them along the footpaths turning and falling away from the border with South Africa: 'Today you tie your testicles. You will not meet a woman until you come back.' Hundreds of ANC recruits passed through Keitsing's hands in this way, on their way to the camps. Born in Bechuanaland, he became an active member of the liberation movement – prominent enough for police to detain and later expel him from South Africa. Although the South African authorities were well aware of his activities just inside the British protectorate – and, later, within independent Botswana – they failed to suffocate this essential lifeline: the Freedom Trail.

Holed up in a house just inside Bechuanaland after making the crossing, Hani and his comrades came face to face with a man he would later regard as something of a nemesis: Modise. The bulk of the man alone was intimidating, his loud voice occasionally slipping into *tsotsitaal* in a way that silenced any doubters. This meeting was innocuous enough. Modise had already briefed MK command about the 'parcel' they should expect, and a truck had been arranged to transport the men to the border with Northern Rhodesia (Zambia). Originally, the ANC had managed to charter flights to take cadres into exile. But the South African and British authorities were monitoring everything and placing increasing pressure on operators. Regardless, such transport was also becoming too expensive.

As the flatbed Bedford truck rumbled towards Francistown, the men felt more at ease. Things were now starting to fall into place. The poor condition of the road meant the young men had to pull, and sometimes push, the heavy vehicle. By the end of the day, they were told they were halfway. Some recruits went off and, bravely, returned with the carcass of a zebra. Pap was cooked as an accompaniment. It was something of a surprising adventure, and they braced themselves for what lay ahead.

After a miserably cold night in the bushveld, they resumed their journey, but the road to their destination – Kazangula – was in terrible shape. Tired and worn out, the men finally lumbered into town. Modise was already in Kazangula, this time with money and further instructions for the journey. Again, he arranged a truck for the trip to the Zambezi River early the next morning. The group would cross on the first ferry, hoping the early start would keep them clear of border patrols. The ANC had appointed activist Sam Masemula to be on the ferry to guide them along the rest of the journey. Dropped about six kilometres from the river, the men were made to walk the rest of the way.

A young black Southern Rhodesia policeman happened upon the group. Pretending to be Ndebele does not work when you are speaking to an Ndebele. Still, luck was on their side. The policeman was sympathetic, and promised not to reveal their location, but he confirmed their worst fears. Police were aware of a group of cadres trying to make their way across the border for military training in Tanganyika. Every effort would be made to stop them. The men retreated towards a nearby poultry farm to regroup.

An entire day passed, pitifully slowly. The policeman had promised not to inform on them, but would he keep his word? Something had to be done. Finally, it was decided that Shope, who had a darker complexion and was therefore closer in appearance to the people of Northern Rhodesia, would be sent to try to sort out their situation. His familiarity with the route would also allow him to take the right bus in search of Masemula.

As the hours passed, armed patrols passed by regularly, each one raising the possibility of discovery. The day drew to a close, and another recruit was dispatched to go in search of Shope. Along the way, he saw the last patrol passing by, on its way back to camp. At last, with desperate hope, the coast seemed clear. The men cautiously crept from their hideout and eventually boarded the last pontoon across the river. Two hours later, Shope returned with a truck and a glorious loaf of bread for the famished men. He had not found Masemula, but the transport would take them to Livingstone, 50 kilometres away.

Livingstone was crawling with police, who would not leave the area until the train for Lusaka had departed. But once in Livingstone, the ANC men found that Kenneth Kaunda's United National Independence Party (UNIP) swung into action, arranging refreshments for the weary group and temporary accommodation in a local township. Now wary of the authorities' knowledge of their movement, the group had to take extra precautions.

Taking a train from Livingstone Station was risky. The roads were probably being monitored too, so the train was still a safer option. In Livingstone, Shope had finally seen Masemula, who had dropped an envelope as he passed by. Inside were the train tickets for the men. But the journey was only beginning. A few boarded the Lusaka-bound train at Livingstone station. Others were taken by truck to board at Zimba station – one stop away. Some got on the train even further along the route. By splitting into smaller groups they could blend in with the local population.

Masemula was already on the train. Moving inconspicuously through the carriages, deliberately ignoring the men distributed throughout, he silently made his presence known. Through gestures, he informed his followers of plainclothes policemen in the crowd. Be careful. Avoid contact with each other. Fit in. But the men were eager to speak to Masemula, to be given reassurance, even though attempts to approach him were met by a clearing of the throat, a stamping of feet and a slight toss of the head. 'They' were watching.

As the sun rose over another day, the passengers began to emerge from slumber. The train pulled into Kafue station, where a group of policemen boarded. Immediately, conversation became uncomfortable. Some fell silent altogether. Making their way through the carriages, the policemen asked some of the lighter-skinned men to accompany them. Hani stared straight ahead, the baby on his lap ensuring he warranted nothing more than a cursory glance. Others cottoned on to this strategem; Zola Skweyiya also pulled a child on to his lap. As the train continued its journey towards the capital, Hani's casual glance revealed he was not the only one to have escaped detection.

But their respite was brief. As the small group disembarked at Lusaka station, police were on hand to arrest the rest of them. They had known about the group all along. Those who had been taken off the train at Kafue were already there when the rest of the group walked meekly into their captors' embrace at Lusaka station.

Eager and efficient, the police had done their job well. The operation had been a resounding success. But two irritating and persistent lawyers named James Skinner and Sikota Wina soon appeared to pester the officers. Would the men be arrested? People could not be detained without a charge, they insisted. The appearance of the attorneys was the work of Masemula, who had escaped the police dragnet and immediately sought the assistance of the UNIP. The party had sent the lawyers to see what could be done.

The police had not thought much beyond apprehending the suspects. 'I'm arresting you,' said one officer as he made his way down the line, touching each man on the shoulder. This was exactly what Skinner and

Wina had wanted. The arrested men would now appear before a court and be released, Skinner explained to his new clients.

In the jail cells in central Lusaka, the freedom to talk freely was a gift. Other prisoners, many of them political detainees, welcomed their visitors from the south. Mostly, the men marvelled at the soft touch of their British captors. No batons or sjamboks raised in anger. No indiscriminate slaps or punches. No loud and violent threats. No baas. Not a single firearm on show. And the food! Three square meals a day.

The next day, as planned, the group appeared one by one before the magistrate. The plan was for a crowd of UNIP supporters to gather at the court. Skinner guessed correctly that, once released, the group would again be the targets of police who would try to detain them for entering the territory illegally and failing to leave within the prescribed 24 hours. But things went awry and Sibeko, first up and newly released, was duly re-arrested by the police. Amazingly, he broke free and managed to flee into the jubilant UNIP crowd, before being spirited away by supporters. UNIP had already colluded with the clerk of the court. As soon as Sibeko was set free, the documents prepared for the rest of the detainees were signed and hurriedly taken to the cells, ensuring freedom of the rest of the group.

Soon the men were reunited at a UNIP safe house in the suburb of Silenje. UNIP quickly organised a convoy of brand-new cars to take them to the border with Tanganyika. Just short of the border and in fading light, the men got out of the cars and were guided on foot across into Tanganyika. The drivers of the cars, complete with the appropriate luggage, would tell border authorities in Northern Rhodesia they were transporting samples.

On the other side, there was at last no need for lies. Left a short distance from the border at Mbeya, the ANC men hesitantly accompanied their hosts to the customs post to declare themselves. Laughing officers filled out the paperwork and welcomed the men into the newly liberated country.

Standing, waiting, finally free of anxiety, the recruits saw things they had never seen before. Why were so many women dressed in black, clearly in mourning? Had there been a massacre? It was quickly explained to the South Africans that these were not widows, but Muslims, wearing the traditional dress of married women.

The all-day journey to Dar es Salaam rushed past. At the station, the men were met by the ANC's chief representative, James Hadebe – a friendly face. A comrade. He drove the group to ANC headquarters, and there, sitting amid a circle of desks, was OR Tambo. Extraordinary. All around the office, young South African nurses moved about, sent by the ANC to assist the independent nation. In this distinctly homely enclave, thousands of kilometres away from the life they knew, even the air smelled different. But there was tremendous sorrow in the background.

When Hani and Sibeko left Cape Town, Looksmart Ngudle had taken over as chair of the regional command. But later that year, the entire MK underground operation would be exposed and he would die in detention, with his torturers claiming he had hanged himself with a piece of cord. Govan Mbeki, also detained, would reveal the terrible lie in this, as Ngudle had bravely passed him a note before he was killed, revealing the tragedy that was unfolding.

There were also agonizing ironies. In August 1963, a group of Cape men sent for training were arrested at a roadblock en route to Bechuanaland, and their story that they were on their way from Soweto to a funeral did not fool the police. During the interrogation, someone spoke. Knowing that Ngudle moved regularly from one hideout to the next, the informer told police where the Cape commander was, believing Ngudle would have moved on. But, in a strange echo of Sartre's *The Wall*, Ngudle had apparently fallen ill and was spending an extended period at the house pointed out by the informer.

CHAPTER 4

# THE USSR

The camouflaged men trudged wearily through the snow. Each movement in the forest was fraught with danger. The scouts sent ahead were the tentacles. Even so, the platoon could easily be outflanked. Stop. A quick check on the chart, compass alongside. No, it was no use. They were lost. They had gone wrong somewhere. The group leader tried to recall the months of training in topography, how to determine direction by the way the bark grows on trees or by using landmarks. It had been hours since the group was dropped off in the middle of the forest on the outskirts of Moscow.

Chris Hani checked the compass again. None of the elevations corresponded with what was on the map. The instructors would be disappointed. But there was a village, so perhaps they would be able to salvage their pride after all. Perhaps this was another test – an ideal place for an ambush? The men took cover, prepared for whatever might come next. They waited, and waited. An hour later, the scout returned: the enemy was coming. The men braced themselves. In the dark, they set their sights on the middle of the clearing, the cold wood of the Kalashnikov stock pressed against their jaws, each man with one eye closed, his finger already gently squeezing the trigger.

Too casually, the enemy – a stranger on a bicycle – approached, closer and closer, slowly, unknowingly being reeled into the trap. A cacophony of automatic fire tore through the quiet serenity of the forest. The enemy screamed, dropped his bicycle and fled.

Shortly afterwards the police arrived, but the local military commander defused the situation and explained it was a military exercise gone wrong. The 'enemy' turned out to be a villager on his way home from work. The cadres in training at the Lenin Institute in Moscow had unfortunately got it all wrong, but they would improve as time went on.

\* \* \*

Even the journey to the Union of Soviet Socialist Republics (USSR) some months before had presented unexpected experiences. It had begun as they stepped off the plane onto the sticky tarmac in Khartoum, capital of Sudan, on their way to Russia. They made their way to the air-conditioned respite of the passenger terminal. Standing among tall dark men wrapped in crisp white linen, everything seemed foreign. But it was still Africa. Soon they boarded the 'Camel' – a Russian Tupolev Tu-104 airliner – for the flight to Moscow. It was still winter in southern Africa. The heat of Sudan, and the short stop in Cairo, gave no warning to the 30 MK cadres of what lay ahead. In Moscow, the light was different, the landscape splashed with many shades of green. As the men stared out of the windows of the bus taking them from the airport to the place that would be their home for the next year, the might of the USSR was everywhere visible.

After coming to power in 1953, Soviet leader Nikita Khrushchev had instituted a period of economic reform, which had brought increased growth and a rise in living standards. He had also rid the USSR of some of the fear and gloom of the Stalin era. However, by the time Hani and his group arrived in Moscow, Khrushchev was battling to keep his position, accused of adventurism in the Cuban Missile Crisis of October 1962 and seen as a diplomatic disaster on the international stage. After a particularly bad harvest in 1963, he was replaced by Leonid Brezhnev, his former right-hand man.

Discussions of Soviet policy were lively among Hani's group, which included people like Lawrence Phokanoka, who had been at Fort Hare with him. It was Hani who had sought Phokanoka out at Mandela House, where those recruits drawn to a political life were housed in Dar es Salaam. Hani had convinced him to join the group at Luthuli House, who were destined instead for a military career.

In the USSR now, the men were witnesses to the way a powerful nation was run. For Hani, having joined the Communist Party a mere two years earlier, but having read extensively on socialism and Marxism, it was the culmination of theory, reading, imagining. It was akin to Mecca. The Vatican. The country of Lenin.

There were no beggars and no blatant poverty. The activity in the city was frenetic: houses being built on one side, flats on the other. Later the men marvelled at the fact that education and medical attention were free to all. This was the product of the revolution. All the propaganda, the lies cranked out by the Western imperialists denouncing life in the Soviet Union, had been disproved.

The officers who met the men as they stepped off the Camel seemed genuinely excited to see their fellow revolutionaries from so far away. For some of the cadres, this was the first time they had experienced compassion, understanding and support from white people. This treatment strengthened their will to fight for a nonracial society.

\* \* \*

A continent away, heads of state of the independent African nations had gathered to establish the Organisation of African Unity (OAU), its primary aim to end colonialism and apartheid in Rhodesia, South Africa, Mozambique and Angola. Ethiopian emperor Haile Selassie pleaded that the union last a thousand years. 'Our armageddon is past. Africa has been reborn as a free continent and Africans have been reborn as free men. The blood that was shed and the sufferings that were endured are today Africa's advocates for freedom and unity,' said Selassie on 25 May 1963 at the opening in Addis Ababa, which became the seat of the OAU.

It had been almost a decade since the first groups of MK cadres were sent abroad for training to countries like Morocco, Egypt, Ethiopia and Algeria (where Mandela had trained). A month after Hani's group departed for Moscow, another group of 50 – led by Modise – made their way there too. Theirs was a more arduous journey overland to Juba in southern Sudan, and by boat along the River Nile to Khartoum – where Simon Senna remarked on the true extent of poverty in Africa after seeing a mature, pregnant woman wearing shorts and nothing else. After travelling for almost a month, the men flew to Odessa in what is now the Ukraine.

Those who were sent to Egypt underwent some of the most demanding training, much of it deep in the desert. The cadres were sent on an officers' survival training course and encountered a host of different nationalities during their time there. Not everyone survived. By the time the men returned to Cairo they were emaciated and had to hole up in a hotel for a month to recuperate.

For others going for training, the entire experience, from boarding an aircraft for the first time to meeting white people on a more intimate basis, was completely overwhelming, sometimes with surprisingly comical results. Radilori Moumakwe was 19 years old when he was sent to the Soviet Union, armed with only the six months of training he had received in Dar es Salaam from ANC instructors:

After the plane took off from Nairobi, I felt like going to the toilet. I open the toilet and I see the clouds. I say, I'm above the clouds, no, I can't sit here, man. This thing is going to break and then I will fall down. So I had to go back and hold myself for six hours until we reached Cairo.

In Odessa, Moumakwe saw many white people. In South Africa, blacks were taught that you were not supposed to touch a white man because you would make him dirty. As Moumakwe stepped off the plane to be greeted by a white Russian, hand extended, the Zeerust youngster retreated in fear, finally being reassured that this was a different country to the racist one he had left behind.

\* \* \*

After their arrival in Moscow, the cadres received a thorough medical check-up, in which samples of their blood, urine and faeces were taken. They were given uniforms, boots, overcoats, bags, clean blankets, sheets and pillowcases and civilian suits. They would receive a regular allowance of 25 roubles each, as well as cigarettes and beer.

Hani and his comrades revelled in the Moscow experience, even though they had not gone there as tourists and there was no time to waste. The cadres started their training immediately, with classes in politics, the theory of socialism, the history of the Soviet Union, the history of the Russian Revolution, political economy and the national liberation struggle in South Africa. Instruction in guerrilla tactics, including demolition, would follow later.

The rules were rigid. When working with explosives, everything had to be 'clean'. There should be nothing but deliberate mixing of chemicals. Common household items like sugar and sawdust suddenly took on new meaning as they became ingredients. Mistakes could be fatal. The cadres were also taught communication among guerrilla units using walkie-talkies, and how to fix radios and weapons. Lessons in topography and conspiracy prepared them for working underground and avoiding arrest, using dead letter boxes (DLBs) and keeping clear of detection.

The plan was that this group of men would be in the vanguard of the guerrilla army – well-trained and self-sufficient, with no absolute need for troops at their rear. They would infiltrate South Africa and train small intelligence and guerrilla units to lay the groundwork for a conventional army. The first Moscow group believed these units would ultimately fall under their control. Most of the subsequent training took place in Odessa, but later, with increased demand from liberation organisations across

Africa, a training centre was opened at Perevalnoye in the Crimea, near the city of Simferopol. Here, the instructors drew on the wartime experiences of Crimean partisans, who had fought the Germans in mountains, forest and bush – conditions not unlike South Africa.

* * *

In heated, well-insulated classrooms, the men listened attentively to their instructors. Most of those assembled had not received much formal education. The skills gained herding cattle, organising workers or trading were not called for here. The men were out of their depth, but Hani – a skinny young man – proved to be a revelation. What his comrades did not fully comprehend in class during the day, the highly educated Hani would impart to them at night, ensuring they kept up to speed with their keen Soviet instructors. Often assisted by an English translator, the Russian officers – 'men who loved war' and had survived at least two – were outstanding instructors. The specialised training centre, on the outskirts of Moscow, was headed by a Second World War guerrilla brigade commander. There were regular visits from the SACP Central Committee, with the likes of Moses Kotane and Joe Slovo addressing the cadres in political education.

The compound was run on strict military lines. Rising at the crack of dawn, the MK cadres started the day with a march, returning to the compound to wash and have breakfast before theoretical and military training began. Often, the training involved being driven into the forests and marshes surrounding Moscow to set up camp. From here, utilising their training, the men had to navigate their way to a predetermined location.

With three square meals a day cooked by white women, and being taught by white instructors, this was 'a new world of equality where our colour seems to be of no consequence … where our humanity is recognised,' wrote Hani.

Instruction was not limited to military matters, and included social and cultural education. There were regular trips to museums, concerts and the renowned Bolshoi Ballet. Many of the soldiers came to appreciate visiting the Great Theatre, an imposing white stone building with a massive five-tiered auditorium, ornate chandeliers and plush red velvet seats. The sound of the pit orchestra, the graceful, emotive movements on stage, the costumes and the carefully manipulated sets all worked together to enthral the audience. Works like Tchaikovsky's *Swan Lake* and *The Nutcracker*, Glinka's *A Life for the Tsar* and Khachaturian's *Spartacus* held the audience in raptures. To a man, the cadres gawked at the ethereal beings flitting about the stage. For some, it had been months, even years since they had been with a woman, so the experience of watching such physical beauty must have had a profound impact on their emotions. Over time, these men from so far away came to appreciate and love Russian ballet and opera.

The men were also taken on journeys around Moscow to visit state-run factories and into the countryside to see how the rural areas reflected the tenets of communism. One of Hani's favourite stories from these trips happened during an excursion to the countryside. The cadres were getting off a bus when they saw women running past them towards a church, where they blessed themselves as they watched the young black men. The commanders escorting the MK cadres later explained that this was the first time these rural people had seen Africans; when they saw the likes of Hani they thought the men must be the biblical offspring of Ham, who had been cursed by Noah.

'Now, of course I know that we were not exposed to everything that was happening, but that partial opening of the window into this new society served to strengthen our strong socialist convictions,' Hani explained. The sacrifices of the Russian people during the civil war of 1917-21 also left an 'indelible' impression on the military trainee:

Everything now is covered up by the excesses that followed. And yet for us as people in this country, let us look at those few years after the Russian Revolution in 1917, when power actually was taken from the hands of the rich few into the hands of the working class. And let's forget about the aberrations that happened afterwards … we must draw the important lessons of what appeared to be a popular democracy, the Soviets, the people coming into the streets.

One day, Moses Kotane arrived at the compound. There had been a setback. A catastrophe. Virtually the entire executive of the fledgling MK command had been arrested at Liliesleaf Farm in Rivonia, Johannesburg, on 11 July 1963. The charges against them would relate to preparing for a guerrilla war and furthering the aims of communism. Life sentences would be handed down almost a year later, leaving the liberation movement reeling. The forces at home were in disarray.

Overnight, the six-month training schedule had turned into a year. Nevertheless, with a gruelling daily schedule in place, the generous Russian hosts had ensured their visitors had few opportunities to be idle or get homesick, despite this significant delay. There was one apparent aberration, however – the men were instructed not to learn Russian, as their instructors feared this could pose a security threat for them later. 'When you go back, you dream and you talk in your sleep. You don't know what language you're talking,' Archie Sibeko told us. Perhaps it was the irrepressible South African rebellious streak, but the cadres picked up Russian anyway over time. The conversation of the women in the kitchen proved invaluable in this regard.

Trade unionist Mark Shope was originally at the head of the group when they arrived in Moscow, but he was called to Prague to represent the South African labour movement at the World Federation of Trade Unions. So Sibeko – fondly known as Zola Zembe – replaced him. One day during a volleyball game, Sibeko, a teetotaller, realised that some of the men had got hold of alcohol and were drunk. After a thorough search of every room, a number of bottles were discovered. Someone had even hidden four bottles inside Sibeko's coat. And soon the source of the liquor was identified: those helpful ladies in the kitchen.

After this incident, the men were doing training in the compound when they noticed a hand sticking through the wooden perimeter fence, clasping a bottle of liquor. Armed with basic conversational Russian, some of the men had sneaked off the base to walk into Moscow to buy their forbidden bottles, and the man outside the fence was the black marketeer. 'It was a case of people showing they can be clever when others think they can rule you,' Sibeko recalled, with some humour.

By the time the 30 well-trained cadres returned to Dar es Salaam in November 1964, American civil rights leader Martin Luther King had become the youngest person ever to receive the Nobel Peace Prize, for his peaceful efforts at racial integration. Liberated Tanganyika and Zanzibar had merged to become Tanzania under the leadership of Julius Nyerere. Inspired and enthused by the revolutionary fervour instilled in them through every class, march and cultural visit, the young South African revolutionaries were ready. Freedom seemed but a day away. And for Hani, whose compatriots had come to cherish him during their time in Russia, those early opportunities to teach men who were his seniors in both age and political experience saw the once-timid young man come into his own. His experiences in the land of the Soviets had convinced him.

CHAPTER 5

# KONGWA

When Hani boarded an Aeroflot flight in Moscow in November 1964, he had not set foot on the African continent for more than a year. He took his seat in the plane among dozens of other MK cadres fresh from Lenin's crucible – elated, enthusiastically Marxist, masters of dialectical materialism and the versatile AK47. After more than a year of training in the Soviet Union, their destination was newly unified Tanzania, where Julius Nyerere, the debonair pan-African socialist, had engineered the merger of the infant Republic of Tanganyika and the post-revolutionary archipelago of Zanzibar a scant eight months earlier. A decade before, Nyerere had used the political infrastructure of a civic and student organisation to create the Tanganyika African National Union (TANU). Quietly critical, quickly influential, Nyerere struck a nationalist covenant with the left once total independence was secured, within three years of the British packing their bags.

Hundreds of cadres from southern Africa's liberation movements were arriving in Dar es Salaam, seizing the opportunity for refuge offered by Nyerere, longing for the frontline. Thousands more, ordinary white and Asian citizens of the East African nation, were leaving, their one-way tickets mostly to Britain.

Hani would have spent the long flight from Moscow in conversation with other cadres who had been with him in training. There were no rhetorical barricades with him; he invited argument. Four years later, some say under a death sentence and then expelled from the party, it would be Heraclitus's view – that all is flux – that would underscore his life. But now was a time of heightened consciousness.

The sophistication of Nyerere's novel philosophy of African socialism and *ujamaa* – the traditional classless collective – attracted him. Like democracy, the Tanzanian leader declared, socialism was an attitude of the mind. Hani's admiration for Nyerere, whom he saw reflected in Oliver Tambo in his ability to listen and then judge, was grafted onto an avowed distaste for individual possession of wealth. To his grave, Hani remained precise about his commitment to the marginalised. He wore Nyerere's argument against the forces of political prestige soberly.

Nyerere had already offered the ANC leadership a small patch of land for use by MK at Kongwa, some 400 kilometres south of the capital, on the hot central plateau. He liked to remind his visitors of a Swahili saying: treat your guest as a guest for two days, and on the third day give him a hoe. So the ANC received little assistance from the Tanzanian government in transforming the lonely village – stripped of its meagre assets by departing colonialists – into a camp. All that was left were two abandoned buildings.

Hani was chosen to set up Kongwa, together with Ambrose Makiwane and Lennox Lagu. It was in that capacity, as a commissar in the camp, that he approached Tambo, Modise, and the communists Moses Mabhida, JB Marks and Joe Slovo with the idea of opening up a route into South Africa through the wild, open bushland of Rhodesia.

By Christmas 1964, the MK soldiers were already impatient. They believed the time to go home, to take the fight inside at last, was drawing near, so they viewed Tanzania as a transit point – a passage on the way to war. It was becoming clear to Hani and others that their desire to use their training to fulfil the mandate of an armed struggle, had struck an unexpectedly discordant note within the ANC's leadership. Preoccupied with setting up an administration in exile, while competing with Thabo Mbeki's drive for international solidarity from his base at the University of Sussex, the leadership would be called to account within two years by the young man from Sabalele.

Presciently, he feared the unravelling of the meritocracy within the ANC's top structures, which was slowly becoming apparent, first in Dar es Salaam and then in Morogoro, where the movement moved its headquarters. This troubled Hani, who, as a profoundly conscious young leader of the organisation, was alarmed by the passive nature of some within the administration, and their seeming lack of devotion to the armed struggle, which had been such a hard-won decision at Lobatse.

Hani believed there was nothing wrong with testing the political boundaries of the leadership. He was a loyal cadre, and his questions emerged strictly out of that honourable crusade. He had to state his clearest objectives and prove his reasons for being where he was. So, even if more highly ranked officials demurred at the thought of MK cadres going into battle with the aim of reinfiltration and, ultimately, victory, Hani immediately volunteered to help plan and lead the proposed Wankie campaign, an operation to insert cadres into Rhodesia to open infiltration routes into South Africa.

Accepting a delay as this proposal was debated and then, finally, ratified by a divided National Executive Committee (NEC) in Lusaka, the 23-year-old Hani retreated into the one pleasure he knew would distract him from his frustration, and engage him. He read whatever he could find, while also initiating the newspaper *Dawn* at Kongwa. Albie Sachs, who knew Hani at various points in his life, remarked on how the man he remembered could never sit still and allow life to unfold around him. This craving for contact with the intellect, with purpose, dated back to when Hani found himself part of the political space that was opening up for the ANC in Cape Town in the early 1960s. 'Physically handsome, Chris was [also] the intellectual person who loved books, thought and ideas,' Sachs told us. 'He was not filled with rhetoric or bluster ... strength was his enduring quality.' Other cadres remarked on how Hani would disappear with a book into the forest outside Kongwa camp whenever he could – just to be alone, to fill his mind. They would warn him that he was going to be eaten by pythons.

Yet Hani was no fading wallflower of the revolutionary movement. He is remembered as much for being sociable – loud and sociable – as for engaging in spontaneous political education. He adored jokes, but he could talk about everything, from Libya – which helped fund the training in the Soviet Union – to the small band of victorious rebels of Fidel Castro's Cuba. Although he gained as much as other soldiers from recalling the terrors and exhilaration of making the crossing into exile, Hani's time at Kongwa was spent emphasising the need to get home to fight. He was certainly among the most militant in the transit camp: he insisted on taking the war to the people. But while he waiting for further instructions from headquarters, he quipped about having to be a worker for the first time in his life, as just about everything at Kongwa needed repairs.

Originally the site of an attempt by the colonial government to start a groundnut farm, Kongwa had only a rudimentary kitchen, toilets and showers. Shifting the filth to start building was the first task; then came supplies of two-man tents and equipment, mostly from the USSR via the newly constituted OAU. In an interview with historian Luli Callinicos, Hani described the camp:

There was only one structure there and then we began to build other structures, build armouries we set up. We pitched tents, we built a wall. We began to cultivate the hectares of land that had been made available. We built recreational facilities, playing volleyball, table tennis and all that. We learnt a lot of skills. There were a few comrades who had skills in building, but we didn't know how to make cement, to drive wheelbarrows, and it was good for people like me, who had never had an experience of being workers, just got out of university … This was another educational centre for us. The need to integrate your intellectual knowledge with manual and physical labour.

The first group – Hani's group – split into three platoons. Work was done on a rotational basis. Some cadres did the cooking, mostly on open fires, others hauled in and raised tents. Latrines had to be dug, buildings constructed and an uncertain water supply fixed. Hani told Callinicos:

For us it was also the beginning of important lessons in self-help, because you remember that Nyerere also attached a lot of importance to self-help projects, to community development. We were given basic infrastructure. It was important for you to build for yourselves, to plant food, tend to chickens, pigs and all that sort of thing.

Meanwhile, the cadres, conditioned to the uncompromising physical rigours of their Soviet army instructors, continued with hours of military exercises. Hani was peculiarly fond of fitness routines. Even when his life was under threat, and right up until the final morning of his life, he started most days with a run, just as he had at Kongwa. In spite of all this activity, however, morale in the camp was generally low. Kongwa was a tough and uncomfortable environment for the MK volunteers.

\* \* \*

ANC veterans like Ike Maphoto admit that their years of deprivation in exile, waiting and waiting for a chance at victory, left scars. We drove to Polokwane, the capital of Limpopo province, to see Maphoto, to talk about war, to get a sense of what Hani had experienced.

Maphoto had gone into battle at Spolilo, during the campaign that complemented Wankie in 1967. A taciturn man, he remarked that it was obvious why he lived in the spartan manner he did – with no frippery or ornament, and barely a hint of the man inside. He had had nothing for close to 30 years. Nothing, except his commitment to the ANC. Like most men and women who crossed the border to join MK and devote themselves to the liberation of this country, he had not owned anything in those decades, had never had a job or a long relationship, although he did father a son when he was based in Zimbabwe, some time after eventually leaving Kongwa.

Coming home was a shock for Maphoto. He was suddenly able to experience so much that had been denied him, ever since those tough days in Kongwa, yet he found he had no place or need for possessions – or even, really, for people – in his life. So now memories, war stories, were his most meaningful form of engagement. And he could remember everything, at least from his point of view.

Maphoto spoke to us for a long time about Kongwa – 'a filthy place, no women, no food, no proper clothes, mosquitoes ... the place was primitive' – where he was stationed at the same time as Hani. Although he tried to make us believe that the young commander was 'very much afraid of me,' he warmed when he remembered Hani as 'a very handsome boy, morally very good,' who developed a close friendship with a young white woman journalist from Britain while they were in the transit camp.

As Maphoto recalled, the journalist had arrived there to write about developments in Nyerere's young state. He claimed the spark between Hani and the woman – who we could not trace – was instant. Later, in Lusaka, Hani began a relationship with another British woman, which lasted his lifetime. Maphoto confessed that he had not had a relationship himself since returning from exile, although he was looked after by a young woman housekeeper from Zimbabwe. When we left, he stood in his driveway, feet together, arms straight at his sides, wearing his MK fatigues and cap, a pair of soft, dark blue slippers on his feet.

\* \* \*

Although the ANC leadership, particularly Tambo, Marks and Mabhida, visited Kongwa fairly regularly, the dissonance of their lives in houses allocated to the movement in Dar es Salaam and Morogoro became more and more of a disturbing force within the ranks. Rumours spread about the suspected high life of members of the NEC. It was said they danced and dined at hotels with white women. Cadres who operated clandestinely in Zambia returned with reports that Kenneth Kaunda had dubbed some in the NEC 'chicken-in-the-basket revolutionaries'. 'Telephone revolutionaries' was another insult.

Meanwhile, the cadres at Kongwa were often beset by illness, especially from malaria and paralysing eye infections, even though a properly supplied clinic was set up when Jackson Mbali, who had trained as a medical assistant in the USSR, was installed as the *muganga* (doctor). Tanzanians from the villages around the camp increasingly preferred to have a card at the camp rather than at the government hospital in the town.

The cadres cultivated a surprisingly large vegetable farm, and concocted a way to pipe water using a reservoir at the bottom of a mountain. Using picks and shovels, with help from Tanzanian engineers, they laid pipes for the camp, which allowed them to irrigate the vegetable farm. Hani had had experience of planting and cultivating vegetables during his childhood when he had spent hours in the fields of lower Sabalele, usually with his mother. So he understood the fragile life of the pawpaw and the mielie.

The number of cadres returning from training in Moscow and Odessa was growing. By 1965, there were close to 500 soldiers in the camp, all promised enhanced training, particularly in underground work and security. Hani got caught up in teaching adult basic education to counter the high rate of illiteracy among the cadres. But he also worried about the children, some as young as 12, who, driven by undeniable political maturity, had made their way bravely into exile, so far from their mothers' embrace. He wanted to see that the youngest of the combatants at least received a good education.

He was also involved with *Dawn* and the establishment of a tone of vigorous analysis in its articles. He wanted to see the publication used to spread the message of freedom, and to reveal the terror of apartheid. Although Africa should always have been at the forefront of coverage, particularly given Hani's admiration for Nyerere's inclusive vision, the internationalist tone intensified. An event like the *World Marxist Review*'s conference in Cairo in 1966, where ANC and SACP leader JB Marks delivered a memorable dirge for Western influence within the liberation movements, was an irresistible opportunity for debate. That conference also provided an opportunity to examine the increasing rivalry between the USSR and China for the political affection of liberation movements throughout the Third World. Historically, the ANC had supported Soviet foreign policy – in part because of the organisation's need to rebuild itself during the 1960s, for which it needed Russian help. So, from the mid-1960s right up until the end of the 1980s, leaders such as JB Marks, Yusuf Dadoo, Oliver Tambo and Alfred Nzo visited the USSR, Vietnam, Czechoslovakia, Bulgaria and Hungary as part of anti-imperialist solidarity tours and campaigns. Hani would have been interested in all of these developments as he slowly grew within the leadership.

Hani had to be part of the world in this way, for Kongwa offered sparse relief from hardship. At first, the only vehicles were a Land Rover and a Czech motorbike, so it felt as if there was no escape at all. Yet he and other cadres were able to banish pessimism by organising entertainment for themselves. A popular way to lift the spirits of the cadres was by setting up dances and even teaching the villagers to dance two-by-two – as the men had done in the townships at home. And there were inter-camp events every Friday, usually concerts, when soldiers from SWAPO, FRELIMO and the MPLA would compete with each other and MK. The quieter recruits played championship chess or draughts.

There are former cadres today who remember Kongwa – known as the University of Life, after an appellation by Tambo – with conscious, righteous nostalgia. They will say it was a world of its own, a place where you could trust a man with your life. Cadres say that it was even difficult for them to trust people who had not served at Kongwa, because the camp was a true test of the ability to survive. Although there was never enough food, even if they wore only battle fatigues and there were very few women, mostly prostitutes, the soldiers simply got on with it. Even if, at one point, they waited for months for salt to arrive from East Germany, this kind of thing was seen as peripheral, a distraction for the disgruntled. There was a strong sense of global, if not regional, safety. For all its fragility at times, the camp was under the wing of a powerful organisation, which had an international movement behind it, and the not-insubstantial military support of socialist countries.

For the most part, the liberation movements spurred each other on. Next door to MK was SWAPO (South West Africa People's Organisation), its camp literally across the road. Strangely, ZAPU (Zimbabwe African People's Union) and ZANU (Zimbabwe African National Union), despite barely bridled antagonism towards each other, lived as close together as possible. This provided some relief, Hani later told researcher Wolfie Kodesh:

We mixed, we played sport together, we did a lot of things. With Samora [Machel] and others [the language] was easy because some of those guys from Mozambique spoke some Zulu and others had a bit of English. So there was good communication. The chaps from Namibia spoke English too, and Afrikaans, so there was a lot of communication and interaction.

ANC leader Mavuso Msimang, who had also trained in Moscow, recalled an African brotherhood, a solidarity in Kongwa that only those who were in the camps could explain or understand. 'We became very good friends with FRELIMO, with Samora,' he specifically recalled when we met him.

But still, the camp was a camp, and while many freedom fighters were somewhat envious of the sophisticated infrastructure of ZAPU and ZANU, MK embraced what it had built out of the sweat of its men: a straight-up-and-down housing complex with no extras. In MK's zones, only the commanders stayed in brick-and-mortar structures. The men lived in tents. But this was a supportive environment, thanks to Nyerere's teachings of African unity. His government made sure that Tanzanians understood that they were not free until all of Africa was free. Ordinary people were proud to show their solidarity, and close friendships developed with MK and soldiers from other military movements. A few soldiers got married in Kongwa, and some even remained behind.

The sparse existence hurt most when it was obvious that some in the

ANC leadership were getting stipends while the rank and file earned nothing. Those desperate for a cigarette or the occasional beer would sometimes have to sell a shirt or a jacket for some money. Hani saw how rebellion could brew out of this discontent, and, in April 1966, the frustrations indeed boiled over. A group that included combatants Justice Mpanza (Gizenga), Philemon Biyela (Pangaman) and Edgar Duma (Problem) stole trucks, planning to go home to Natal and fight. They were arrested in Morogoro by Tanzanian soldiers and an ANC tribunal was set up to investigate their actions. But it only reprimanded them.

At this time, the liberation movement was in the last stage of its political honeymoon, with some in the leadership still believing that, as recruits streamed in and were trained to seize South Africa's liberation, freedom could be secured within a reasonable period of time. So they ignored the seething discontent that could boil over into rebellion. Therein lay the tangled roots of later anger – including Hani's own, when he penned the Memorandum, which was highly critical of the leadership, and which led to the Morogoro Conference in 1969. In the 1980s, the furious, bloody mutinies in the MK camps in Angola reopened these old wounds.

By 1967, several comrades had already deserted to Kenya. Although the notion of solidarity was constantly reinforced, warning signs had been there for some time. Many soldiers confided in Hani about their emotionally precarious position. Although his rivals sometimes accused him of being pompous, too self-assured, many others remember Hani's ability to listen and to try and solve the common, human battles.

He understood why resentment had developed towards those sent abroad to study. Rumours flew about nepotism, targeting especially the 21-year-old Thabo Mbeki, who was studying in England at the University of Sussex. Yet there was respect for Mbeki's own struggles in 1963, even if his relative privilege rankled. At the time Hani was training in Moscow, Mbeki was watching the Rivonia Trial unfold, with his father in the dock facing what most were sure would be the gallows. When the trial began in November 1963, Thabo Mbeki surprised his fellow students by adopting an apparently natural ambassadorial quality, speaking on radio and spurring on an international solidarity campaign to support the Rivonia trialists. He led a now-legendary two-day march from Sussex to London, arriving at 10 Downing Street on 13 June – the night the sentences were handed down in the Pretoria Supreme Court.

The concern about what was happening to the movement exacerbated simmering tensions between cadres. Covert meetings, convened along tribal lines, were even said to have included Modise and Batswana, Bapedi and Basotho soldiers. ANC officials, like controversial camp commander Ambrose Makiwane, issued warnings against rebellion. But Makiwane was also being watched, with some cadres alleging that while he was a good camp commander and politically strong, he had a penchant for taking trips into town and having the odd drink. Sometimes, it was claimed, he would drink too much, get back to camp around midnight, and wake everybody up for emergency military exercises. Other cadres insisted that Makiwane would even go so far as to sjambok those among them who were seen to have broken discipline.

Although educated men like Makiwane, Hani and Lennox Lagu were among the original 40-odd cadres who had set up Kongwa, the next group were not as well-educated. They had been trained in Odessa in more formal military structures, and were destined to be unit commanders. The differences between the two groups sometimes led to conflict and power struggles. These power struggles were symptomatic of the growing dissatisfaction, among even the most talented of the cadres. It is said that when Joe Modise first turned up in Kongwa, Ambrose Makiwane's cousin, Tennyson – later a notorious dissident, shot dead in 1980 – completely ignored him, possibly due to an inflated sense of self borne out of education, and not necessarily out of experience.

But the mood began to shift in late 1966, when Hani was moved to Zambia and rumours grew that MK was, at last, going to go into battle to secure a way home. Already, other small groups – one of them under veteran Josiah Jele – had left Kongwa for Lusaka to prepare to return via Mozambique. Hani later said that when he finally left Kongwa he was not sure of the nature of his mission. All he knew was what had been proposed in terms of taking the fight for liberation home, and that he had been summoned to report to Lusaka for discussions with the leadership there. 'The others didn't know because I was not at the camp. I was briefed when I was already in Zambia about what I was going to do.'

But Hani's passage to Zambia, where he was to liaise with old Kongwa comrades from ZAPU before they embarked on a joint training programme to ready themselves for entry into Rhodesia, was never going to be easy. He had to re-enter Botswana – where he had first crossed into exile – and was arrested by the immigration authorities: 'I was detained for about two weeks and then sent back to Lusaka,' Hani said. He had been travelling on a falsified document, which led to his arrest. 'They knew me because I had gone through Botswana and ... they had photographed me and taken my details. When you left Botswana, you were assumed to be deported. So they arrested me and said I'd come through, that I was a political immigrant.'

Although known to only a handful of people, Hani's departure, and that of others, for Zambia, created a sense of anticipation in Kongwa. Soon, the soldiers had a nickname for the Land Rovers that arrived periodically to fetch comrades who were being moved south. They called them 'the Chinaman', because the load represented something of a lottery for the men. By extension, the name reminded them of home, of the Chinese fah-fee games they used to play in the faraway neighbourhoods of their childhood.

\* \* \*

By early 1967, the activist academic Ben Magubane and his family had opened their home in Sunningdale, a suburb around the campus of the University of Zambia, to Chris Hani – 'a young man who wanted to spend some quiet time and consult'.

This request had come from Tambo and Thomas Nkobi, who knew other academics at the university – people like English professor Zeke

Mphahlele and Jack Simons, who was the head of political science.

Ben Magubane's townhouse is full of books, floor to ceiling. And, unlike Ike Maphoto, there is so much of him and his past in his house. His identity as a writer, an ANC supporter, a champion of ideas, is everywhere. In pictures, old posters, photographs, monographs, magazines, masks. And he relishes the influence of memory: who said what when? Where were they? The textures of the moment.

Magubane had arrived at the university only a year before, and had found a large, sympathetic South African black community there 'from the PAC, the ANC, the Unity Movement, people trying to find better prospects'. He had been living in the United States with his wife Thembi and their three daughters before coming to Zambia. When Tambo asked for his assistance, it was partly because the ANC was looking for families with children to host the soldiers. Magubane offered space in his house, located about ten minutes from State House, to Hani and to Barbara Masekela. Even the university administration was not formally aware of the fact that South African academics were protecting MK cadres.

A few years later, there would be a party to mark the return of the heroes of the Wankie campaign after their two years in prison in Botswana. Magubane had been wary about hosting the party, as he had been asked to do, unless the ANC could guarantee security. 'I didn't want to be responsible for any mishap,' he said. But Magubane did it anyway, and it was a gathering that would have made for a compulsive portrait. Among the guests were Tambo, Nkobi, Simons and the soldier and raconteur Eric Mtshali.

Despite Hani's relative youth, he had the confidence to engage with luminaries of the movement. But he was never a flamboyant man. Respected academic and writer Mbulelo Mzamane, who knew Hani over many years and whose wife Nthoana is the sister of Hani's widow, Limpho, told us he watched how Hani would go to parties, play out the necessary pleasantries and then disappear as soon as he could into a bedroom where there were books.

So this party, to mark the survival of the Wankie soldiers through war and prison, would not have been Hani's choice. Yet it was his first official honour. When Hani first stayed with Magubane, 'they were being prepared for the 1967 campaign,' Magubane explained:

There was another chap who was around us a lot, a Coloured chap, Basil February, a quiet, studious fellow, who had started with Jack Simons at UCT before he decided to join MK. He wrote poetry, essays ... he could have done anything. He was one of the brightest ... Chris was ever so quiet. If people came around, he would retire to the bedroom with his book.

There was plenty of private political discussion on campus, usually over lunches or dinners, where the conversation would stray equally into agitation and laughter. There was never silence. The white and black academics, their families and other comrades presented a world to Hani unlike that which he had known in his childhood, although he had become accustomed to white and black people treating each with genuine regard when he was in Cape Town, before going into exile.

Friendship between black and white children in Sabalele was rare. Yet Hani's first political and intellectual influences were undoubtedly white priests and nuns, who he admired for the way they practised their faith. Even as a boy, he respected their commitment, their truth and stability within a complicated ethical framework. They concentrated on developing cultural empathy and attempting social reconstruction, walking for hours over the iron-hard tracks of Sabalele, healing, talking, listening. These were the qualities Hani liked, and which he later developed in his own character. Discipline about ideals, much more than dogma, was Hani's instruction.

Magubane recalls how he and his family – Hani being regarded as something of an older son – would meet at the Simons's place most Sundays to discuss the evolving political situation in southern Africa. Magubane said it was on Sundays like those that he truly discovered the depths of the young man who occupied a room in his house. At first, he and other academics were taken aback by the complex young cadre's spontaneous yearning to indulge in the classics. It was just so unusual to come across anyone of Hani's age and background who responded to the political and social worlds of ancient Rome and Greece, or the English poets struggling with the chaos of industry. Hani was able to quote entire pieces of writing, exquisite passages from the Romantics, from Shelley and Keats, such was his precision and exact observation. For the intellectuals of Lusaka's bohemian African underground, Hani was a revelation.

CHAPTER 6

# WANKIE

The Tunisian officers showed him the weapons. French, American, British, Russian, you name it. They had it all, and he could choose any. The bill was already settled. Archie Sibeko had spent almost a week in the military barracks in Tunis. And considering his relative confinement there since his arrival, it could have been almost anywhere in the world. He could hear orders being given in French and Arabic, but he had had only glimpses of the city on the way to and from the airport in a military vehicle. He might have seen the statue of the celebrated Arab scholar Ibn Khaldun, near the gateway to the ancient Medina. Not far away stands the majestic Ez Zitouna, the ancient Mosque of the Olive Tree. Tunis was a place of sacred truth.

But Sibeko had an urgent, and critical assignment, so when he was picked up from the airport by his military hosts, the understanding was that he was to remain in the barracks for the duration of his stay. It had been only days before that Tambo had summoned the trusted MK commander to his office in Dar es Salaam. The struggle had to evolve, he said to Sibeko, as the enemy was strengthening its grip politically and militarily. And the time had come to forge closer bonds with other liberation organisations, especially in southern Africa, with a view to mapping out and securing routes for the infiltration of cadres back home.

Tambo confided in Sibeko. The planning for a joint ANC–ZAPU campaign into Rhodesia, using their military wings, MK and ZIPRA (Zimbabwe People's Revolutionary Army), was already well under way. The men were being selected, and one of the commanders, an illustrious young man, was Sibeko's old friend and comrade – Chris Hani.

Sibeko, who was one of the first MK cadres to have been trained in the Soviet Union, was mandated to draw up a shopping list for weapons, consulting with the leadership and the men who would run the operation. He would then fly to North Africa to assemble a serious cache for the campaign. As there was no ANC representation in Tunis, Sibeko first had to travel to Algeria to collect a visa, and he would have to follow the same route home.

\* \* \*

Sibeko's stories about that trip are absorbing, as we discover when we meet him in a hotel on the outskirts of Benoni. Sibeko perches on the edge of the bed, indicating with some amusement the kitchenette, which has cups and all the accoutrements for coffee but no kettle. 'And that bottle of wine,' he gestures at the dressing table, 'will be just like that when I leave. I'm not going to have it.'

We're aware of how fortunate we are to be able to spend time alone with the legendary trade unionist. Sibeko is in South Africa for a congress of the South African Transport and Allied Workers Union, of which he is the honorary president, and he mingles as easily with COSATU's general secretary, Zwelinzima Vavi, as he does with ordinary delegates, such as the young unionists from the Western Cape who seek out his charming counsel.

He lives in England with Joyce Leeson, his wife of many years, whom he met in Zambia where she was an academic at the university and he was in exile. The congress is a chance for Sibeko to spend time with his children and revisit places to which he undoubtedly attaches meaning. We spend three afternoons with him, encountering a man of formidable political independence, unafraid to express a point of view markedly different from that of many in his company at the congress.

Sibeko relates the story of the roundabout route he had to take to get to and from Tunis, and, like most of his other stories, it is high on entertainment value, expressly detailed. As it turns out, his return journey from Tunis included a substantial delay in Algiers, where he remembered his dislike for bureaucracy. He had been classified 'alien' on the passport he had collected from a covert venue, and this attracted the attention of the woman in passport control. She decided she needed back-up, and paid scant regard to Sibeko's protestations.

'So I did what we Africans tend to do in these circumstances because we know it will work,' smiled Sibeko. 'I spoke very loudly, I told it to her straight – that this was rude, and did she think that just because I was a fellow African, a black man, I could be treated like this? She got anxious and asked me to sit down while she summoned some other officials.

'Needless to say, I wasn't going to sit down, and soon they let me go on with my journey, I think just because they couldn't bear to have me around anymore.'

The delay, which had been preceded by a stopover in Algiers, meant that by the time Sibeko arrived home in Dar es Salaam, the weapons shipment from Tunisia had already arrived.

\* \* \*

The ANC was indeed taking its relationship with liberation organisations to an entirely new level at the time. This was a process that had started in December 1961, at a meeting at a secret location in Johannesburg, when leaders of the ANC had officially declared war on the apartheid regime. Peaceful protest had been abandoned in the wake of the Sharpeville and Langa massacres in 1960, which had led to the banning of the ANC and other liberation movements.

At the same time as the secret meeting in Johannesburg, another one was taking place in Highfields, Harare. At that meeting, the founders of ZAPU ratified the formation of their party, and Joshua Nkomo – a trade unionist and maverick entrepreneur, popularly known as Chibwechitedza ('the slippery rock') – was installed as its first president. Nkomo was later detained by Rhodesian police, and found himself sharing the confinement with a revolutionary, Robert Mugabe, who later became the leader of the rival organisation, the Zimbabwean African National Union (ZANU).

The same year also saw the establishment of the PAC's military wing Poqo, meaning 'standing alone', the precursor to the Azanian People's Liberation Army (APLA), as well as the Movimento Popular de Libertação de Angola (MPLA), which would take about 15 years to achieve the liberation of Angola from Portuguese colonial rule.

At the time neither ZAPU nor the ANC knew what the other was doing. Within a year, however, volunteers from the two liberation organisations, en route to military training in the USSR, met on what was known as the Great East Road to Tanzania. Young soldiers and their leadership from the Basotholand People's Party, ZAPU, Mozambique's FRELIMO (Frente de Libertação de Moçambique), Namibia's SWAPO, the MPLA and the ANC all descended on Dar es Salaam. ZAPU and the ANC opened offices in the city, and the organisations became close. Over the next two years, recruits trickled in, but it was not until 1963 that actual camps were set up in Tanzania.

\* \* \*

Sibeko doesn't eat any lunch when we meet. He occasionally threatens to have a bite later, but, instead, the conversation continues. We want to know the logistics: how the weapons selected in Tunis were directed to their destination – Lusaka, Zambia, where Hani and his unit were waiting to receive them.

He describes it as though it has just happened, with a truck roaring down a dirt road at breakneck speed, dust swirling in its wake. The driver, Lefty Mabula, clutched the wheel with determination. Ahead, a speeding Land Rover set a furious pace. The main route from Dar es Salaam into newly independent Zambia had fallen into disuse since Rhodesia's Unilateral Declaration of Independence (UDI) in 1965, and the threat of ambush from Rhodesian forces was very real. Sibeko recalls how 'the first few times' were nerve-wracking. The tall, well-built Mabula's experience at driving heavy vehicles was invaluable when it came to handling the specially adapted Leyland truck. The speed of their passage meant the two vehicles stayed ahead of the thick dust cloud they sent up.

The precious cargo being transported to Lusaka had come a long way from Tunis. There had been problems when the consignment of arms arrived in Dar es Salaam and an overexcited local official had decided the weapons could be put to good use in the recently formed Tanzanian army. Tambo's intervention put the arms back where they belonged. Sibeko was tasked with planning transport with Eric Mtshali, whose debonair personal style was a surprisingly consistent asset. Mtshali even managed to politicise men who could make or break the journey into and out of Tanzania. Across the border, the Zambian officials presented a somewhat different challenge. There was little sympathy for freedom fighters among officialdom there, where trade relations between Kenneth Kaunda's government and the regime in Pretoria saw to it that the ANC's presence in Lusaka was necessarily discreet.

At the border, Zambian officials insisted on searching the truck. As he stepped down from the passenger seat, Sibeko warned Mabula in Xhosa to get ready to flee, as Sibeko would not be able to show the officials that he was armed. Taking advantage of the confusion, Mabula turned the truck around and sped back to the Tanzanian side. Sibeko was arrested but later released after intervention from the ANC's Lusaka office.

Transporting the weapons at high speed was essential: too slow and the checkpoints that had been established along the route would contact Hani, who was in overall command of the operation, to alert him to a possible security breach. It was dark by the time the MK crew reached its final destination, the Lusaka suburb of Lilanda, a medium-density area next to the larger, older suburb of Matera, where the ANC, FRELIMO and MPLA all had residences. Hani was waiting when they got to the house in Lilanda, and he and his men took the truck to hide the weapons at a secret location. No questions asked. The next morning, Mabula and Sibeko returned to Dar es Salaam with the empty truck and the Land Rover.

\* \* \*

By the end of 1966, preparations for war were well under way. Urged on by the young guns, particularly Hani, the ANC's chief diplomats – Tambo, JB Marks, Moses Kotane and Thomas Nkobi – had negotiated with their ZAPU allies to send a joint force into Rhodesia. The two movements had grown so close that, at times, when the one could not be present at an international conference, the other would deputise. When the ANC was setting up its headquarters in Lusaka, ZAPU was instrumental in helping the ANC to move personnel. A joint high command was established, led by Tambo and ZAPU vice-president James Chikerema. The planning for the Wankie operation was done by Hani and ZIPRA commander John Dube. Dube was a large, jovial man, and he and Hani had already become close in Lusaka, where they had socialised together and found common ground.

\* \* \*

There is no emptiness in the woodland of the Zimbabwean bush, but there is an uneasy silence in its vacant golden meadows. The quietness reaches out of the thick dry sand of the Kalahari and between the flat, high rocks. It twists between the clutter of mopanes and the sausage trees, with their strange wild fruit. It's a deceptively open space that hides a profusion of wildlife – elephant, lion, leopard, cheetah, buffalo, zebra, giraffe, rhino, wildebeest, baboon, cheetah, hippo, wild dog and many birds.

In the late 1960s, following UDI, the Rhodesian bush became an area of operations as troops battled the forces of the liberation movement. Among the units deployed in the 'bush war' was the Rhodesian African Rifles (RAR), a black infantry regiment officered by whites. The regiment was one of the oldest fighting forces on the continent, with a history dating back to 1916.

The RAR became a prime adversary of Chris Hani when he assumed command of MK's legendary Luthuli Detachment. In August 1967, the Luthuli Detachment was to enter the Wankie Game Reserve (now Hwange National Park), on the first covert mission of this size and stature, with the mission to establish unassailable infiltration routes deep inside Rhodesia back home to South Africa.

But while Hani would emerge a hero, Tambo would later describe the campaign as Umkhonto we Sizwe's 'heroic failure'. It could not be judged more fairly. Confident in lending his name to the proposal to ANC headquarters in Dar es Salaam to use Rhodesia, specifically the game reserve, and strike a strategic alliance with the liberation forces of Zimbabwe, Hani had actively petitioned for a chance to take control of the men. However, he later told Luli Callinicos that those in Kongwa 'didn't have a profound understanding of the problems':

Most of us were very young, in our early twenties. We were impatient to get into action. We were saying: 'Nobody must tell us that there are no routes. We have been trained to explore and establish routes. We must be deployed to find these routes. Why can't we go through Mozambique, Rhodesia, Namibia? Let us hack our way through these countries.'

These were our arguments. And I think these strong feelings that were conveyed to the leadership resulted in the building of a formal alliance between ourselves and ZAPU, which was beginning to fight an armed struggle in Zimbabwe. In the meantime, the waiting was eroding morale. Some comrades deserted to places like Kenya. People were feeling that they were wasting their time.

When the decision was made to embark on the Wankie campaign, the approach of the ANC was one of selecting the best cadres. This was the first time we were working together with ZAPU military cadres and in order to avoid misunderstandings and conflicts, it was important for the organisation to go for its best cadres.

I was already commissar of the camp, and I had been given a number of responsibilities within MK at that stage. I believe I was one of the most vocal in terms of the need to get involved in Zimbabwe to open a route to infiltrate the cadres. So without being called to volunteer, because I openly supported the move, I was selected.

You must remember that 1966 to 1967 was the lowest point in terms of the ANC and the Congress movement as a whole. The movement was, politically speaking, decimated, so there was a very strong feeling that the guerrillas should use their presence inside South Africa to begin to build the ANC underground, to train combat units and later to move into active military operations against the regime.

It was a strongly held view that when you have an army, you cannot wait for a favourable situation. In our camps we had been shooting at paper targets. Now we were going to get involved. I was very happy.

The NEC, under the chairmanship of Tambo, was not an elected body at that time, although it occasionally co-opted members from the senior ranks of the movement. And it was the only body that could consider the action. Although the decision was made to send MK cadres into combat, it was not taken lightly, nor without dissension. Trade unionists and communists like Moses Mabhida and JB Marks, the firebrand Tennyson Makiwane, veterans Joe Matthews, Alfred Nzo, Thomas Nkobi and Robert Resha, and Mzwai Piliso – later vilified as the boss of MK's notorious security wing, Mbokodo – were among those who gave the campaign the go-ahead.

The SACP was certainly not ideologically opposed to either the armed struggle or MK looking for routes home to take the battle into South Africa. In an internal memo in 1967, the Central Committee spelt out the duty of a communist in the national liberation army:

For decades it has been a cardinal principle of the revolutionary party of the working class to support the struggle for freedom and democracy. For this reason, our party has given primary importance to the building of a united front of national liberation centred around the ANC ... this struggle has now entered the new phase of armed revolutionary war. It is the duty of communists to set an example of hard work and zeal in the performance of their duties ... and always to be the first to volunteer for the most difficult tasks.

Revolutionary struggle is not an invitation to a picnic ... There is no duty nobler than the fight for the liberation of the masses. This noble fight must not be sullied by arrogance and immoral behaviour such as theft of property, molesting of women or drunkenness which would lower the prestige of the movement and also endanger its security.

**SACP leader Joe Slovo admitted that it had become clear in the late 1960s that**

... we were entering the second phase, which was the attempt to reconstruct the political underground and to attempt to return to the country those activists who had been trained in the art and science of people's military struggle.

The post-Sharpeville and post-Rivonia successes of the enemy had created such a demoralisation that without the beginnings of armed activity, without a demonstration of our ability to hit at the enemy, it was difficult to conceive of people getting together in any large measure, to reconstitute the political underground.

From 1965 and 1966 onwards, the attention of MK and its leadership, the ANC, was devoted to attempting to get our trained political and military cadres back, even though, at that stage, South Africa was still surrounded by a cordon sanitaire of imperialist-dominated states: Angola, Mozambique, Rhodesia. We were completely cut off from the borders.

Undoubtedly, there was hesitation from the NEC, because of the fear of cadres being killed by the RAR. Soon, lingering uncertainty was entrenched by the utter failure of similar campaigns into the so-called frontline states. An attempt to use Botswana as an access point in March 1967 was a disaster. Two cadres were arrested and the trail they were working on had to be allowed to go cold. A second foray, this time into northern

Mozambique, had an even more unsettling outcome in May 1967, when movement stalwart Josiah Jele led a joint MK–FRELIMO unit, only to be violently repulsed by Portuguese colonial forces based in Niassa province. A second MK-led detachment was attacked in the neighbouring province of Cabo Delgado, and forced to retreat.

In an analysis of these early failures, the Russian academic Vladimir Shubin – a vital politico-military link between the ANC and the Soviets during the struggle – reflected that, even on paper, the Mozambique attempt was hopeless. The exceptionally rough terrain exhausted the troops, whereas the well-armed colonial troops were used to the demands of operating in the bush. The language barrier was also a problem. Finally, even FRELIMO, although its influence was growing, lacked strength outside the north of Mozambique. An alliance with ZAPU – whose membership was culturally closer to the ANC – made better sense.

Hani was determined to succeed in Rhodesia by drawing on the experience of the liberation struggle in Vietnam, in particular the theory of the 'bridge' as a method of supply. The 'bridge' was a network of routes designed by the Vietnamese National Liberation Front (NLF) to supply cadres operating in the jungles of South Vietnam. This complex replenishment method was accessed by foot, bicycle, truck and water. Dubbed by the Americans the 'Ho Chi Minh Trail' – after their archenemy, North Vietnamese president Ho Chi Minh – the network ran from North to South Vietnam through the neighbouring kingdoms of Laos and Cambodia. The NLF called it the Truong Son Road, after the mysterious mountain range that was their central marker.

The 'bridge' was undoubtedly one of the most formidable military strategies of the 20th century, but while the method was impeccable in theory, in practice it could not succeed for MK. Yet the ANC's military wing naturally aspired to it, in awe of the way in which the communist insurgents of the NLF had supported themselves with arms and men against the might of the United States and its South Vietnamese ally.

By comparison, MK's attempt to open routes that would facilitate its re-entry into South Africa was a brave but improbable effort. Even under the command of a military zealot like Hani, the effort was hampered by practicalities. The unit did not have enough weapons or men. Maps provided were wildly out of date, and there was unconvincing on-the-ground intelligence, with only the most fragile penetration of the villages along the proposed route. More controversial was the perception that ZAPU was less than prepared for the campaign. But the two organisations were partners in war, and diplomacy dictated that neither reveal the difficult truths about what happened in the bush between them.

\* \* \*

By the mid-1960s, the morale of the nascent liberation forces in southern Africa had been profoundly damaged by state repression. In South Africa, John Vorster had succeeded Hendrik Verwoerd as prime minister following the latter's assassination in Parliament on 6 September 1966. Both Vorster and Rhodesian Prime Minister Ian Smith were determined to eradicate their enemies, but Smith was under a different kind of pressure by 1967. International economic and diplomatic sanctions had been applied to Rhodesia after UDI. Smith was fortunate that Pretoria was willing to cushion the blow, as analysts described it. So an alliance was created that would meet the political needs of both leaders: their armies and security forces would assist each other in defeating the liberation movements.

The year 1967 was also challenging for Tambo, who became the acting president of the ANC after the bizarre death of the ailing Chief Albert Luthuli, who was hit by a train on 21 July while crossing a railway bridge. Luthuli's death presented some complexities. Although he had opposed the establishment of MK by Mandela in 1961, Luthuli was revered by the troops. But he had been banned by the apartheid state for such a long time that his influence had begun to wane, in spite of himself and in spite of the unqualified loyalty of the ANC.

The reluctant accession of Tambo to the role of supreme power broker within the ANC was given credence on the banks of the Zambezi, shortly before Hani and his soldiers entered Rhodesia. Standing there in darkness, the soldiers breathed deeply as they prepared themselves for the crossing. Tambo took a central position for a short address, such was the solemn nature of the moment. The acting president quietly declared them to be the Luthuli Detachment, in honour of the leader who had died.

* * *

Although Hani embarked upon war in 1967, it was only in the 1970s that he and the leadership of the armed wing would be able to expand with realistic ambition – thanks largely to the coming to power of Mozambique's FRELIMO and Angola's MPLA and the unexpected influx of thousands of Young Lions, following the Soweto uprising of June 1976.

In 1967, the groundwork for a people's war seemed plausible. But Hani had studied the complications. He was concerned about staging classical guerrilla warfare, even in the rural areas of South Africa. Yet he understood the restlessness of his fellow MK cadres. On this, Hani was adamant: 'Once you have trained an army, you have to deploy it. You cannot afford a moment of idleness with soldiers.'

ANC veteran Graham Morodi has also spoken about how the cadres implored the leadership: 'Now we are trained and we feel we are okay. We are commanders and we feel that we can meet the enemy anywhere.'

Hani, who admired Tambo, believed that he could set the example by persuading the leadership that another campaign to go to war and win a route back home could succeed. So by the time he left Kongwa in 1966 to go to Zambia to plan, he was doing it with clarity about what could happen. He feared insurrection, and he could feel its stirrings. 'I met Tambo now and again,' he recalled of that period in Lusaka:

Tambo is actually commuting between Dar es Salaam and Lusaka, and we have got an office in Lusaka by now. He [Tambo] becomes an integral part of this discussion of our preparations and we report to him. He was totally involved in the whole military strategy of preparing for the trained combatants to go back into SA. He would be involved in the smallest details.

We were about 30 from the ANC, and about 20 or 30 from ZAPU … [and] Tambo becomes the brains behind this, the organising spirit behind it. He comes to stay with us. We were actually deployed not far from the Zambezi River, away from the cities [and] we had prepared for three months, physically, politically and militarily together with ZAPU, so that we should know one another, and get to know the language, the customs, and the traditions of Zimbabwe.

We spent a few days on the banks of the Zambezi River, about two kilometres from the river – and Tambo stayed with us, slept there with us, in the open, not even in tents. We were just sleeping in the bush. And this convinced us again of the type of leader that Tambo was. A practical leader, an exemplary leader, and one who was prepared to share the hardness of this very difficult and demanding task with his soldiers.

The operational planning for the Wankie campaign was divided into four areas: personnel, reconnaissance, logistics and intelligence. A camp was established near Livingstone for joint training; 30 men from MK and 70 from ZIPRA trained together for three months, exercising night and day to ensure the unit was physically and mentally sharp and well-disciplined. The reconnaissance team set up a base on the Zambezi, familiarising themselves with the river and looking for possible places for the unit to cross. They were joined by two expert swimmers to gather knowledge about the river crossing, including the likely behaviour of animals and people living in the vicinity, and the terrain within the crucial first eight kilometres on the Rhodesian side. ZIPRA's Dumiso Dabengwa – popularly known as the Black Russian – led the reconnaissance team. Some MK members of the team, unfamiliar to the local Zambian police, were repeatedly arrested, only to be rescued by their ZAPU comrades, who were well-known in the area. The intelligence function was also left to ZIPRA, which was tasked with preparing the local population to assist the liberation force passing through.

Hani had gone out of his way to get to know the ZIPRA leaders and had made some of the initial overtures towards a joint operation. In Lusaka, he had to keep the morale of his hand-picked detachment high as they waited for their training to start, cooped up in the houses with few distractions for months. During this time Hani occasionally even clashed with the outspoken MK cadre Basil February, as frustration set in.

Another difficulty was that ZIPRA was locked in a bitter rivalry with ZANLA (Zimbabwe African National Liberation Army), the armed wing of ZANU, which threatened to upset the entire operation. This rivalry was to be exploited by Rhodesia's Central Intelligence Organisation (CIO), which carried out acts of sabotage and assassination that had the two liberation organisations blaming each other.

But Hani worked tirelessly to forge strong bonds with ZAPU, to the point that when the MK contingent finally arrived at the ZIPRA camp near Livingstone – which had been named Da Nang, after the US base in South Vietnam – the Zimbabweans slaughtered an ox to celebrate their arrival. Weekly reports were submitted to the political leadership on both sides.

Meanwhile, Hani had travelled to Swaziland, where he met secretly with Gasson Ndlovu, head of the PAC's Poqo, to discuss possible co-operation with MK. Although Ndlovu weighed up the strategic advantage – the possibility of finding a reliable, protected route home through hostile Rhodesia, with liberation movement checkpoints and the support of co-operative villagers – he simply could not negotiate the ideological bend. Although he and Hani had a certain rapport, they could not secure agreement on political motivation – or the outcome of the revolution.

We met Ndlovu – still a handsome man, proud of reaching the milestone of 80 years at the time we met him – at his house in Cape Town. He told us that he confronted Hani, asking him how, as an MK commander, he could approach the PAC about an amalgamation of sorts when they differed so profoundly as to how to run a rebellion against oppression.

Although Hani regularly visited the strip of land between Zambia and Rhodesia where the MK–ZIPRA force would enter enemy territory, the PAC had its own intelligence. Enemy agents were watching and waiting, and this was something Ndlovu was able to share with Hani.

The MK–ZIPRA plan involved setting up three crossing points along the Zambezi in order to stretch the enemy forces. The first crossing, which involved Hani's group, would take place near Livingstone, another near Lake Kariba and a third near Feira. As the men prepared to cross, ANC NEC member Ruth Mompati went through the group's luggage, ensuring there was nothing to incriminate them, such as a Soviet-made watch or shirt. Nevertheless, there was a problem.

By the time the almost 100-strong contingent was loaded onto trucks under cover of darkness for the 25-kilometre journey to the crossing point, trucks had ferried their equipment to the same point, so it seemed as if preparations had been more than adequate. But once they arrived, it became clear to Hani that there was insufficient weaponry. Marching at the head of the Luthuli Detachment with Tambo and fellow commander Mjojo Mxwaku, Hani told Tambo that this was a serious enough issue to stall the entire campaign. Mjojo backed up Hani's assertion.

Earlier, the MK commander-in-chief, Joe Modise, had turned down a request from the men for additional ammunition. Now Tambo himself made the request. By the next day, each man had been given an additional magazine, a grenade and 300 rounds of ammunition. The detachment was now armed with an assortment of SKS rifles, AK47s, submachine guns, light machine guns (LMGs), rocket-propelled grenades (RPGs), Makarov pistols and small radios. Finally, the mission could get under way.

As the group made their way towards the river, February, fiddling with his rifle, accidentally let off a shot. The men stopped dead and fell silent. Hani investigated the source of the noise, as the report could have carried across the river to patrolling enemy troops. But there was no turning back now. As they approached the riverine escarpment, the echoes of the wild broke the night air. The howl of a jackal, the hollow bark of a hippo. Hearts pumped furiously with excitement. Fear. Anticipation. Far below, the men could hear the sound of rushing water.

The crossing point had been carefully selected, with the thinking being that the enemy would not expect the liberation fighters to cross at such a difficult spot. 'Lizwe?' came a call from the darkness. 'Lolo,' replied one of the men in the detachment. Emerging from behind a tree was their comrade, Boston Gagarin, a short and stocky man in swimming trunks. His team would lead them from Point Lolo across the river to Base One. Hani was the first to climb down. The rope snaking 200 metres down the side of the steep gorge allowed the men to quietly clamber over the rockface, although they occasionally flinched as rocks loosened by those above them hurtled downwards. Moments before Dabengwa reached the bottom, a climber above him slipped, sending a small boulder tumbling down, which knocked the ZIPRA commander unconscious.

At the foot of the rockface, the comrades gathered on the narrow shoreline. The occasional shimmer revealed the 35-metre-wide, fast-moving obstacle before them. On the opposite side of the river, by the sliver of light available, some could discern the figure of Hani. He was already doing exercises.

Moving close to 100 men across on inflatable boats was a tedious business, but the entire contingent finally reached the Rhodesian shore by 5am. Having successfully concluded the first phase of its operation, the Luthuli Detachment saluted its leader, Tambo, still standing, watching and waiting, on the opposite shore.

Thus, 2 August 1967 saw the start of one of the most courageous, if ill-fated, adventures in the history of the ANC. Those who were there remember the unity as night descended again, and the men resting quietly in the shadows of the mopane trees came to life. At the head of the column, Hani set a blistering pace. Marching only in darkness, the soldiers navigated using the stars and their compasses. But trouble struck early. Their food and water started running out, and the men were soon reduced to one meal a day. Two days into its mission, the detachment was forced to make contact with locals in order to supplement their rations.

After a week, as planned, a smaller combined MK–ZIPRA unit of 21 men broke away and headed towards Lupane in the east. It was planned that this group, led by Andries Motsepe, would establish a northern and central Zimbabwe base for the future infiltration of cadres to the home front. Two weeks after entering Rhodesia, Motsepe and his group made contact with the enemy on the banks of the Nyatuwe River, between Wankie Game Reserve and Dett. The battle raged for 10 hours. Pinned down on the banks of the river, the small group put up a spirited fight, but were no match for the Rhodesian troops.

Far away from the fighting, the main Luthuli contingent listened to the battle on their radios. They had been plagued by setbacks, the most serious of which was when a cadre went missing, and three others were sent to look for him. None rejoined the group. The ever-jovial Hani, however, lived up to his role as commissar, continually encouraging the men under his command and cracking jokes to keep their spirits up. He knew it was only a matter of time before they engaged the Rhodesians. Until then, it was a case of marching at night, sleeping during the day.

After almost two weeks, the pace and conditions were gruelling. The men became exhausted. On one of the stops, cadre Lawrence Phokanoka, also known as Peter Tladi, discovered he had left his weapon behind at a camp where the men had rested in the middle of the night. He had to return to find it, and eventually the contingent moved on, leaving him behind. He, too, did not rejoin the detachment and was ultimately arrested.

By now deep inside the reserve and without any contact, Hani's show of bravado, fiercely marching on with a knapsack that seemed featherlight, began to lose its inspiration. Marching on empty stomachs and critically short of water, the weakened soldiers found themselves stumbling through acacia thorn bushes, which tore at their uniforms and at their flesh. At one point, a contingent – including James April and John Dube – went in search of water.

Although they used pangas to mark trees along the way, the group soon lost their way in the dense bush. This was the dry season, so there were almost no rivers or streams. Their survey maps, which dated from the 1940s, were hugely inaccurate. April told us of how the sight of water one morning caused utter disbelief. The pan was shining and unbroken, reflecting the sky, and the men were emotional as they approached it.

Being in a game reserve also presented a unique set of challenges. Hani said he regarded the elephant, lion and giraffe as part of a greater harmony, the way in which he and his men would know if water was safe to drink, or if there were other people in the vicinity. During night-time training sessions, the troops had often encountered game animals and had come to understand their behaviour. At one point, a rogue elephant chased the group, eventually singling out Mjojo Mxwaku, who fortunately managed to escape.

Rhodesian forces had by now picked up the invaders' trail, and were following close behind. The distance covered by Hani's detachment was dropping each day. The soldiers were getting weaker. The time to attack was fast approaching.

Despite the hardships, Hani's view was that so far everything had gone according to plan. By mid-August, however, spotter planes began to track their movements, prompting the detachment to prepare for battle. The men fortified their positions, dug foxholes and organised defence lines, just as they had been taught in training.

The enemy waited. Two weeks later, they struck. Aircraft circled their position early one morning. Trucks packed with soldiers started arriving at about 10am, passing only about 100 metres away. The Luthuli men took up their positions, but there was some concern for two cadres who had gone to fetch water at a dam. When, hours later, the group heard an exchange of fire, Hani realised the two men must have been killed. For a long time afterwards, the air was silent.

Then, at about 3pm, a burst of gunfire was directed at the Luthuli Detachment positions. The Rhodesians shouted for the 'terrorists' to surrender, and so the taunting began. Hani's command insisted that nobody was allowed to pull a trigger before a target was clearly identified. There had to be economy of ammunition. Every bullet was precious. But the silence worried the enemy, and they opened fire. Caught in their first-ever battle, the Luthuli men were terrified as bullets landed at their feet and whizzed past their ears. 'It was like the chopping of hearts against the ribs,' said Hani later. The unspoken understanding within the detachment was that there would be no surrender.

The silence had given the Rhodesian troops a false sense of confidence, even arrogance. Standing up from their firing positions, some of their soldiers called out, trying to get a better view of the enemy. Finally, with the RAR clearly in their sights, some cadres opened fire. Two Rhodesians fell, and immediately there was panic in the RAR ranks. Hani led the Luthuli unit as they broke from their positions to pursue the fleeing enemy.

Then, like pirates, the men descended on the supplies left by their attackers. Cheese, biltong, meat, condensed milk and an assortment of other rations were a feast for soldiers who had, for days, teetered on the brink of starvation. Also among the booty was a brand new LMG, new uniforms and boots. In one RAR soldier's bag, they found an unfinished letter to a girlfriend.

\* \* \*

The liberation force's success in this early battle resounded across the continent. Tambo and Chikerema released a press statement shortly afterwards, respectful of the fierce fighting that had taken place:

From the 13th of this month, the area of Wankie has been the scene of the most daring battles ever fought between freedom fighters and the white oppressors' army in Rhodesia. Only last night, the Rhodesian regime admitted having been engaged in a six-hour battle yesterday.

In fact, the fighting in this area has been going on continuously for a full six days. Both the Rhodesian and the South African regimes have admitted that South African freedom fighters belonging to the ANC have been involved in these courageous battles, fighting their way to strike at the boers themselves in South Africa.

Ben Magubane recalls reports on the BBC World Service and Voice of America, in which it was said the men were encircled. He also read about Wankie in the newspapers, 'and it was actually exciting, but in order to get a copy, you had to be at the shop very early'. The descriptions of bombs falling and bodies shaking underpinned dozens of almost-mythical adventure stories about Wankie. For the oppressed peoples of southern Africa, this benign energy and idealism offset some of the humiliation and violence to which they were subjected.

Albie Sachs – who was living in London at the time, having decided to go into exile – said he can remember 'vividly' how Tambo announced this grand move forward with the armed struggle. The meeting at which he made the announcement was held at Peace House, which was actually a Quaker meeting house:

We were not told what it was all about, but it was very important to get a big crowd. He [Tambo] said armed combatants were proceeding to South Africa and managing to roam undetected … that they had engaged in combat.

People cheered and cheered, then a man shouted, 'That's murder!' a couple of times. It was a well-elocuted voice from the back. But we wanted to know, who was this provocateur? Then Tambo responded.

He said, 'yes, we have become killers. We sought by every means possible a peaceful solution. This was met by more and more repression. We were a peace-loving people …'

Sachs said Tambo ended up telling the gathering about the implications of the campaign: the ANC was not only going after installations now, but was using weapons of war. He said he sensed a 'very close understanding between Chris Hani and OR Tambo – a great moral and personal respect that each had for the other'. Wankie had turned Hani into 'an admired leader … he'd been in combat and now had a different kind of authority, an unofficial, intangible sense of authority'. Sachs said one of the outstanding things about Nelson Mandela is that he 'stood out, physically – he had a kind of stature'. The judge explained that Hani also had 'that standout quality'. 'You know that excitement when a person [like that] enters a room. They have an allure, a charisma. He had physical courage, intellectual clarity, a strong sense of morality.'

When he spoke later about the fighting, Hani believed this was indeed the moment at which the detachment was transformed into a fighting force. The men's reaction to the enemy attack recognised courage and faith, he would later say. And the initial triumph also gave hope to those fighting for liberation all across Africa, echoing throughout South Africa and inspiring a new generation. The legend of Chris Hani was born.

\* \* \*

A week later, around 25 August, the Luthuli group stumbled into their second engagement. This time, the Rhodesians deployed helicopters and Buccaneer jet fighters, which bombed an area about two kilometres from the MK–ZIPRA position. Troops were then sent in to mop up. Confident after their previous victory, the Luthuli Detachment surprised their enemy – and notched up another victory. But, at least two members of the detachment were killed and several were wounded in the engagement.

The next day, the RAR did not fight, instead using the lull to collect its dead. After emerging victorious from the two skirmishes, Hani believed the detachment would now be taken seriously. This had been the first time the RAR, more familiar with weak, poorly organised resistance, had suffered defeat. Major-General Ron Reid-Daly, commanding officer of the elite Selous Scouts, described these encounters as 'assuming the proportions of a military disaster'. The Rhodesian troops had become demoralised. They needed assistance and called in reinforcements from their willing neighbour to the south.

With supplies critically low, and the lack of water weighing on the troops' physical condition, Hani knew the men would not be able to complete the march south. So, led by Dube, the remaining members of the detachment made their way towards the Botswana border. Hani explained later that the decision to veer away to Botswana was informed by the combination of a depleted supply line, the build-up of enemy reinforcements and the knowledge that terrain ahead was even more barren and waterless:

We decided it would be futile to continue fighting because the enemy was bringing in more reinforcements. So we deliberately took a decision to retreat. The aim of this decision is important to emphasise. This was no surrender to the paramilitary units of the Botswana government.

But by this time, the South African regime had pressurised the Botswana government to prevent us from getting into Botswana. We found a situation where the Rhodesian security forces, joined by the South Africans, were pursuing us. And within Botswana, the paramilitary force had been mobilised to stop us from entering Botswana.

Botswana is a member of the OAU and in theory, it is committed to the liberation of South Africa. So we came to the correct political decision that we were not going to fight them. When they came to meet us, they played very conciliatory and friendly, saying they had not come to harm us. They said their instructions were not to engage us and that all they wanted was that we surrender and our fate would be discussed amicably. They also promised that we would not be detained.

So we accepted their bona fides and surrendered, only to discover that they were being commanded by white officers from Britain and South Africa. All of a sudden, we were manacled, handcuffed and abused.

**Ex-combatant James April, who now lives quietly in suburban Pretoria, surrounded by books and pictures of his children, is sanguine about the Wankie operation:**

We might have taken on too much with this long march. You see, instead of going south, we should actually have stayed, all of us, and established ourselves in Zimbabwe and moved south gradually. We could have been close to our rear bases.

It was important to be able to retreat to the bases and get supplies, because sometimes the locals are so intimidated by the security forces, terrorised by them, you know, it is difficult to get co-operation. But we could only do it over time.

Hani, too, remarked on this, saying that one of the lessons learnt from Wankie was that it is important for soldiers in any military operation to have sufficient data – about the operational area, the attitude of the local population, the state of enemy forces, and so on. The insufficiencies of the Wankie operation earned the men of the Luthuli Detachment two years in prison, and created a legacy of embitterment that would divide the liberation movement, and change it from the inside.

CHAPTER 7

# THE MEMORANDUM

Lying on his single bed, Hani was restless. Cold air blew through the openings at the top of the cell wall. Although reduced to wearing short pants, a jacket and a jersey, he found prison almost luxurious after months in the Rhodesian bush. Porridge in the mornings, meat, vegetables, sometimes even fish – a veritable feast. Still, this was not how it was supposed to be.

Hani had crossed into newly independent Botswana with three other top soldiers in early September 1967, following a month of running battles with Rhodesian security forces. The men were already heroes, as the progress of the Wankie campaign had been widely reported. It was, after all, the first time South African liberation forces had properly engaged a substantial enemy force. But the skirmishes had taken a severe toll on the joint MK–ZIPRA force, which had started out with 100 men. By the time Hani and his fellow commander, Zimbabwean John Dube, had set off into the night to look for water, leaving half of their group behind, there were only eight in their company.

It was a time for reflection and re-appraisal. And it was a time for Hani, who was at a critical juncture in his development as a fighter and a leader, to consider how he and his fellow soldiers had been sustained and championed during the campaign and afterwards in prison – and by whom. Hani was typically reflective afterwards, saying in an interview that the Wankie campaign had 'failed to achieve its main objectives, militarily speaking'. But this was also a factor of his lack of ego: he could have elevated himself to the position of hero, because that is surely what he, and his men, had become. Instead, he described Wankie as 'an important experience for the organisation':

We were able to have a taste of military action. We were tempered in battle, we were tested under difficult conditions and I think we succeeded. [The standard of the soldiers] was excellent. Our moral qualities, our conviction and our toughness were exceptional, and we maintained a discipline and unity which very few armies would have under those circumstances. I mean, no regular army would have endured, you know, marching all the way from there without proper logistics.

By the time the mission was over, the detachment had covered more than 200 kilometres through dense bush and thorn trees, using the most fragile of supply lines:

I mean, you judge yourself, being around, crossing from the Zambezi River near Livingstone and then to Botswana and going all in zig-zags, see. And not moving straight along a road. Although it was a turning point in terms of the struggle in Zimbabwe. The people of Zimbabwe felt the impact of that. The enemy couldn't suppress information about it. So although we didn't succeed, I think we inspired the population.

We also inspired people politically in South Africa because the press in South Africa, which had inquired about the ANC for so long, now began to say ANC guerrillas are crossing into Zimbabwe, running battles fought around Wankie. So our people inside the country got the message that the ANC had been told by the media that it was kaput when actually it was in there and fighting. And this was followed by an upsurge in student activity, in the formation of the Black Consciousness Movement and SASO [South African Students Organisation]. Our trial in Botswana got a lot of media coverage ... So in a way, directly now, we had actually begun to influence and inspire young people about armed struggle.

This was exactly what Hani had wanted when he had fought for the right to take the war for justice forward when he was still at Kongwa. But it had been a year since that desperate crossing into Botswana, to what was assumed to be safety. Hani and Dube had buried their weapons after stopping at a trading store close to Francistown to buy civilian clothes, and had presumed their negotiations were on even ground when they were confronted by Botswana security forces in a dry river bed.

They had reasoned that the Botswana government would be sympathetic to their cause. But it was also important not to jeopardise the country's newfound independence by giving the Pretoria regime an excuse to invade. Surely the weary guerrillas would not be convicted? The men were sentenced to prison terms of between one and six years, and the Botswana security forces later convinced Dube to reveal the location of the buried arms cache. If Dube refused, he would be handed over to the Rhodesians and probably face the hangman's noose.

Two years into independence, Botswana's first democratic president, Sir Seretse Khama, was under considerable political pressure, both from within his own country and from Britain, whose closest regional ally was apartheid South Africa. But the OAU and the ANC's highest official, OR Tambo, were determined to engage Seretse's government for the group's early release.

In Gaborone jail, Hani, too, was agitating. At least the men had graduated from reading Enid Blyton books – all that was available in the beginning – to serious novels like Henry Fielding's *Tom Jones* and other classics, supplied by a benevolent Oxford University, friends in the United States and Britain, and the library in town. Ironically for the communists among the MK and ZIPRA cadres, someone had generously donated a Monopoly game for some capitalist entertainment. Ruth Mompati secured a Scrabble board and sent it to the prisoners.

For the first time in years, Hani had the luxury of time to read and read for the pure delight of it. And here, inside the cell, he also found a ready ear for talk about politics. Conditions were not harsh in the beginning. Prisoners were not abused and spent their days doing manual labour, Hani being assigned to water the plants and to do general garden maintenance. Unlike the government, which had vacillated in its approach, the warders were sympathetic to the liberation fighters from across the border.

Describing his time in prison, Hani later said to Wolfie Kodesh:

You know it's important that you prepare yourself for a long grind in prison … a long grind. I was ready. I was not demoralised. There was slight demoralisation on the part of a few, but we would actually run up our spirits. There were comrades who felt bad about it. It's very difficult. It's degrading. Even the uniform is humiliating. You wear those pants without underwear. You don't have shoes. You sleep in those dirty blankets. It is a punishment, but we take it. You take the punishment in your stride, you see, because you know, if I want freedom, then I must be ready to make a certain sort of essential sacrifice.

In prison, together with comrades, I have had no food to eat. I really feel it and I become helpless because I know how another must be feeling.

But the revolution had to continue, even in prison. An escape attempt led to stricter conditions and no yard time. And inside the cell Hani shared, there was dissension. The anger and frustration at not receiving any contact from their comrades at headquarters in Lusaka was borne out in plans to rebel against their captors. The instigators of the campaign of non-co-operation later came together to take on a more formidable challenge: the ANC leadership itself.

When it was finally clear that the men of the Luthuli Detachment were to be released, Tambo approached an old friend and confidant to house Hani. The young man had great potential but needed to be intellectually stimulated, the argument went. The responsibility fell to Livingstone Mqotsi, an intellectual and devoted struggle exile, who refused offers of money and welcomed the fellow Xhosa-speaker into his home.

After 18 frustrating months in jail, Hani would be a son for Livingstone and Nzimazana, and an older brother for Yvonne and Laurantia. But whenever visitors came to the Mqotsi home, the quiet Hani would go to his bedroom with a book. When the house fell silent, he and Mqotsi could again engage in discussion on the political situation in South Africa and on what needed to be done. A romantic, Hani enjoyed the writings of Shelley and Keats. Initially averse to classical music, Hani would over time come to appreciate the sound. Sometimes, when reciting poetry in his bedroom, he would engage in animated conversation with himself. But soon, the graduate of the battlefield had more than his fair share of visitors.

\* \* \*

Across Woodlands, the academics enjoyed the quiet of the middle-class Lusaka suburb. By 8pm on a week night, most residents were settling down for bed. By midnight, the entire campus neighbourhood was usually aslumber. A rumbling diesel engine would have seemed amiss at any time. But the grinding of gears and the throaty roar of the truck engine put paid to any further attempts at sleep.

A light went on at number 10. An older man swaddled in his robe peeped through narrowed eyes. 'Is Chris here?' the young man at the door asked. He had been there many times before, like so many others, to enjoy the company of the 'eldest son' of the Mqotsi household. But this time, something was wrong.

When Hani and his company had returned to Lusaka from jail in Botswana, a party was thrown for them at 250 Zambezi Road – the home of communists Jack and Ray Simons. Ben Magubane threw a party, too. But surprisingly, disturbingly, there was no other official welcome.

The silence from the leadership began to eat at Hani. Within months, his confusion turned into a desperate kind of fury. Finally, he put his name at the top of a list of seven signatures in the Memorandum, a document that sought to expose the rot within the ANC's highest administration.

The signatories, all former cellmates in Gaborone, gathered in Mqotsi's home in Lusaka, mostly at night after the dinner dishes were done and doors were quietly closed in the house as the children went to their rooms. In the lounge, Mqotsi and his wife would listen to Stravinsky and Beethoven on the record player and read quietly. Later, they would turn off the lights and the radio, check the locks on the doors and the window latches. The door to Hani's room would be closed, but inside there was a buzz of hushed conversation.

For months, the comrades had discussed the betrayal of the revolution. The time had come for talk to be turned into action. A memorandum. A document that would honestly address matters. The risks were high. Dissidents often disappeared. But it was their duty, the duty of any true revolutionary. No one would be spared.

The Memorandum contained explosive allegations. And that was why the emissary arrived at the Mqotsi house at midnight that night. Hani had become a target, and the reason was only too obvious.

In the document, names were named. It was claimed that one Thabo More – the name by which Joe Modise was known – paid more attention to commercial enterprises like a furniture factory in Lusaka and a bone factory in Livingstone. Initially fronts for the ANC's underground activities, the businesses were now run as true commercial ventures. More, or Modise, took a salary and owned a posh 'militarily irrelevant' car. He was becoming middle class. More's relative, Shadrack Tladi, was part of a trio that was openly flirting with members of the US Peace Corps, an alleged 'CIA front'. At the time, Tladi and Joseph Cotton, the son of ANC treasurer-general Moses Kotane, handled much of the organisation's highly sensitive information and transported war materiel. It was also stated that the wife of a prominent ANC official worked for an Israeli intelligence-gathering agency.

The Memorandum reflected the sense among some cadres that the ANC chief of security, Duma Nokwe, was indifferent and cynical towards battle-weary comrades. It was understood that his apparently cold demeanour had upset Hani. In the camps, combatants who had offended the leadership were rumoured to have been dumped in dugouts half-filled with water, without any protection from the elements, for weeks at a time. There were secret trials and secret executions. MK commander-in-chief Modise was reputed to have become a law unto himself, arbitrarily appointing and dismissing people, leading to the entrenchment of a culture in which sycophants prevailed.

Particular rancour was directed at the ANC Youth League, and one of its leaders, Thabo Mbeki, was singled out. Hani and Mbeki were ideological opposites. While Hani went to war in Wankie, Mbeki was studying at the University of Sussex, funded by the National Union of South African Students (NUSAS), the white liberal student organisation. It felt as if there was clear nepotism going on. A hangman's noose had ended the life of MK cadre Vuyisile Mini, while Wankie hero Basil February had died in a gun battle with Rhodesian police. Countless others had been killed, sacrificed to the greater good. Meanwhile, some of the children of the ANC leadership were studying in Europe. Hani and others believed they would enjoy the comforts abroad, and return home only once the battle was won. For this, he detested them.

Quietly plotting in the Mqotsi home, the eight men resolved to demand a truly representative conference between the ANC's leadership and MK. One by one the men signed their names at the end of the seven-page Memorandum, and the document was delivered to the ANC leadership. A reply came soon enough.

The knock on the door in the middle of the night was not uncommon. As a South African exile in Lusaka with strong links to the ANC, Mqotsi would occasionally get visitors, such as Tambo, who kept odd hours. In recent years, more and more of those familiar faces knocked on his door to visit Chris. But no one had ever come visiting in a truck before.

'Is Chris here?'

Something inside Mqotsi told him to say no, and it seemed the young men were reluctant to push the point anyway. Without much left to be said, they clambered back into the Russian truck – and drove off. But that was not the end.

The next morning, after Hani had completed his routine run, Mqotsi sat down with him at the kitchen table. He described the midnight visit, his sense of trepidation, how he'd lied ... Hani thanked him, without offering an explanation. Yet for Mqotsi, there was more going on than Hani was prepared to reveal. Mzwai Piliso, head of the ANC's feared security department, Mbokodo, had been another midnight caller just 24 hours earlier. He had come to plead with Mqotsi, his old Fort Hare classmate. Piliso knew Hani and his friends respected the intellectual, so he begged Mqotsi to use his influence to convince the group to apologise to the ANC leadership. They had committed a grave offence.

'I've been sent here by the leadership. This boy is mine,' said Piliso. Desperate, he waved a document in his old friend's face. It was the Memorandum.

* * *

After Hani returned to Lusaka from detention in Botswana, he spent much of his time at Luthuli camp, 130 kilometres out of the city. At first, he did not talk about what had happened in Wankie, but later he addressed the men in the camp, telling them about the glorious victories won during the campaign and the time spent in prison. He gave advice on what to avoid should any of them be involved in similar missions.

The men enjoyed these vivid accounts. In their distant camp, with little to occupy them other than military routine, feelings of isolation were not uncommon. From here, the familiar sounds of Radio South Africa could be heard on radio, and people coming from Lusaka would bring newspapers. Every column inch of local Zambian and international news was devoured by this eager audience.

Still, there had been no debriefing session, no formal call from the MK leadership – and, therefore, the ANC and SACP leadership – for those who had survived Wankie. No one had officially asked them to share their experiences. Even more disheartening was the fact that no other missions seemed imminent. The battle-hardened cadres were in a state of limbo. In the meantime, all that was visible to the rank and file was the leadership, flying from world capital to world capital, enjoying the high life.

'They thought that we were going to just applaud everything they did and say, "hallelujah",' Hani recalled. Instead, 'we blew our tops'.

As news spread by word of mouth, and copies of the now-famous Memorandum started circulating, a certain fear ran through ordinary members of the ANC. Never before, not in their time as members of the organisation, had the movement been challenged so sharply from within. The document would surely do irrevocable damage.

The contents of the Memorandum were pulled apart and criticised by groups in conversation. The language was crude. It was not ANC. It was tribalist. All the signatories come from Transkei. Still, many agreed with the main sentiment. The struggle had indeed stagnated, with the leaders flitting about the world stage. Facetious remarks about 'telephone guerrillas' and 'chicken-in-the-basket revolutionaries' seemed to have a basis in fact.

But in the ANC's culture of consensus, so carefully fostered by Tambo, many felt that making the Memorandum public was tantamount to an open rebellion. In the end, two documents emerged: a second Memorandum detailed the background of the first. There was a view that, although the second document had been produced by Hani and his comrades, Jack Simons had assisted them. It was agreed that the group's independence had to be asserted, so three of the signatories were sent out to interview Duma Nokwe, while arrangements were made to discuss a meeting with other members of the executive.

An incensed Nokwe – who was enraged at being singled out, and who felt his wife had been vilified – was predictably hostile. He tried to deflect attention from the real issues, saying these were 'trivial'. He insisted on seeing the signatories as individuals, not as a group, and asked his representatives to arrange a meeting with the NEC. Eventually, six members of the NEC met as a delegation, and copies of the Memorandum were prepared. These were first typed, stencilled and duplicated, and then given to members of the executive and select members of MK, with the latter cautioned to be careful with the fire they had in their possession.

The signatories were to have a second meeting with the executive. But this time, representatives from military headquarters and the regional administration were present. The executive explained that they had been summoned because the Memorandum was now also in the hands of soldiers, but almost immediately, some of the military men grew threatening.

To this day, there are rumours that dire punishment, and even the death sentence, was mooted. Dungeons were said to have been dug, perhaps upon the orders of Modise, or even Nokwe, but an upset Tambo ordered that these be closed. He wanted the matter to be discussed again, and insisted a meeting be convened for this purpose. His view was that the Memorandum was not the work of the eight signatories, but rather that the men were being used as proxies by others, who were as yet unknown.

Eventually, a military tribunal consisting of NEC members Mzwai Piliso, Jonas Matlou and former PAC member Sipho Mthembu was convened in Livingstone, and a majority voted for the execution of the signatories. Despite his formidable reputation, Piliso is said to have been the person whose determination and intervention saved Hani and the others from the firing squad. Others say it was Ray Simons. Apparently she had heard about the decision of the tribunal – and was livid. She took on Thomas Nkobi, then the ANC's chief representative in Zambia, and said there would be serious consequences if anything happened to Hani.

Having heard the news of the possibility of execution, Hani's 'father' in Lusaka, Livingstone Mqotsi, launched his own appeal – to the East German and Soviet ambassadors. He wanted them to use their influence to stop the ANC from killing the young men. Even at this relatively early stage of Hani's life, a legion of admirers came to his rescue.

Finally, the NEC met and overruled the tribunal, even though the decision to punish the men had been confirmed at the Morogoro Conference in late April 1969. The men attached to the Memorandum were suspended from the organisation. But a hornet's nest had been stirred up. The fact that there were some, notably within the NEC, who had bayed for the blood of Hani and his cohorts clearly showed that the leadership did not like being criticised. So although the knock in the dead of night at Mqotsi's door did not ultimately lead to Hani's imprisonment or death, it did compel a rearguard action on behalf of the NEC. Vocal in this were the likes of leading SACP members Joe Slovo and Yusuf Dadoo.

* * *

By the time 70 delegates had gathered in Morogoro, Tanzania, on 25 April 1969, from stations across the world, 41 African states had gained independence. But Mozambique, Angola, South West Africa, Rhodesia and South Africa were still in bondage. 'The countries of southern Africa have not yet broken the chains of ... racism which hold them in oppression,' read a statement adopted at the conference.

The ANC affirmed its purpose at Morogoro. Certainly, it was a revolutionary movement, which had adopted an armed struggle, but its battles were primarily political. The use of force was something not entered into lightly. The organisation's goal was not militarism. For the ANC, political leadership was the sublime good. All other structures were subordinate, as it was strongly felt that the armed struggle alone could not bring about success.

The propaganda of the apartheid regime was fierce, and had to be countered. At Morogoro, where race issues played out to devastating effect, it was clearly spelt out that whites were unified as the enemy, with the ANC in unison that 'all significant sections of the white political movement are in broad agreement on the question of defeating our liberation struggle'. It argued that the battle along colour lines had been created by the enemy, and the tragic consequences of it would be hard to eliminate. In a different situation, the white working class might have come to understand that its fate was intertwined with that of the black working class. At the same time, the conference called on the liberation movement to assist in breaking the policy of racial domination: 'Our policy must continually stress in the future (as it has in the past) that there is room in South Africa for all who live in it but only on the basis of absolute democracy.'

The mainstay of the conference, and these statements, was the Strategy and Tactics document, engineered by Joe Slovo, which secured the recognition that the main aim of the revolution was the national liberation of the African people as the most oppressed group, a belief which should govern every aspect of the struggle. There was a powerful call for unity among oppressed people, lauding the sacrifices of the likes of Basil February and the many Indian and Coloured political prisoners. 'We are revolutionaries, not narrow nationalists,' stated the document. 'Committed revolutionaries are our brother to whatever group they belong. There can be no second-class participants in our movement.'

The Strategy and Tactics document then looked forward to the eventual emancipation of the masses of South Africa, arguing for economic and political emancipation as the first phase of the military struggle. 'To allow the existing economic forces to retain their interests intact is to feed the root of racial supremacy and does not represent even the shadow of liberation.'

Hani saw, however, that the Memorandum – which was necessarily suppressed in favour of the Strategy and Tactics document – had had a more immediate effect. In the aftermath of the conference, the allowance paid to members of the leadership – which he and the other signatories had found so repugnant – was stopped, and a number of camp commanders were removed from their positions. The movement was tightening its belt and refocusing itself on its primary mission.

By the time the week-long conference came to an end, the ANC had decisively reinvigorated itself and the liberation movement, deciding with renewed vigour to infiltrate South Africa both militarily and politically.

But other African governments were seriously wavering in their resolve to isolate the apartheid and colonial regimes. Although not militarily successful, the battles of Wankie and Spolilo – a second MK–ZIPRA infiltration campaign, lasting from December 1967 to July 1968 – had sent a clear message. The liberation movements were inextricably intertwined and were ready to confront the enemy with force. However, barely two weeks before Morogoro, the fifth summit conference of East and Central African states had produced the Lusaka Manifesto, which dealt a crushing blow to the liberation movements of southern Africa.

For more than a year, Zambian president Kenneth Kaunda had been engaging South African apartheid leader John Vorster in talks about normalising relations in return for the release of Mandela and engagement with the liberation movements. The Lusaka Manifesto, which took this into account, was believed to have been largely authored by Julius Nyerere, and was eventually adopted by both the OAU and the United Nations General Assembly. The manifesto declared:

> If peaceful progress to emancipation were possible, or if changed circumstances were to make it possible in the future, we would urge our brothers in the resistance movements to use peaceful methods of struggle, even at the cost of some compromise on the timing of change.

But the liberation movements read it differently. It seemed the African heads of state were threatening to pull the plug on the armed struggle in return for a protracted withdrawal of oppressive colonial and apartheid rule.

The ANC leadership responded with deafening silence. Since Zambia was hosting the ANC and several other liberation organisations, they could hardly allow themselves to fall foul of Kaunda. But the African leaders changed their tune a year later at their conference in Khartoum. The colonial and apartheid regimes of Portugal, Rhodesia and South Africa had not taken up the invitation to hold discussions with the respective liberation organisations in their countries, prompting the heads of state to again increase their support for the revolutionaries.

Watching from the sidelines, disillusioned but still involved in the history unfolding before him, Hani tried to make sense of the politics in play. In an interview that later appeared in *Mayibuye*, he is documented as saying:

We were all bitter about the Lusaka Manifesto, about the negotiations between Kaunda and Vorster. But we thought it would be wrong to denounce Kaunda for a number of reasons. Though he was continuing with his negotiations, he was keeping us in Zambia, and for us this was important. So we had to weigh up our priorities. We thought, let him; he was entitled to do what he was doing, but basically, it was important for us to retain Zambia as a base for the ANC in order to continue with our strategy. That was Kaunda's strategy. He was not hostile to the ANC because he was talking to Vorster.

We felt let down. We would have preferred a situation where Africa would totally isolate the apartheid regime. Because this was our strategy, that South Africa must be isolated continentally and internationally. But we knew that some African leaders were having secret talks with the regime because of their dependence on South Africa economically, and [the fact that] they traded South African goods.

I think Kaunda this time had problems with Smith, because Smith had declared unilateral independence, and Zambia had closed its borders and everything with Smith. I think he was playing South Africa against Zimbabwe in order to ensure that Zambia, which was a landlocked country, did not suffer the long-term effects of the blockade that Zambia, with the support of the international community, had imposed on Zimbabwe.

On reflection, though, 1969 was marked not so much by Strategy and Tactics or the Lusaka Manifesto. By far the most influential catalyst for far-reaching decisions was the Memorandum. As Hani said later to Wolfie Kodesh:

Our detractors would not say that we had contributed, but if we had not spoken out, in my own view there would have been no Morogoro Conference. Our criticism created a crisis within the movement which jolted them. And again [prompted] a clear definition of the objectives of the ANC. The ANC began to say the working class is the backbone of our struggle. And I would want to believe that our erratic, if you like, criticism and anger did contribute to this sort of thing.

The post-Morogoro ANC depended more on developing revolutionary structures inside South Africa to mobilise the masses. Importantly, the rank and file had gained in stature.

* * *

Hani's suspension from the movement hurt him deeply. In late 1969 he retreated to Zambia's Copper Belt region, feeling betrayed by the organisation to which he had dedicated his life. He had done what had to be done for everybody. His actions were patriotic. Why, then, was he being punished? Some had called him arrogant. Some even labelled him a traitor. 'It was a painful moment for me. Very, very painful,' he would confess. 'I had come from a traumatic experience.' From the time he had left Sabalele almost a decade before, the ANC had been his home. Now, left in the wilderness by his 'family', it was expatriate friends in the Copper Belt who provided refuge.

After the Memorandum had become public, many comrades travelled there to speak to him, to try and persuade him to see things differently. Yet even though the Morogoro Conference agreed that the Memorandum signatories should be reinstated, Hani remained cautious, even bitter. He felt he had been discarded, and his closest friends said that he fell into a depression that lasted for some time. He seriously considered his options outside the liberation movement.

Hani's old comrade James April also went to the Copper Belt to try and persuade Hani to return to the fold. As ever, Hani commanded total loyalty among his friends. But, believing that April had been sent by the ANC to further punish him, his response was merely civil. Finally, April gained more intimate access to Hani and persuaded him to listen. These were not merely overtures. Eventually, Hani returned:

For me it was a continuation of the struggle. I refused to be bitter. And I also refused to leave the ANC and go to school. Other people opted for school. I refused. I continued. I wanted to prove the point that I was not a traitor, that I was not being selfish. There was no personal aggrandisement in my complaining. So I remained there.

At the end of the nightmare, only one of the eight signatories remained outside the movement – Wankie veteran Leonard Nkosi. In the interim, he had returned home to South Africa, where he found his father had been sentenced to imprisonment on Robben Island and his mother was barely able to make ends meet. The disillusioned cadre was fertile ground for the Security Branch, which quickly pounced. Some say he was betrayed, tortured and forced to turn against the ANC. Whatever the truth, Nkosi testified in a number of trials against his former comrades, including James April, who was detained in Durban in 1971 after infiltrating the country. Nkosi was even reported to have taken part in police raids, acquiring a reputation as a particularly dangerous askari – a Swahili word meaning warrior or soldier, but which came to mean a guerrilla who had been 'turned' by the police. It was generally accepted that MK played a part in the assassination of Nkosi in 1977.

\* \* \*

In the wake of the Morogoro Conference, another group of dissenters, this time originating within the NEC itself, made itself heard in a spat that became a war and ended in bloodshed. Known as the Group of Eight, these men were strongly opposed to the Morogoro decision that ANC membership be open to all races. They were also enraged by what they perceived as the undue influence of the SACP on the ANC and the liberation movement as a whole. Ultimately, the group's leaders, Ambrose Makiwane and Themba Mqota, were suspended from the organisation for a period for trying to galvanise an alternative faction.

For some time, the group – which comprised Mqota, Makiwane, his cousin Tennyson Makiwane, George Mbele, NEC member Jonas Matlou,

OK Setlapelo, Pascal Ngakane and Thami Bonga – had criticised the ANC from the relative safety of a base in London. Even after personal sit-downs with Tambo, discussions in the NEC and a specially convened conference, they felt that nothing had been done to address the issues they had raised. Despite this, Tambo went so far as to reappoint those among them who were former members of the NEC, and most of them were assigned 'comfortable' jobs as organisation representatives.

Still, the Group of Eight used the occasion of the unveiling of a memorial to the vocal Africanist and anti-communist Robert Resha as a megaphone for their criticism of the ANC. Their main complaint was that the ANC had been hijacked by non-Africans and communists. Yet, for at least three years prior to Morogoro, debate had raged about greater inclusivity. So when it was decided there that non-Africans could become members of the ANC external structures, but not be elected to the NEC – with the NEC whittled down from 18 members to just 9, excluding the likes of the Makiwane cousins and Mqota – their fury was ignited.

A Revolutionary Council was created after Morogoro to coordinate the armed struggle. The council included numerous members of the SACP, as well as whites, Indians and Coloureds. This annoyed the Group of Eight, who also couldn't help remarking that Strategy and Tactics, the key document at the conference, had been drafted by members of the SACP and was now hailed as the most important document to emerge from the ANC in more than a decade.

'The trouble the African people have at present is that our strategy and tactics are in the hands of and dominated by a small clique of non-Africans,' Ambrose Makiwane read at the unveiling ceremony for Resha. But the group was quick to rebut the view that their attitude was racist:

The label of racist which the non-African clique uses against all Africans who oppose the control and the manipulation of the ANC by non-Africans, is an anomalous one. It is anomalous because Africans suffer from the jackboot of white racism from the cradle to the grave; in their own country they are made aliens.

Going further, the group plainly stated that 'the Africans hate the domination of the Communist Party of South Africa'.

Many of those who now so vehemently criticised the ANC had been regarded as among its brightest stars. Tennyson Makiwane, a former Treason Trialist, had been Tambo's right-hand man in Dar es Salaam and later in Lusaka. Ambrose Makiwane had been the first camp commander at Kongwa, and, like his cousin, had sat on the NEC.

But the group's criticisms became a problem for the ANC. Both the international and South African media latched onto the issue, which spoke of the fractious nature of the movement and its apparent domination by the communists. Months later, pushed into an untenable position, the NEC took action: 'Every effort was made to try and persuade these ringleaders to desist from their acts of subverting the struggle, but the tolerance and constructive approach of the movement was mistaken for weakness on its part, and rewarded by these conspirators with an intensification on their part of attempts to sow division and confusion,' read a statement delivered by ANC veteran Alfred Nzo. 'Let it be made abundantly clear that the policies of racialism and anti-communism have been and still are diametrically opposed to the policies, traditions and practices of the ANC.' The organisation summarily expelled the eight.

But if the ANC's response was professional and measured, that of the SACP was scathing. Under the headline, 'The enemy hidden under the same colour,' the Central Committee of the SACP mocked the eight for being a carbon copy of the 'failed' PAC. The party pointed out that two of the group had testified in the 1969 trial of trade unionist Dorothy Nyembe and 11 other activists in Pietermaritzburg, helping to condemn them to prison. The article adopted a snide, biting and often mocking tone:

Can it be that the Group of Eight is saying that Indian and Coloured comrades on Robben Island and white comrades in Pretoria prison, some serving terms of life imprisonment for their part in both armed and unarmed struggle, should not have played a part, but should have restricted themselves to organising only among their own communities? ... Are they saying that non-African revolutionaries like Basil February, killed alongside Patrick Malaoa in Umkhonto's fighting ranks against racist troops, had no right to participate in the ANC's External Mission, or even to be a member of the ANC's Revolutionary Council? But, of course, they are saying all this.

Years later, Tambo exhorted comrades to

... wage a relentless war against disrupters and defend the ANC against provocateurs and enemy agents. Defend the revolution against enemy propaganda, whatever form it takes. Be vigilant, comrades. The enemy is vigilant. Beware of the wedge-driver, the man who creeps from ear to ear, carrying a bag full of wedges, driving them in between you and the next man, between one group and another, a man who goes round creating splits and divisions. Beware of the wedge driver, comrades. Watch his poisonous tongue.

The Group of Eight and a motley crew of fellow dissenters attempted to form an alternative ANC, but failed to garner any real support. And of the dissenters, all except one eventually made their peace with the party. The exception was Tennyson Makiwane, who left the ANC and sought employment with the United Nations in Swaziland – a move that was opposed by the movement. Makiwane later took up residence in Maseru, Lesotho, where he lived at the same time as Hani during the 1970s. Although there are indications that the two were close at one point, Hani had to review his feelings about Makiwane later on when, ostracised and embarrassed, Makiwane rushed into the embrace of Transkei homeland leader Kaiser Matanzima, who bestowed on the former NEC member the title of 'roving Transkei ambassador'. Suspected of revealing sensitive information to the apartheid state, Makiwane was shot dead in Umtata in July 1980 by ANC hitman David Simelane.

\* \* \*

Hani survived the pain attached to the Memorandum and remained in

Lusaka for a while, helping to build the internal organisation and once again revelling in debate. Although not a member of the Revolutionary Council, he worked closely with it, and was especially reliant on his relationship with Jack and Ray Simons. Hani was also involved in discussions on the implementation of the Strategy and Tactics document. In time, the Memorandum came to be regarded as historic, even monumental. Meanwhile, having further enhanced his reputation, Hani's growing stature within MK did not go unnoticed. Within the ANC and SACP, his talents were being recognised, and at the SACP conference in 1970 he was duly elected to the Central Committee at just 28 years of age. Of the relationship of politics to the armed struggle, he reflected later to Wolfie Kodesh:

Undoubtedly politics plays a central role in maintaining the high morale and conviction and dedication. Politics, politics ... A guerrilla army is important because it is a disadvantaged arm. It is not an army that has a support network. You know the American armies kept supplies of refrigerated cold drinks. The guerrilla army marches on conviction. You must understand why they're hungry, why there's a shortage of food, why they do not have blankets, why they have to sleep outside and why they can't have three meals a day. They must learn how important it is to share even a morsel of meat, so that you, as a commander, don't have the lion's share. So politics shapes the outfit of the revolution.

CHAPTER 8

# LESOTHO

Hani had walked for two days, using a compass and the stars to guide him over the Botswana border to Zeerust, 55 kilometres inside South Africa. It was 1974, and he thought it might be a good idea to use his fragile Afrikaans, interspersed with 'baas', to throw off the white Afrikaner stationmaster:

I spoke to the guy in the ticket office in broken Afrikaans thinking he would be more helpful to a Bantu trying to speak Afrikaans than a smart kaffir trying to speak English. I called the fellow 'baas' and, well, it seemed to work, because he became very helpful, suggesting I take a bus to Mafeking and the train from there to Johannesburg, where I arrived the next morning.

The typical Hani comedy in enemy territory succeeded. Perhaps his good mood was informed by the fact that days earlier he had married Limpho Sekamane in a quiet ceremony and reception in Dar es Salaam, attended by only a few friends. It had been almost a year since the risky decision was taken to try and infiltrate South Africa from The Island, as Lesotho was known. The mountainous ramparts of the tiny landlocked kingdom would help to protect Hani's launching pad for operations back home.

He had been preparing, militarily and ideologically, for this moment for some time. He had spent three months in the German Democratic Republic (GDR), undergoing training in guerrilla command at a dacha (country house) outside Berlin. One of his instructors and mentors at the time was Joe Slovo, who discovered that the young Hani had never learnt to ride a bicycle. Slovo advised Hani that he should know how to cycle if he was going to do underground work, and duly took it upon himself to teach his protégé. 'Hani came off the bike many times and there was Joe pushing him along, and encouraging him to get his balance. And there was Chris, complaining that Joe was trying to kill him,' recalled Ronnie Kasrils, who was an MK regional commander at the time, with a laugh.

Now Hani was ready. From the moment he clambered over the fence from Botswana and entered South Africa, he knew the journey would be dangerous. Armed with a bundle of cash, he was on his way to Johannesburg to set up underground cells and spearhead a new wave of infiltration, the first since the ill-fated Rhodesian campaign of 1967. It had been seven years since he had confronted the adversary head-on in the Wankie Game Reserve. Now he had to call on all his training to sow the seed for wide-scale insurrection. He later described the situation:

I arrived in Johannesburg and found that conditions for survival were not ideal. It was a question of safe places. Friends and relatives were very scared to accommodate me. They stopped just short of kicking me out because I was a relative.

Paranoia was running high. The Security Branch had informers everywhere and the risk of betrayal was ever-present. After four months, setting up cells in small groups of two or three – to prevent an entire chain of activists being betrayed by a single capture – Hani finally made his way across the border into Lesotho, the diplomatic survivor.

\* \* \*

Lesotho was founded by the first King Moshoeshoe, who had united tribes defeated and displaced by the onslaught of Shaka, and forged the Basotho nation. Through shrewd diplomacy, Lesotho withstood external threats, eventually becoming a protectorate of the British crown in 1884. Following independence from Britain in 1966, King Moshoeshoe II became locked in an intense power struggle with a minor chief, Leabua Jonathan, leader of the Basotho National Party (BNP). The king was ultimately pushed into exile and, on his return, was forced to behave as a constitutional monarch as Jonathan entrenched his control of the tiny nation. With Jonathan installed as prime minister, the new government cosied up to its powerful neighbour, South Africa.

By 1970, Jonathan and Lesotho's honeymoon was over as the opposition Basotho Congress Party (BCP) won a clear majority in the first post-independence elections. Much of the Basotho voting sentiment was centred around greater autonomy from South Africa, which effectively controlled much of Lesotho's administration. Jonathan, prompted by apartheid South Africa – which feared the BCP would offer safe haven to liberation movements – suspended the constitution, jailed opposition leaders and ruled by decree. Jonathan's actions would give rise to the Lesotho Liberation Army, the armed wing of the BCP, a small group of fighters who first trained alongside the PAC and then, in a cynical about-turn, became allied to apartheid South Africa's infamous Vlakplaas.

For the ANC, quietly observing from the periphery, increasingly aware of The Island's strategic significance, the time was ripe. There were other signs, too. In January 1973, a group of 2 000 workers from Coronation Brick and Tile Works went on strike in Durban, rallying for a living wage. By the end of that month, more than 30 000 workers became involved, bringing much of the industrial and municipal sector in Durban to a halt. The strikes were largely spontaneous, and occurred after black workers became conscious of their poor wages and living conditions. Their efforts were aided in part by various attempts at mobilisation and moves towards nonracial trade unions. However, according to Russian academic Vladimir

Shubin, the SACP Central Committee had also taken a decision, at a 1973 meeting in Moscow, that it was time to take the battle to the enemy.

By the time Hani arrived in Lesotho's capital, Maseru, in 1974, the mood in Lesotho was changing. The ANC had been allowed to exist quietly and unobtrusively in Maseru since the 1960s. Comrades such as Lehlohonolo Lambert Moloi were already firmly established in the country, and a skeleton network existed.

At the time there were many theories as to why Hani went to Lesotho. Many in the exile community believed he had gone to visit his father, Gilbert, who had been living there in exile since 1963. The Security Branch, who knew Chris Hani variously as Temi, Thembi, Heni or Hani, believed he had escaped to Lesotho after he botched the unfortunate Operation J, a valiant attempt to deliver cadres by sea to top-secret locations where they would be met by fellow operatives who had already infiltrated by land. Trained at Soviet naval bases, the group was supposed to depart from Mogadishu, Somalia, in a vessel packed with arms, explosives, communications equipment and cash. During this time Hani – who had become assistant general secretary of the SACP in 1972 – and a number of high-ranking SACP executive members visited the specially trained cadres in the Somali capital. But the plan had to be abandoned, leaving many of the original group attempting to infiltrate South Africa by land, many unsuccessfully.

Hani had always been one to draw on his own knowledge and resources, and, in this foreign place, his father Gilbert's assistance would prove invaluable. When Chris Hani arrived in Lesotho, Gilbert Hani was running a small shop in lower Thamae, Mafeteng, where he was living with Elizabeth 'Rocky' Mafikeng – herself a well-known trade unionist who had been banished from the Cape – and some of her eight children. Every Sunday afternoon Chris would arrive with some money, supplies and the Sunday papers. As Mafikeng's younger children climbed playfully all over Chris, father and son would discuss the politics and other news of the day as Hani senior cooked a meal for the large family.

For those in the exile community living in Lesotho at the time, it was plain to see where Chris's keen sense of humour came from. Although Gilbert Hani seemed, at first, somewhat unassuming, a legend grew around his favourite pastime: he liked to call up his old foe, Kaiser Matanzima, who had driven him out of Sabalele and later out of Cape Town, forcing Gilbert to live in exile. Gilbert would goad him with words like: 'You know, I have more brains than you in my sleep.' An audibly angry Matanzima would respond with threats of coming to Maseru to beat up Gilbert. 'Ah, there you go talking in your sleep again,' would be Gilbert's response.

'When you saw Gilbert, you saw Chris,' said Linda Mti, former MK security chief in Lesotho. But Gilbert Hani was also a strict parent and disciplinarian who never lost sight of his political objectives. He had not spent his time idly in Lesotho, and quickly went about introducing his son to valuable contacts, including Lesotho parliamentarians.

Sitting in the yard of the Lebentlele family, a favourite rendezvous in the suburbs of Maseru, the sight of two men exchanging ideas in Latin was not strange. This was the place where the intellectuals met, especially the student class – those who were voluntary or involuntary exiles, those who were looking for company, those looking to speak their own languages in this familiar but foreign land, those with nowhere else to go. On one side of the compound was a clutch of *mkhukhus* (shacks), for those students who could not afford the journey home during school holidays. More importantly, the yard was a place of political discussion, conducted in relative safety in a heavily populated area. Two young men would occasionally separate from the rest, their animated discussions of Greek and Roman culture of little consequence to those with more pedestrian interests.

It was natural for Hani to gravitate here. It offered a perfect balance of connectivity to what was happening back home, politics and his fascination with the classics. Hani would seek out the company of Mbulelo Mzamane, the two quoting 'chunks and chunks' of literature to each other. 'This was the ethos, the milieu into which we were growing,' said

Mzamane later. But there was another reason the two young men became close: the Sekamane sisters.

Lithe, forthright, light of complexion, Limpho Sekamane drew admiring glances. Some described her as 'wayward', others merely as 'strong-willed'. But, by all accounts, she never allowed herself to be dictated to. From a politically active family with strong ties to the BCP – her brother, Tjaoane, went on to lead the LLA – Limpho was a good political match for Hani. 'Limpho got whatever she wanted. Chris Hani was a soldier, a lover, a fighter. He would have looked for someone with chutzpah. There were few people, politically speaking, who were more suited. You could not tell Limpho who to love or who not to love,' said Mzamane, who went on to marry Limpho's sister, Nthoana.

Hani was able to blend in with the Maseru exile community, assisted by his wife – who probably arrived soon after Hani, a handful of ANC operatives and his own growing group of contacts. Trained and retrained in guerrilla tactics, Hani knew how to maintain a low profile, as he later explained in the interview with Wolfie Kodesh:

We first crossed into South Africa, discreetly met comrades in South Africa, to begin the process of building the underground from Lesotho. We were actually invited to come to Lesotho at night. We didn't sleep for evenings [on end]. We were discussing the whole evening, strategies for building the underground and then we'd send the comrades and drive them back into South Africa.

Combatants crossed illegally near Quthing and Qacha's Nek. Even much later, relating events to Luli Callinicos, Hani spoke about the young recruits coming from all over South Africa to be trained and reinfiltrated:

Now we were actually building a number of units from Lesotho into the country … We built a network of structures inside the country. We trained people in guerrilla affairs, in politics, in intelligence and everything else …

Those were exciting days for me because I was receiving these cadres coming from the Transvaal, from the Orange Free State, from the Cape and Natal. I was in touch with trade unions. Absolutely, I was in dynamic touch. I used to go in and out. Meet comrades at Sterkspruit in Transkei. I used to send some of my colleagues from our collective in Lesotho to Cape Town, to Johannesburg, to Durban for a few days.

We had little meetings. We discussed strategy … we had been joined by dynamic young people like Thenjiwe Mthintso and many others. We began to build education groups inside Lesotho. We prepared them in terms of understanding the ANC and our struggle. We would select the best to send back into the country underground.

We would say, go and form a cell or two, then come back. We are giving you a week … all the theory that we had acquired in our training and our limited experience we began to apply creatively in a new situation. And for me that was a turning point in terms of our struggle.

MK's increased focus on Lesotho as a training ground, recruitment centre and infiltration point ensured Hani's operation quickly grew from a sideshow to the main theatre of operation at the time. His work did not go unrecognised by those in Lusaka. In 1975 Hani was promoted to army commissar and was co-opted onto the ANC's NEC, along with Thabo Mbeki. They became that body's youngest-ever members. Because of his high-risk status, Hani's appointment was not made known until a year later, when he was embedded in Lesotho. He described the early days of the mission:

We led a very frugal, disciplined existence in Lesotho. For a long time, for instance, we had no beds. Both comrade Lambert and myself were sleeping on mats or on small foam mattresses. And it was very difficult. We had no money, we were struggling. But we were soldiers.

This situation improved. Comrade Slovo initiated contact with us and we were able to receive resources from abroad. And we moved from place to place. We never stayed long in one place. I began to learn the language, and after some time I was fluent. After two years we were intercepted by the Lesotho authorities, because South African security was working very closely with the Lesotho security and even within Lesotho.

Yes, I was arrested – we were arrested – in Maseru [in early 1976] and I was detained under the 60-day detention law then and badly tortured [by the Basotho]. For almost 90 days. Solitary confinement. The Jonathan government was very repressive. There was no social life whatsoever.

Jonathan's government suspected Hani and Moloi were funnelling money to the banned BCP. The foreign minister of Lesotho also complained that Hani and Moloi were using forged official Lesotho government papers as part of their operations.

Of course, this was not the first time Hani had been sent to jail. In Cape Town, he was fortunate to have escaped the violent prison gangs due to their respect for political prisoners. In Botswana, Hani had been frustrated by the apparent lack of urgency on the part of the ANC to secure the release of the Wankie veterans. The man who was subjected to torture at the hands of the Lesotho security forces was a hardened fighter, fully aware of the risk of capture, and trained to endure just such a situation.

However, by ANC standards for the time, action followed swiftly. Lennox Lagu, another veteran of Wankie, was dispatched to Maseru brandishing a letter from Tambo himself to try and secure the pair's release. The two were eventually released, with the ANC narrowly averting their deportation to South Africa. Although Jonathan was ignorant of just how big a fish Hani was at the time, he knew via his regular contacts with Vorster's security forces that the MK operation in Lesotho was responsible for a number of missions inside South Africa.

By this time Jonathan's relations with his erstwhile benefactor had cooled and he was increasingly warming to the liberation movement. In 1971, South Africa's unilateral decision to devalue the rand and suspend foreign currency transactions had hit Lesotho hard. Jonathan turned to those most reviled by Vorster – the ANC and the PAC. He pushed for the liberation movements to be represented at the United Nations, and in 1975 went so far as to call for the international isolation of apartheid South Africa. A year before, Vorster had allowed BCP leader Ntsu

Mokhehle to flee into Zambia through South African territory. Many of Jonathan's actions can be attributed to the threat from the BCP, and his change of heart would probably not have been prompted by his advisers, who had urged him to rule by decree.

Lesotho turning its back on South Africa was also, in no small part, due to the intense political lobbying taking place elsewhere on the African continent, as well as that orchestrated by Hani, which reached as high as Jonathan's private secretary, Daniel Sixishe. In 1976, the ANC finally managed to secure an official presence in Lesotho, with Hani as their chief representative in Maseru. It could not have happened at a more fortuitous time. The revolution that the liberation movements had so meticulously planned would soon be overtaken by events within South Africa itself.

* * *

With the ANC and PAC both banned and their presence in the townships heavily suppressed, a new revolutionary banner had unfurled in the late 1960s: Black Consciousness. Shaped by the environment and informed by the writings of Frantz Fanon, WEB Du Bois, Léopold Senghor and others, Black Consciousness appealed to many young black students, for whom the liberation movements had seemingly failed. It helped them to define themselves and their role within the oppression of apartheid.

Then came the Soweto uprising of 16 June 1976. There had been no warning and no instigation from political parties. The action by the 20 000 students who took part in that historic march against the forced imposition of Afrikaans was the match to the powder keg, setting off protest action across the country. Oliver Tambo later described the impact of 16 June on the ANC:

[The ANC] had not recovered sufficiently to take full advantage of the situation that crystallised from the first events of June 16. Organisationally, in political and military terms, we were too weak. We had few active ANC units inside the country. We had no military presence to speak of. The communication links between ourselves outside the country and the masses of our people were still too slow and weak to meet the situation such as was posed by the Soweto uprising.

At the time, the charismatic Black Consciousness Movement (BCM) leader, Steve Bantu Biko, was still criss-crossing the country, despite a banning order restricting him to King William's Town. One of the people he called on was Linda Mti, then a fervent follower and organiser in the BCM. Mti was not at home, and shortly afterwards Biko was detained. At 31, having inspired a generation, Biko died in a Pretoria prison cell from brain damage after a series of horrific interrogations. That fateful visit to Mti's home had unknowingly put police on the young activist's trail.

By 1977, Mti and the entire leadership of the BCM had been detained and their organisation banned. During a brief spell out of jail, Mti decided to follow what was now becoming a well-worn path into Lesotho. For the liberation movements, the trickle of students who had come across the South African borders into exile, many fleeing from police for political or other reasons, turned into a river in the wake of 16 June. Hani later explained:

1976 was the watershed in the ANC and in the armed struggle because we began to receive big numbers of cadres from inside the country. A different type of cadre – angry, impatient – and a cadre who wanted to see the demolition of apartheid as soon as possible. With huge expectations and readiness to sacrifice, they didn't want to waste their time outside. They wanted to go back and confront the monster.

For many of those wishing to go into exile, lawyers like Durban-based Griffiths Mxenge and his contacts within the legal fraternity in Maseru were key. Through this network, transport and even fake passports were arranged. When Mti arrived at the border crossing, he watched as Basotho and South Africans passed back and forth, unhindered:

Some Lesotho people were coming from drinking in South Africa and going back in the evening. I was angry because I didn't realise it was that easy. Donald Woods had darkened events, even dubbing the river 'crocodile-infested'.

Mti said this was simply not true: most people made their way across without a problem. 'When I got across the Telle River, I even dumped my fake passport,' he said.

Those who entered Lesotho were invariably accommodated at a safe house before finding their feet within the growing exile community. Technically, those who had fled the repression in South Africa were refugees. With limited resources, the ANC encouraged all exiles to register with the UN High Commissioner for Refugees. The monthly stipend provided by the UN allowed the liberation movements to continue their work, without the expense of having to feed and clothe the new arrivals. Still, entrusting money to young people who had never before had to take care of themselves often led to a knock on a comrade's door for help towards the end of the month.

Invariably Hani would appear, rumbling down the road in an old VW Beetle. He was a believer, a true believer with an unwavering faith in the ability of the youth. At all hours of the day or night, he would go and meet new recruits. Often he would have been given details by friends of the person arriving, yet he always perplexed his audience with his intimate knowledge of the arrivals and the political situation in their specific location. 'He made me feel as if he had just arrived from South Africa, instead of me,' recalled Thenjiwe Mthintso, an SACP stalwart and later South African ambassador to Cuba.

Many of the young people crossing into Lesotho had heard of Tambo, Jele, Nkobi and Nzo but not yet about this young commander, Chris Hani. For them the ANC was an abstract idea, with many feeling their political home in the BCM was more closely aligned with the PAC. Hani had to draw on all his powers of persuasion to recruit for life out of this pool of politically conscious young people. He later remarked to Luli Callinicos:

[But] actually, the ANC fared better than most organisations in terms of influencing the young people in the country. The majority of the activists and leaders from the BCM or the MDM movements opted for the ANC. It was possible because we were able to communicate with them. It was also possible because we engaged them in discussions and we came with a clear ideological approach.

We had a coherent and concrete programme of struggle. We were not sporadic. We followed a strategic path and that is why we were able to influence trade unions and youth organisations.

One after the other, those recruited by Hani would speak about his amazing powers of recollection. He would invariably have learnt something about his subject before meeting them, meticulously going about the business of identifying people who could be useful to the Lesotho operation. Those who chose to join the ANC or MK would be taken through months of political education to give them an understanding of the basic tenets of the organisation. 'The engagements would be interactive, slowly bringing the new recruits to gain a proper grounding and appreciation of the organisation they were joining. Part of this work would be to identify the brightest and most disciplined to be drawn into the ranks of the SACP at a later stage.' The words, 'there is a need to yolk the national democratic revolution with the class struggle,' was a refrain on Hani's part.

Later, those who were recruited into the SACP came to understand their overwhelming influence in drawing up key documents relating to the direction in which the ANC was guided. Being invited to join the party was a badge of honour, silently carried and reserved for only the most promising of cadres.

Slowly at first, the recruits were utilised for underground activities. Many started off in the production of literature. The tasks were strictly divided, each person along the production line ignorant of what the others were doing. One person would be involved in photocopying, others in loading the material, others engaged in setting up transport. Security was paramount. The first briefing to new recruits was always about basic security arrangements. The enemy was within and all around. Each new recruit had to memorise his or her legend, a fabricated life story with all the pertinent details that went along with a new identity. During the debriefing, cadres had to relate their legend until it came naturally, until it became intimately their own.

Members of the Lesotho command themselves had pseudonyms, Moloi being 'Comrade A', Hani being 'Comrade B', and so forth. Cadres trained for reinfiltration were divided into cells consisting of no more than two or three members. There was only one commander, who would be in communication with Hani, making it clear where the orders came from. Everyone understood that the lifespan of each tightly woven cell was no more than three years, a lesson learnt by Soviet guerrilla forces operating behind German lines during the Second World War. Survival of a cell required operatives to be highly mobile and to live and travel lightly. Operatives used public transport to blend in. Hani asked each recruit which part of the country they would like to be deployed to.

Part and parcel of communicating securely involved the use of dead letter boxes (DLBs). For example, a combatant would buy a specific item at a general dealer, such as a packet of sugar or flour, that had a message hidden inside. Occasionally, physical handovers occurred, with operatives meeting behind a bus with a specific number. If the contact had not arrived within five minutes, the meeting was immediately abandoned, the assumption being that the operation had been compromised. For more conspicuous items, like weapons and ammunition, the Lesotho operation used the local graveyard. For the most part, graves at the cemetery on the outskirts of Maseru were numbered, making it easy for the recipient to find a location and dig up a package that had been planted there. Operatives always used fresh graves, as soil that had been disturbed was not as obvious – and easier to dig up.

Hani never believed in the ordinary door-to-door distribution of revolutionary literature. 'There must be a political oomph!' he would tell cadres. The 'oomph' involved training recruits in bomb-making, the explosions to accompany the distribution of pamphlets.

During the first few months following 16 June, Hani's operation in Lesotho, like those in Swaziland, Mozambique and Botswana, was caught off-guard by the massive influx of aspirant soldiers. As always, Hani led from the front, making many trips into South Africa from his base in Maseru. Even though his face was not generally known to those hunting for him, Hani would cross into South Africa using the inaccessible routes through the mountains that were the domain of cattle rustlers and dagga smugglers. Hani always made a point of never sending people on missions into territory where he himself had not been. During these missions, Hani would swaddle himself in a heavy overcoat and wear a balaclava, like most Basotho in the highlands. 'Comrade A', Lehlohonolo Lambert Moloi, once told recruits of a mission where he was wearing a balaclava and had just crossed into South Africa. A passerby offered him a lift and immediately remarked that he looked like a terrorist! The footpaths cutting through the mountains were often shrouded in thick mist and whispering with a persistent drizzle. The clandestine nature of the missions meant Hani and the other operatives were denied the comfort of a fire.

Hani's insistence on doing much of the reconnaissance personally did much to enhance his reputation as a frontline commander. It was not uncommon for him to appear suddenly in a remote village, knocking on the door of a family he knew all too well but had never met. He would personally come to tell the family of a cherished life sacrificed to the liberation of South Africa – the life of their loved one.

During one of his earliest missions, Hani proved his powers of recollection by remembering that a relative of Livingstone Mqotsi – his host and 'father' in Lusaka – lived near Neethling in the eastern Cape. Knowing the Mqotsis gave him unfettered access, and the old man upon whose door he knocked slaughtered a goat to celebrate the occasion of Hani's visit. The commissar had come on official business and, using the knowledge gained from locals, identified a series of caves on the banks of the Tsomo River to hide weapons for later use. But the Security Branch and its network of informants found out about the clandestine visit. The old man was arrested, taken to Butterworth and tortured at length about his association with Hani. He died a few months later, probably as a result of the abuse inflicted by the police.

As the people became aware of the secret battles being waged for their freedom, more and more sought an understanding of events shaping their lives. Students from Wits University, academics who preferred the protection of anonymity, miners ... Hani welcomed them all, in language they could understand, involving them in confidential exchanges about how to organise themselves.

* * *

Having been co-opted to the NEC, Hani was kept informed of most of the policy decisions taking place within the leadership of the ANC, and he would surely have been envious of the October 1978 mission to visit what was then the pride of communism: Vietnam. Although it was a Third World country with limited resources, Vietnam's mastery of guerrilla tactics had defeated the United States and united its citizenry. 'We thought we could learn something from the Vietnamese, their ability to unite all these people, north and south, their combining the military side with the political side, the way they moved their supplies,' Thabo Mbeki later remarked about the trip:

The relationship between the political and the military was very important, because, as you know, the Communist Party was in the leadership of the liberation front, and therefore of the military struggle, so what we could learn from the Vietnamese was how to organise. We then decided that a task team should be formed that could then prepare a document which could draw up these lessons from Vietnam, to say what could be done to intensify the struggle, if we wanted to achieve the same level of mass mobilisation.

Upon their return from Asia, the likes of OR Tambo, Joe Slovo, Joe Modise and senior ANC leader Cassius Maake revealed they were mesmerised by the strategies employed by the legendary General Vo Nguyen Giap, whose forces had defeated the French at Dien Bien Phu in 1954 and later fought the Americans to a standstill.

At home, too, the leadership was reinvigorated, and a fresh approach to African revolution was captured in the Green Book, named for the cover it sported when first unveiled by the Politico-Military Strategy Commission, which had been tasked with drawing up the document. The document emerged after a report-back session to the NEC, which in turn mandated a further commission to canvass opinion among the alliance and the membership abroad.

Emissaries were dispatched to The Island to gather Hani's thoughts. He spoke of the primary importance of political work when recruiting MK members, to make each cadre self-sufficient. This in turn translated into shelter from attacks, increased survival periods, better collection of intelligence and better advice. He also spelt out the stringent security under which the Lesotho operation existed, where units worked in isolation, with each individual accountable to the leadership in Maseru. Facilities had been established for cadres to undergo short periods of military and political training before their reinfiltration, with an emphasis on trade unionism, underground political organisation, conspiracy and security. In addition, an intelligence network had been created to keep the leadership in Maseru abreast of potential threats.

Ever the propagandist, Hani established an effective, articulate and vocal propaganda machine that produced content in the language of the distribution area, with local units encouraged to produce unique material. The Lesotho operation had already initiated discussions with the anti-apartheid Democratic Party in Transkei and was seriously debating engaging the Labour Party, which they believed could be used as a tool for mass mobilisation among the Coloured community. The Lesotho command urged integration in mobilising Coloureds, by nurturing supporting ANC cells and strengthening SACTU's mindset among Coloured workers. They also recognised the cleverly subversive entreaties of brave anti-apartheid sporting bodies like the South African Council on Sport and the South African Rugby Union in the Coloured community.

The Strategy Commission praised Hani for 'creating an organisational structure which, from top to bottom, is designed to plan and coordinate all aspects of internal work under the immediate direction of a single political collective, serviced by specialist departments'.

The Green Book took all of these recommendations on board, while largely re-affirming what was stated in the Strategy and Tactics document at Morogoro in 1969, calling for a reinforcement of the struggle inside South Africa with ever more intense political mobilisation. It called for the broadening of the liberation front, importantly taking a softer line on what were usually referred to as 'collaborators', warning that the liberation movement should not 'mechanically reject all participation in government-created bodies, if such participation will advance our revolutionary aims ...' Building on what commanders like Hani were already trying to implement, the document called for mass support that would project internal rear bases for MK. But the main thrust, the true influence of The Green Book, was politics; the armed struggle was clearly seen as secondary, its role being to 'keep alive the perspective of people's revolutionary violence as the ultimate weapon for the seizure of power'.

\* \* \*

From The Island, exiles were taken to Swaziland before escaping across to Mozambique and beyond to other ANC camps in Africa. Limpho Hani acted as a guide for many youth into Swaziland. Her involvement in MK was becoming increasingly pronounced, and by 1978 she was a veteran operative, running coded messages across the Cape Province. During one such mission, carrying messages between Ladybrand and the western Cape, she was arrested. For months, Limpho was detained under the Terrorism Act, tortured first in Cape Town, then in Bloemfontein. Ultimately, she lost their baby in a brutal miscarriage. This was the first conception with Hani. When she was eventually released and returned to Maseru, Limpho retreated to the home she, Hani and her daughter Neo shared in Qoaling, on the outskirts of Maseru.

They called the house Moscow, and it would never really be their own as Hani was always welcoming visitors – MK recruits, academics, workers, students, all those who had heard the gospel preached by the man known simply as 'Chris'. Comrades knew that alcohol was not permitted at the Hani home. December 16, the anniversary of MK's founding, was commemorated in stages, with groups of cadres arriving at the house throughout the day to join the passionate celebrations.

Security was paramount at Moscow. The entire operation could never gather at the same time for fear of attack by the apartheid forces. No visitor could approach the front door undetected. Hani's dogs, which numbered more than a dozen, made sure of that. The animals were a collection of abandoned and bedraggled mongrels nursed back to strength by Hani, and were fervently protective of their master. Numerous attempts were made to kill the dogs with poison. But as soon as one died, it was replaced by another.

For Hani, each morning started in exactly the same way. Dressed in a tracksuit, Hani went for a run, accompanied by two bodyguards wearing oversized sweat tops to hide the Makarov pistols they carried. The route was never the same. Perhaps as a taunt to would-be killers – or perhaps just as a personal preference – Hani often wore a red tracksuit.

Comrades speak of spotting Hani from some distance during his morning jog. It was terrifying for those who had to protect him, but the continual change of route also made it difficult for the Security Branch to plan a hit on the MK commander. Would-be Hani assassin Hendrik Prinsloo later testified to this effect before the Truth and Reconciliation Commission. But attempts were made nonetheless. On two occasions, shots were fired at Hani while he was driving. None penetrated the vehicle or injured him. Nevertheless, the assassins did not give up.

\* \* \*

The apartheid regime had slowly become aware of the threat from Hani's Lesotho operation. With the exodus of 16 June recruits and an upsurge in activities emanating from the kingdom, so came increased scrutiny from the agents of the regime who also arrived in Lesotho, determined to integrate themselves into the enclave.

The task of eliminating Hani fell to Hendrik J Prinsloo, a junior officer in the Bloemfontein office of the Security Branch, originally tasked with examining the many incidents of large-scale propaganda being distributed in the eastern and western Cape as well as the Orange Free State, often via the postal service. Prinsloo had pored over military and national intelligence reports and had been one of Limpho Hani's interrogators in 1978. At that time, he had presented her with handwritten postal addresses, '90% convinced' the handwriting belonged to one Martin Thembesile [sic] Hani, 'the main person of the ANC MK structure in Lesotho'. She did not demur.

In 1980, Prinsloo was called into the office of the divisional commander, Lieutenant Colonel Eben Coetzee. Hani had to be eliminated, and Prinsloo immediately accepted responsibility for the task. For three months, he observed, planned and collected information on his subject. The man responsible for dealing with operations inside Lesotho was Colonel JJ (Johan) Viktor, who had already carved a niche for himself as an operator who got the job done. In 1979, Viktor became the first commander of the infamous Vlakplaas.

Prinsloo also made contact with Sergeant Karel de Bruin at Ladybrand police station, De Bruin having within his operation a man who was close to Hani and could assist. Prinsloo eventually settled on a car bomb to do the job because the 'sly' Hani did not follow a regular daily routine – other than getting into the car every morning with his bodyguards. (Hani's routine had been to load his family into the car and drop them off in Maseru before he attended to MK affairs.) De Bruin's man was Ernest Ramatolo, who was apparently promised the price of a taxi in return for planting the bomb. For months, Ramatolo fed his handler information about ANC activities and, more specifically, about Hani's movements. But it was difficult to reach Hani.

Two kilograms of explosives were packed into a cake tin and hidden in a special compartment of a Valiant automobile. Security was tight in and around Maseru at that time, in response to the activities of the South African-backed Lesotho Liberation Army (LLA), the exiled offshoot of the BCP. To avoid detection, Prinsloo purchased the Valiant for Ramatolo, who collected the car at the border and made his way to the target while his handlers waited in the veld for their emissary to return.

Having somehow crept into the yard, without being detected by Hani's dogs or by Hani himself – despite the MK commander not feeling well on the day and having to occasionally dash to the outhouse – Ramatolo knelt next to Limpho Hani's car. As he had rehearsed with De Bruin and Prinsloo, he attached the cake tin underneath the passenger seat, using a magnet. Attached by wire to the cake tin was a little black box containing the detonator, which had to be placed underneath one of the rear wheels. The plan was that as soon as the car started rolling it would exert pressure on the box, setting off the explosion.

Ramatolo was nervous. As he knelt, he accidentally depressed the detonator, and was caught in the ensuing explosion. Years later, he re-created the scene when he testified before the TRC:

> As I lay in the yard after the bomb went off, he [Hani] picked me up and took me into the house. He then wrapped me in a blanket. Mrs Hani was reprimanding me but her husband told her to stop.

At the time of the blast, the impact of which blew out the front and back doors of the house, Hani and Limpho were inside together, changing infant Nomakhwezi's nappy. Hani called the Lesotho police, who arrested Ramatolo and took him to hospital. But the askari escaped to South Africa and later re-emerged at Vlakplaas.

Mac Maharaj visited the Hanis at Moscow some time later, by which time the terror of the assassination attempt had receded. Hani handed Maharaj an exercise book in which his daughter Neo had written an account of the attempted hit. Her story, told from a child's point of view, revealed Hani's fury as he shouted and punched the man who had tried to kill not only him but his entire family. Later, while visiting his confidante, the lawyer Phyllis Naidoo, Hani stated repeatedly: 'We don't do this. We don't target women and children.'

Less than a year later, in June 1981, Hani's driver Sizwe Kondile was abducted by security policemen while driving Hani's car near Bloemfontein. The young Eastern Cape activist was taken to the Jeffreys Bay police cells, where he was tortured at length. Vlakplaas commander Dirk Coetzee happened to be in the area when he ran into Major General Nic van Rensburg and noticed the clearly traumatised Kondile handcuffed to a bed in a back room of the police station.

Coetzee's testimony to the TRC reveals how Van Rensburg 'told me that they had brought in a doctor friend [to look at Kondile]'. 'He told them there was blood on the brain and that if they wanted to avoid a second Steve Biko case, they would have to do something about it,' Coetzee told the commission. He said it was alleged that Kondile had agreed to cooperate with the regime's operatives, but they realised this was a ruse after the discovery of a note, penned by Kondile, in which he stated his loyalty to the ANC. The activist then apparently tried to jump through a window with his hands cuffed behind his back, causing great injury. Or so his captors said.

Hani's driver had been given the name of a police operative in Lesotho who he was to contact. This person would be compromised if the young activist was set free. So Kondile was taken to Bloemfontein where a show was made of his release. But the horror was only just beginning. He was immediately recaptured by Coetzee's men, who took him to within 10 kilometres of the border with Mozambique, drugged him and then shot him dead. His body was later burned while the policemen drank and had a braai nearby.

The attempt to turn Kondile was again designed to put the Hani family directly in the firing line. The car-bomb attack compelled the family to leave Moscow. They moved to Kuena Flats, closer to the city centre. Closer to the expatriate community. Closer to safety.

\* \* \*

Moving to Kuena Flats was an adjustment for the family, who had so enjoyed the relative freedom and space afforded by Moscow: the countless visitors, the dozen or more dogs prowling the yard. The flat was a far cry from the house on the road to Mafeking. And here, on the third floor, it was difficult with two young girls around. So Comrade Gene agreed to change apartments with Hani. As part of the swap, Hani gave him a set of chairs. In an environment where furniture or any physical possessions were scarce, the chairs gave Gene bragging rights in the tight-knit expatriate community – even more so because the chairs had once belonged to Hani.

By early 1982, a number of attacks had been attributed to the MK operation in Lesotho: a bomb explosion at the Langa Commissioner's Court on 20 March; another bomb explosion in a lift at the President's Council building in Cape Town on 4 June; a handful of acts of sabotage in the eastern Cape. These attacks would not go unanswered.

Hani was removed to Lusaka by the ANC leadership, as the attempts on his life became more numerous and his killers drew closer. Following Hani's departure, uncertainty reigned over who was actually in charge of the Lesotho operation. Zola Nqini, known as Bra Z, was a former Robben Islander who had been dispatched to replace Hani as the chief representative of the ANC in Lesotho. But those aligned with Hani now found themselves at loggerheads with those in the Moloi camp. People started exerting their authority according to the camp they were in, dispensing supplies only to their group. Tensions ran so high that all MK operatives were disarmed. But divisions had set in well before Hani's departure. Tokyo Sexwale's brother, Lesetja, who was part of the Lesotho operation, had written a letter complaining of the untenable situation that had developed as a result of the rivalry between Hani and Moloi.

In response to the activity emanating from Lesotho, the regime had initiated plans for a major operation. It took almost four months of planning, with the targets constantly shifting and changing. The security forces examined countless photographs, conducted practice assaults in specially modified houses, and even made a few sorties across the swollen Caledon River. Clandestine operatives wormed their way into the refugee community or posed as salesmen, building up networks of contacts and informants. One senior commander even claimed to have succeeded in ingratiating himself into Hani's jogging entourage.

For the raid itself, a team of 70 specialist operators was assembled. A command centre was established 10 kilometres from the Lesotho border. Several times, the operation was postponed, usually for unforeseen logistical reasons. In one instance, the operation had to be delayed by almost a month because of the imminent approval of a loan to South Africa from the International Monetary Fund.

The men crossed the Caledon by boat on the night of 9 December. Their faces smeared with black boot polish, they carried silenced submachine guns and poisoned boerewors – for any dogs they might encounter – as they crept toward their targets. Word had arrived a week earlier that Hani was back in Maseru. He was hastily added to a list of targets that included the entire command structure of MK.

On 24 October, Hani had sent a short letter to Naidoo, telling her he was back for 'political and personal' business and that he was trying to keep as low a profile as possible. He had to deal with family problems that were 'strictly personal'. A few days later he appeared at her door, across the way from Kuena Flats.

Limpho Hani had known this moment would come. She and Chris had spoken about it many a time. She knew what had to be done. As the men ran up the stairs, heading for Hani's flat, shots rang out in quick succession. Then a pause. Shouting. More shots. A different sound this time. The gunfire continued. It seemed the boers were killing everybody in Kuena Flats.

People were ordered to lie on the floor. Anybody taking an inquisitive peak was quickly dissuaded with a rifle butt. One black operative emerging from the building told another: 'I shot her, boss.' One of the men walked towards the VW Beetle standing in the parking garage on the ground floor. He tossed a device inside, flames immediately licking along the upholstery.

Afterwards, SADF chief General Constand Viljoen acknowledged to the media, in a statement partially prepared before the raid, that 30 ANC 'terrorists' had been killed in the Maseru raid, along with 12 civilians, including women and children. In the morning, Lesotho security forces found the bullet-riddled body of Comrade Gene outside the block of flats. Close by lay the body of Matumo Ralebitso, the daughter of Lesotho's ambassador to Mozambique. Zola Nqini was dead, and media reports confirmed that Limpho Hani was also among those killed in the raid. The back of the Lesotho operation had been broken.

Western nations condemned the attack but stopped short of calling for further sanctions against the apartheid state. The UN Security Council strongly condemned the attack, demanding that Pretoria pay reparations for the damage and loss of life. King Moshoeshoe II begged the UN to stop South Africa from 'pursuing a strategy of naked terrorism against a whole subcontinent'.

A week later, at a Heroes' Day meeting, ANC secretary-general Alfred Nzo condemned the callous actions of the assassins in killing innocent civilians and ANC people in their homes:

Our popular army under the leadership of the ANC, heroic combatants such as Solomon Mahlangu, have not sought out white South Africa in its bedrooms, claiming that these bedrooms were military bases. We have not sought to attack the diplomatic missions of the apartheid regime as it has in our case when it assassinated Boy Mvemve in Zambia, Joe Gqabi in Zimbabwe, the Nyawoses in Swaziland, and now Zola Nqini in Lesotho – and bombed ANC offices here in London.

We have done none of this because we are not terrorists. We are combatants for the emancipation of millions from racism, national oppression, superexploitation, fascism and war. As such we shall continue to intensify the offensive against the apartheid enemy of humanity on all fronts.

In that offensive, the enemy will increasingly suffer the kind of losses in its personnel that it suffered during our attack on its Komatipoort garrison two weeks ago ...

The attack on Maseru did not go unanswered. On 20 May 1983, two MK operatives detonated a car bomb at the entrance to the South African Air Force (SAAF) headquarters in Church Street, Pretoria. The ANC command had decided to strike a public blow against the heart of the apartheid regime. Nineteen people were killed, including 11 SAAF officers. More than 200 people were injured. Afterwards Tambo said: 'The policy of the ANC is to intensify the struggle, attack the enemy, avoiding civilians where possible, but intensification involves not just sabotage but attacking the enemy forces.'

The response came swiftly. Three days later, the SAAF bombed a number of buildings in the suburb of Matola, just outside Maputo. The SADF later claimed to have killed as many as 64 'ANC terrorists', with the Mozambican government showing journalists the debris of the Somopal jam factory and a crèche, destroyed in the rocket attack. The Mozambican government reported that six civilians, two children and two women – one of them pregnant – had been killed and 40 injured.

The tit-for-tat attacks between MK and the SADF shifted the struggle dramatically. Civilians were increasingly targeted. Now there would be no respite.

*   *   *

Limpho Hani was breathless. She was excited to be with Chris. 'I was so scared after the raid that I rushed to Maputo with the children,' said Limpho later. Working for the Lesotho Tourism Board, she was still in Maseru when she heard of her own demise during the events of 9 December. Jacob Zuma, then a commander in the Mozambique operation, asked Albie Sachs to allow Limpho and the girls to live with him for a few months. Neo, the eldest, was sent to boarding school but would visit during the holidays. Unlike the numerous other activists who intermittently stayed with Sachs, Limpho quietly went about her business – cooking, working, looking after the children – introducing a measure of calm to what had become a frenetic life.

Standing on the landing of Sachs's third-floor apartment in Julius Nyerere Avenue, Maputo, she couldn't speak fast enough to get the story out about the night the boers came hunting for them, how the commandos were shouting as they were coming up the stairs. 'They were shouting, "We're coming to get you!" And then Neo said, "Get down. Remember, Mommy, Daddy said get down!"' Limpho and the children could hear the assassins were attacking the wrong people. The menace in the race up the stairs, boots thumping, men yelling. Then the firing … and it all went quiet.

Later, she reminded Hani about a Mr van Vuuren, who lived in a flat close by. They had thought he was a spy, but instead he showed them love and support. Limpho and her daughters had survived the attack only because the nightwatchman at the Kuena Flats had shown Pretoria's killers to a different apartment – an apartment with the wrong number. It hadn't been a political act, just pure fear and confusion. Sachs watched Limpho telling her husband about this. 'And I felt, here was this man listening quietly while she narrated, and the only reason these people they loved so much were in danger was because of him.'

CHAPTER 9

# KABWE

The Church Street bombing of 1983 unsettled the military status quo and drove the apartheid government to greater violence. PW Botha, who assumed the newly created post of State President in 1984, stepped up the regime's cross-border raids and internal repression. National Party propaganda began to target Hani around this time, using pliant media organs such as *The Citizen* and the SABC to portray Hani as a bloodthirsty black communist, committed to the murder of white women and children.

But Hani – who displayed both insouciance and disappointment at this false depiction of himself – opted always for the truth. The end had to be nigh for the comforts enjoyed by white people: the braais, the movies, the five-star hotels. In an interview published in *The Times* of London and the *Weekly Mail* in 1988, he told journalist John Battersby that whites supported the system because it guaranteed happiness and comfort for them, but this would have to come to an end: 'Their life is good. They go to their cinemas, they go to their braaivleis, they go to their hotels. It guarantees a sweet life. Part of our campaign is to prevent that sweet life.'

Careful words, careful phrasing. But whites had to be conscientised. When Hani talked about it later in an interview with the *Christian*

*Science Monitor*, he reflected on the campaign with a ready responsibility. He was MK chief of staff at the time of the Battersby interview, and in 1985 he was the army commissar, so he was charged with life and death. Cadres who infiltrated the country and participated in operations inside took their orders from Hani, even if this was via their regional politico-military councils.

In Swaziland, Mozambique and Zimbabwe, the leadership came from Joe Slovo, Jacob Zuma, Siphiwe Nyanda, Lennox Tshali, Bogart Soze, John Nkadimeng and Sello Motau (Paul Dikeledi) – the latter assassinated by Pretoria in Swaziland in 1986, together with MK's admired chief of ordnance and logistics, Cassius Maake (Job Tabane). Ronnie Kasrils and Ebrahim Ismail Ebrahim chaired the coordinating mechanism in Swaziland following the signing of the Nkomati Accord in 1984.

'When we began to attack targets in the white areas, for the first time white South Africans began to sit up and say, "this thing is coming",' Hani told the *Christian Science Monitor*. In an interview with the ANC journal *Mayibuye* in 1985, he articulated the impetus for extending the war into white areas, in detail:

So far, the theatre of war in our country is in townships where our people stay. Our townships are presently occupied by the SADF, the security police and all sorts of military units of the enemy.

We have seen the sadism, the murders and the viciousness of the SADF. Every day, if you … read South African newspapers, you come across tales of cruelty, of murder of the young and the old. You come across horrifying stories of the rape of our women, of the beating up of schoolkids, of a situation where the residents of our townships can't be sure whether they will see the next day.

It's a situation of complete ruthlessness, of acts of atrocities against the blacks in our country. Now, in the face of that situation, it is important that the whites should realise that our country is in a state of civil war, because nothing is taking place where they stay.

Their suburbs are still pictures of peace and stability and the usual rhythm of life continues. Their lives are not disturbed.

That was indeed true. Yet a group of prominent white South Africans were, at the very least, concerned. This led to secret talks between businessmen and the ANC leadership at Mfuwe Game Reserve in Zambia's Luangwa Valley. The respective delegations were led by the chairperson of Anglo American, Gavin Relly, and ANC president Oliver Tambo. The ANC group included Hani and fellow NEC members Pallo Jordan, Mac Maharaj and Hermanus Loots (better known in the underground by his *nom de guerre* of James Stuart). Yet the man who was running the show was Thabo Mbeki.

Tambo selected Mbeki and Hani almost as twin political brothers, destined to take divergent paths. There have always been those who assert Mbeki's assiduous nature, insisting he was Tambo's diplomatic equal – a man who could burnish the ANC's reputation by building tactical relationships. His detractors say he was a sell-out, which, they suggest, is partly explained by a remark Mbeki made in the late 1980s. Asked when he thought the ANC and the National Party government would begin to seek some sort of accommodation, he said two years. When Hani was asked the same question at about the same time, he said 10 years. Hani remained doubtful about the capacity of Pretoria to go beyond its habitual reponses. When it came to negotiating about Namibia's independence, there were so many clauses – related to Angola and the withdrawal of the Cubans, for instance – and so many late conditions that it seemed the goodwill was on one side only.

Certainly, it may be said that this duality – Thabo Mbeki, the son who would do the unpopular things, and Hani, the son who would refuse to bow to the minority view – must have suited Tambo on some level. It gave him the best of both options – negotiate or fight.

Mbeki had persuaded a sceptical Tambo to meet with the businessmen, at a time when Tambo was quite torn – ideologically, mostly, but also personally – between the camps that were developing within the ANC and the SACP. The issue of whether or not the SACP should predominate within the liberation movement, and, in fact, the true nature of the communism practised by the South African left, had started to alienate Mbeki, and his response annoyed and upset Slovo.

Those who have attempted to suggest that Mbeki and Slovo argued over race, as it pertained to the SACP, were wrong. Africanists like Tennyson Makiwane – who could not understand how whites could be African and why they should be taken seriously within the movement – eventually broke away and were then expelled by the ANC. And after Kabwe, where the issue of white members of the ANC came up again and was deemed positive by leaders like Tambo and Hani, there should not have been a question – if you were a loyal member of your party.

So Mbeki's decision to resign from the SACP in the late 1980s – his apparent impatience with the Stalinism that was occasionally present in the SACP another reason to go – was in keeping with his efforts to engage white capital. Hani, on the other hand, may not have been seduced by the more prescriptive aspects of the party's communism, but he was devoted to the communist cause. He was not yet wedded to a particular means of post-apartheid government, because he did not believe South Africa would achieve democracy as soon as Mbeki seemed to think it would. But his preferred means would have been more worker-centred, a more collective leadership. Nonetheless, he allowed Tambo to persuade him to attend the first rendezvous with white business, chaired by Mbeki.

Hani later reflected on this to historian Charles Villa-Vicencio. He was not thrilled that Tambo was allowing himself to be drawn in by Mbeki – for whom the liberals and social democrats of Britain were major influences. And it was not only Hani who felt this way. But his attendance at Mfuwe was mainly an attempt to please Tambo, even if it did not happen again. Mbeki ultimately left the SACP while Hani went on to become its leader.

Journalist and Mbeki biographer William Mervyn Gumede asserts that Mbeki – who had been a member of the SACP's Central Committee – was inherently a centrist, and that it was simply 'fashionable' to be a member of the Communist Party in the 1970s and 1980s because it had overtones of intellectualism. Hani was never a member of the party because it was in vogue, although he did admit in the *New Statesman* that 'being young, there was something romantic about belonging to a cell of the SACP – a party cursed by our apartheid rulers. I felt there was basically something good about a party hated by the people we hated.'

Hani's unease about relationship-building exercises like Mfuwe was palpable. It went back to the Convention Alliance, put forward by Frederik van Zyl Slabbert of the Progressive Federal Party. Hani was especially concerned that so-called reformist solutions would, in fact, leave salient aspects of the apartheid system intact. Angry and at odds with the intentions of Mbeki, who had been at the centre of the clandestine meetings, Hani did not join the ANC's delegation to meet the Institute for Democratic Alternatives in South Africa (IDASA) in Dakar, Senegal, in 1987, or at subsequent meetings in Paris. The papers of Phyllis Naidoo contain a recollection from Alex Boraine, a founder of IDASA, of a chance encounter he had with the army commissar in Dakar:

He sat next to me and ordered a drink. I didn't know who he was so we didn't start a conversation until he nudged me, put out his hand and said, 'Hi, I am Chris Hani'.

He was very quiet, and I think he wanted to see for himself whether we were genuine, rather than simply taking the word of others who had told him of our visit. He was a hardline Marxist and we talked mainly about economic justice in South Africa. Certainly, at that juncture, he was deeply committed to a socialist structure for the economy.

He didn't attend the gathering in Dakar and I never met him again, but my impression, from that meeting and some of his speeches that I read, was that Hani was a highly intelligent, serious man who would certainly have been a strong rival to Mbeki and others for the presidency of South Africa.

\* \* \*

White South Africans retreated into naked racism and fear after the 1983 bombing of the SAAF headquarters, but the ANC regarded the attack as being against a military target. Ten MK cadres – including Aboobaker Ismail, commander of the ANC's Special Operations Unit – explained as much when they applied to the Truth and Reconciliation Commission in 1997 for amnesty for a series of blasts, including that in Pretoria. Ismail told the commission he regretted the deaths of innocents, saying: 'We did not target civilians. However the policy of the ANC at the time was that we could not, for the sake of saving a few lives, be prevented from striking at the power of state, the apartheid state.'

He then quoted from a speech made by Tambo at a funeral for ANC members killed in an SADF cross-border raid into Mozambique in the same year. Although Tambo was later to vacillate between two positions – the moral and the military – in his argument about civilian loss of life, he told the mourners in 1983 that the time had come at last to take the battle to the white suburbs. It was inevitable that whites would have to have a taste of the pain of reality for black South Africans.

In July 1985, when the National Party government declared a partial state of emergency in order to bring the townships back under control, Tambo went on Radio Freedom – broadcast on Radio Lusaka, Radio Luanda, Radio Madagascar, Radio Ethiopia and Radio Tanzania on shortwave at different times throughout the day. His was an unequivocal message: 'We must take the struggle into the white areas of South Africa and there attack the apartheid regime and its forces of repression in these areas which it considers its rear.' Hani, who had been appointed deputy army commander in 1983, supported Ismail and other bombers, explaining later that:

... the bombs were to tell the whites: we can creep and crawl next to you. Be careful, we are developing and we will be able to do something big in your areas. It is a position of armed propaganda and demonstrating to our people that we are still around, and to white people, that they are going to have to live in insecurity as long as Botha is there.

\* \* \*

In 1985, the rand started to feel the pressure as the West finally began to engage its disinvestment campaign, after nearly 20 years of campaigning by lobbyists. The Commission of the European Economic Community called for economic sanctions and 10 EEC states withdrew their ambassadors, while France announced its own ban on investment in South Africa. Within a year, the rand's value had plunged 12 percent. Although the United States Senate had voted to repeal the Clark Amendment of 1976, which prohibited aid to any private groups engaged in military involvement in Angola, the House of Representatives now voted in favour of a comprehensive series of sanctions against South Africa. And the financial bars applied by American banks – particularly Chase Manhattan, which stopped rolling over hundreds of millions of dollars in loans to South Africa and recalled credits – exerted considerable pain on the apartheid state. A lack of capital and a freezing of unused lines of credit created a serious balance-of-payments problem that certainly focused the National Party government's mind on a negotiated solution.

Naturally, there were those who tried to suggest that the true victims of sanctions would be black South Africans. Tambo hit back angrily, saying this notion 'is used by those who are, in fact, more likely to suffer more – that is, those who are getting the best out of the status quo, out of the system. They will suffer.' The ANC put it to its supporters that those who gained from foreign investment in racist South Africa were 'the mining magnates, those of their ilk and the oppressive state. They all went laughing to the bank when black families were torn apart by influx control and poverty.'

Botha's response to sanctions was hardly measured. He threatened to expel migrant workers and cut trade and economic ties with southern African countries. But the National Party was compelled to change its position when the impact of sanctions started to be felt. Botha would later promise to cross the Rubicon, giving rise to an unexpected optimism that he quickly scotched.

The moral position of concerned senators in the US was that Congress should be appalled by an apartheid government that kept on inventing new ways of repression, but the legislation that was finally enacted against South Africa, in the form of the Comprehensive Anti-Apartheid Act of 1986 and the Budget Reconciliation Act of 1987, was only partly recommended by novel apartheid legislation that sanctified violence. In particular, the first of successive states of emergency, slammed into place just after the ANC's historic Kabwe conference in Zambia in June 1985, should have had an influence. The security crackdown was largely a response to the ungovernability of the townships as MK structures and front organisations, commanded by Hani out of Harare and Lusaka, began to take hold.

Champions and patriots of the US insist it was President Ronald Reagan's reaction to Pretoria, through the actions of Chester Crocker, Assistant Secretary of State for African Affairs, that tilted the hourglass. Anti-imperialist forces may disagree, but the pro-American point of view is that Crocker's policy of constructive engagement – initially aimed at direct involvement in Namibia and Angola – worked. Yet there was tremendous suspicion around Crocker, much of it centred on the relationship the US administration was building with Mangosuthu Buthelezi and his Inkatha Freedom Party (IFP). There were certainly those in the US (and elsewhere) who would have preferred Buthelezi rather than Tambo as leader of the liberation movement.

Under Ronald Reagan, US policy in southern Africa focused on the need to contain the Soviet Union, mostly through resisting what were seen as the proxy Soviet forces in Angola. A uniquely regional, yet divisive, quid pro quo was the route put forward by Crocker and others. For Namibia to get independence from South Africa, the Cubans would have to withdraw from Angola, and so would MK, despite the fact that Angola was a sovereign state whose leader Agostinho Neto had invited the Cubans to help defend his country against the invasion of Pretoria's army.

\* \* \*

The SACP held its sixth congress in Moscow at the beginning of 1985, a jubilant reunion where it was ratified that the party would intensify recruitment and entrench its commitment to the armed struggle. Hani received the highest number of votes for a seat on the Politburo. This was a foreshadowing of events at the first NEC conference after the exiles' homecoming, held in Durban in 1991, when Hani drew the highest number of votes – 94.7 percent of the total – and a public poll showed he was the most popular leader in the ANC after Mandela.

The year 1985 also saw the ANC convene the Kabwe Conference. This was an important moment for the ANC, in which its NEC became fully elected for the first time. Thus, support for Hani there, too, was more than meritorious; it was symbolic of his stature. Indeed, at Kabwe, the overwhelming demand from cadres for the democratic accountability of the leadership was the reason why the new path – voting by ballot – was introduced.

The election also proved the complete integration of communists with the ANC, as 24 of the 29 elected members were from the SACP, including chairperson Joe Slovo, and Politburo members Mbeki, Moses Mabhida and Hani, who had been a member of the Central Committee of the SACP in exile since 1970. Upon his election, Hani was also MK's deputy army commander and commissar and a member of the ANC's Politico-Military Council (PMC).

Hani had been on the ANC's Revolutionary Council since 1976, again along with Slovo, Mbeki and Mabhida. Now, he had multiple roles, which allowed him access to, and influence over, every organ of the liberation movement. This was a direct result of the conference of front commanders and commissars in Luanda in early 1983, when the lack of coordination between the political and military wings of the ANC came under fire. Frustration at the dominance of the political wing, which was deemed by the troops to be largely ineffective, had been implacable at Morogoro in 1969 and at other extraordinary meetings afterwards. Joint planning and control had been unequivocally demanded in Luanda, with MK – under commander Modise and chief of staff Slovo – insisting upon the consolidation of military structures inside the country to prepare the ground for a true people's war.

So the PMCs were created to replace the Revolutionary Council, and became the executive arm of the NEC, although by the end of 1986 the councils were under strain. Insurrection across the borders, with MK and internal forces in collaboration, was becoming dangerous and difficult to sustain due to the ubiquity of the regime's forces. The delivery of ordnance was near-impossible, but Hani remained motivated, especially by the support for MK's goals by the masses inside the country and by ordinary township residents

There were other successes. The blurring of the political lines between the ANC and the SACP meant that American demands for negotiations with the liberation movement – an aspect of its constructive engagement policy – created a fairly unique situation given the Reagan administration's support for anti-communist movements elsewhere in the world. Unity was critical, and disunity had to be masked with a certain diplomacy. By the time of Kabwe, the SACP had been through substantial argument within itself, particularly between Slovo and Mbeki. Both Mbeki and Hani were members of the Politburo, but they tolerated their disagreements, particularly on one major obstacle: whether the SACP should dominate the alliance, over the ANC. This was Slovo's contention, and Hani, his second-in-command, sided with him. Although Mbeki was alienated as a social democrat within the structures, Hani later defended him to Slovo, and insisted on Mbeki being welcomed back into the Communist Party fold. By 1986, Mbeki was back.

\* \* \*

The Oasis Motel sits on the city limits of Gaborone, Botswana, the latticed green shadows of its palm trees enticing visitors to the cool inside. Its simple retro sign belies the splendour of its visitors' book: Kenneth Kaunda slept here, as did Nelson Mandela, Bill Clinton, Queen Elizabeth and the late Samora Machel.

For all its high-profile visitors over the years, the Oasis Motel has also been a comfortable stopover for those who need a certain secrecy. It was never a place where a lot of questions were asked, yet the idea of assassins masquerading as tourists would probably have been deemed unusual – even if theirs was a mediocre cover.

In the mid-1980s, Gaborone offered rare access to long weekends in another African country for South Africa's state-controlled middle class. Few of the staff of the Oasis, neatly positioned on the road southeast from Gaborone to the satellite town of Tlokweng, would have thought it strange for white South African men to check in. Black South African men, even less so. The well-armed visitors to the Oasis Motel probably looked like tourists or hunters, yet their ruse was complete, linked as they were to other men entering Botswana – through the Kopfontein border post and Gaborone airport – at about the same time. Their arrival was the prelude to a deadly attack that left 14 people dead.

The political atmosphere in southern Africa was peculiarly charged after March 1984, when South Africa had signed the Nkomati Accord with Mozambique. The threat of economic embattlement had undoubtedly assisted Maputo in agreeing to expel senior ANC and MK officials from its borders, with the agreement then being the conclusion of the relationship between South Africa and its puppet force, RENAMO (Resistência Nacional Moçambicana). This compelled MK to withdraw its cadres back into South Africa as quickly as possible.

When Swaziland was revealed to have signed its own accord of this nature with the South African government, even earlier than Mozambique, the regional command of the ANC panicked, and some MK cadres on their way to conduct operations, primarily in Natal and the Eastern Transvaal, were reinfiltrated too rapidly. There was often insufficient risk management. Nonetheless, MK was more active than ever inside the country, and the SADF was invigorated to realise its goal of total destruction of the armed wing's bases and resources. This was the seed of the Gaborone operation.

The SADF employed members of its elite special forces – 5 Reconnaissance Regiment and 44 Parachute Brigade – for the operation. The soldiers were trained for just this kind of attack. Agents planted in Botswana had monitored ANC activity in that country for years, living and working there without detection. The detail they provided was such that, in the final briefing for the soldiers, it was clear that targets that had been identified would still have to be hit, even if they no longer existed.

The troops were heavily armed with RPG7s, R5s, stun grenades and shrapnel grenades, 9mm pistols, Kevlar flak jackets and helmets. They had long-range two-way radios, and the stand-by evacuation support of the SADF's Puma helicopters.

In April 1985, Botswana police had raided ANC safe houses in Gaborone, in keeping with the government's long-standing agreement with the movement's leadership that MK was not permitted to keep, and especially not conceal, arms caches. The police operation reportedly netted thousands of rounds of ammunition, hundreds of grenades, pistols and mines, as well as plastic explosive and TNT.

Two months later, with MK defanged, it seemed no one could stop the SADF soldiers, their mission made easier by the fact that Gaborone's street lights went off by timer at midnight. They struck in the darkest hours of 14-15 June 1985. The recces had split the city up into zones to be attacked at particular times and focused on the ANC's weakened security structure. The official postmortem of the Gaborone raid was that 14 people were murdered. Four Botswana nationals were among the dead, as were a child and three women. At least six were injured, including a child and a woman.

After the mission, the troops held a victory party in the border town of Zeerust, the departure point for so many border crossings by aspirant MK cadres. There was a certain cheer among the men as most had received bonuses of up to R850, a fair amount for that time. Agent Manual Olifant told the TRC that the men had stood around at the party, recalling how their victims had cried and screamed before they were shot, and that no one had been able to fight back or offer any kind of armed resistance.

\* \* \*

The Gaborone raid took place just two days before the ANC's momentous Second National Consultative Conference at Kabwe, Zambia, on 16 June. As he stepped up to the podium to open the conference, Tambo immediately expressed his utter despair, his fury at the death squads deployed by Pretoria, and his impatience at the regime's total onslaught on black South Africans. The Kabwe Conference, which had been organised in the firm belief that the conditions for a people's war were at last at hand, became nothing less than a war council of 250 delegates from home, the rest of Africa and the ANC's 21 foreign missions.

Although the ANC had declared 1985 the 'Year of the Cadre', within the country it had been a year of bloodshed. Among the most devastating events was a massacre in Uitenhage on 21 March, the anniversary of Sharpeville. Police in the small southern Cape town opened fire and shot dead 17 people. Nearly 30 organisations were banned in March 1985 alone. From September 1984 to March 1985, 10 000 people had been arrested. The report of the South African Institute for Race Relations for that year recorded that more than 400 township residents had been killed by members of the security forces. Violence was accelerating in the townships, targeting especially the Uncle Toms of local government: at least 12 state-supported councillors had died since the end of 1984, and more than 20 members of the security forces had also been killed in the townships.

*Mayibuye* published an appeal to black soldiers and policemen to stop killing their own people. It asked:

Are you not living in shame? Rejected and isolated by your own people? The racists care less about you because they see you as kaffirs, coolies and hotnots at their beck and call, cannon fodder to be sacrificed in the townships. You can liberate yourself from this shameful life and become part of the people once more. Choose now, before it is too late!

That year, the ANC dispatched some of its finest soldiers into the war zone, among them Sibusiso Sihle Mbongwa – known by his *nom de guerre* of Mntungwa – as the commander of Operation Butterfly. The operation was an ambitious attempt to set up joint internal and external military and political command structures in Natal by reorganising the underground, as had been envisaged at Kabwe, and was to be expanded on a national scale. But it was a lesson in failure, dogged by delays, security breaches and, ultimately, arrests and betrayal.

However, it had become critical for guerrillas to be able to enter South Africa more easily. The failure of one operation could not be allowed to derail the war effort, and a landmine campaign was planned to destabilise white border farming areas, despite the tight control exercised over these areas by the SADF and local commando formations.

By the end of 1985, MK commander Joe Modise was in Zimbabwe, commanding infiltration efforts. The decision had been taken for Hani to leave Zimbabwe, where he had been based on and off, to travel clandestinely into Botswana to run the military operation on South Africa's northern borders with Zimbabwe and Botswana from there. Cadres from Swaziland would run attacks into the eastern Transvaal.

MK units had to operate very rapidly once inside the country, due to the heavy presence of the SADF and commandos in the border zones. This meant that many campaigns were not as successful as they should have been, and could not be sustained. So Hani's call to ordinary people to organise themselves into small mobile units had a strongly positive reaction. He believed it had become incumbent upon all freedom-loving South Africans to realise that revolutionary violence was the key answer to the reactionary violence of the enemy. In a *Mayibuye* interview, he said:

We know our people are disadvantaged, [so] they are not to be compared with … Botha and his army. Our people are not armed. But we are saying to our people, use every weapon that you can lay your hands on – from a stone to a Molotov cocktail. From a stone to a grenade, submachine gun and anything you can lay your hands on. Use everything that is available to fight back, to inflict casualties on the enemy.

Hani urged an understanding of the tactics of war – such as 'sneak and surprise'. The mobile units of which he spoke would emanate from within communities, especially 'our youth in schools, universities, factories, farms and mines [who] must make the fullest use of their physical capabilities to run, hide, trap and strike at the enemy when it is not expecting an attack'. Yet it was vital, said the commissar, that people do not present themselves as targets to the enemy: 'The people are very angry. They are in an emotional state of mind and that anger is understandable ... but it should not substitute cool, calculated planning.'

The question was, would these mobile community units be distinct from MK, or part of it? Hani was adamant, saying there was 'no dividing wall'. He saw the involvement of the oppressed as expanding the people's army: 'We are saying, not everybody will get hold of a sophisticated weapon. Not everybody will get a chance to train outside. Not everybody will be within the MK units, but the guidelines of MK must be used as a basis.'

Hani had conceptualised the idea of 'grenade squads', and ensured these were armed as far as was possible, their duty being to harass the occupying army, collaborators and police. He also emphasised the importance of creating no-go zones – areas where the enemy would not be able to enter or operate. And he warned against 'opportunists' who would attempt to engage people on getting involved in the system, who would become what Botha called 'moderates', but whose task was to ensure that the ruling class remained in power. In this way, with a clear ideological directive, Hani began to build his legend among ordinary South Africans.

The strategy from MK headquarters was clear on the complementary relationship between the forces within and the forces outside. Hani instructed that the mass movement should not be strengthened at the expense of the underground: 'We need a strong ANC to strategise and put before the people the correct tactics.' This became increasingly Hani's own role from outside, as his unbendable position became the rallying cry. He was not there in body, but the people in poverty-stricken rural communities like Sabalele, and the people tormented by strife in urban areas like Alexandra, began to revere him from afar.

\* \* \*

The Kabwe Conference, which saw Hani sitting on the main podium with the top leadership, was the first for the ANC in 16 years. Nothing of the kind had happened since the dramatic national conference at Morogoro, Tanzania, in 1969, and yet, in many ways, the reasons for the two meetings were similar. Although Tambo and the leadership of the ANC were driven to assemble at Kabwe primarily in order to gather their forces for war, the mutinous mood that had developed in the MK camps in Angola during 1984 had necessitated dramatic political soul-searching.

MK needed to consolidate itself as a true revolutionary army, and its soldiers needed to view themselves as being in the vanguard of military combat. The ANC's Operation Zikomo, which began in mid-1985, had been refined as a campaign to integrate MK cadres into the townships in order to guide militants there, and this was, of course, Hani's vision.

The terror inflicted upon the ANC by Pretoria was a subject of intense consideration at Kabwe. In the past, cross-border raids had been carried out only by the SADF. Now, the Security Branch and its askaris were also violating the sovereignty of frontline states. Pretoria had not known the conference would take place at Kabwe, a mining town of about 1.6 million people, originally known as Broken Hill, some 140 kilometres north of Lusaka, on the road to the Copper Belt. There is no airport there, just a main road that carries thousands of trucks each year. Yet, for all its relative anonymity, Kabwe was the political stronghold of Kenneth Kaunda's UNIP and, indeed, of many of Zambia's other political parties and freedom fighters. Kabwe's greatest appeal was the presidential chalet, and other villas for government and the wealthier members of Zambian society. There was also a barracks there, housing a large contingent of Zambian soldiers.

Although the joyous ambience of freedom fighters reunited was not one of war, the discussions of war were unmistakable at Kabwe. Tambo and the NEC, emboldened by a vocal Hani, would no longer watch the doom unfold. Tambo's opening statement at Kabwe, made on the ninth anniversary of the Soweto uprising, was rich with strong emotion about avenging the martyrs of 1976 and all the other massacres. He mourned the patriots being killed every day on the streets and in the rural backwoods of home:

Gathered here are professional revolutionaries, military commanders, commissars and cadres, diplomatic representatives, trade unionists, workers, peasants, royal persons, intellectuals and students, men and women. We have come here from all corners of the globe, bringing with us our varied experiences, but united by a common and militant resolve to ensure the 1980s do indeed become our Decade of Liberation.

The war was finally, relentlessly, on, although the distinction between soft and hard targets would continue to be discussed – as it had been in the months prior to Kabwe – in ANC offices around the world. Tambo spoke with the poetry of his own pain:

Over the past nine to ten months ... there have been many soft targets hit by the enemy. Nearly 500 people have died in that period. That works out at 50 a month: massacred, shot down, killed secretly. All those were very, very soft targets.
 The darkness that has shrouded our country for so long is now lit by flames that are consuming the accumulated refuse of centuries of colonialism and racism.
 For us, these flames are like beacons which draw us faster towards our goal. Botha prefers darkness and the night. But his nights are festivals of nightmares. All that his fearful eyes can see is a desolate road that ends in an abyss.
 For our enemy, the age of illusion is coming to its ignoble end.

The liberation of the masses could no longer be postponed, argued Tambo. His tone was consistent with the mood that had to be instilled in Umkhonto we Sizwe: that the end of the oppression was imminent. The enemy's defeat was inevitable. He spoke of 'qualitatively new initiatives consonant with the situation in our country'. And those assembled at the conference – the leadership, the soldiers, the diplomats – were left in a stunned silence, just for a moment, as he ended his cry for justice: 'We express our confidence that you will carry out your tasks in a manner befitting our movement, our revolution and our times.' And then the room erupted.

CHAPTER 10

# ANGOLA

The 1980s was a decade filled with so much horror for so many that those who experienced it sometimes refuse to talk about it anymore in order to protect the born-free generation. If white South Africa had thrived on the misery and enforced poverty of black people for 300 years, by 1983 it had created a hell.

The terror really began to unfold after 1978, when John Vorster was compelled to resign as prime minister following the massive cover-up of the Information Scandal. Defence Minister PW Botha stepped into the breach, and the constitution was rewritten to combine the functions of head of state and of government, giving Botha total control over the armed forces and intelligence services. Under Botha, South Africa moved toward complete militarisation of the state. The SADF had already been considerably bolstered by Vorster in successive budgets, and Botha also began directing more resources into covert operations involving the police, SADF, newly assembled covert death squads and the brutal Koevoet, the South West Africa Police Counter-Insurgency Unit, which engaged in many bloody cross-border operations through the 1970s and 1980s.

When Botha made his speech accepting the post of prime minister, he described to the National Party's constituents how critical it was for the state to engage in cross-border destabilisation. Angola and Mozambique, independent since 1975, were now controlled by governments hostile to Pretoria. He did not mention the covert injection of firepower into the regime's puppets – Jonas Savimbi of UNITA in Angola and Afonso Dhlakama of RENAMO in Mozambique – nor the State Security Council-designed military plots and intricate cover-ups to protect white supremacy.

The regime's propaganda focused on the concept of the 'total onslaught', the looming threat to South Africa from International Communism and its pawns in the liberation movement. At its most basic level, this propaganda involved priming the white electorate to back the National Party and its policies. White schoolchildren were ordered to stash the accoutrements of siege – a shopping bag with their own plastic cutlery and plate, cup, face cloth and toothbrush inside it – in a special cupboard in their classroom, and they were compelled to take part in regular drills on the school fields. Every white child underwent Citizen Preparedness Training, essentially a form of brainwashing. White teenagers were instructed to attend 'veld school' – tough rural boot camps at which they slept on open concrete floors, were taught to leopard-crawl for long periods, track each other at night and observe what instructors insisted were the secret signals of Red terror. In every aspect of this, black people were posited as the enemy. Fear took root and flourished.

\* \* \*

The mid-1980s also saw a new crisis within the liberation movement, when violence and mayhem erupted in some of the MK camps in Angola, which were established in the late 1970s following the independence of Angola. Hani would play a key role in quelling the violence and soothing the discontent of the MK soldiers. In no small part this added to the legend that had steadily built up around him.

The arrival of thousands of aspirant soldiers after 1976 had reinvigorated the ANC's campaign for liberation under the man who became first their army commander and commissar and then MK chief of staff – as he set up and managed the complex infiltration campaign into South Africa from Lesotho while frequently returning to structure covert operations right on the home front.

These achievements deeply entrenched his heroism. Yet they were also the reason why he was recalled to Lusaka in 1983 – for his own safety. In those years, when Hani engaged in spontaneous political education of his troops, he always pointed to the revolutionary inspiration of the People's Republic of Mozambique, which was born on 25 June 1975, and the People's Republic of Angola, which celebrated its freedom a mere six months later, on 11 November 1975. Particularly uplifting for Hani was the triumphant installation of the FRELIMO government in Maputo under his old Kongwa comrade, Samora Machel.

Tanzanian President Julius Nyerere had long provided the ANC with space and facilities. Its Morogoro mission was now one of the busiest transit points on the continent, and a former sisal plantation, given to the movement for the specific purpose of building a school, was slowly but surely gaining significance as a mecca for young recruits. The school was later named the Solomon Mahlangu Freedom College, named for an MK cadre hanged by apartheid's executioners in April 1979 for a murder he did not commit. The Tanzanian sites were overwhelmed by the end of the 1970s, so Kenneth Kaunda also offered the ANC formal space – its own building in Lusaka to set up headquarters.

Angola's first president, Agostinho Neto, installed at last in the modern port capital of Luanda, should have been at the beginning of a magnificent opportunity to transform the country. Instead, from the start of socialist rule in the mid-1970s, Angola was involved in a bitter and brutal civil war. The country was invaded from the south by the armoured columns of the SADF, together with its satellite rebel force, Jonas Savimbi's UNITA movement. Pretoria was ostensibly acting to destroy the threat from SWAPO, but ensured that the well-armed UNITA forces created the impression of civil war for years to come. Although the SADF and

US-sponsored mercenaries were eventually driven into retreat by the efforts of Angola's armed forces, FAPLA (Forças Armadas Populares de Libertação de Angola), this would not have been possible without external help. Neto appealed to Cuban president Fidel Castro, who sent thousands of troops, as well as arms and supplies.

The Cuban intervention in Angola is regarded as a bellwether for internationalism. But it also provided Pretoria with a lever. The apartheid regime could demand negotiations around key assets, such as the status of South West Africa (Namibia), on the pretext that it was protecting South African interests from the Cubans.

In 1984, Angolan president José Eduardo dos Santos sent a letter to the Secretary General of the United Nations, Dr Javier Perez de Cuellar. In it, he stated Angola's position on two critical matters: the objective of guaranteeing the independence of Namibia through the full implementation of UN Security Council Resolution 435/78, and the withdrawal of South African forces from the south of Angola. He referred to a visit paid by De Cuellar to Luanda on 23 August that year, and reiterated his country's rejection of what the regime called linkage – seeking to make the implementation of Resolution 435 contingent on the prior or parallel withdrawal of Cuban soldiers from Angola.

Up to 15 000 Cubans defended the south of Angola. Dos Santos did, however, point out that if South Africa ceased its attacks on Angola, Angola would, within an adequate period, initiate the progressive withdrawal of Cuban troops. This had in any case already been agreed between Angola and Cuba in 1982 and again in March 1984.

\* \* \*

In 1984, Hani found himself in the middle of a military and political nightmare. Inside South Africa, townships like Sebokeng, Duduza and Langa were caught in a terrible cycle of violence. The apartheid-sponsored Black Local Authorities were in an inevitable shambles, with sustained pressure on the councillors to resign. The campaign to make the townships ungovernable was intensifying.

Yet the people's courts and the naked horror of 'necklacing' by youth militia, the *amabutho*, required the leaders of the mass movements to intervene. Bloodshed on this scale disturbed Hani. Phyllis Naidoo recalled how he had spoken of his distaste for this kind of death, not to mention the state's gallows, in 1988 in Harare:

We are about life, Phyl. If our morale is maintained through killing off comrades on Death Row, then we should not work against the death penalty. We should accept it and wish for more bodies to keep up our morale …

Since the late 1970s, the levels of violence had steadily risen. A foretaste of the violence of the 1980s happened with the unspeakable horror of Operation Reindeer in the autumn of 1978, when 200 SADF paratroopers hit a SWAPO transit camp in Kassinga, Angola, killing 600 Namibian refugees. It was a tale that chilled the MK leadership, already struggling to pacify their restless troops in the camps, who were insisting, more and more, on being sent into battle.

In the MK operations report in the ANC's second submission to the Truth and Reconciliation Commission, Tambo's pained words were added:

This means the conflict is escalating. We always thought it was going to be a bitter, brutal, vicious struggle, almost as a necessary precondition for the liberation of South Africa. We have to go through that. The conflict is reaching new levels. There is to be much destruction, much suffering, and a lot of bloodshed which will not be confined to South Africa.

In 1980 we signed the Geneva protocols and said that if we captured any enemy soldiers we would treat them as prisoners of war. The fact is we are not against civilians. We do not include them in our definition of the enemy. The ANC was non-violent for a whole decade in the face of violence against African civilians. What do we mean by civilians? It really means white civilians. No one refers to Africans as civilians and they have been victims of shootings all the time. Even children. They have been killed in the hundreds. Yet the word has not been used in all these years.

Now it is being used, especially after the Pretoria bomb [at the South African Air Force headquarters]. But implicit in the practice of the South African regime is that when you shoot an African you are not killing a civilian. We don't want to kill civilians. But some will be hit, quite accidentally and regrettably. I am sure we are going to lose many civilians and many innocent people, as happens in any violent situation.

We do not boast about it in the way the SA regime boasts about its killings ... I think South Africa is going to be a very happy country one day and we will avoid all avoidable loss of life but – harsh though this sounds – we cannot allow the system to persist for the sake of saving a few lives. It is not so harsh when one considers how many lives apartheid has destroyed.

The TRC was later to find that gross violations of human rights and other unlawful acts were indeed perpetrated on a broad scale, especially during PW Botha's time, by members of the South African Police and the SADF. These included murder and attempted murder, torture, forcible abduction, covert logistical and financial assistance to organisations opposed to the ANC, and acts of arson and sabotage.

Throughout the 1980s, Botha's government dispatched assassins and troops to deliver mayhem inside and outside the country. Among the more high-profile ANC members who were killed, were Hani's driver and confidant Sizwe Kondile, ANC representative in Harare Joe Gqabi, and Durban-based lawyer Griffiths Mxenge, all murdered in 1981. The following year, Pretoria sanctioned the attacks that led to the deaths of Ruth First, by parcel bomb in Maputo, and the ANC's representative in Lesotho, Zola Nqini, who was killed in the raid on Maseru.

Joe Gqabi was gunned down in the white middle-class suburb of Ashdowne Park, Salisbury (the name was changed to Harare in 1982). It was a year after Zimbabwean independence, and the quiet life of the suburb cast into relief the violence that had gone before. Black families were slowly moving in around the whites. No one was expecting the sound of gunfire when Gqabi – sent to Salisbury by the ANC to represent its interests – reversed out of his driveway. He was ambushed by three gunmen and shot 19 times, the fatal wound either in the head or the chest, his killers leaving only shards of glass and cartridges from ammunition similar to that used in Uzi submachine guns. Zimbabwean Prime Minister Robert Mugabe immediately issued a statement vowing Zimbabwe's continued support for the just fight, and blamed South Africa for the murder. Gqabi was given a state funeral by the Zimbabwean government. In 2004, his remains were exhumed, repatriated from Zimbabwe and reburied in his home town of Aliwal North, Eastern Cape.

After Hani's assassination, it was impossible not to note the similarities between their murders. Gqabi was on his second official mission for the ANC in exile in Zimbabwe, his first appointment having been in Botswana. The same secret agent dispatched as part of the Pretoria-sanctioned death squad to gun down Gqabi allegedly helped plan Operation Lebanta, the 1982 attack on ANC targets in Maseru that was designed to kill Hani. Many years later, Gray Branfield – who was linked to both incidents and was alleged to have been connected to the SADF raid on Gaborone in 1986 – died in Iraq, where he was working as a security contractor.

At Gqabi's funeral in Salisbury, Tambo said the fact that Zimbabwe had treated Gqabi's death in the way it had, relayed the message that it would not be frightened off from the struggle for liberation:

On the contrary, the more the enemy strikes at Zimbabwe, the greater will be the determination with which Zimbabwe responds. The people of this region, correctly reflecting the positions of the African continent, have stood firm in defence of their commitment to the total liberation of our continent.

The fact is, the more the racists have stepped up their aggression, the more united have been the people of the entire region, the greater the support that has come from the international community.

In a way, therefore, while we mourn the departure of Comrade Joe, because it occurs in the context of an ongoing struggle, it has been the occasion for the further consolidation of the unity that binds the people of Zimbabwe and the people of South Africa.

And we, in South Africa, inspired by this act, are grateful for what Zimbabwe does today. For, if it was ever necessary for Zimbabwe to demonstrate her commitment to our struggle, no better method could have been found than to take this single militant of our struggle and give him a state funeral.

As the 1980s wore on, the list of the fallen grew longer. The Internal Security Act was a green light to banning, detention and torture, while state killers carried on their deadly covert operations. In 1983, Vlakplaas commander Eugene de Kock received a medal for organising the hit on Swaziland-based ANC leader Zweli Nyanda. The pursuit of activists became ever-more violent with the murders of the Cradock Four and Victoria Mxenge in 1985; the Pebco Three and Mamelodi activists Florence and Fabian Ribeiro in 1986; secretary of the Mamelodi Civic Association, Stanza Bopape, in 1988; and David Webster – the anti-apartheid activist and social anthropologist at the University of the Witwatersrand, in 1989. Agents increasingly violated sovereign frontiers in assaults on individuals: in 1984, agents planted a bomb that took the lives of ANC member Jeanette Schoon and her young daughter Katryn, in Angola. Four years later, Albie Sachs lost an arm and suffered extensive injuries in another bomb blast orchestrated by the state in Maputo. Also in 1987, one of the ANC's most senior leaders, Cassius Maake, was killed in Swaziland in a hit that claimed top cadre Paul Dikeledi. That year, another ANC member, Theophilus Dlodlo, was to die in Swaziland, too. In 1988, Dulcie September, the ANC's representative in Paris, was murdered.

Among others murdered in this decade were: MK cadre Patrick Macau and a seven-year-old girl who died in an explosion in Manzini, Swaziland, in 1980; 13 members of the South African Congress of Trade Unions (SACTU) and MK in an attack on safe houses in Mozambique in 1981; MK cadres Petrus and Jabu Mzima in a car bomb in Swaziland in 1982; SACTU leader Vernon Nkadimeng, also in a car bomb in Botswana in 1985; and Zimbabwean Tsitsi Chiliza who was killed by a bomb in a TV set meant to blow up her husband, R Mzimba, the ANC's chief representative in Harare, in 1987.

In spite of the onslaught orchestrated by Pretoria, the ANC itself was more active than it had ever been, with an increasing number of donors and political sponsors having given their support to the chief diplomat, Tambo. It had offices and representatives in 34 countries, economic, academic and cultural boycotts in place and there was sustained diplomatic pressure on Botha's government. However, the insidious tactics of the apartheid regime inflicted deep damage on the ANC in exile, effectively preventing it from following in the footsteps of the MPLA and FRELIMO.

* * *

After being set up in the mid-1970s, the camps in Angola now held more than 10 000 MK soldiers, trained and ready for war. But few had been given the chance to serve, so uncompromising was the protective shield thrown up around white South Africa by the SADF and Pretoria's death squads. The inactivity of the soldiers in the camps produced a devastating outcome for the ANC itself, casting deep despair on its own beleaguered military leadership.

There could be no doubt that the regime's reign of terror inflicted arduous challenges upon the ANC, even as it fell under the fragile if loyal protection of Angola, Zambia and other African states during the 1970s and 1980s. It was inevitable that the regime's constant subversion would give rise to the increasing fear, and then outright paranoia, of being infiltrated by enemy agents.

When Hani returned to Lusaka, following the Lesotho operation, he found himself indirectly charged with dealing with serious discontent spreading in the camps. Recruits pleaded for him to represent their interests, Hani being the only senior leader who was still willing to bed down with them in the tents and train with them, who still behaved like an ordinary cadre. The leadership's profound neuroses about spies and the perpetual concern about being attacked had led them to overlook the fact that the cadres in the camps were volunteers and not prisoners.

In the depths of despair at being holed up in the camps for years, under punitive conditions, discontented soldiers often found themselves on the wrong side of the ANC's iron-fisted security section, marshalled by veteran Mzwai Piliso. In 1984, a mutiny took place at Viana camp. The mutineers were persuaded by Hani to end their siege, but the ringleaders were detained. Ultimately, 32 men were arrested, charged, found guilty of their crimes and imprisoned at Luanda Maximum Security Prison. Two died between February and July 1984. In a bold and aggressive mutiny in Pango camp, also in 1984, the mutineers used machine guns and other heavy weapons to kill the camp commanders and other soldiers, setting off a series of events which devastated the movement.

Years later, the TRC was to find that between 1979 and 1989, the ANC had been responsible for committing human rights abuses against its members in exile. Many abuses were committed by its security department, established in the mid-1970s and known by the acronym NAT – for National Security – and as Mbokodo, meaning 'crushing the boulder'. The commission noted the operational report submitted to it by NAT in which it claimed credit for uncovering an espionage network in 1981, in an operation known as Shishita. A subsequent incident of mass poisoning of MK members had contributed to an atmosphere of paranoia about infiltration by agents of the regime, and it was in this context that a number of ANC members were first detained and tortured. Some died as a result of these assaults, and a few were executed.

To examine what had gone wrong, and why, the ANC constituted no less than three enquiries: the Stuart Commission in 1984; the Skweyiya Commission in 1992; and, under Nelson Mandela in 1992, the Motsuenyane Commission. The focus was especially on the detention camp known as Quatro, which was named after the Fort prison in Johannesburg – with 'fort' being transliterated to 'four', hence 'Quatro' in Portuguese. The camp was originally called the Morris Seabelo Rehabilitation Centre, or Camp 32, and had been set up in 1979.

The Working Committee of the NEC in exile first established a Special Commission under convenor Hermanus Loots (James Stuart). Included on the commission were Sizakele Sigxashe and Aziz Pahad, their job being to investigate the root cause of the 'disturbances', the nature and genuineness of the grievances, outside or enemy involvement, their aim and methods of work connection in other areas, and the ringleaders and their motives.

The Stuart Commission spent three weeks in Angola, interviewing soldiers at Viana, Pango, Quibaxe, Caxito and Caculama camps, where the disturbances had so recently taken place. It also interviewed 33 cadres detained in the Luanda Maximum Security Prison as well as members of the MK Military High Command, the regional command and the ANC's chief representative in Angola.

Stuart said, however, that the commission's final report was not exhaustive; due to pressures of time, it was unable to carry out its investigations as fully as desired. Still, the members felt that their report was a true reflection of the situation in Angola. In general, the report found those living in the camps to be desperately unhappy by 1984, and laid the blame for the situation on the arrogance of camp administrators. There were numerous problem areas, ranging from the supply food and cigarettes to the treatment of female comrades and disciplinary methods.

The camp administrators enjoyed separate housing, cooking, eating and other facilities, and regularly slaughtered pigs, ducks and chickens while the ordinary soldiers rarely received meat. Cigarettes were not available in the camps for long periods, but the administration had sufficient supplies. They had access to alcohol, yet drinking by cadres was severely punished.

The issue of women comrades was peculiarly painful in some camps, as it affected single and married women and their partners, who could be harassed and, if need be, transferred to another camp if someone in the administration wanted it to be that way. The administration would invite women to private parties in their section. It was known that some trainees had tried to commit suicide because their girlfriends had been taken away from them. The women singled out by the administration, on the other hand, were said to have received special treatment.

A portrait of Chris Hani, SACP General Secretary, *circa* 1991. (Rashid Lombard)

Alban Nyimbana, Hani's former school principal, rings the bell outside Sabalele Primary School. Hani skipped a year at the tiny school, the SACP leader later admitting that he had an edge on his fellow pupils as a result of instruction from his school-teacher aunt who taught him to read and write. (BONILE BAM, *THE STAR*)

The bell tower at Lovedale's main administration building. It was at Lovedale that Hani met a young Thabo Mbeki and was recruited into the ANC. (BEAUREGARD TROMP)

The dignified avenue of oak trees at Lovedale College. This was the route Hani walked every day when he was at school there. Lovedale, and, later, Fort Hare, went a long way towards shaping Hani's awakening to the struggle for liberation in South Africa. (Beauregard Tromp)

Chris Hani at about 22 years old in the back garden of Joyce Leeson's house in Lusaka, Zambia. With him is his lifelong friend, Archie Sibeko, aka Zola Zembe. The two went into exile while out on bail in Cape Town and later underwent military training in the former USSR.
(Supplied by Joyce Leeson and Archie Sibeko)

Archie Sibeko, who first met Hani in the 1960s in Cape Town, went with him into exile and was later involved in the preparations for the Wankie Campaign. (Mujahid Safodien, *The Star*)

James April, who was a member of the Luthuli Detachment during the Wankie Campaign in 1967. Both April and Hani were subsequently imprisoned in Botswana. During engagements with Rhodesian soldiers, April was often mistaken as being Chinese, creating the belief among Ian Smith's soldiers that communist China had joined forces with the liberation movements. (Jennifer Bruce, *The Star*)

Hani at 27 in the garden of Livingstone Mqotsi's house in Lusaka in 1969. Mqotsi is on the extreme left, his late wife Mzimazana on the extreme right and their daughters Yvonne and Laurantia are on either side of Hani. Hani stayed with the Mqotsis after his release from prison in Botswana following the Wankie and Sipolilo Campaigns in the then Rhodesia.
(Supplied by the Mqotsi family)

Hani on a march in the streets of the GDR in the 1970s during his counter-insurgency training, before he was sent to Lesotho to head up operations in what would become known as 'The Island'.
(From the ANC Archive at Fort Hare)

Hani at a rally in the late 1970s. (MAYIBUYE CENTRE, UWC)

Hani in disguise. He was renowned for his trips into South Africa, even as a senior leader within the ANC and SACP, easily passing for a common Basotho farmer or, at times, a businessman.
(MAYIBUYE CENTRE, UWC)

Hani with Zambian statesman Kenneth Kaunda and fellow members of the ANC's NEC and the SACP in the late 1980s. Kaunda later became highly critical of the ANC's inability to infiltrate South Africa, at one point referring to them as 'chicken-in-the-basket revolutionaries', seemingly in reference to the snack baskets available in hotel lobbies. (ANC ARCHIVE, FORT HARE)

Hani carrying the pouch containing his Makarov pistol on his way to the airport in Lusaka to meet Nelson Mandela in 1990. He is flanked by Joe Modise on his right and his bodyguard Pule Matakoane on his left. Already a cult figure by this stage, Hani was at first disparaging about moves towards a negotiated settlement with the apartheid regime.
(SUPPLIED BY PULE MATAKOANE)

Tokyo Sexwale took Chris Hani on a tour of Johannesburg after his return from exile.
(Alf Kumalo, *The Star*)

Hani with, among others, some of the recently released Robben Island leadership, including Nelson Mandela and Ahmed Kathrada, as well as such luminaries as Trevor Huddleston, Cyril Ramaphosa, Alfred Nzo, Albertina Sisulu, Thabo Mbeki, Trevor Manuel and Winnie Mandela. (ANC ARCHIVE, FORT HARE)

Hani with Joe Slovo and Joe Modise in 1990 after their return from military exile in 1990. (ANC ARCHIVE, FORT HARE)

Hani with ANC militant Harry Gwala on his left and trade unionist John Gomomo on his right. (Rashid Lombard)

Hani (*second from left*) with (*from left*) Trevor Manuel, Jay Naidoo, Joe Modise and Frene Ginwala (*in the background*). (Rashid Lombard)

Hani greeting members of the crowd after his return from exile. A reluctant returnee, Hani was recalled to join the rest of the ANC leadership to help negotiate a settlement and to prepare the way for the returning MK fighters. (RASHID LOMBARD)

Hani in deep discussion with Harry Gwala. The firebrand ANC and SACP leader from the then Natal would later be censured by both organisations for his militancy. While Gwala, a former Robben Island prisoner, was seen as a warlord by some he was indeed a major player in the bloody and costly battles between the IFP and ANC during the 1980s and early 1990s. (RASHID LOMBARD)

Hani (*extreme right*) with (*from left*) Joe Modise and Jacob Zuma. Although Modise and Hani would clash as early as the 1960s, when Hani publicly criticised his commander in his now famous Memorandum, the two later seemed to mend their relationship. Zuma, Mbeki's number 2 in Swaziland, went on to become the president of South Africa. (Rashid Lombard)

After Nelson Mandela's release for prison in 1990 Hani often travelled with the stalwart to the rural areas of South Africa as they prepared the people for the first democratic election and spread the torch of freedom to all corners of the country. (PictureNet)

...ani (*second from right*) with (*from left*) Joe Slovo, Winnie Mandela and John Gomomo at the time of the Codesa ...egotiations. (RASHID LOMBARD)

...ani with (*from left*) Thabo Mbeki, Joe Nhlanhla and Aziz Pahad. (RASHID LOMBARD)

Hani speaking to journalists including Patrick Laurence (*right*) on the fringes of the Codesa negotiations.
(Rashid Lombard)

Hani with, among others, Ruth Mompati Joe Nhlanhla and Jay Naidoo on a plane (destination unknown).
(Rashid Lombard)

SACP leader Chris Hani during a pro-Cuba demonstration march in downtown Johannesburg in 1992.
(PAUL VELASCO/PICTURENET AFRICA)

Chris Hani and Joe Slovo enjoying a good laugh together at the Eighth Party Congress of the SACP, 5–8 December 1991. (ANC ARCHIVE, FORT HARE)

Hani at an ANC anti-violence rally in Khayalitsha in the Eastern Cape in 1990. Hani was called to intervene in the hotbed that was KwaZulu-Natal in the early 1990s, when trade unionists and members of the United Democratic Front clashed with Inkatha. (RASHID LOMBARD)

Hani addressing supporters at a joint ANC-SACP rally. (RASHID LOMBARD)

Hani outside Parliament with jubilant ANC and UDF leaders Allan Boesak, Walter Sisulu, Cheryl Carolus and Ronnie Kasrils at the ANC's 'People's Parliament' march through the city on 24 January 1992. (Rashid Lombard)

Thabo Mbeki and Chris Hani, *circa* 1990s. (Joe Sefale © Johncom)

Hani lies dead in his driveway at his home in Dawn Park after assassin Janusz Walus shot him four times.
(ALF KUMALO, *THE STAR*)

The nation grieved in the days after Hani's assassination. All over the country, communities gathered to express their anger. (Rashid Lombard)

The women of the Black Sash staged a peaceful demonstration to mark their grief at Hani's death. (Rashid Lombard)

The hearse arriving at the FNB Stadium. (KEN OOSTERBROEK, *THE STAR*)

From left: Adelaide Tambo, wife of OR, Hani's widow Limpho and his daughter Nomakhwezi (*second from right*). (KEN OOSTERBROEK, *THE STAR*)

Kenneth Kaunda mourned with OR Tambo, Walter Sisulu and Govan Mbeki at the FNB Stadium in Johannesburg on 19 April 1993. Thousands crammed into the venue and hundreds more battled outside with peace-keepers and police. (KEN OOSTERBROEK, *THE STAR*)

Hani's grandson, Aluta Tembisile Martin Thunyiswa Hani, holding the only picture he has of his grandfather – a poster given to the family after Hani died. Aluta was born three months after the assassination. (BONILE BAM, *THE STAR*)

Hani's grandson Aluta reading in the bedroom of the house that was allocated to his grandparents – Hani's parents – in Sabalele, Cofimvaba, Transkei.
(BONILE BAM, THE STAR)

Nolusapho Hani, the widow of Chris Hani's older brother Victor, tending the graves of his parents Mary and Gilbert in Sabalele, Cofimvaba, Transkei, in March 2008. She and her husband endured constant harassment at the hands of security police searching for Chris. (BONILE BAM, THE STAR)

(*From left*) Tokyo Sexwale, Zwelinzima Vavi, Blade Nzimande and Limpho Hani at the memorial service held at the South Park Cemetery in Boksburg to mark the 15 years since Hani's assassination. (*The Star*)

Limpho Hani laying a wreath at the tombstone of her late husband Chris during the memorial service. (Antoine de Ras, *The Star*)

Chris Hani as everyone will remember him – a man of the people leading comrades in dance, 20 years before Jacob Zuma would popularise this. (GALLO IMAGES)

The administration resented doing chores, like fetching water for their daily wash, cleaning their rooms, and washing and ironing their clothes, and this resulted in a general abuse of authority. Their failure to discuss solutions with the rank and file led to a strong belief that they did not pass on cadres' complaints to the leadership, and that the senior officers may even have doctored reports to suit their own interests.

Extremely limited organisation of political or cultural life became more and more of a problem. Meanwhile, the provision of military training was problematic in some instances. Mock attacks, sometimes using live ammunition, resulted in casualties, and there was improper deployment of personnel.

As far back as 1979, as Stuart and his commission discovered, almost all disciplinary problems were 'resolved' by severe punishment and beatings. The aim of the punishment, said the commission, 'seems to be to destroy, demoralise and humiliate comrades and not to correct and build'. Soldiers had to carry sacks full of soil while doing exercises, sometimes being forced to enter swamps at 2am while carrying the sacks. Cadres were severely beaten with knobkieries, kicked, lashed with cables and wires, and then tied, half-naked, in trees, sometimes for as long as 24 hours, under all weather conditions. People were locked up for days in windowless goods containers lacking any form of ventilation, which was extremely dangerous. And there were beatings with pistol butts on the slightest pretext.

Food had always been a source of antagonism in the camps. The soldiers ate mostly tinned meat and rice, and sometimes only soup, for months on end. Fresh fruit and vegetables were rare, even though some camps were located in fertile agricultural areas. This meant that the soldiers developed skin diseases and other ailments. Because of a lack of salt and spices, food had been prepared in the same unappetising way for years. In some camps, the water supply was too far away, not clean or not available at all. Stuart noted that simple equipment like pumps would have helped to alleviate the problems.

After the death of the ANC's long-time camp doctor, Nomava

Shangase, there was only one fully trained medical doctor on hand. The doctor had not been to any camps outside Luanda, so the camps were serviced by medical orderlies, many of whom were trained on the job. Stuart found that the last general medical checkup had been in 1977, so the rate of illness was high. Malaria was rife, despite the fact that nets, coils and insecticides were available. There were outbreaks of bronchitis, and many soldiers developed asthma, kidney problems and tuberculosis, which was widespread. Mental illness was often neither recognised nor treated; the underqualified, insensitive medical staff tended to tell patients they were 'malingering'.

Hani, regarded throughout his leadership as the one man to whom cadres could turn, and who would listen, was flagrant in his criticism of those terrible years. He told Charles Villa-Vicencio that:

> ... not for one moment [am I] suggesting we have been ethically above reproach. There have been injustices and wrongful deeds committed in our name. The detention and torture camps are among them.
>
> I have been a vocal and persistent critic of such action, as have several other members of the national executive of the ANC. We have repeatedly argued that we could not morally demand that the regime release our political prisoners while we continued to detain people without trial.
>
> Our people were targets of assassination, our people were being poisoned, our camps were being destabilised by agents of the South African regime and there was an urgent need for us to get to the bottom of this. There were spies and government agents working among us.
>
> [But] we recognised that in any movement or government, the security forces should be given clear directives and that they obey these directives.

The ANC's second internal inquiry, the Skweyiya Commission, conducted investigations, interviewed witnesses, visited detention camps and led evidence. Advocate L Skweyiya – a relative of Zola Skweyiya – was appointed chairperson, and ANC leader Brigitte Mabandla was included on the commission. Its frame of reference was the ANC's Code of

Conduct, adopted after Kabwe in 1985, which set out standards for the treatment of detainees.

But the Skweyiya Commission was criticised by Amnesty International for its limited terms of reference. It did not assign individual responsibility for abuses within the ANC, nor did it analyse the chains of command within the security department and MK or between those bodies and the ANC leadership, in order to establish political responsibility for what had happened.

The independent Motsuenyane Commission of Inquiry was appointed by Nelson Mandela in 1992, with broader terms of reference than the Skweyiya Commission. It heard testimony from 50 witnesses in open sessions, and its report (issued the following year) supported that of Amnesty International. The Motsuenyane Commission, too, said there was a lack of accountability for excesses, and attributed this to the lack of clear lines of demarcation between MK and Mbokodo. It said the leadership had not dealt adequately with the complaints that led to the mutiny and it was concerned that Quatro personnel had not been adequately trained and did not have sufficient maturity or experience. The commission was clear: the ANC was only halfway into its task. The victims of the abuses had not yet received the full measure of justice due to them.

The NEC responded in 1992 by saying: 'We acknowledge that the real threat we faced and the difficult conditions under which we had to operate led to a drift in accountability and control away from established norms, resulting in situations in which some individuals within the NAT began to behave as a law unto themselves.'

\* \* \*

Hani was better placed than most to understand the political conflagration in the camps. Years before, after his release from detention in Botswana, he had experienced frustrations similar to those of the cadres in the camps in Angola. He had, after all, also faced the threat of the supreme punishment of the movement for his part in penning the Memorandum, in 1969. He could perceive the consequences with an insight to which even Tambo was not privy: 'Some of our cadres began to question what they were doing fighting in Angola rather than being allowed to take the fight into South African territory.'

Hani strongly believed that part of the reason why the soldiers were filled with unease, indeed dread, about their circumstances was that their political education had not continued in the camps, and leadership – true, proper leadership – was sorely lacking. When the camps first opened in the mid-1970s, there was recreation and an organised cultural life, with high-level military instruction from Cuban instructors and MK stalwarts. Political training and development had been given priority, and discipline had been maintained by constructive punishment and the involvement of the cadres themselves. The relationship between the administration and the rank and file in those early days was described to the commission as having been firm and comradely. And this resulted in a revolutionary atmosphere of high morale and combat readiness. However, the situation deteriorated considerably in 1979 after one of the major camps, Nova Katenga, was destroyed in a South African air raid. Stuart had found that, after 1979, the senior comrades who could solve problems politically and timeously were no longer as available as they had been at the beginning. This contributed to the gradual development of the explosive situation that finally erupted in December 1983.

Hani later told Wolfie Kodesh that the 'disgruntlement' and 'dissatisfaction' in the camps also had to do with the shortage of food

> ... and life in the bush, and the stupid attitudes by the security departments of the ANC – [their] harsh punishment. [The mutineers] also incited people around the criticism of our involvement in fighting UNITA. Because UNITA was actually trying even our security in the camps and we felt that we couldn't just expect the Angolans to defend us.
>
> We are soldiers. We should defend ourselves. We should continue training in

Angola, we must secure our own places ... we had begun to suffer casualties in fighting UNITA.

The leadership didn't want them to fight at home. They wanted them to fight and get finished. So these were some of the emotional issues. And a few people were taken up – quite a number, not a few, more than 100 ... and they killed our people. They attacked our people ... staunch members of the ANC – senior officers. And they took over our camps.

MK commander Teddy Williams, also known as Wellington Sejake, told the TRC in 1996 that when cadres refused to go into battle against UNITA Joe Modise told them they were 'half-baked'. Williams was also sent to Quatro.

Hani, whose 1969 Memorandum had neither advocated violence nor intimated it, admitted, however, that he could never condone the decision by the Pango mutineers to seize control by murder. He said that their ruthlessness, even in the face of real problems in the camps, made him 'reach the end of my tether'. He told Charles Villa-Vicencio:

We had no alternative but to recapture the camp and assert authority. Lives were lost on both sides in the process. This is very sad because the rebels, like us, were members of the ANC, fellow South Africans, fighting for the same cause.

In an interview with *Work in Progress*, he described 'a situation of overall suspicion':

In other words, if, for instance, we had sent people into the country and 60 percent of them were either arrested or killed, sometimes the wrong conclusion should be drawn that those who handled the operations were working for the enemy.

People began to lose a balanced approach in terms of combating the infiltration of the ANC by the regime. And that situation actually caused problems where, in my own view, the innocent and the guilty were sometimes lumped together.

'A mutiny in the army is a serious thing,' he said to Wolfie Kodesh, who asked: 'Do you have a clear conscience yourself of the strong measures that had to be taken there in the camps during these mutinies?' Hani's response was immediate:

I'm ... very critical of the strong measures we used at Quatro. We had no experience about life. We thought that anybody who was said to be a spy or was suspected, must be treated harshly. I know some people have criticised me for talking about Quatro, [but] within the NEC as far back as '85, '86, I raised my own serious reservations about the way we handled Quatro.

Hani was deeply affected by what happened. The Stuart Commission chair, Hermanus Loots, went to Pango with Hani, and they set up a meeting there in an open hall. But what remained with them both were the images of walking into the camp and seeing armed mutineers still running around in a state of violent confusion.

Years later, Hani confessed that he had never quite recovered from Pango and the events thereafter. At the time, when he was called to participate in the tribunal to investigate and try the Pango mutineers, he had withdrawn. He was overwhelmed by the decision the tribunal then took: to execute the men. The Skweyiya Commission referred to his 'feelings of revulsion' upon hearing, in the mid-1980s, that some of those thrown into Quatro had been kept for up to two years without trial. He said that he and others had inquired about why the code of conduct that emerged from the Kabwe Conference in 1985 had not been adopted. They then insisted upon it being held up as the model, and being implemented.

He told that commission that some members of Mbokodo were 'really vicious' and that the ANC, which had built its troops and its reputation on the quest for human rights, had to admit and then make redress for the sins of the past. His view was that a mechanism had to be found in order to prevent future abuses of this nature.

Thabo Mbeki, who was deputy president of South Africa at the time of his testimony to the TRC in 1996, told the commission that the ANC had executed at least 34 of its cadres for mutiny, murder and rape in Angola between 1980 and 1989. A list of the names of people executed by order of the military tribunal was provided in the ANC's 100-page submission to the commission. These included the name of a cadre found guilty of raping an Angolan woman. Another military tribunal ordered that he be executed by firing squad, and sentence was carried out in 1984 in Luanda. Two other cadres also faced a firing squad, in 1989, in Malanje, Angola, after they got drunk and shot randomly at shoppers at a local market, killing two Angolan women and injuring a woman and a child. Seven Pango mutineers who shot officers and other cadres were given the death penalty by the tribunal to which they were summoned. None among a second group of eight was executed, said Mbeki, 'despite the fact that some wounded cadres the morning after the mutiny began finishing them off'.

'I rushed back to Lusaka and asked the leadership to stop the executions,' Hani told Villa-Vicencio. 'The leadership, in all fairness, intervened, but by that time, comrades had already been executed.' Hani told Kodesh:

As a communist, I've always believed that we need to respect the human rights of individuals. And I thought we should not use torture or beatings even against those we thought were our enemies. I annoyed a lot of people in the NEC, but I was not the only one speaking out, there were others. But I think I was the most consistent because I had seen it myself, I'd been to Quatro.

In 1993, the Douglas Commission, established by the De Klerk government to investigate Quatro and the ANC's abuses in the camps, pointed the finger at Hani, as did certain writers. In *Comrades Against Apartheid* (1992), Stephen Ellis and Tsepo Sechaba tried to lay some of the blame for what had happened there on him, and to suggest that Hani was not only witness but also party to violence and torture. Hani's response to the Douglas Commission was clear in his conversation with Kodesh: 'They don't know why I visited it and what I did after visiting it. Anyway, that's not their business. I was not doing the work for them.' Loots substantiates the unbridled emotional resonance of the events around the camps at that time. He said Tambo had cried when he had discovered the nature of the abuses.

* * *

Comrade J would have been a millionaire if he had been a free man from the start. He's got a superb business brain, a way of seeing through the obfuscation of others, and he admits that he is most pleased when he sees the race to the finish. Somehow, he is unmistakable when he walks into the News Café in Midrand. We stand up to greet him, and he is immediately reticent. He clearly understands that his lack of warmth can be a problem, so he indirectly apologises for it by reminding us of how difficult, and painful, it is to have to recollect his memories from the camps in Angola, particularly Quatro.

His spectacles, grey hair and impeccable suit also help to give him away: what we do know, we intend to interrogate; what we don't know – his view of Hani's role in dealing with the mutinies at Pango and Viana in 1984, and, indeed, how he perceived Hani in general around this time – we must probe. It's not easy. It's intrusive, corrosive, but we have it on impeccable authority that Comrade J is the best candidate for an interview. Nervous at first: that checks out. Gregarious as the conversation gets going: that also checks out.

He had been a trade unionist and small-time businessman in the 1970s, when he started recruiting and moving in and out of the country, 'making arrangements'. After making his way into exile through Mozambique, he wound up in what was known as 3rd camp, Engineering, in Luanda.

It was the beginning of a struggle within a struggle for Comrade J and others based there. There was not enough food, a common complaint in most of the camps, and the recruits often found themselves having to rely on the Angolans to provide. Comrade J, a bit of a wheeler-dealer, decided to intervene and approached a bakery near the camp. It required a letter from the Minister of Defence in order to supply more than the rationed amount of bread, and ANC NEC member Cassius Maake organised this, so that there would, at least, be sufficient supplies of the staple. Comrade J also managed to organise a few bags of pineapples now and then from the nearby Hotel Tropico. The senior members of the camp were concerned about the teenagers of 12 and 13 years old who had come from Natal and the Transvaal, and needed to eat properly as they were still growing.

Day-to-day medical attention in the camp was scarce. The political and military training, which had been expected by recruits, was irregular. Perhaps less important, since it is a factor of most refugee camps, there were no luxuries at all. None of the rank and file could afford sweets, cigarettes or even salt.

Comrade J said he heard recruits at the time wondering what they had got themselves into: 'They felt they had been dumped there. There was nothing happening, no food.' Recruits sat around most of the time. Some tried to play soccer. They were not allowed to venture out, particularly nowhere near the basic brothels – a row of one-roomed units – that lay on the periphery.

What irked many was that their uniforms resembled those of UNITA. When they had to go to the hospital, for instance, they were more comfortable in civilian clothes. But this required money and the ability to go out into town and buy.

When they found an old Russian radio, their outlook brightened slightly:

We connected it and, surprise, surprise, it worked. So we used to stand outside on the stoep relating the news from Radio Moscow, the United Nations, even South Africa. It was a bit of political education to get people to know what was happening out there in the world.

Later, ANC veterans Mark Shope and Jack Simons put together a political education campaign, but it was inadequate when compared to the expectations and the promises made by the leadership, let alone MK's own manifesto, which guaranteed proper training.

Relationships with the Angolans, who ran the kitchen, were often difficult. Comrade J recalls that although the South Africans were deeply respectful and appreciative of the Angolans' generosity – politically, socially, financially, in every way – there were cultural differences that were heightened by the uncomfortable circumstances in which the cadres found themselves.

'People complained. They found the Angolans to be dirty. They spat all over the place so that even where there is food, you feel you cannot eat it.' Later, an approach was made, and a compromise agreed whereby the kitchen was shared.

But as soon as these issues were resolved, others arose. Comrade J said newly trained MK cadres were arriving in the camp all the time, 'very nice and well-fed, especially if they came from the German Democratic Republic. Some even had dollars and could buy sweets and drinks.' On special occasions, he managed to secure the camp some Angolan beer, the deal with the taverns being that he could have five glasses of beer as long as he bought a plate of food.

He did not remain silent about conditions in the camp, and became more and more outspoken. In 1980 he found himself rounded up with a few others from the 3rd camp and sent to the detention centre, Quatro. The most feared visitors to the camp were Joe Modise, Mzwai Piliso and Andrew Masondo. Comrade J's testimony in this regard matches many other reports about Quatro:

Modise used to assist with interrogations. He would arrive in a Land Rover, sometimes with trucks escorting him. And when he came, we knew we had drama. They would demand we write confessions, sometimes they would say they would write them for us and all we had to do was sign. The aim was for us to confess to being collaborators and enemy agents, but my position was always the same: they could beat me with sticks, they could do what they wanted, but I would never sign. I told the other men in my cell the same thing.

We had no water, no toilets except plastic containers where the top was cut off and we had to use this for 16 of us. The cell should have fitted about four. Remember, we were near the equator, so it was hot in there. We would start beating on the door, and if they opened it, our only exercise was to run down a 60-metre hole alongside the building. And the guards were standing all along it, bearing their AK47s.

Comrade J recalls a particular incident when he and five other detainees were sent to pull a water tanker filled with 20-litre containers. 'We were being beaten up while we were doing it ... even 16 men would have still battled to push it up, and we were five.'

To this day, he is shocked by the fact that the ANC leadership could condone the methods of interrogation at Quatro. 'This was something people learnt in the GDR, interrogation. It could be a specialisation after military training and they had teenage boys doing this there.'

\* \* \*

In these difficult years before De Klerk unbanned the liberation movements in 1990, there was a clear move from the younger leadership, led by Hani, to carefully examine the political status quo within the ANC and begin to plot a way forward. The military and political leadership of the party had met in Luanda in 1982 with just this aim. At this meeting, the decision was taken to create Politico-Military Councils (PMCs) to advance the organisation and prepare it for governing. The Kabwe Conference of 1985 was another step forward.

By the late 1980s, the ANC was, at last, a well-funded organisation with sufficient resources. Yet the mutiny at Pango and the testimony that later came out of the camps in general, and particularly out of Quatro, revealed the underbelly of a movement that was persistently beaten down by its enemy. Although many cadres had been plunged into war chasing UNITA, there was widespread dissatisfaction about not being able to get home.

Uppermost in the minds of most soldiers was the longing to take the fight to the enemy, to do battle in the streets of Johannesburg and Cape Town, if need be. Many felt they were ageing, without having realised their revolutionary dream of overthrowing apartheid. So an insurrectionist attitude continued to fester after Pango, and the leadership in the camps simply could not adjust.

Hani was against the idea of only using the MK troops to fight the enemies of the Angolan revolution. But there were issues in the background, most notably Tambo's close relationship with Samora Machel and FRELIMO, which had been developing since Kongwa in the mid-1960s. Tambo urged the NEC to consider its regional allies, and the fact that war on one was akin to war on another. This concept of internationalism, which Tambo supported, had allowed the Cubans and the Soviets to become embedded within the liberation movement. Ronnie Kasrils, later Minister of Intelligence in the Mbeki government, reflected that 'Chris got on enormously well with the Cuban and Soviet advisers. But many cadres in the camps had lost their energy for fighting others' battles.'

It hadn't always been that way. The Stuart Commission found that the need to defend MK base camps had, at first, developed into a general political understanding of the need to participate in the struggle against imperialism and bandit forces. It had also served the need to get out of the camps, and away from the boredom. Some comrades had been in the camp since their arrival in 1977, and there was a desperate need to gain combat experience. So MK cadres became involved regularly in mine-clearing operations, laying ambushes, raids into the villages, going out on patrols. The backup they gave to FAPLA forces provided the impetus for MK participation in an attack on UNITA bases across the Kwanza River in December 1983.

Hani was vehemently opposed to this campaign. His experience in the Wankie campaign had shown him that going into battle without proper reconnaissance data was a recipe for failure. He felt the solders would be fighting an enemy they did not know, without an understanding of the weapons they would face, the organisation of the rebels or their means of reinforcement. Even more dangerous was the lack of knowledge about the terrain. Just as had happened at Wankie, there were no proper maps.

All that was certain was the enthusiasm of the men.

Hani expressed his disappointment at his superiors' insistence on continuing the campaign, so Lennox Lagu took over. Lagu was instructed to cross the Kwanza to answer the security needs of FAPLA and the Angolan government. Almost immediately, MK's soldiers were scattered within different FAPLA formations, and could neither fight nor defend themselves as a cohesive unit. Problems of ill-discipline or insubordination were impossible to handle because of the dispersion of the force.

Unfortunately, as had happened at Wankie with ZIPRA, the FAPLA troops used in the Kwanza campaign were poorly trained. On average, each man had received only about two weeks' training, and Captain Sabastiao, the brigade commander, was singled out for his inefficiency in planning operations. During one operation, a joint force of MK and Angolan troops nearly starved when they spent three days marching in enemy territory with insufficient food. The lack of reconnaissance meant that every time they arrived at a UNITA base, it was deserted, or they fell easily into ambushes. On the day after Christmas, an ambush claimed the lives of five comrades who were taken into the operation on the basis of scant information about a bandit base in the operational area. The rest of the MK cadres, about 12 in number, said the FAPLA troops ran away. A decision was taken that the dead bodies should be retrieved, but it was distressing for the other cadres to see their comrades' mutilated and decomposing bodies. Soon, the MK soldiers were refusing to participate in further operations with FAPLA, and the arguments over going home to fight became stronger.

In early December 1983, the Angolans requested a reinforced company of MK soldiers to take a defensive position in Cangandala village, 28 kilometres from the capital of Malanje province. While FAPLA was to go on an offensive, some comrades went out to the village to buy booze or dagga. This meant many did not sleep in their positions.

Lagu travelled to Cangandala for a three-day meeting with the comrades, who demanded to know, again, why there were no operations happening in South Africa. He did not get a satisfactory answer, and moved on to Musafa village, where two MK platoons were stationed to defend a base. Incidents of random shooting had taken place there, and the soldiers told Lagu much the same thing as their comrades in Cangandala. But then an MK soldier was blown up by a mine near the defence position on his way to a makeshift toilet. Soon, news reached Cangandala about the five men killed in the Kwanza ambush and they also heard about a recruit who had died after being punished in another training camp, Caculama. The situation was intensifying, and the soldiers' demands to see the leadership became louder and more insistent. In mid-January 1984, the incidents of random shooting into the air became more aggressive, and even took place in the village streets, eroding the good relations between MK and the locals. The Stuart Commission found that almost everybody in Cangandala camp, including some commanders and commissars, was involved in the lawlessness, with the camp administration unable to stop it.

A forced withdrawal was ordered from Cangandala and another camp, Cacuso. Comrades were taken to Cacuso for interrogation, but they were soon joined by soldiers from Musafa and travelled in two groups to the transit camp of Viana, just outside Luanda. About 40 comrades from Caculama heard of these events and defiantly left their camp too, travelling by train to Luanda to join those already in Viana. The previous occupants of Viana had been moved to a site known as The Plot, a few kilometres away.

The Stuart Commission report details what happened next. On arrival in Viana, the first group of about 60 men were persuaded to surrender their personal weapons, as this was a general rule: the camp administration had to secure arms for the duration of a stay. But 15 men refused to give up their guns, saying they needed them 'for their self-protection from the security department men'. When the second, larger, group arrived at Viana, they too refused to hand in their weapons.

At least one soldier, Solly Sibeko, died as these events unfolded. Although described as mentally unstable and troubled with fits, he had been detained in a container in the camp for several days. Soon a rumour began that Sibeko's corpse had been 'riddled with bullets by the security men', adding heat to the comrades' fury about the freedom of action enjoyed by Mbokodo. Sibeko's death could not have happened at a more dangerous time. Viana was on a knife-edge, and its administration – which had allowed dagga smoking and drinking, as well as the slaughtering of livestock – was losing control through sheer lack of respect. Arms were brandished openly, said the Stuart Commission. It was a situation that could easily have been taken advantage of by enemy agents.

On Sunday, 5 February 1984, Julius Mokoena, the regional commander, and regional commissar Edwin Mabitse, who was also the regional chief of security, visited Viana camp and told the soldiers there to prepare an agenda for a meeting. On the Monday, cadres at The Plot – loosely organised by Kgotso Morena – called a meeting under the pretext of ironing out irregularities. But instead, the question of the comrades from Cangandala was raised, and the decision reached was that they should all go to Viana, to listen to the complaints of those from Cangandala.

At Viana, a Committee of 10 – comprising chairperson Zaba Maledza, Bongani Motwa, Kate Mhlongo, Jabu Mafolo, Sipho Mathebula, Grace Motaung, Moss Thema, Simon Botha, Sidwell Moroka and Morena, from The Plot – assembled to work out the agenda and discuss issues with the regional command. They wanted to know why there had been so many lies and distortions. They wanted to bury Sibeko themselves, and they wanted to talk about the security department and contact with the leadership.

Stuart described the atmosphere at the meeting as 'emotional and electric. The participants were armed with a variety of weapons and some individuals made provocative and inflammatory statements.' It was decided to have another meeting. But this did not materialise as FAPLA forces moved in on the Tuesday with the intention of disarming Viana camp.

As soon as the FAPLA troops appeared, some cadres formed a circular defensive position at the back of the camp. It was a critical moment, and without the intervention of some of the members of the Committee of 10 a serious battle could have broken out. One comrade was killed during a brief exchange of fire at the beginning, and a FAPLA soldier was injured by an RPG shell. There were no other FAPLA casualties. Some of the cadres in the circular defence position surrendered their arms, while others stored their weapons in the nearby bushes.

Meanwhile, some members of the security department went to a flat in the centre of Luanda where the propaganda unit was housed. They intended to disarm everybody there, apparently because of uncertainty about who was loyal and who was not. But as soon as Mbokodo entered the flat, a soldier, Diliza Dumagude, ran into the bathroom armed with a hand grenade. Another comrade, Soyisile Mathe, was already in the bathroom. He shouted, 'the police have come to arrest us!' Afraid, Dumagude pulled out the pin of the grenade and shouted, 'We'll all die!' Mathe grabbed the hand with the grenade and tried to talk to Dumagude, then tried to break a window in an attempt to escape. He managed to prise open the door, holding on to Dumagude's hand which still clutched the hand grenade. Dumagude then released the grenade and was severely injured in the ensuing explosion. Witnesses say the Mbokodo agents shot him while he was crawling towards another grenade lying on the floor. While this was going on, comrade Salier Janemzi threw two grenades at the security officers in the room. He, too, was shot, though he did not die instantly and immediately tried to use a second grenade. He was shot a second time – and killed.

The Stuart Commission arrived in Luanda on Monday, 13 February and by the Thursday, most soldiers had been taken out of Viana to either Quibaxe or Pango, while 31 – including the Committee of 10 – were held in detention. At The Plot, cadre Vuyisile Maseko, who was being taken to the ANC's detention camp with Committee of 10 member Morena, pulled out a hand grenade, which exploded in the vehicle. Maseko managed to jump to safety and Morena started running, but he was shot and seriously injured. Lennox Lagu was on the scene at the time.

\* \* \*

Thami Mali is a striking man who drinks Red Bull and chain-smokes during our interviews. He lives out on the plots hidden away among rows of birch trees outside Vereeniging with his wife, a bunch of dogs and a gaggle of ducks. We sit outside on the patio listening to his stories for hours. 'I bought this place when white people were leaving here in droves,' he tells us. That was in the early 1990s, when some whites were building bunkers to stash canned food and supplies, in case of uhuru.

On the other side of Mali's fence live former Selous Scouts who, like him, lead a quiet existence. Neither wants to know too much about the other. Visitors drift in and out during our interviews, and Mali periodically takes calls on two cellphones. He's got a lever-arch file crammed full of telephone numbers. There's no one he doesn't know who was in the camps in the 1980s, and he knew Hani very well. He even wrote a biography of Hani, *The Sun that Set Too Soon*, a year after the murder. It was published by the Sached Trust in 2004.

Mali agrees that this time was undoubtedly the most complex chapter in Hani's life: the years after Lesotho, when he was based in Zambia and touring the regions, particularly Angola, ultimately as MK chief of staff. Truth and lies circle around him in equal number, and there is indeed an enigmatic quality to Hani's leadership at this point. But Hani remains the hero, and Mali, who spent years in the camps himself, is well placed to present another side to the way cadres lived. 'Frustration was building, that's for sure. We were monitoring the news bulletins and we knew that more and more of our people were dying, but we persevered.'

He described life in the camps in detail, from the 4.45am bell every morning to the 10pm curfew at night. When the camps were functioning well, each day had its activities, beginning with roll call at 5am, followed by ablutions. The usual military procedures were demanded: shiny boots, clean uniforms, checking of tents. Political education classes – covering world events, socialism, Marxism, the history of the ANC and other liberation movements – started at 6am and ran till 1pm, when the soldiers broke for lunch. The cadres would gather under trees for their lessons, with their guns in their laps, ready for combat.

There were classes in tactical manoeuvres and physical training, and Mali remembers well how the soldiers were warned: 'Tambo has no car to take you to South Africa. These [and he pats his legs] are your car.'

From 2pm to 5pm, the soldiers did manual labour, cutting wood, fetching water, cleaning their weapons and any other activity required of them by their commanders. From 5pm to 6pm, they would have supper, and then relaxation until 7pm. From 8pm to 10pm, there was a different programme for certain days.

On Mondays, time was set aside for music, specifically listening to jazz or singing revolutionary songs like '*Umshini wami*', which was an outright favourite in the camps. On Tuesdays, there would be political discussions about specialised topics. Mali remembers a night of great debate over the issue of the US and Nicaragua, with the role of labour in the broad political struggle being a particular point of argument. On Thursdays, culture was the theme, with soldiers from different parts of the country expressing their traditions in music and dance. On Sundays, there would be a sports programme, dominated by soccer, with teams named as the Bolsheviks or the Mandelas.

Revolutionary holidays were the only time when the combatants could have a little alcohol – at least on an official basis. These days included: ANC Day (8 January); Sharpeville Day (21 March); May Day (1 May); Youth Day (16 June); the anniversary of the Freedom Charter (26 June); Women's Day (9 August); Tambo's birthday (27 October); and MK Day (16 December). On these holidays, the Cubans in the camps would donate whisky, vodka and Angolan beer. Only those on guard duty or who had to operate the anti-aircraft guns were excluded from the revelry – they would get to celebrate the next day.

Neither Christmas Day nor New Year's Day were celebrated, as MK did not recognise religion. This was also true of the culture and traditions of cadres in general. Those who had not been through initiation as teenagers, for instance, would only be able to perform the ceremony once they were men, and out of the camps. (Alban Nyimbana, Hani's teacher from Zigudu, said Hani had been through initiation while he still lived in Sabalele.)

Mali remembers that when Hani arrived on a visit to the camps, the mood lifted. He would laugh, make jokes and ask people where they were from, something of their past and what was happening in their lives in Angola. In order to allow soldiers to escape the ambience of perpetual politics, he would occasionally play chess or Scrabble with cadres. Mali recalls that:

[H]e would speak to you like a brother. He would ask, 'Do you know how your girlfriend is feeling? Did you say goodbye?' He seemed to understand how heavily affected people were by having to be there. He was interested in all kinds of things about people. What subjects people had chosen to do at school, what would happen if they were sent home with a gun.

\* \* \*

Mali believes Hani's fervent desire was to re-establish a culture of tolerance and co-operation in the camps. Yet there are still those who have tried to discredit him. Although Hani had no history of authoritarianism, allegations about his role in abuse, torture and murder emanate mostly out of the writing of disgraced former ANC cadres, and the one name that comes up often in their testimony, with which they intended to damage Hani, is that of former MK commander Thami Zulu.

A Sowetan by birth, Zulu – whose real name was Muziwakhe Ngwenya – died in Lusaka in late 1989, apparently shortly after being released from detention by Mbokodo. There were reports that he had been very ill and under close confinement. After his death, traces of an organic pesticide were found in his body, giving rise to rumours that he had been murdered.

The ANC convened a commission of inquiry – whose members included the esteemed Albie Sachs – and found that the regime's security agents were responsible for Zulu's death. However, anti-ANC former cadres have insisted on casting aspersions on Hani, who, together with Joe Modise, saw Zulu in the hours before his death.

These same sources make claims about the death of MK cadre Sipho Phungulwa, who had once been a bodyguard of Hani but later took part in the mutiny in Viana, which led to his internment at Quatro prison camp. Upon his release from Quatro in November 1988, he was taken with other former mutineers and ex-Quatro inmates to Tanzania, to a camp called Dakawa, where ANC secretary-general Alfred Nzo addressed them, and told them that the time had come for them to play a role within the ANC again, if they desired. Different roles were thus created within Dakawa, and Phungulwa participated in culture and sport.

A year later, in September 1989, another enormous challenge faced the ANC in exile, even though it was only months away from being unbanned by the regime. Elections were held for the regional political committee (RPC) in Tanzania, and several ex-mutineers and former Quatro prisoners were selected, but this resulted in some dissension within the NEC, and the RPC was dissolved while discussions around it took place.

By the end of December, there was fury inside Dakawa, and Hani and NEC member Stanley Mabizela were sent there by Tambo from Lusaka to talk to the soldiers. Hani slept in the same room as his bodyguards, for protection, and they related to us how Hani entered a packed community meeting at Mazimbu, near Dakawa – some five hours' drive from where they lived – and found dozens of soldiers already waiting to tell him their central problem: they felt they had been abandoned.

But in January 1990, two groups fled out of Tanzania, one to Kenya, another – which included Phungulwa – to Malawi. This second group was arrested by April 1991, and Malawian government forces negotiated their handover to South Africa. Once the men had been processed, the renegades were released in Johannesburg, and they staged an impromptu press conference at which they expressed their fear of retribution. The TRC later reported that their actions then had included approaching the ANC, the SACP and COSATU, as they claimed they wished to expose the hardships they had endured in Angola.

A journey to the ANC offices in Umtata created a legend around Phungulwa that persists to this day. The story goes that, when he and another former comrade, Luthando Nicholas Dyasop, left the offices, having been unable to see any officials, they were tailed by assassins. As soon as they emerged from a taxi they had used, they were fired on and Phungulwa was killed.

In February 1991, a year after its unbanning, the ANC adopted a resolution to release everyone it had apprehended as 'secret agents, spies, agents provocateurs and hired assassins in the employ of the SA government's security services'. By August of that year, 32 men labelled as 'the most notorious' suspected agents and infiltrators, who had been detained in various ANC detention camps, returned to South Africa where they met the leadership. The men fingered for Phungulwa's murder – Ndibulele Ndzamela, Mfanelo Matshaya and Pumlani Kubukeli – were granted amnesty by the TRC in 1998 in connection with the incident.

* * *

The tail end of exile meant a move to Uganda for many cadres. It was an unexpected development, based on the political difficulties Angola was experiencing in reaching agreement, through UN Resolution 435, for the withdrawal of South African troops and the independence of Namibia. No matter how distasteful this was, and how unjust the behaviour of South African foreign minister Pik Botha had been when he had shifted the conditions at the eleventh hour to include the isolation of MK, Angolan president Dos Santos had to bend.

So Hani travelled to Uganda on a mission. Would the government assist him, and the ANC, by hosting armed MK troops? A move for the combatants was all but inevitable. They had to leave Angola, and no other African country would take them. The prospect of admitting armed soldiers was unpalatable for most, and their position was understandable.

Emmanuel Maphatsoe, better known as Kebby, was one of the combatants who experienced what was to become an unhappy period in the lives of soldiers who were desperate to go home. Today a senior leader of the MK veterans, Maphatsoe trained in Angola from 1985 and understood well the mindset of the Young Lions Detachment, some of whom had been no more than children when they had arrived, and who would now have to make the transfer to Uganda.

The MK veteran recalled how the youngest of the recruits would occasionally ask even Tambo for sweets. It was agonising – they were so mature, yet still steeped in childhood. The older soldiers played a dual role: mentors and parents-in-proxy. It was enormously difficult to juggle for emotional balance. So stability became a core concern, and moving to Uganda, rather than going home, was a dislocation.

Many of the Young Lions had been sent to Cuba for specialist training, and others to Moscow, but all of them wanted to get back to South Africa and fight to the finish. Instead, many had been dispatched to the Northern Front of Angola to fight not directly for their own people's freedom, but against UNITA. Maphatsoe said there was indeed antagonism about this, with the final, glorious batch of post-1976 recruits becoming the next generation to question the leadership, in much the same way as Hani and his fellow soldiers had done, for much the same reasons, in the 1960s.

Hani constantly had to play the role of military diplomat as these events unfolded, both within the Angola camps and on the broader, regional political level. He would even go so far as to visit soldiers on the border battlefield, travelling there in perilous convoys that were frequently ambushed. 'Comrade Chris always seemed to be being baptised by fire,' Maphatsoe remembered:

[B]ut it took a man like him to make us understand why we should carry on doing what we were required to do. At times, this was only about taking food to the Northern Front because the regime's response was to disorganise the revolutionary troops at the rear. Even when morale was low, when he was around, everybody would be in there. It would be like Christmas Day.

He would sleep in the camps, do his morning run there, attend classes, eat beans and rice with us and not with the leadership … that kind of thing. He would never come without doing hours of talking, there would be a gathering wherever he was.

When the time came for Hani to discuss the move to Uganda, he was typically concerned about how the cadres would feel. 'He told us, "it's up to you. I cannot take you out if you want to stay",' recalled Maphatsoe. And so the camps became very tense. 'He explained to us that the victory of Namibians was also our victory, that it was also part of all our sacrifices.'

Hani used unusual methods of persuasion, though, including the prospect of lots of Coca-Cola and better living circumstances in Uganda. 'We started ululating,' Maphatsoe said with a smile. 'He said there would be bungalows, and everybody was happy.' Although there was significant reluctance on the part of the troops to up and leave Angola without the option of choosing the war at home, most decided to throw their lot in with Hani. When they left, they were in civilian clothes – white shirts, blue jeans, old shoes – with their uniforms packed away until they arrived at their new camps.

But Hani was betrayed by his own organisation almost from the start. The arrangements were poor, almost non-existent, and this damaged the morale of the men. The soldiers had to leave Angola on the long journey to Uganda without even eating a meal. All they were given was a small piece of cake and a Coke for the four-hour plane trip to Kampala. Maphatsoe described their arrival:

When we arrived, we hoped there would be buses waiting for us, but we had to get on trucks, loaded on there like cattle, and escorted by the military intelligence of Uganda. We drove the whole night until the morning. At one time, we asked the driver if we weren't maybe in Sudan now. We were hungry, hungry, hungry, so we began to say that we wanted to be taken to Entebbe Airport. We wanted Comrade Chris to come and see what was going on with us.

Hours later, the soldiers arrived at the transit camp to which they had been assigned – and it was a hellhole. Once used by Idi Amin to dispose of dissidents and perceived enemies, the place was scattered with forgotten graves and fragments of bones. This disturbing, brutal environment began to dramatically affect the mental state of many among MK's displaced. The promised bungalows were nowhere to be seen. There were only tents, and no blankets. It was a raw place, and hard on the soul. If there had been too little food in Angola, here there was next to nothing – a cup of hard beans per day. 'We began to believe that if we stayed there any longer, we were going to produce mercenaries. It was like a slaughterhouse,' said Maphatsoe.

But the signal for help had gone out, and soon Thenjiwe Mthintso arrived. Apparently she burst into tears when she saw what was going on. Some of the troops were using the skulls of the dead as ashtrays. But after Mthintso's intervention, the soldiers were moved to a camp in Ngoma. Maphatsoe described the new camp:

There were rondavels there, and because, practically from the time we left Angola, we had no rest, we were exhausted. So we just lay down on the beds provided, which were constructed out of two sticks shaped like a 'V' with a grass mattress on top. Immediately we lay down, we leapt up again because there were red ants with eggs inside those mattresses. They got everywhere, even between your toes. You call them *mabidaganye*, and they were terrible. So this time, comrade Chris came to help us. We couldn't live like that. He had already been briefed by comrade Thenjiwe. But no one else from the leadership came.

Comrade Chris confirmed that he was our commander and that he understood our needs as soldiers. The way he was loved! He would ask:, 'What is your view? Give me your ideas.' He re-established our ranks there. He asked, 'Who do you serve, comrades? You serve the people of South Africa.'

For the first time in the history of MK, there were luxuries – tomato sauce and Oros. The lone white cadre in the camp, known as Craig, was the only one who didn't quite appreciate the nuances of *masatamato* (tomato mix), preferring plain beans and rice. But the overall mood was improving. There was an edge, with Hani indicating that the time for homecoming was approaching.

By 1992, the first contingent had left Uganda, while Bantu

Holomisa – upon request from Hani – had sent Transkei Defence Force officers there to assist in the integration of training needed to prepare the MK fighters for South African life again. 'We experienced all of this like a kind of family,' Maphatsoe said. 'And Hani was for us at the head of it.'

\* \* \*

By 1988, Hani was living in a house in Woodlands, Lusaka – close to the ANC's new military headquarters when it opened in Avondale – with two permanent teams of bodyguards. The last time he had lived in Woodlands was when he had stayed with Ben Magubane and his family, as he prepared himself politically and philosophically for the Wankie campaign.

We travelled to Bethlehem, a dry, voiceless little town on the eastern margin of the Free State, to meet Pule Matokoane, one of Hani's guards during that time. Matokoane – a quiet, serious man, still in the army, who had just turned 40 years old – was preparing for the possibility of peacekeeping duty on the continent when we met him. He was fiercely proud of his young family and of his history, but still in pain about aspects of it that remain unresolved.

He smiles at the memory of being around Hani, a man he clearly respected for his humanity. He liked him as a man. He misses him. 'But, ja, he was tough to look after. It was very stressful,' Matokoane recalled. He had been selected as a bodyguard from Residence 1 Luanda regional command. He described life with Hani:

It was hard work. He would wake up at 5am, and then we'd have to go on a 10-kilometre run – even when his life was under threat like that. But he wanted to try and live as normal a life as possible. His family visited in the holidays, December-time, and they went to the USSR.

Another Lusaka bodyguard, Andile Haneae, says Chris took pleasure in seeing Limpho Hani and their children, Neo, Nomakhwezi and Lindiwe, when they visited him. Limpho would prepare 'good food' and do her husband's washing. She brought new clothing for the bodyguards, and Coke.

There was also the rare occasion – a surprise, in fact – when Mary Hani arrived in Lusaka to visit her son. Haneae was on duty with Hani when she arrived. 'She was sitting on the couch by the door, and he walked straight past her without actually seeing her, to go to the bathroom. When he came out, she got up off the couch and she cried. They embraced each other and she stayed for about a week.' But Hani being Hani, unable to relax, unable to set himself apart from his comrades, carried on working throughout his mother's visit. He might have been away from her for nearly 30 years, but his priorities – long shifted – remained in place.

The experience of his bodyguards was that Hani was 'very humble at home'. He would clean the house, and 'if you wanted something to be done, you asked Comrade Chris'. Matokoane said Hani and the bodyguards dressed in civilian clothes, with Hani always carrying his beloved Makarov pistol in a leather pouch on his body. He recalls that 'there was always at least one person on duty, one driver and another for cooking. We mostly ate rice, meat and porridge and we always ate together, except breakfast. He only had tea.'

'There was always lots of laughter around Comrade Chris. Even when he was by himself, he could sit around laughing,' Matokoane remembers. 'Because he liked doing this, he liked reading Bill Cosby.' Haneae remembers Hani as an authentic African jazz fan. He had a preference for Stimela, Bayete and Sankomoto, and he felt no shame in singing freedom songs out loud when they were all in the house, 'and dancing'.

Matokoane recalls several moments of complication while he was on duty, particularly the rather strange activities of people who moved into a half-built house next door. A Zambian woman living there, who worked at the Angolan mission, appeared to have a house guest in the form of a man known to the bodyguards as 'Dala Boy'. Dala Boy, in turn, seemed to have an inordinate interest in the comings and goings of the men at

Hani's house, so they put him under surveillance for three months, while keeping the dogs in their yard on full alert. Soon after the bodyguards finally confronted him – 'you can just tell if somebody's from your country' – he left, 'and we did not see him again'. But there was a persistent air of trepidation around Hani getting too close to anybody who had not been thoroughly vetted.

The chief of staff's social encounters were few. He chose the company of Pallo Jordan and Steve Tshwete, but Hani was not one to indulge. He refused to keep alcohol at his house, not only because he didn't drink, but because he had no patience with those who did. Sometimes he played soccer in the yard with his bodyguards.

Then, one morning in early 1990, Hani called his men into the kitchen and advised them that there was a strong possibility they would be going home. For the loyal Matokoane, that was the beginning of the end. His most distressing, pervasive memory – and the one that causes him the most discomfort all these years later – is not from his time with Hani, but rather from his time without him, when Hani had become inaccessible, as the movement coalesced at the headquarters of the ANC in Shell House in downtown Johannesburg.

Although Hani had already been sent home, on a provisional amnesty order from FW de Klerk's government, his bodyguards from Lusaka only arrived in June 1990. They landed at Jan Smuts Airport and found that no arrangements had been made to collect them; perplexed, they were stuck at the airport without money or contacts. They couldn't reach Hani and were advised that he was out of the office and too busy to get hold of them, and so it went on for a couple of days until they were approached by a member of the Security Branch who was monitoring the airport and had noticed their continued presence.

Ironically, he was able to assist them by contacting Shell House, and the order was for them to return to Lusaka for the time being. 'We knew this had nothing to do with him,' Matokoane said. 'He was always looking after our best interests. He used to try and tell us to go off duty and be with our girlfriends. But there was no way we could do that.'

Three weeks before he was gunned down, Hani had spoken to Haneae about reforming his protection structures. Of course, this very issue was at the core of the ANC's inquiry into his assassination on Easter Saturday, just days after the two men had met quite by chance in Johannesburg when Haneae was between jobs, a couple of years out of exile. Hani was delighted to see him. 'He made me promise I would join him again. He wanted to start working with me again. He even said he had servant's quarters in Dawn Park if I had nowhere else to stay.' But they never had a chance to talk about the finer details of working together again. Days later, Hani – who told Haneae that 'if ever the boers arrested him, he would fight' – was killed.

The shock of Hani's murder still shatters Haneae, and Matokoane: 'We were so vigilant in Zambia. We were battlefield-ready for anything. We were the big brothers, always there. We were young then, 20, and not afraid. We knew what we were doing.' Haneae and Matokoane say that there was never a moment when Hani was alone after the formal implementation of his security detail in Lusaka in the late 1980s. Bantu Holomisa said the same thing in reference to the protracted period in which Hani lived in the Transkei again in the early 1990s. Based in Umtata, Hani was never without a team of Transkei government-sponsored bodyguards, day and night. Holomisa said it was their honour to protect him. Hence, neither the Lusaka security detail nor the Umtata security detail will ever understand how it was allowed, or how it happened, that Hani was killed when he had bodyguards: 'We understood that this was the man who would die for us. He was really dedicated to the freedom of our people. So it wasn't a difficult situation for us. We would also die for him.'

CHAPTER 11

# COMING HOME

The men were seated around the lounge, the radio blaring in the background as always. It was a time to relax, the Lusaka suburb having settled down to a languid afternoon. Hani liked hearing the news, so the radio had always been important during the years of exile. When he wasn't in earshot, he would expect his bodyguards to listen and give him a detailed bulletin. This came out of an abiding need to be in touch with the world, the secret places of exile sometimes being so remote or so parochial as to serve only the narrow interests of those within an inhabitable radius. Now there was another dimension to this need to be informed. Hani had experienced such a wrench when he and many others in the NEC had seemingly been left out of a key decision, completely contrary to ANC policy, so that he was unsure that he really knew everything that was happening.

Later when he went into the kitchen with his bodyguards – dinner had just been set down – he confessed what was in his heart. 'Gents, I have this feeling we are going home. I don't know when, but we are going home,' Hani said. And so the discussion began again about how Hani and others in the ANC's top structure had been left flabbergasted when news first broke of the negotiations between the movement and white Afrikaners – mostly businesspeople – in London, the movement being represented by Thabo Mbeki.

According to Mbeki biographer Mark Gevisser, Hani had erupted over this at an ANC National Working Committee (NWC) meeting in late February 1988, from which Mbeki was absent because of this rendezvous. 'On whose authority has Comrade Thabo entered into discussions? I cannot understand why the NWC and PMC were not apprised. Let the minutes record that we register our extreme displeasure that Comrade Thabo has unilaterally gone to London without any ... consultation and without a mandate from the NEC.' But even these words, which were recorded, did not convey the full force of his anger.

In October 1987, Govan Mbeki and Walter Sisulu had been among a group of ANC leaders released from Robben Island. In January, they made their first trip outside the country in more than three decades to meet their comrades in Lusaka, before travelling to Stockholm to see their ailing leader, Oliver Tambo.

Like most of the MK soldiers who had spent years in the camps – some for nearly 25 years – Hani had retained a militant approach to his commitment, even if militarism, as an ideology, had been stripped from MK's lexicon in favour of the politicisation of the whole soldier. He believed fervently in the armed struggle. It had to continue.

Then came 2 February 1990. The news from Parliament was astonishing. The ANC and other liberation movements had been unbanned and Mandela and others were to be released from Robben Island. The exiles could begin coming home.

Lawyer Phyllis Naidoo took many in the movement by surprise with the news on that day. *Daily News* editor Dennis Pather had called her from Durban. She was at home, in exile in Harare. Had she heard? The announcement was met with utter disbelief. Pather immediately faxed through a copy of De Klerk's speech, while Naidoo was already on the phone to the ANC's head office in Lusaka.

Hani was knocked off his feet by the news. This had been only a borderline possibility within the debating circles of the ANC's highest echelons, mistrustful as they were of FW de Klerk's motives. What would this mean for the cadres?

\* \* \*

It was the opening of Parliament, and the apartheid State President got up to make the boldest announcement of his career – one that sent waves of excitement around the world: 'The season of violence is over. The time for reconstruction and reconciliation has arrived.' He called for a normalisation of relations with the country's southern African neighbours and, indeed, the rest of the world. And, with elections having taken place a year before, comment had to be made about the opinions of the recalcitrant whites. De Klerk took it on: 'Underlying this is the growing realisation by an increasing number of South Africans that only a negotiated understanding among the representative leaders of the entire population is able to ensure lasting peace.'

By the end of his speech, the president had changed the course of history for the ANC, the SACP and the PAC. Their imprisoned members would be released, although there would have to be discussions about the future for those convicted of offences like terrorism, murder or arson. The release of Mandela was to take place as soon as was administratively possible.

From Sweden, Tambo responded with caution. While welcoming the decision, he called for the international community not to let up the pressure on the South African regime until the system of apartheid had been dismantled. He criticised the fact that some political prisoners would not be released, that the State of Emergency would persist, and that the practice of detentions without trial would continue. Immediately, a meeting was convened in Stockholm between the NEC and released leaders to chart the way forward. And it would not be long before that way forward was given a guide.

On 11 February 1990, before a jubilant crowd that had been waiting outside Victor Verster prison in Paarl, and later at Cape Town's Grand Parade, Nelson Mandela took a graceful step on his epic walk to freedom as he was finally released. The process of dismantling apartheid had now been firmly set in motion, but there was great trepidation on both sides. An air of mistrust, built up over generations, hung over them, thick and daunting.

Towards the end of May 1990, a group led by the liberal politician, Frederik van Zyl Slabbert, and including a number of serving and former apartheid security force leaders made a trip to Lusaka to meet the ANC. The topic of discussion had been clearly set out. With moves toward a democratic South Africa, a way had to be found to work towards integration, including that of the defence force.

With so many issues still outstanding, Hani was opposed to the immediate abandonment of the armed struggle. 'Calls for our unilateral abandonment of the armed struggle in the face of a battery of laws preventing free political activity are unrealistic,' he said. But by the end of the Lusaka meeting, there had been some agreements: the phasing out of military conscription; a 50 percent reduction in force levels; the scrapping of the commando system; restrictions on the carrying of weapons; the police to be trained to use minimum force for crowd control; and efforts towards the formation of a new South African defence force, integrating the SADF, MK, homeland armies and the armed wings of the other liberation movements.

Importantly for the apartheid regime at the time, and for some sitting across the table from them, was that there would be no retributive Nuremberg-style trials. From his vantage point in Lusaka, Hani viewed the National Party as bruised. Its powers were waning and it was seriously divided at a time when the ANC was gaining greater acceptability and stature. The organisation had been courting black business leaders and homeland leaders.

He lauded the irony of the state of emergency for strengthening people's resolve against the government of the day. Already, Transkei leader Bantu Holomisa was distancing himself from the apartheid government, a move which Hani re-emphasised on numerous occasions. Now 'the big powers' were pressuring all parties to negotiate, but the movement was determined to proceed with care. It would be perilous simply to ditch the policy of armed struggle, when this had so inspired the youth.

'Armed struggle is the mobiliser, the inspirer,' urged Hani. Clinging to the importance of MK, he argued that it had instilled a sense of pride among young South Africans who were able to stand up and say they were fighting back, even though they had only meagre resources. Importantly at the time, the armed struggle had also sown insecurity among whites, and unsettled the sweet life that had allowed them to refuse to see the truth inside.

'I am sure the ANC won't call off the armed struggle because it has been unbanned,' assured the MK chief of staff at first when the troops asked him the tough question. Yet, ever the pragmatist, he knew in his heart that if the ANC called for its army to cool it, the organisation would have to address the morale of the cadres. He was concerned about its stock of weapons. There were still very real threats that the SADF could oppose De Klerk's reforms.

Meanwhile the time would be used to educate cadres politically and prepare them for the task of demobilisation, while also keeping them at a simmer should it be necessary to build covert units inside South Africa if everything went horribly wrong. 'We must also teach cadres that there is a need to fight and talk, and if talks fail we must go back and fight. I think we must struggle very hard for our comrades not to feel that sitting down with our enemy is betrayal.'

On 4 May 1990, the state and the ANC signed the historic Groote Schuur Minute. It was a sober-minded setpiece. The ANC and the government would work towards stemming the violence damaging the country at the time, as well as a definition of political offences and the release of political prisoners. There would be temporary immunity from prosecution for members of the NEC, and specific ANC members, in order for them to work towards a political solution and help establish and maintain political activity. The government would review current security legislation with a view to lifting of the State of Emergency. The two would establish effective lines of communication between the ANC and the government on all levels.

With the foundations now seemingly laid for the return of exiles, Hani landed at Jan Smuts Airport on 28 April, setting foot on South African soil for the first time in years – since the days of covert operations from his base in Lesotho. PWV regional chairperson Tokyo Sexwale – himself recently freed from Robben Island – welcomed him home.

Later, dressed simply in blue slacks, leather shoes, a golf shirt and a jersey for the dry Joburg cold at that time of the year, Hani marvelled at the city as he strolled down Fox Street, past the Carlton Centre, briefcase in hand, accompanied by Sexwale. There were those within Hani's closest circle who resented Sexwale's presence, and still do – the most virulent of his critics decrying him for being an opportunist who milked what was, in fact, a fairly new relationship with Hani. But the destinies of the two men would forever be intertwined.

Soon, Hani and Sexwale were at the core of what resembled a train station – and sometimes a police station – at Shell House in downtown Johannesburg. Although Hani relinquished his post as MK chief of staff in the interests of supporting the objective of peace, MK headquarters was a blur of voices and experiences, with everyone wanting his attention, until late into the night. Returning cadres had been instructed to check in at Shell House as they had to be documented. And soon, the building was a rendezvous for the brave, the embittered and the beleaguered.

Hani quickly formed a tight partnership with Mandela's wife, Winnie, and their iconic pairing – both wearing MK fatigues and boots, caps on their heads, striding side-by-side in a choreographed suite – aroused the expectant nation's imagination. Their relationship was, of course, anathema to white South Africans, who had been reared to hate Winnie. Her rise only served to entrench their empty terror of Hani, and the linking of the two leaders provided the perfect opportunity for the regime's propagandists. A fantastical tale was concocted which, if designed to destroy them, was more comical than catastrophic. It was certainly a tale with divisive intent: Winnie Mandela and Hani planned to set up their own political party as a rival to the alliance.

By the time she met Hani upon his return from exile, and opened her Soweto home to him for a period, Mandela had been charged with kidnapping and assault in the case of the 14-year-old child activist Stompie Seipei, who had been found dead under disturbing circumstances. She was convicted in May 1991. Later, the Truth and Reconciliation Commission heard details about how the ANC president's wife had allegedly fomented violence and torture among her bodyguards, notoriously known as the Mandela United Football Club. All of these facts were a triumph for her enemies, whose campaign against her became iniquitous when Nelson Mandela divorced her.

But when she and Hani spent months on the road as revolutionary lobbyists of the first order – their first goal the liberation of the nation, their only drive the victory of the ANC – Winnie Mandela was the queen. After Hani's death, the disinformation turned spectacularly vulgar. Winnie was said to have indicated that 'moderate' ANC leaders had been involved in his assassination. It was stated, as if she had said it, that these leaders were the only ones who could have known the details of his comings and goings and the movements of his bodyguards; thus it was only they who could have collaborated with the regime's National Intelligence Agency to have him killed.

There was indeed a similarity in the characters of Winnie Mandela and Chris Hani. Although she was the firebrand lacking in diplomacy, and he the soldier who preferred to listen, they were principled about their purpose: justice. There would be a time for back-slapping and a time for fury. Hani exemplified both. Where those involved in the negotiations with the National Party were quickly learning the art of diplomacy, he could be the rapier.

\* \* \*

Hani was also inspiring the SACP, among whose young leadership was

Blade Nzimande. Disturbed by the bloodshed in the Natal Midlands at the time, Hani was often called upon to intervene, to visit, to deliver words that could help make sense of the terrible strife there. Hani was becoming more involved in the grassroots development of the SACP, working with influential leaders, such as the ANC's Harry Gwala, as well as younger communists like Nzimande, who were developing their own roles within the democratic movement. The fratricidal strife between the ANC and the IFP required supreme peace efforts, the dominant one steered by Jacob Zuma, who was delegated to the task by Nelson Mandela.

Hani had been elected to the position of SACP secretary general in 1991, after Joe Slovo had suffered a stroke and anounced he would not be available for re-election. Hani wanted to prove his competence as Slovo's successor, and he more than did that with his affable, self-contained but expansive personality. He liked to get to know the people within the Communist Party's structure as intimately as he could, so as to direct the right attention to the right places. Nzimande, a former academic who left the gilded university halls to become a proper rabble-rouser for the just cause, rues the fact that he never got to know Hani as well as he would have liked, 'but I felt like I had known him for years':

He was a warm and truly kind person, he would meet you with his arms open. Even today, we are guided by his definition of socialism, which was never about big words but about what you did for the people who had nothing.

Nzimande recalls how a small delegation of SACP leaders once had to travel to Johannesburg for a meeting, and, due to a lack of funds, had to find accommodation in the townships and suburbs. He got to stay with Hani:

We would stay up late and have very lengthy discussions. But when it came to the morning, he would wake us up in a tracksuit – sweating. He'd been for a run, but he'd also made us breakfast. That was the giant in the man, I was just the laaitie.

\* \* \*

At every turn, Hani would remind those across the table that the ANC was an opponent at the very least equal to their regime. And both sides were keeping their options open. While the protagonists in this protracted battle circled each other, the country was bleeding.

On 13 July 1990, a right-wing bomb attack in Johannesburg injured 27 blacks. The racists, too, wanted their detainees released, and the threat that emanated from them felt imminent at that time. A month later, Hani, addressing an audience at the University of Transkei, warned that the ANC might have to 'seize power' if the government did not make concessions. He also had his eye on the lunatic fringe, but his every comment, no matter how measured, no matter how balanced and justified, provided fodder for the disinformation campaign that intensified against him.

The next step in the negotiating process was the signing of the Pretoria Minute, on 6 August 1990. Furthering the broad objectives put forward at Groote Schuur, the agreement would see the resumption of the release of political prisoners on 1 September 1990, with the plan that this process be completed by 30 April 1991. The agreement was clear. There would be indemnity for groups from October 1990, with the process to be completed by the end of 1990.

Most importantly, the ANC announced the suspension of the armed struggle. Mandela had convened a meeting of MK commanders and other ANC leaders in Cape Town to discuss the issue of the suspension of the armed struggle. This was one of many tightropes the ANC leader had to walk. 'The general perception at the meeting held in Cape Town was that the ANC should talk but retain its right to continue the struggle by training people,' recalled ANC spokesperson Jessie Duarte.

But the threat posed by right-wing Afrikaners was very real. Most were armed. They could – and did – launch many more attacks. Mandela argued that the ANC could not be part of an atmosphere of tension. It had to demur. It had to build. But the emotional life of a long-battered people was fragile. The Boipatong Massacre of 17 June 1992 led to an extended period of devastating violence, especially on the East Rand and in the Natal Midlands. Mandela argued that the South African government should be held responsible for the security of the people and thereby become part of the solution, too.

As part of the Pretoria Minute, the ANC had undertaken to suspend armed attacks, and to stop the infiltration of soldiers and materiel, the creation of military underground structures, statements inciting violence, threats of armed action and military training inside the country. The regime agreed to accept that MK was not only legal but also that membership of it was not a crime. It knew MK had arms caches inside the country and that it might continue to recruit. The government agreed that the ANC was entitled to maintain its existing structures, and, to this end, the government would review sections of the Internal Security Act 74 of 1982 that restricted the activities of political organisations.

In this political chess game, the De Klerk government was keen to muzzle the likes of Hani, who was already seen as a bogeyman by white constituents, thanks to a rancorous campaign against him. Less than two weeks after the signing of the Pretoria Minute, the temporary indemnity from prosecution for those involved in the negotiation process expired, and Hani, Ronnie Kasrils and senior leader Mac Maharaj had their freedom effectively revoked. Maharaj was already in detention for his part in masterminding Operation Vula, the final master plan to build an underground military network throughout South Africa. Kasrils, a fellow Vula leader, was in hiding. By the time Hani heard the news of his new position under the law, he was, fortuitously, in Transkei, under the protection of its leader, Bantu Holomisa.

'This is just another attempt to intimidate me ... the struggle continues,' rallied Hani, criticising De Klerk for not taking action instead against the military's so-called Civil Co-operation Bureau, whose members were assassinating anti-apartheid activists. In that week, at least 371 people were killed in clashes between ANC and IFP supporters in townships in the Transvaal, particularly in KwaThema and Tembisa. The mood in the country was dark.

In a wide-ranging interview with the *Financial Mail* in September

1990, Hani had called for police levels to be increased:

The tensions of the past are not going to evaporate all of a sudden. Police are trained to control situations without violence. In Britain, police patrol without weapons and that is what we ultimately desire, whereas the army is trained to shoot only when they feel their lives are threatened. This matter should be dealt with by the police together with the [relevant political] organisations; we should sit down together to work out a strategy to solve it. I don't think this violence can be resolved by the use of force. It is a consequence of a number of problems, such as unemployment and other economic and political problems. We need to establish a culture of peace.

In the meantime, with negotiations progressing at a pitiful pace and resistance from the apartheid regime towards integration of the armed forces, the cadres were trickling back into the country. The few still remaining in camps in Uganda and Tanzania were agitating to be brought home:

They [the SADF] think Umkhonto we Sizwe is just a rag-tag army. I don't think those views are useful. They need to be broad and objective and realise that the ordinary black person in the country regards Umkhonto very highly and that Umkhonto has been fighting for their freedom. They would never accept the exclusion of MK.

Hani saw affirmative action in the army and police as the only way to ensure it was representative of the country and instil a new confidence among the population in a new security force:

A new South African army must be loyal to a democratic government and accountable to parliament, or, if you like, civilian authority and the constitution of that country. That army must never be used by any political party to entrench itself in power. Armies must be seen as the helpers of the people, who help during natural disasters, build bridges ... We would not want a future army to be deployed to stop people from exercising their right to demonstrate.

Hani called for tighter gun control and greater emphasis on crime control and crime prevention. All of this implied the creation of a new mindset:

> What we need in South Africa is for egos to be suppressed in favour of peace. We need to create a new breed of South Africans who love their country and love everybody, irrespective of his or her colour.

By the end of that year the ANC took stock of the progress towards negotiations and was sorely disappointed at the moves made in relation to the objectives defined in the Harare Declaration – an initiative of the OAU, adopted at its meeting in Harare in August 1989, which laid down the principles and modalities for possible negotiations between the liberation movement and Pretoria. Among the issues outstanding were the unconditional release of prisoners, the unconditional return of exiles, the repeal of repressive security legislation and the termination of political trials – all of which had created a climate simply not conducive to peaceful negotiations.

The violence was part of a campaign by the state and its allies to destabilise the ANC, they concluded. When the ANC's National Consultative Conference closed on 16 December – the anniversary of the formation of MK – it mandated the NEC to continue talks about talks, but that all obstacles should be removed by the end of April 1991, failing which the ANC would consider the suspension of negotiations and engage in mass action and other actions.

The meeting also resolved to embark on mass campaigns to bring an end to the violence and to continue to recruit and train people for MK in order to defend 'our people' and prepare for integration into a new army. There was an undertaking that there was a need to build the underground to ensure the ANC did not suffer serious setbacks during this period. Meanwhile, the legend of Chris Hani was growing.

\* \* \*

In November 1990, journalist Shaun Johnson, writing for the *Saturday Star*, visited Transkei, and was struck by Hani's cult status among everyone he encountered. The SACP general secretary had become part of the graffiti, with the words, 'Viva Hani!' 'On the streets of Umtata (and especially among younger men),' wrote Johnson, 'the mention of Hani's name elicits a grin, a thumbs-up sign and, not infrequently, a loud impression of the sound of AK47 gunfire.' Hani had always been keen on working with homeland leaders and convincing them to be sympathetic to the cause of the ANC and the broader Mass Democratic Movement (MDM). In his pursuit of these alliances he had struck up an especially good rapport with Holomisa. Having deposed the oppressive regime of Kaiser Matanzima, Holomisa had rid the Xhosa homeland of a personal enemy of the Hani family. Beyond this, he showed a willingness to engage the movement and had even provided assistance in training MK personnel in Uganda.

When Hani's indemnity was revoked by Pretoria, Holomisa had met with Mandela and Sisulu and suggested they exploit the extradition treaty in place between the Transkei government and Pretoria, which was a cumbersome bureaucratic process. Hani drove from Johannesburg to Transkei and when he was safely in Umtata, Holomisa got a call from Foreign Minister Pik Botha. 'My friend,' said Botha, 'my president is very angry.' But Holomisa would have none of that. He told Botha that due process needed to be followed. 'Imagine that,' he huffed in the interview with us, 'a dictator lecturing a democrat?'

During his time in Transkei, Hani was permitted to address members of the Transkei Defence Force and police about their future in the SADF. Holomisa also granted an exemption to MK cadres on carrying weapons in execution of their duty of protecting Hani. 'Why Pretoria's verbal attacks on Hani, then?' asked Johnson of Holomisa at the time. Holomisa replied:

I think they're scared of him. I can understand that point of view, because to some of them, even cabinet ministers, it must be frightening to suddenly realise that yesterday you were planning to attack this person, now he must no longer be regarded as an enemy. They also had to make noises [about Hani] to satisfy a certain audience, to appease them.

At the time, Minister of Defence Magnus Malan – a former Chief of the SADF and a notorious proxy for De Klerk – dismissed Hani as 'some sort of secretary' in a war of words that carried on in the media for years.

In the meantime, on a broader consultative front, the negotiations between the ANC and NP government were creeping along. When they finally arrived at a resolution it would have far-reaching implications for MK.

\* \* \*

The Working Group created to iron out the details of the Pretoria Minute finally concluded their deliberations in February 1991, months after their deadline. With regard to MK, the group agreed that the democratic process obliged all political parties and movements to participate peacefully. It therefore accepted the principle that in a democratic society, no political party or movement should have a private army. It noted that the ANC had, in good faith and as a contribution to the process of arriving at a peaceful settlement, announced the suspension of all armed actions, with the presumption that the process would lead to a complete ceasefire. By virtue of the fact that Umkhonto we Sizwe was no longer an unlawful organisation, its cadres could parade their membership openly. A phased process would have to be initiated to enable the ex-combatants to begin to have normal lives. And then, there was the matter of the weapons. The parties would have to agree to legalise control over the arms.

Still, by early 1991, negotiations toward a democratic South Africa were going nowhere. The major obstacle at the outset of negotiations had been, and continued to be, about who would draft the new constitution. If it was something brokered between the NP government and major parties, it would surely prolong white rule and lead to power-sharing.

If it was opened to the masses of South Africa, it would be the death knell for minority rule.

Then, suddenly and without warning, De Klerk announced that his government would repeal all remaining apartheid laws. And it was this and the signing of the DF Malan Accord on 12 February that led to the continued release of political prisoners and the return of exiles.

The men who had spent years, decades even on Robben Island were itching to be released. The first few leaders had left towards the close of 1989, and were followed by others in a slow but steady procession. And then the tap was turned off. So, in February 1991, the political prisoners decided to embark on a hunger strike, dubbed 'Operation Go Home', to force the regime's hand and put pressure on the negotiating parties. The strike lasted 22 days before the wheels were finally set in motion.

MK veteran and lifelong cadre Zakes Molotsi explained to us how it worked. A number was called out. Then you would be led to the ticky box – the payphone – to call a loved one to let them know you were going to be released. Then, prisoners received a bundle of clothes, and the singing began. The exhilaration was almost uncontrollable. On 21 March 1991, a large crowd of prisoners was at the Robben Island dock. Three boats were moored in the harbour, waiting to take the passengers on one last trip across the bay to the mainland. Some of the prisoners had taken the trip before, usually for medical checkups or a visit to the dentist. For security reasons on those occasions, the prisoners were held below deck. But not today. Today the men were on deck, singing freedom songs, dancing, toyi-toyiing. Some cried as they approached Table Mountain.

As the men approached the dock, a familiar, beaming figure stood out among the small group waiting to welcome them to freedom. It was Chris Hani. For days after that, Hani and UDF leader Trevor Manuel visited the men at a rendezvous point where they were prepared for re-integration into society. The prisoners were released in time to take part in the ANC National Conference, held 2-6 July at the campus of the University of Durban-Westville, and the first to be held on South African soil in 32 years.

The occasion in itself was historic, but the conference would also pit two foremost champions from a new breed of leaders against each other and forever determine the direction the organisation would take as it stood on the brink of democracy. On the eve of the signing of the Harare Declaration in 1989, Tambo had suffered a massive stroke, which effectively prevented him from attending to his duties as ANC president with the vigour and resolve he had shown for close to 30 years. It was time to hand over the responsibilities of leadership, and it was obvious to the conference that ANC deputy president Mandela would take over from Tambo. Who would step into the position of the deputy president was a question that quickly became contentious after Thabo Mbeki made his availability known, prompting others to push Hani forward as a candidate for the same position.

The leadership was faced with a critical problem that could easily have divided the organisation. In Mbeki, they saw a consummate diplomat who had led many of the negotiations with the apartheid state up until then, and been instrumental in rallying much of the world behind the cause of the ANC. Nonetheless, so covert were many of the negotiations undertaken by Mbeki – even if these had been sanctioned by Tambo – that some in the organisation were taken aback at the pace of change, and viewed Mbeki with more than a little suspicion. Hani was the voice of those who believed the Nationalist overtures at parleying were nothing more than a gambit and could not be trusted. When the time came, the ANC would have to be ready, gun in hand, to embark on a new era of warfare.

When it came to voting for a new NEC, Hani proved to be the second most popular leader after Mandela, narrowly edging out Mbeki by 34 votes. With the election of the National Working Committee, the tables were turned, with Hani dislodged from the top spot by a single vote going the way of Mbeki. The impasse was resolved when Walter Sisulu, who had previously informed the leadership of his reluctance to serve, was convinced to take up the seat of deputy president. With such an auspicious personality vying for the job, all other takers took a step back, the young bulls returning to their pens.

In opening the meeting, and in his farewell address as president, Tambo said:

We did not tear ourselves apart because of lack of progress at times. We were always ready to accept our mistakes and to correct them. Above all we succeeded to foster and defend the unity of the ANC and the unity of our people in general. Even in bleak moments, we were never in doubt regarding the winning of freedom. We have never been in doubt that the people's cause shall triumph.

* * *

Two months earlier, the ANC had suspended negotiations with the Nationalists as waves of state-sponsored violence rocked the townships, often involving IFP members under the protection of the police. Part of the problem were the self-defence units (SDUs), which had been set up in the 1980s, at the behest of the ANC, to confront the regime's security forces. Originally consisting of community activists, these groups – armed with little more than knobkieries, rocks and petrol bombs – attacked those seen to be proxies of the state, such as policemen and councillors, and dug trenches to slow down the movement of security personnel in their areas.

According to activist Tsepe Motumi, youths later joined the SDUs, using them to wield power and influence. In township vernacular they were commonly referred to as 'com-tsotsis'. Hani was vocal about reverting to the original mandate of the SDUs and making them accountable to the community structures they were intended to serve. Instead, the SDUs became a tool in settling long-standing feuds between individuals, and in carving out areas of influence, along the lines of criminal gangs. This, Hani urged, could not continue.

The SACP leader took on many battles, and represented many interests – but only those in which he had a firm belief. When he returned to South Africa, one of the first places he visited was Death Row although by that time capital punishment had been suspended. Here, he would listen to the prisoners' concerns and their anxieties about negotiations, and he would often reprimand them on their behaviour, encouraging them to act like disciplined comrades. 'Your training is not for the battlefield. It is discipline to be applied at all times,' Hani encouraged.

In May 1991, he focused on the case of Robert McBride, who had been sentenced to death four years earlier for the car-bomb attack on the Magoo's and Why Not bars in Durban on 14 June 1986. The two bars were popular with members of the police, and the explosion claimed the lives of three white women. In 1988, in conversation with McBride's then-wife Paula, Hani spoke passionately of the need to save her husband from the gallows as he had not betrayed anyone. As Hani walked into the cells at Pretoria prison, the inmates greeted him with song, with some warders even joining in. Again, he was faced with the depth of human insecurity and disappointment as the prisoners, one after the other, complained of being left to rot as the parties held negotiations.

In December 1991, negotiations for a democratic South Africa finally started, when the first session of the Convention for a Democratic South Africa (CODESA) got under way at the World Trade Centre in Kempton Park. In the same month, at an altogether more important congress for Hani and those within the SACP, general secretary Joe Slovo stepped down as party leader after being diagnosed with bone marrow disease. But his successor had been anointed well before, and the election of Hani to the position as leader of the organisation was a fait accompli.

While CODESA was an attempt to bring all the relevant role-players into the fold, bilateral negotiations went on between the ANC and the NP government, to the dismay of the Conservative Party and the IFP in particular. In February, the ANC and PAC held anti-CODESA demonstrations, their prevailing argument being that the future of South Africa was being negotiated among a small elite.

The NP was also facing revolt from its otherwise tenacious constituents. Hints of this came strongly when it lost a by-election in Potchefstroom on 19 February 1992. The ruling party saw this as a sign of frustration and discontent from its supporters, prompting De Klerk to call a referendum to decide if he should continue negotiations. Former president PW Botha, the 'Great Crocodile', commented: 'I cannot participate in what I perceive as a direction of suicide for my own people.' Yet De Klerk promised to resign and lead his party in an election against the Conservative Party, which was still the official opposition, should the referendum return a No vote.

The referendum, held on 17 March 1992, showed that 68.7 percent of white South Africans supported De Klerk's reforms, prompting him to declare in the aftermath of his victory: 'Today we close the book on apartheid.' Armed with his mandate, the stalemate on power-sharing became more defined than ever before.

After months of deadlock and continued violence, the ANC broke off the negotiations. The catalyst was the Boipatong Massacre on 17 June 1992, in which nearly 50 people were killed. It was this kind of bloodshed that gave rise to a campaign of rolling mass action, starting on 16 June, to force the regime's hand. In the UN Security Council, Pretoria also drew criticism for its failure to deal with the incessant violence around the country. Part of the ANC's campaign was to work towards the dismantling of the homelands, areas to which they were being denied access to mobilise support. Ciskei, Bophuthatswana and KwaZulu would be the targets.

\* \* \*

Hani was marching at the front of the procession, arm-in-arm with Ronnie Kasrils and his old friend Steve Tshwete, representing the ANC's top leadership. Behind them, in the second row, followed the regional command structure. As always, Hani tried to keep the mood light, saying he was enjoying the exercise and that the whole event, the mood, reminded him of the old days.

On the morning of 7 September, close to 80 000 people had gathered at Victoria Stadium in King William's Town. For weeks, people had been roused and rallied in villages dotted throughout the Ciskeian homeland. The night before, members of the alliance – the ANC, SACP and

COSATU – had gathered in King William's Town to make the final preparations for a mass march to Bisho. Late that evening, Ciskei homeland leader Oupa Gqozo filed an urgent interdict at the Bisho Supreme Court, trying to stop the march from happening. The matter was referred back to Zwelitsha Magistrate's Court which affirmed the right of the alliance to march to the Bisho Stadium.

Bantu Holomisa sets the context, his view being that in the months leading up to that September, relations had soured with the ANC in Ciskei, as some members of the party had started to incite villagers against the age-old headman system. In Transkei, there had been similar complaints:

After Oupa Gqozo had taken control of Ciskei [in 1990], he had created a political space for the liberation organisations, but now it was like a Coca-Cola bottle that had been shaken up. People throughout the villages were wearing ANC T-shirts and toyi-toyiing in an expression of suppressed political activity.

Headmen had then approached the Ciskei government, also my government, complaining of this unruly behaviour, and this was around the time Hani had arrived in Umtata.

Holomisa says he implored the MK leader to speak to the people, and made a helicopter available to him for this purpose:

Really, he did a very good job for Transkei. The trick worked as Hani persuaded his colleagues to act in a disciplined fashion. The agreement between the ANC and Transkei was that discipline must be the order of the day, meaning that the bantustans should not be used as a springboard to launch attacks against the apartheid regime.

Both of us understood that the Transkei Defence Force would quickly crumble in the face of Pretoria's military might.

But across the border in Ciskei, things were quite different. Relations between Gqozo and the ANC were all but shattered. The ANC was encouraging political activity and resistance, and the march grew out of that.

Leaving King William's Town, the march swelled to an enormous crowd. Instructed as to the order of the protest action, the marchers set forth at 11am, heading for the Ciskei border. An hour and a half later, they met South African troops and homeland soldiers, who were deployed along the border. Although the enemy portrayed the crowd as a mob, in fact the people were as organised as possible – and calm. It was the regime's soldiers who adopted an aggressive posture. Rolls of razor wire laced the border. Soon the phalanx of soldiers was herding the massive crowd down the road towards Bisho Stadium. But only part of the crowd was able to enter the stadium, which was fenced in. Spotting an opening in the fence, the rest of the marchers, led by Kasrils, moved towards the gap, toyi-toyiing closer and closer to the edgy Ciskei Defence Force soldiers.

'At first I thought they were releasing firecrackers. But some comrades around me were on the ground screaming,' said one of the marchers. 'People started running, screaming. Some shouted that everybody should fall to the ground.' Bususiwe Dingaan-Stofile, regional leader of the SACP, recalled how people started running towards Hani. 'They wanted to protect him but he was asking them to lie down.'

Immediately, word spread that the soldiers had shot Hani. Panic gave way to anger. Hani had to move around the massive crowd to reassure them, and as he moved, everybody else followed, fearing that the next volley of shots might strike down their charismatic leader.

'Today I have seen the Pied Piper of Hamelin because I seem to be one,' he joked. But tragedy was imminent. Four minutes of machine-gun fire left 28 people dead and more than 200 injured.

Dingaan-Stofile described the scene as nightfall approached:

When it was becoming dark, a decision had to be taken as to what was to happen that night. The people were worried that more people might die. The national and regional leadership met. I was one of the people who felt that we must stay because at least we have achieved something that we were still there – even though [Oupa] Gqozo had said we won't set foot there.

But on the other hand, we had lost because some of us were no more. Comrade Tokyo Sexwale was angry with this perspective saying we must avoid more bloodshed. Comrade Ronnie Kasrils wanted to know why we wanted to desert those who marched with us to Bisho by leaving their spirits alone. We had to get Comrade Chris's version, [and he] simply reminded us of the objective and the programme of the march, which included sleeping over at Bisho.

We unanimously agreed to stay till the following day, but those who were not allowed to come over by the SADF, we agreed that they must stay at the Victoria Stadium. While we were there, the SADF arrived in huge numbers and their objective was to disperse us because they said we were holding an illegal gathering. When they arrived, some people were terrified but when Comrade Chris started a freedom song, we all forgot about the SADF and chanted.

As the night settled, the scene shifted. The lights went on, some people sat, while others lay down. Most were exhausted. Fears that the crowd might become discouraged began to subside, and after a while, the soldiers and the masses reached equilibrium. The army remained on guard. The people sang, almost through the night. Fires were lit, and Hani never stopped mobilising and mustering morale. Kasrils joined him, walking through the crowds. Walking, stopping, talking.

At 5am, said the regional command, the people were woken with a rousing revolutionary song. By mid-morning, the marchers had drifted into a mournful kind of peace. But the fallout would be dramatic. Faced with a massive amount of international pressure fuelled largely by media images, De Klerk would appoint eminent judge, Richard Goldstone, to investigate the events of that day, with the subsequent commission condemning the callous actions of Gqoza, for refusing to allow the march to go ahead, and his defence force for their fatal behaviour on the day. Kasrils would also be strongly criticised for irresponsibly leading a group through the gap in the razor-wire fence with the behaviour of other senior ANC figures present on the day also being strongly condemned for placing people's lives in danger. Ironically, the Bisho Massacre finally led to a resumption of talks, three months after the agony of Boipatong.

CHAPTER 12

# THE ASSASSINATION

Janusz Walus waited for Hani at a hotel one afternoon, days before he became an assassin. Or so the story of a rehearsal goes. It was late summer, around the end of March, a time when highveld rains and white skies lashed by lightning create an eloquent drama. Walus – tall, lean, blond, austere – was an inconsequential figure. Or so it seemed. When he took up his position in the foyer of the Johannesburg Sun, he was probably carrying only his car keys, wallet, and – according to descriptions – a small bag, compact but sufficient to conceal a weapon. But this was just for practice. It was not the first time a hotel had been used as a rendezvous for a hitman seeking out Hani. In the 1980s in Gaborone, Hani was once confronted by a man reported to have been a British hired gun. Memory has it that Hani drew his own weapon in response.

Walus may have wanted to size up the man he was going to kill, to understand his presence – how tall he was, how strong, how formidable. And if the continuity of events was true, by that afternoon at the hotel, Walus and Clive Derby-Lewis, formerly an MP and then member of the President's Council, had already discussed the means, the target and the rationale.

In court, their defence would suggest that they had hoped national grief would emanate out of the assassination of Hani, that this would extend into violence, that the violence would rupture into anarchy, and the anarchy into a political miasma out of which the CP – which had narrowly lost the last election to the NP in 1989 – could again rise, seize power through an embittered military, and destroy the communist threat it so desperately feared.

There was no doubt the party they supported, the CP, had been in the ascendant, reflecting the self-deceptive mood of a white nation. The NP itself later admitted that the last election in which both had participated had been bitterly tight. Three years later, in 1992, the CP said it was driven to war talk – and apocalyptic propaganda – after the referendum that gave President FW de Klerk plenipotentiary powers to hold talks with the ANC and other liberation movements. This was anathema. This was an omen. But on that afternoon, Walus did not yet have the weapon. That would come a few days later.

Hani had never become inured to the enemies gathering around him, their shadows a subliminal force in his life. Even when he was seemingly at his most powerful, back home from exile, growing daily in stature, he was at his most insecure. 'Some people they've recruited, some comrades have come to me to say the security forces don't want to kill me in an ordinary way,' he revealed to American journalist Jerelyn Eddings just days before the reported encounter with Walus in the hotel lobby. 'They'd like to kill me so that it would appear as an accident,' Hani said. Then, with the prescience of a man who had lived with death all his life, he spoke his most prophetic words: 'I think they are calculating that if they kill me, the whole country might go up in flames.'

When the former MK chief of staff appeared in the lobby of the Johannesburg Sun with a small entourage, including his bodyguards, he was exhausted. Hani had been caught up for weeks, if not months, in a relentless peace tour for the ANC, the son of the village having only just returned from his beloved Sabalele. He had been campaigning abroad for the SACP too, most recently in Cuba, keeping company with Fidel Castro, and then in Britain, where the Anti-Apartheid Movement and British communists clamoured for his approval.

## THE ASSASSINATION

At 51, Hani was still young enough to represent a coming generation of socialists. Although he never seemed to show his age, he was certainly feeling older, experiencing deeply the psychic strain of his own mortality. More than once, he confided in friends that he felt his life was fragile. He was becoming worryingly introspective and increasingly philosophical about it. He made some tenuous demands about what he wanted for his own life. Surrounded by comrades, he expressed a longing to be alone with ordinary people.

At the ANC headquarters in Shell House, barriers were in place. The ordinary people couldn't reach him, they were not allowed to get close to him, as he was rightly regarded as a security risk. Yet Hani craved interaction with people, as he had done with the cadres in the camps when he was commissar and chief of staff. He could never quite understand why he was so important that he had to be cosseted and buffered.

But there was no time for contemplation. Just days before Walus stepped out of a red Ford Laser in Hakea Crescent and took aim at his target, Hani had delivered a final clarion call for peace. He chose the battered East Rand, where he addressed a restless, adoring crowd. His subject was one that had become a kind of crusade for him: the need for discipline and a calm purpose on the part of self-defence units (SDUs). Hani was troubled by these structures; he had felt their incipient power in the 1980s, when the reach for ungovernability was yoked to the highest cause. But these structures could also be subverted and used for criminal activity, and he believed the SDUs should account to their communities. People were dying, with infighting tearing communities apart. He urged, encouraged, insisted, cajoled, and his words rang as clear as ever, even into the year after his death when the East Rand was aflame.

This was the way Hani showed his leadership. Before HIV/Aids became the next struggle, he was already urging education, treatment and support. While many of those around him were contesting for influence within a future army, he was rallying for a stronger police force. He spoke about wanting to be part of an anti-corruption forum – and he warned about the lure of the gravy train.

Meanwhile, family life was but a delicate flutter on the periphery, an elusive promise of loveliness in the embrace of his three daughters. Even when he knew he had to be with them, Hani found himself surrounded. From those trapped in the rancorous violence of the Natal Midlands to the loneliest villagers, marginal in their poverty, everyone clamoured for his presence.

As negotiations between Pretoria and the liberation movements all but crumbled, Hani vowed to keep the centre that would not hold. Yet privately, those closest to him had an understanding that his need to intensify the role of the SACP, and to entrench socialism in communities wherever he went, was beginning to dominate his engagement. The revolutionary consciousness was not enough. Slogans were shallow. Only true mobilisation to roll back poverty could lead to the complete political transformation that the country needed. Nearly two decades later, Hani's voice on this is as loud as ever. It echoes, but the echo may be too late.

\* \* \*

Since Walus knew he was going to kill Hani – whether the next day or the next week, when the moment was right – the minutes in that hotel lobby were less an intimate reconnaissance than a denouement. Hani was to face death a final time. Before the arrival of the SACP general secretary that day, one can imagine Walus sitting alert on a couch as guests socialised in the bar.

The hotel was a privileged enclave, but had quickly earned the heightened atmosphere of the suddenly unforbidden. Into this milieu, Hani's familiar smile would have been an endorsement, an assurance of solidarity. Yet, no matter how many people recognised him, few were privy to the private gaze behind his sunglasses. He had become comfortable in loose, open-necked shirts, insisting on projecting a relaxed, open persona. Yet he missed the sensation, the security, of his Makarov pistol at his waist. The apartheid state preferred that neither he nor his bodyguards be given licences for guns. At the same time, Hani's protection was not considered a priority by the police force. Ironically, where Hani's bodyguards would surely have followed the line that they had to remain unarmed, with their party concerned to stay true to its decision to talk to Pretoria, Walus was able to obtain an illegal weapon.

It's likely that when Walus saw Hani, he would have thought the Communist Party leader taller and broader than he had imagined, as most people did on meeting Hani for the first time. Although he was not particularly tall, Hani's physical presence took most people by surprise, as had that of Nelson Mandela when he emerged from Victor Verster Prison just three years earlier. Like Mandela, Hani insisted on remaining fit and strong, no matter the circumstances. The only time anyone could recall Hani losing his physique was when he spent extended periods in the USSR in the chill of winter. He would put on weight then, sometimes surprising those who hadn't seen him for a while, and would joke about eating too many potatoes and not being able to run in the snow. Where Mandela exercised strenuously, Hani ran almost every day. In the months before his death, he was said to have started a more rigorous fitness routine, twice a day. But Hani's life was accelerating almost out of his control in the weeks before his death. So the run, the harmonious balance of time and need, was not always possible. He regretted it.

The wiry Walus, who prided himself on his practice of martial arts and marksmanship, apparently stepped right up to Hani in the hotel. Hani's bodyguards, primed by several recent death threats, immediately edged closer. It was unimaginable, too difficult, to protect someone so hated by so few, but with the few being so dangerous.

Walus's menacing appearance came partly out of a crystal-coloured gaze that was curiously vacant. Nonetheless, Hani would probably have readily extended his hand to his murderer who, it was said, had pretended to be a journalist on that afternoon. And then the moment was over, apparently a few seconds of curiosity. But the bodyguards were shaken, and were reportedly devastated when they saw photographs of Walus in the media in the weeks after the murder.

Journalist Amrit Manga, who revealed the astonishing events at the Johannesburg Sun in the newspaper *Sunday Nation* six months after Hani died, speculated that it was 'no chance meeting'. Just as Hani had suspected, his movements were being monitored. A surveillance operation was in place.

Within a couple of weeks, Walus would finally pull the trigger of the stolen 9mm pistol, not at targets on his brother Vitold's plot outside Pretoria – as he was said to have done in the days before the assassination – but at the real thing. The flesh and blood. He would shoot Hani at least four times with the ice-cold terror of total belief. There was a seething darkness in his mission, so pitiless in its intention that Joe Slovo was compelled to describe Walus and Derby-Lewis as cavemen, 'the savages of our land'.

* * *

On 7 November 1994, the state heard case number 586/93 in the appellate division of the Supreme Court of South Africa. Accused Number One Janusz Jacub Walus and Accused Number Two Clive Derby-Lewis had been sentenced to death the previous year in a sensational trial that had thrown up intense emotions in South Africans everywhere.

The appeal began with a redrawing of events as these had unfolded at the original trial when Walus and Derby-Lewis had been charged jointly with Derby-Lewis's wife, Gaye Derby-Lewis, for four crimes. Count one was the murder of Martin Tembisile Hani. Count two was a contravention of section 18(2) (a) of the Riotous Assemblies Act 17 of 1956 by conspiring to murder nine people – including Hani – whose names had appeared on a list found in Walus's flat in Pretoria. Count three was a contravention of section 1 of the Arms and Ammunition Act 75 of 1969 of the unlawful possession of a 9mm Z88 pistol. Count four was a contravention of section 36 of the Arms and Ammunition Act 75 of 1969 of the unlawful possession of five rounds of 9mm ammunition.

The co-accused had pleaded not guilty on all counts, with each

## THE ASSASSINATION

represented by their own counsel. At the close, Walus had not given evidence. Neither had Derby-Lewis, although he had called two others to testify on his behalf: a long-standing friend of Walus's, and a ballistics expert. Gaye Derby-Lewis testified for herself.

By the end of the trial, Gaye Derby-Lewis had been acquitted on all counts. Walus and Clive Derby-Lewis were acquitted on the alleged conspiracy to murder nine people, and Walus was acquitted on the illegal possession of the ammunition – a charge for which Clive Derby-Lewis was found guilty. But, for the rest, the trial court recorded unanimous guilty verdicts for Hani's murder and the illegal possession of the Z88 pistol. Sentences were imposed for each conviction. For the unlawful possession of the gun, Walus was sentenced to five years. For the same crime as well as possession of the ammunition, Clive Derby-Lewis was sentenced to five years in jail. For the assassination of Chris Hani, both were sentenced to death.

Walus decided to appeal only against the death sentence, while Derby-Lewis wanted to appeal against his conviction for murder and the death sentence, and against the five years' imprisonment for possession of the weapon and the ammunition.

The description of the play of events at times resembled a movie script, the props including two cars – Hani's white Toyota and a red Ford Laser hatchback, registration PBX 231T, driven by Walus. The court document sets the scene:

Immediately after the shooting, the deceased's attacker got into the red Ford and started reversing out of the driveway. The shooting of the deceased and the imminent departure of his attacker were observed by a passing motorist, Mrs MJ Harmse. In a remarkable display of self-possession Mrs Harmse stopped her own car and reversed it far enough to obtain a closer view of the red Ford's registration number.

Trying to memorise the registration number, she drove at once to her nearby home from where she telephoned the flying squad. She gave the red Ford's registration number as PBX 237T. In the event, her information to the police proved to be sufficient. Armed with Mrs Harmse's description of the assassin's vehicle, two policemen in a patrol car were able, within minutes of the killing and in a locality some 6 kilometres distant from the deceased's home, to spot the red Ford and to make it pull over and stop by the roadside.

Retha Harmse was hailed as a hero on the night of Hani's death in Nelson Mandela's statesmanlike speech, which sought to quell the fury pulsing through the nation. But not long after the assassination, Harmse and her family admitted they were selling up in Dawn Park. The pressure from the white right was too frightening. They said they were the victims of racist invective, and were receiving death threats. Retha appeared to be traumatised, spiritually damaged by what she had seen.

Retha's husband Daan said at the time: 'I am angry. Retha did the right thing. She did what any normal person would do.' Magda Smith, a neighbour who waved good morning to Hani every day on which he ran past her family's neat corner home, told us she was not sure where the Harmses were, anymore. Perhaps they had gone overseas and stayed there? Perhaps they had moved to Kempton Park? Perhaps Cape Town?

Three years after his appeal failed, Walus finally revealed some of the anguish of Hani's final moments. His testimony came before the TRC after the commission had presented the impossible glimpse of an eleventh-hour reprieve from imprisonment. Freedom, such a privilege, was clearly too tantalising for a killer to ignore. Both the trial and appeal courts and the commission heard Walus's biography: a life's summary of a banal, embittered white reactionary.

\* \* \*

When he killed Hani, Walus was 38 years old. An immigrant from Poland, he had made a life for himself in South Africa over 10 years – and he was not doing badly. He still had business activity in the homeland of Qwa Qwa, where the apartheid government had once allowed significant concessions to white immigrants, especially those who fled Eastern Europe.

The *Sunday Times* reported that, at one time, when the Walus family were living in Qwa Qwa together running a glass-cutting business, their turnover was more than R1.5 million a year – a huge sum for the time. They lived in an affluent area there, and Walus's father Tadeusz owned a luxury home in upper-class Waterkloof, Pretoria, and had another factory in Harrismith.

It was in 1989 that things fell apart. Walus's father blamed this on the politics of Pretoria, which had decided to unravel the homeland system, and was cutting back on loans to foreigners. The game was over. The father went home to a Poland in economic free-fall, but his sons remained in South Africa. Janusz worked for a transport company, and had a fixed address – a flat in Pretoria. He had few friends, but he had a lover, Maria Ras, in the capital city, and a wife called Wanda and a daughter named Ewa living in the city of Radom in Poland. When Walus killed Hani, Ewa was the same age as Hani's middle daughter, Nomakhwezi.

Walus's interests were primarily in right-wing activity and Shokotan karate. He did not appear particularly intelligent, and was disturbingly deadpan about his childhood pain: the wrench of being forced to live in a particular way because of a ruling ideology. Few believed him. Few sympathised. The appeal court reiterated:

According to the defence's evidence, the appellant found the yoke of communist rule in Poland intolerable. He and his family suffered much deprivation and frustration. It was in order to escape from the rigours of life under a communist regime that the first appellant settled in South Africa which he saw at the time as a political haven.

He became a South African citizen. His political views were strongly rightist. The political changes in South Africa heralded in February 1990, and thereafter put into effect, appalled the first appellant and outraged his staunch anti-communist sentiments. He was friendly with his two co-accused. In the course of her evidence, Mrs Derby-Lewis told the court that the first appellant did not have many friends; and that she and her husband 'were probably his closest friends'. They called him by the familiar name of 'Kuba'.

By the end of the doomed process – a trial, an appeal and a plea for amnesty at the TRC – the Derby-Lewises had denigrated their former friend. His loneliness, a corollary to the openness to infamy, was exposed, while Clive Derby-Lewis's wide popular network of support was elevated. As it happens, neither image was quite correct. But certainly, Derby-Lewis had gained some influence within the far right. Ex-NP member of the Transvaal Provincial Council and member of the General Council of the CP since 1982, he became a CP MP in 1987, two years later being nominated to the President's Council.

When he was arrested for murder, he was still a member of the council, which was collapsed soon after Hani's killing. Derby-Lewis was nearly 20 years older than the man with whom he elected to collaborate. On the surface of it, the 57-year-old with the comical moustache lived a peculiar life attempting to adjust his insufferable Englishness to a penchant for Afrikaner supremacy, such as that practised by the white right-wingers within the CP and on the fringes of white society. Derby-Lewis shared a home in Acacia Park, Krugersdorp, with his wife – an Australian former nun and ex-gay club owner – who was the editor of the English section of the racist weekly newspaper *Die Patriot* and the press officer for the CP.

Lawyer George Bizos, who confronted Gaye Derby-Lewis at the TRC hearings where he represented the Hani family, told us, 'she was smart, she was the brains, and I detested her'. This was no straightforward murder case. This was war – and it was profoundly personal. Hani's beloved 15-year-old daughter Nomakhwezi had been present when the gunshots rang out. 'Hey daddy, he's greeting you,' the *Sunday Star* of 11 April reported her as having said when she saw Walus approaching. These words cut to the bone, although later there was hesitation about what had really happened. Nonetheless, the country wept.

Later on, after her father's killers were sentenced to death, Nomakhwezi said in an interview that she felt she was robbed. 'I miss him very much. Some days I feel he has just gone overseas and one day he will come back. And some days you tend to believe he is gone, but I have not accepted that he is dead.'

Her younger sister, Lindiwe, said in the same interview in the *Sunday Star* that she couldn't understand why Walus had to come all the way to South Africa to kill one black communist. 'I am sure it makes no difference at all to him, but to me, it's a world of difference.'

'I am a Catholic,' said Nomakhwezi, 'and I believe there is a God, and He is supposed to be powerful enough to protect good people. It puzzles me that God did not stop these killers. My dad did nothing wrong to anyone, but God took him away. His crime was that he cared for people.'

\* \* \*

On the morning of 10 April, Walus set out from leafy Muckleneuk, in the shadow of the Union Buildings. The Shokotan karate enthusiast claimed he was heading for the Stan Schmidt Centre in the vicinity of Bramley, Johannesburg, but found it closed as it was Easter Saturday. So he drove on to the Gun Exchange in Corlett Drive nearby, emerging with 25 rounds of 9mm subsonic ammunition.

He said that the morning's journey had been planned to take a final look around the Hani home, which was situated on a gentle curve where few other houses were in view of its secluded driveway. But, as he pulled up close to the house he now knew so well, Walus saw that Hani was leaving home. On impulse, Walus said, he followed him. Whether by coincidence or design, Hani was without his bodyguards. The air was fresh, the morning still. It was a holiday and few people were around. On his tail, Walus saw that Hani wasn't going far, mere blocks away to the local strip mall. So when he saw that Hani had stepped into a café, probably to buy the newspaper, Walus realised he did not have much time if he was finally going to do it.

'At that moment I decided it would be the best opportunity to execute my task and that this opportunity would never be repeated,' Walus admitted. 'I decided not to do it in the shopping centre because there were a lot of people.' Walus quickly veered off on a different route back to Hakea Crescent so that he would arrive just before Hani returned in his Toyota sedan. A former rally driver, Walus got to the house only a couple of minutes before Hani. He quickly pulled on his gloves, and armed himself. He was ready:

I put the pistol in the belt of my trousers behind my back. Seeing Mr Hani move away from the car I did not want to shoot him in the back. I called to Mr Hani. When he turned I … fired the first shot into his body. As he turned and fell down, I fired a second shot at his head.

Nomakhwezi's gaze had fallen immediately on the terrible scene, at the same time as Retha Harmse, who was driving past slowly in her car. By the time the two realised what was happening, seconds after Walus took aim, it was already too late. It was over.

Nomakhwezi had longed desperately for this time alone with her father. When he had fetched her in Lesotho on the previous Thursday, leaving her mother and sisters behind, they had planned to spend the weekend together; he would be all hers.

Now she began to scream as Walus walked, with an eerily confident stride, straight back to his car. Retha Harmse drove off as quickly as possible, pulled into her driveway and rushed inside for the telephone. Walus got into his car and pulled away, as silently as he had arrived.

Nomakhwezi ran into the road, screaming louder. The neighbours quickly began to make sense of the heartbreaking sound, and as they started to filter into their gardens and driveways, Hani's bewildered, terrified daughter headed in the direction of the home of Noxolo Grootboom, a TV journalist, who was in her kitchen. Grootboom flew outside and threw her arms around the child, holding her tightly, trying to calm her down. What was going on? What had happened? Where was her daddy?

The *Sunday Star* reported Nomakhwezi's words: 'They shot my daddy. I saw it. It was a white man … my mommy is not here.'

Since no one had heard the shots – Walus having used subsonic ammunition – there was confusion initially. But it didn't take long for people

# THE ASSASSINATION

to realise what had caused Nomakhwezi's desperate sobbing.

As the neighbours rushed to the house, they saw Hani, lying in a thick pool of his own blood in the driveway. And so the wailing started there in the crowd gathering on the neat paving of the house in the small suburb. By evening, grief had overcome the nation. Chris Hani was dead.

\* \* \*

'What child should witness such a barbaric crime?' Nomakhwezi confided in a private piece, which was read out for the first time at her own funeral, by her younger sister, Lindiwe. Nomakhwezi died, apparently from an asthma attack, in 2001. Tokyo Sexwale was one of the first people called to the scene after her death at a friend's house, just as he had been after her father was murdered. Sexwale says he found Nomakhwezi with a blanket covering her, resting in exactly the same position that her father had been in after he was killed. 'Her right hand was under her face and her other hand was on her side, as though she was trying to clutch something.'

'I want to be with him just one more time,' wrote Nomakhwezi, who was confronted with her father's killer again when the murder trial began at the Rand Supreme Court in Johannesburg, and again at the TRC, when ANC supporters danced around Walus and Derby-Lewis, taunting and booing, and hissing at them outside the hearing chambers at the Benoni town hall.

\* \* \*

Blood spattered on Walus's clothing and gunpowder on his gloves worked to damn him, but there was plenty more evidence. Walus had been alone in the red Ford when the police boxed him in. He stopped the car and sat still behind the wheel, his hands in his lap. On the back seat of the car was a carry-bag, perhaps the same one as he had been holding when he had approached Hani at the Johannesburg Sun. Inside the carry-bag was the

Z88 pistol. Just behind Walus's seat was a silencer. The police immediately took him into custody, and kept the red Ford under police guard. The next day, police found a bag in the car containing self-adhesive plastic letters and numbers that could be superimposed on registration plates. This was not the purchase of a man who killed on a whim. Walus knew he was going to do it when he did. He knew how.

'There has been widespread condemnation at the assassination of the general secretary of the SACP, Chris Hani,' reported André Jordaan for SABC radio in bulletins that grew ever more agonising as the day wore on. 'The news that he was gunned down in the driveway of his Dawn Park home on the East Rand shortly after 10am was greeted with grief and shock.' Every broadcast featured the words of South African Police Brigadier Frans Malherbe, who was the first person to officially confirm the assassination, saying: 'I am unfortunate to announce that Mr Hani died instantly.'

Malherbe's words reflected the profound human grief expressed by Tokyo Sexwale. The former Robben Islander had not known Hani long, but knew him well enough to weep. 'There is a time to cry,' he said, standing in the road outside the Hani house. 'I saw Chris Hani dead … in the driveway next to his car, his body lay.' Without hesitation, Sexwale warned: 'He was a revolutionary, and the hand that pulled the trigger was merely a hand.' Then, television agencies captured Sexwale as he began to sob, his voice faltering even as he was determined to tell the world Hani's message. 'People wanted all the time an image of chief of staff to remain on him so he would be a man of war, but Chris stood for peace.'

With South Africa very much in the international news at the time, word of the killing quickly resounded throughout the world. Connie Lawn reported from Washington for the SABC: 'The Americans view this as a grave event not likely to be passed in a few days. It has made front-page news in every American newspaper and the hope is that terrorism will galvanise the parties towards peace.' She said that US President Bill Clinton had taken 'a personal interest in the matter'.

From London, Keith Chortley spoke to the ANC's representative,

Denis Goldberg, who said the killing was a big shock for De Klerk, and that 'every political leader would have thought: "My God, it could have been me." This was a man whose greatness, true greatness, was still to come,' said the former Rivonia trialist. Chortley reported that prayers were being said in churches all over Britain.

At the scene, ANC spokesperson Gill Marcus pleaded with the media to show some dignity as photographers jostled for position, some on tiptoe, around the pool of blood in which Hani lay. Not long afterwards, Oliver Tambo – ailing, unable to speak – arrived. There was absolute silence as he stepped out of a limousine, in a bright, silky, red-patterned neckerchief, and strode as boldly as possible down the guard of honour towards the mortuary van to see Hani before his body was taken away. Tambo's wife, Adelaide, could only take a glance before she burst into tears, and was comforted by Walter Sisulu.

'*Hamba kahle Umkhonto, Umkhonto, Umkhonto we Sizwe*.' The chant wafted across the horrified gathering. 'We heard it,' Racheal Lerutla, who was living nearby, recalled to us. 'Everybody was running. Everybody was emotional. Everybody was crying. You could see it had struck everybody. Nobody was speaking to anybody. People were in a state of shock. It was a spontaneous reaction.'

\* \* \*

How much did Gaye Derby-Lewis know, during the first three months of 1993, about her husband's plan to kill Hani? Life went on, she said, dismissively. Yet Clive Derby-Lewis must have had many conversations with strangers, or in secret, in their Acacia Park home – circumstances that would have attracted the attention of a wife.

In a crucial prelude to the catastrophe, her husband had taken the trouble to source an unlicensed firearm, part of a cache stolen in April 1990 from the South African Air Force armoury in Pretoria by rightwing rebel leader Piet 'Skiet' Rudolph. On 10 March 1991 – exactly a month before Hani died – Clive Derby-Lewis met with right-winger

Faan Venter, who also lived in Krugersdorp, at the Derby-Lewis home. At that meeting, which was recalled for the TRC in 1997, Venter said Derby-Lewis had asked him if he could get hold of a firearm, preferably an unlicensed one. His reply to Derby-Lewis was that 'we are stocking up' – this, Venter claimed, meant that guns were being gathered for 'the battle that lay ahead'. Venter was already in possession of a 9mm pistol, which had been given to him by a friend he named as Gene Taylor – a right-winger who was in detention at the time in connection with the theft of the weapons cache.

SAPA reported after the TRC hearing that Venter had admitted the gun he gave to Derby-Lewis 'was stolen from the defence force', and that while he had kept it in his house, he did not really want it 'as I already had a firearm – it was a nuisance'. Derby-Lewis asked him to deliver the pistol to the Krugersdorp home of another right-winger, Lionel du Rant. The understanding, according to Du Rant, was that the parcel contained a pullover for Derby-Lewis, so when Venter arrived with the gun hidden inside the parcel, Du Rant was not surprised. At Derby-Lewis and Walus's trial, Venter, Du Rant and his wife Elizabeth appeared as witnesses for the prosecution. Although Venter had told Elizabeth Du Rant that the pullover belonged to Derby-Lewis, she was curious enough to open the parcel, and found a gun in a plastic bag. She immediately rewrapped the pullover to make it look just as it had when Venter delivered it, and took it to Derby-Lewis at his house the next day. Bizos would comment: 'We will submit that you know much more than what you are prepared to admit.'

Two more men, both Capetonians, entered the picture around 22 March. Derby-Lewis approached one Keith Darroll to get a silencer fitted to the Z88. Darroll took the stolen gun to one Gavin Smith, who ran a gunsmithery from his home in Tokai, and it was Smith who fitted the silencer, returning the firearm to Darroll with the silencer and a cap that could be screwed onto the muzzle. Smith also supplied Darroll with five rounds of subsonic 9mm ammunition. The gun and its deadly accoutrements were delivered to Derby-Lewis in Acacia Park in late March.

Smith testified that he had fitted a silencer to a Z88 pistol only once in his entire career and that the weapon used to kill Hani was that pistol. He recognised the silencer as being of his own making and he told the court at Derby-Lewis's trial that he had machined the barrel of the Z88 in a particular way so that the metal cap, which he had also made and modified, could be screwed onto the muzzle. Smith's testimony was damning. So were the words of state witness Elizabeth Motswane, who had worked as a domestic worker for the Derby-Lewises for five years.

Motswane said Walus was known as 'Kuba' in the household. When she arrived at work at about 8am on 6 April, she was not surprised to see Walus sitting in the kitchen with Gaye Derby-Lewis, who was making breakfast. Walus then had breakfast with the Derby-Lewises, and after that, Gaye Derby-Lewis left in her car. Motswane started washing up, and Walus and Clive Derby-Lewis moved into the lounge, but Motswane was interrupted soon after by Derby-Lewis who said she had a phone call.

On her way to the phone, Motswane saw a strange and chilling scene. 'I saw accused number one [Walus] holding a gun downwards on the lounge table,' Motswane testified to the Supreme Court. And although Derby-Lewis's counsel, Hennie de Vos, tried to refute, or at least diminish Motswane's testimony, he did not succeed. Derby-Lewis claimed the woman, who had worked for him for several years, could not have seen anything inside the sitting-room as the phone was kept in the study. Motswane quietly disputed this. The phone was, in fact, kept on a long cord, and the Derby-Lewises generally left it in the passage – right at the entrance to the lounge. So she would have had a clear view of the interior of the lounge. Motswane told the court that Walus and Derby-Lewis had a table between them, and there was a briefcase on the floor. She believed she saw Walus holding a firearm with its butt in his hand and with its barrel pointing to the floor.

On Easter Saturday, a few days after the rendezvous described by Motswane, Clive and Gaye Derby-Lewis had arranged to have tea and apple tart at 10am at the home of Faan and Maureen Venter. Just before

11am, as the Derby-Lewises were preparing to leave, the phone rang. Maureen Venter answered, and Gaye Derby-Lewis said she heard her say: '*Chris Hani is doodgeskiet.*' It was the Venters' son on the the line, and he had just heard the news on the radio. Hani had not yet been dead for two hours.

Whether Faan Venter made any connection at that moment with the memory of the gun he had procured so recently for Derby-Lewis is unknown. Whether he and Derby-Lewis even traded glances can only be imagined. But Maureen Venter later told the TRC that Clive Derby-Lewis did not display 'any noticeable reaction', although, in a statement to the police soon after Hani's death, she indicated that Derby-Lewis had looked 'extremely surprised'.

Had Gaye Derby-Lewis's husband not been one of the killers, the behaviour of the pair following the phone call would probably have seemed rather normal for conservative white South Africans – unmoved, untouched by the tragedy. Gaye Derby-Lewis couldn't remember exactly how she and her husband spent the rest of that Easter Saturday, only that they had shopped and eaten lunch at home. Later, at around 3pm, the pair had gone canvassing for the upcoming Krugersdorp by-election, which Clive Derby-Lewis hoped to contest. No one could have known what was going on inside Clive Derby-Lewis's head, convinced as he was about what Walus would do.

Walus, meanwhile, was undergoing a relentless interrogation. He later claimed he was conned into believing his interrogators were on his side – that they, too, feared Hani's influence and hated communism, but that they were only doing their jobs. Within just a few hours, Walus gave police the name of his mentor, Derby-Lewis.

\* \* \*

An hour's flight and a two-hour drive away, in Qunu, Transkei, Nelson Mandela had been hoping to spend a rare, quiet Easter weekend with his family. Now, suddenly, there was utter despair and desperate tears.

Mandela and Hani had become close – not like father and son, as it had been for Hani with Govan Mbeki and even Oliver Tambo. Rather, they were true comrades. Mandela had an urgent need to connect with a younger generation, to know what they were experiencing and what they expected from their ANC. Hani provided that critical wisdom. Rumours about the closeness between Winnie Mandela and Hani were quickly refuted.

For Hani, the relationship with Mandela was born out of impassioned loyalty and admiration. The Robben Island leadership had always been as important as that based in Lusaka. It was always consulted on major decisions, considered in everything – despite the long delays in receiving replies and answers. Without Mandela, there was no Tambo. So Hani knew the honour he had been given was true. On the day Hani was assassinated, Mandela's emotion was already close to the surface by the time he called Bantu Holomisa. When Holomisa took Mandela's call, it had already been a long day. He had just arrived back in Umtata by chartered jet, after honouring Mandela's request to represent him at a wedding in Swaziland at the invitation of King Mswati III.

The day should have ended quietly too for Holomisa. But he was surprised to see another jet glinting on the tarmac. As he stepped down from the plane, he was advised that Mandela was in the VIP lounge, waiting for him. Two hours later, coming down the stairs at Jan Smuts Airport in Johannesburg, he saw the sombre faces of Joe Slovo, Pallo Jordan and Cyril Ramaphosa. Mandela had sat him down in Umtata to relay the news that crumpled both men: 'They have assassinated Chris Hani.' That night, Mandela had his first experience of addressing the nation on television, in an attempt to contain the violent backlash that was sure to follow. It was a stirring, unforgettable speech, without hyperbole, told from the tightrope. In solidarity, the South African embassies in London and Washington flew the flag at half-mast.

Much earlier in the day, not far from Qunu in the village of Sabalele, nothing unusual was expected to happen on that Easter Saturday. Hani's old friend Nondala had switched on Radio Transkei to keep him company while he built a new kraal outside his rondavel. 'I dropped everything when I heard the news,' he breathed softly when he related the events to us. A few hours later a helicopter appeared in the sky with Mandela on board. The ANC president had come to bring comfort to the family.

But before that, the children had yelled into every open doorway of every rondavel until there was no one left who did not know Hani was dead. Then they had tumbled like boulders back down the hill to the house where Chris's elderly parents, Gilbert and Mary Hani, lived. 'Victor [Hani's older brother] was mad that day,' Nolusapho Hani recalled. She adjusted the blanket on her back to keep her sleeping granddaughter warm as she recalled what had happened. 'Tata [Gilbert] was very difficult: they couldn't believe it. Victor didn't shout. He believed in action but he couldn't do anything because we had nothing.'

The family travelled to Johannesburg a few days later for Hani's funeral, held at the FNB Stadium, and they heard Mandela reminding the millions watching of the place where Chris Hani truly belonged:

Sabalele is … well known to me. Not for its beauty, but for its harshness. Yet this small, virtually unknown village produced a Chris Hani, whose life shook the whole country and impacted on the world's stage.

[His] passion for justice, for addressing the problems that plague the rural poor, were rooted in his childhood. His roots were so deep, so true, that he never lost them. Through three decades of exile Chris Hani remained steadfast in his commitment to free our people from bondage.

\* \* \*

Hani rarely ate breakfast, even though he took pleasure in making it for other people, but he enjoyed a cup of tea, first thing. He'd always make his bed, but strangely not on the day he died – at least not until Nomakhwezi called him back to do it. She was up early that day too. She'd planned to go to Spruitview with her father, and she'd have her hair done there.

Then, they would visit a few people, talk to people on the streets – as always happened when they were together – and then they'd return home together. It was school holidays, and the world was a better place for a teenage girl.

Her father had never told her about an attempt that was made on his life just three months before, as he was leaving the SACP offices in downtown Johannesburg. On that occasion, his bodyguards had tackled the suspect. But those who knew about the incident, which was kept under wraps, felt ill at ease. The shadows were drawing closer.

When Walus gunned down Hani, he was himself a married man with a daughter. But those relationships – of husband and father – were evidently not foremost in his consciousness. After he was arrested, Walus's wife Wanda spoke as if their marriage was still strong, despite the vast distances that separated them. Mother and daughter had flown to South Africa twice to make an attempt at family life together. But Wanda told the *Sunday Times* that she had been unable to bear her unhappiness and alienation, and so she had left. Yet she was adamant: the assassin was not the man she knew. She recalled to journalist Peter Malherbe how Walus had once attacked his father, Tadeusz, for killing an unwanted litter of kittens. He had never been a soldier because he had a chronic stomach ailment.

Wanda Walus heard about the assassination when she was watching television on the day it happened. She told the *Sunday Times*: 'We were all sitting around the table watching the news when suddenly they said my husband had been arrested for murdering a political leader.' Immediately, Wanda tried to protect their daughter. 'My husband served as a small stone that started an avalanche. He was the ideal victim because he had [not] been in the country long enough.'

Wanda Walus was wrong about her husband, and misguided to imagine that their marriage was intact. Janusz Walus's lover, Maria Ras, was unashamed in court, saying that their relationship had been going on for ten years, and that they knew the Derby-Lewises well enough to share the occasional braai. Ras related the events of Easter Saturday with precision.

She had woken up with Walus at 7am at his flat in Muckleneuk. He told her was going out to practise his karate at the Stan Schmidt studio in Johannesburg and that he thought he would be back in Pretoria around 11am. She had no reason to doubt him.

But Ras's testimony about what happened a little later in the day was most absorbing. She said 11am came and went, and it was getting closer to the afternoon when the phone rang. Clive Derby-Lewis was on the line, and wanted to know where Walus was. Ras said she expected him home soon. Derby-Lewis declined to leave a message, but asked Ras to ask Walus to call him the moment he got home. By this time, Walus had already been arrested, and a huge crowd was assembling outside Hani's Dawn Park home, where Tambo was arriving in the limousine.

Insisting that she knew none of that, Ras was beginning to get worried about her boyfriend, so much so that by 2.30pm, she had already called a few hospitals and the police, in case there had been an accident. Then Derby-Lewis called her again; although Ras told him she was afraid that something had happened to Walus, he was dismissive, saying he simply wanted to invite her and Walus to a braai the following day.

Ras had no reason to disbelieve Derby-Lewis, and, since it was Easter Saturday, she went to see some friends as a distraction. On her way home, Ras wondered if Walus had arrived back at his flat. She decided to stop in – and he had indeed returned. Inside, he was surrounded by plainclothes policemen and the chaos of a full-scale search. Amid the apparent pandemonium of papers and files, fingerprints and plastic sample bags, it was clear that the raid was going well. And Ras, who would suggest she was confused by the events that afternoon, and who may still know more about Walus than she ever suggested, was immediately drawn into the investigation.

\* \* \*

The police were in a feverish state. They had already found significantly more than they had expected – a typewritten list with annotations in pen, in the top drawer of Walus's desk. Nine names appeared on the list: Nelson Mandela, Joe Slovo, Mac Maharaj, Karen Brynard, Pik Botha, Richard Goldstone, Ken Owen, Tim du Plessis – and Chris Hani.

When the list was analysed, it became clear that this was no random selection. These people were enemies of the right-wing state. *Sunday Times* editor Ken Owen was regarded as a traitor by the right wing. Journalist Brynard was vilified by the same constituency as having been the reason for the CP losing a by-election in the Germiston suburb of Primrose. Tim du Plessis was generally seen as an implacable enemy of white racists for his stance in print.

Only Slovo's name did not have an address attached to it on the list, while Mandela's name was followed by an entire page of details, which included:

Note the house, situated in an oak-lined road, is deliberately not numbered, but is easily recognisable by the wrought-iron black fence which has had black metal sheeting placed behind it to limit the view from the road. It has high-tech electronic surveillance systems throughout, including a television camera mounted at the gate behind a glass panel. The gates are electronically controlled.

Also on the page was a colour photograph of a double-storey house with a red tiled roof. Later, when Gaye Derby-Lewis admitted that the list emanated from her, she insisted she had simply intended using it to write a piece for *Die Patriot* in which an ironic point would be made about the lifestyles of the ANC and SACP leadership. She had hoped Mandela's house would take on special contrariness to the party's projection of a struggle hero. But the court was sceptical. The view was that the description of high security devices 'excites suspicion as to the purpose for which [the] list was designed'. The court found that such information would really only be of great interest to someone with more nefarious activities in mind than commentary by a journalist about relative wealth.

The list was punctuated with remarks written in pen, and of particularly grisly interest was that a number had been given to each name.

Mandela was number one, Slovo number two and Hani number three. Next to Hani's name were the letters and numerals: BMW 525i PWY 525T. These were the details of the car driven by one of Hani's entourage. State witness MC van Zyl testified at the trial of Walus and the Derby-Lewises that he, Van Zyl, and others often used a BMW 525i with that registration tag to drive Hani to meetings. The last time he had done so, said Van Zyl, was less than a month before Hani died. So Hani and his bodyguards had been followed, they had been under surveillance – just as Hani had indicated several times to different people in the weeks before he was shot.

The Derby-Lewises seemed horrified at the suggestion that the document was effectively a hit list. But although the court was unable to prove that it was a hit list, the document has been referred to in this way ever since.

Detective Sergeant Anton Grimbeek, who took part in the raid on Walus's flat, later revealed that when they drove away after their first search, Walus made a revealingly laconic remark to the leader of the investigation, Warrant Officer Mike Holmes. 'Mike,' Walus said, 'I think something made you happy, you found something'.

On the Monday after Hani's murder, a right-wing journalist and CP supporter named Arthur Kemp had lunch with the Derby-Lewises. He had known Walus since the late 1980s and the Derby-Lewises for even longer, becoming particularly close to Gaye Derby-Lewis when they worked together at *Die Patriot* from mid-1989 to mid-1992. Then Kemp left *Die Patriot* and took up a post at the reactionary English-language daily, *The Citizen*. He claimed that his first real contact with Gaye Derby-Lewis after that came when she phoned him at work in January 1993. She wanted him to help her find addresses for prominent ANC and SACP leaders, as well as journalists, activists and even mainstream politicians, whose actions had upset their conservative cabal. Gaye Derby-Lewis allegedly faxed Kemp a list of 19 names, from which Kemp drew up another, much tighter one comprising nine names and eight addresses. Soon after that, at the end of January 1993, Gaye Derby-Lewis met Kemp at the Rotunda in Braamfontein, Johannesburg – where buses arrive and depart day and night – or so she said.

Gaye Derby-Lewis had a ticket for a bus to Cape Town, and just before she got on, she claimed, Kemp arrived and handed her an envelope. Inside it was the typewritten list. Kemp would always claim that Gaye Derby-Lewis had never explained to him why she needed the information he gave her, but he proffered the suggestion that it may have been used to rally members of the CP to protest outside the houses of the individuals on the list 'for propaganda value'.

Gaye Derby-Lewis was most emphatic about this, saying she opened the envelope only once she got to Cape Town, when her husband was with her. There, she claimed, they perused it together, before spending two weeks in the Mother City. They drove home to Krugersdorp at the end of their trip. As if to show she then lost interest in it, Gaye Derby-Lewis said she put Kemp's list in a room they used for filing. The Derby-Lewises said they both were obsessed at the time with the campaign for the Krugersdorp by-election, and that the registration of voters was all-consuming. They only thought about the list again in late February, when, they said, a canvasser noticed it, attracted by the picture of Mandela's house.

Arthur Kemp apparently had his own encounter with Hani earlier that same month. On 6 February, South African Airways flight 232 took off from Johannesburg en route to London with Hani – and a small group of SACP representatives – on board. They were on their way to Cuba via London. It is unlikely that Hani would have known or even noticed Kemp on the flight, but Kemp – travelling on unrelated business – would certainly have experienced a shiver of recognition when he spotted Hani, if it was purely coincidental. By that time, Kemp had already drawn up the list, which was later reshuffled and redrawn in order of priority.

Within three months of giving Gaye Derby-Lewis the list, Kemp had, on the face of it, become involved with her in what they called an exchange of business ideas, related to her mail-order outfit and his invoicing sideshow, which he had started upon his resignation from *The Citizen*. That 'exchange' was ostensibly the reason for a lunch the Derby-Lewises arranged at their home with Kemp the Monday after Hani's assassination. Before Kemp arrived, Gaye Derby-Lewis had bought a copy of *Beeld* – and said she was left cold to the bone.

There was a description of a list that had been found in Walus's flat, and, more disturbingly, an allusion to her husband having a connection with Walus. This built on similar suggestions that had been made in some Sunday papers. The couple laid an indignant complaint by phone with the newspaper. Then Gaye Derby-Lewis started to look for Kemp's list, or so she said. And it was gone. The Derby-Lewises quickly insisted that they had never discussed the list, but on Monday 12 April, they were at last compelled to do just that. They were determined to make it seem as if they had no idea how it had come to be in Walus's possession. He must have picked it up when he was in the house, they said – but this assertion contradicted their insistence that the last time Clive Derby-Lewis had seen Walus was in December the previous year.

By the time Kemp arrived for lunch, there must have been palpable tension, if not anxiety, in the Derby-Lewis household. The day before, the Sunday newspapers had already linked Clive Derby-Lewis to Walus, so when a call came through from a reporter at the *Pretoria News* while they were eating lunch, the mood probably became anguished. The journalist apparently had a reasonable rather than provocative question: did the MP know if Walus was a member of the Conservative Party? But the fact was that a link with Walus was beginning to emerge, early in the investigation. This meant that even a relatively harmless question related to Derby-Lewis's presumably powerful position in the party, and the intimate knowledge he had of its membership, took on a different tenor.

When Derby-Lewis put down the phone, Kemp was apparently prompted to ask if the list of nine names he had given to Gaye Derby-Lewis nearly three months before was the one which was now being connected to Walus. The couple shot back and denied it, but Kemp persisted. Eventually, Gaye Derby-Lewis admitted it was, but they had not wanted to tell him. 'I was a little scared,' she said at her trial of this moment. 'We were, after all, high-profile CP people, and I could not see ourselves being implicated in anything so devastating as Mr Hani's murder.'

Clive Derby-Lewis then suggested they tell the police that the list was Kemp's. Later portraying themselves as anxious and conflicted, Kemp and Gaye Derby-Lewis were completely against the idea. So, whether for effect or out of fear, Clive Derby-Lewis was said to have uttered the fateful words: 'Not to worry, Mr Walus would not speak ...'

Straight away, the MP felt ill. He needed to lie down. Five days later, at 6pm on Saturday 17 April, a week after Hani was killed, Clive Derby-Lewis was arrested. It took another six hours for him to finally sign a statement which, in part, said that he had been convinced that, the matter being serious, he was not expected to say anything that could be used against him. So all Derby-Lewis would confess was that he knew 'a certain Walus', and that he had seen him last on 22 December 1992.

Again and again, contradictions surfaced to Clive Derby-Lewis's statement to police on 17 April. For instance, Gaye Derby-Lewis would confirm her domestic worker's testimony that she and her husband had had breakfast with Walus on 6 April, but the wife of the killer also said she had no idea why her husband had invited Walus to their house that day.

Gaye Derby-Lewis always emphasised that there were no secrets between her and her husband. Perhaps she had not known about an illegal gun and perhaps she had not known the means by which her husband had got it. In fact, perhaps the entire weapon story was a mystery to her. At her murder trial, the court found Gaye Derby-Lewis was not telling the whole truth about the reasons for having Kemp draw up a list of enemies' names, but it could not refute her statement that she knew nothing about the 9mm pistol. And for that, among other reasons, she was acquitted.

The court found that it was difficult to differentiate between Walus and Clive Derby-Lewis, so it found that they were in it together. The accused were deemed to have arrogated to themselves the right to destroy a life because of their own political perceptions.

Hani died a mere four days after making the appeal on the East Rand for peace, for patience, for tolerance, for the just future that would be created if everyone held steady in their convictions and commitment. His appeal came on the same day that Gaye Derby-Lewis had made breakfast for her husband Clive and their associate, Kuba. That was also the day, as Motswane testified, that Clive Derby-Lewis had provided Walus with the gun. At the rally on the East Rand, Hani had said:

I don't accept people calling for war because I feel we have achieved something in this country where those who oppressed us in the past are actually talking to us and showing a readiness to negotiate for democratic elections. I am saying to these comrades here that everyone should be a combatant – a fighter for peace.

By 21 April, five more suspects – including Kemp – were in custody, and police were unequivocal in saying they believed there was a conspiracy behind the assassination. All but Kemp had been arrested in Krugersdorp. Kemp was held in Benoni. Newspapers were clear in their reports about the 21 April police press conference. When journalists asked if police believed there was a plot, spokesperson Brigadier Malherbe said: 'We believe there has been a conspiracy, yes.' Malherbe also revealed that the additional suspects – Gaye Derby-Lewis, Kemp, estate agent Venter, property speculator Du Rant, and self-employed computer expert Edwin Clark – had been picked up after Clive Derby-Lewis had given statements to police following his arrest on 17 April. Clark – who was described at the TRC as being an intelligence official in the Afrikaner Volksfront – was at that time alleged to have been involved in fund-raising for the killers.

The brigadier emphasised, however, that the five were not yet considered as co-accused, although the police 'would not arrest anyone for no rhyme or reason'. He was quoted as saying: 'When the police arrest a person, they already have a lot of information.' Apparently, Clive Derby-Lewis had been 'cooperative' during questioning, while Walus had co-operated 'eventually'. Walus claimed he had been plied with alcohol by his interrogators, although video footage of the extensive interrogation showed only very occasional drinking taking place. He blamed Derby-Lewis, just as Derby-Lewis blamed him.

Malherbe was confident enough to say police had completed their investigation into the assassination and were now concentrating on the 'conspiracy phase'. Seventeen top detectives had been assigned. Scotland Yard was involved. Derby-Lewis's links with right-wing organisations were exposed. Apart from setting up his own racist body, the Stallard Foundation, in 1985, which urged the retention of the Verwoerdian dream and which was allegedly given some financial support by Walus, Derby-Lewis was also an honorary vice-president of the Western Goals Institute, based in London, and allegedly involved in stockpiling arms and using British Army veterans to train white South African mercenaries.

Walus's links with the National Intelligence Service came up at this time, with agent Johan Fourie saying he used him as a source to inform on members of the South African Polish community with links with Poland's intelligence service. Another agent said he had once used Walus's business in Qwa Qwa as a support address.

But none of this apparently led the investigation further than the fact of Walus and Derby-Lewis having conspired to kill Hani. Gripping information about a second gunman has never been properly investigated. Journalist Amrit Manga and others went as far as to expose the alleged identity of a malevolent figure attached to a private security company. And there were rumours in newspapers about Boksburg Traffic Department officials knowing more than they revealed. But the most chilling of all were stories centred on a double agent with links within the old Transkei intelligence structures and at Vlakplaas. Still, there has been no deeper probe, and the case is closed.

\* \* \*

There's a perfect circle of a hole just below the middle of the wooden garage door at 5 Hakea Crescent, Dawn Park. Racheal Lerutla, who was a neighbour when Hani was assassinated and who now lives in the house where he lived, pointed it out as she rolled the door up for us to step outside into the driveway. The door rattled and squeaked as it pushed up slowly. It was just Lerutla, the two of us and photographer Leon Nicholas, and we were suddenly quiet. The street was silent.

It was a Saturday morning in Dawn Park, around 9.30am, and we were on the bend of the Crescent, somewhat obscured from the houses around us at the end of the secluded driveway. We felt uneasy in the hiddenness, a loose group lost in thought. Glamorous Lerutla, an ebullient Johannesburg socialite and businesswoman, bought the house from Limpho Hani in late 1993 'because it is significant to the nation'. But as we stood there, a light March breeze lifting the leaves on the trees all around us, Lerutla was suddenly smaller. She folded her arms across her chest and gripped them lightly with her fingertips. She stepped forward and into the middle of the shadow latticed into the stones. 'We know he fell right here,' she said, pointing again, and when we looked around, it was impossible not to remember the SABC TV footage aired on the haunted night of Hani's death. The charcoal facebrick of the house, the tight angles of the driveway, the paving covered in blood.

It was as if the ghosts of the living were there, those fragile and speechless forms, those broken shapes, propping each other up in a flimsy line along the wall. Sexwale. ANC spokesperson Gill Marcus locked in anguish. Eastern Cape activist Ronnie Watson. ANC PWV Peace Desk spokesperson Mondli Gungubele. ANC NEC member Joe Nhlanhla. COSATU deputy general secretary Sam Shilowa, who had been close to Hani, practically shadowing him, such was his reverence. There were neighbours, white and black, drawing nearer.

Siphiwe Nyanda had succeeded Hani as MK chief of staff after Hani relinquished the post to entrench his commitment to the suspension of the armed struggle in April the year before. On that day, Nyanda was filmed in all his rage, jumping around in fury outside the house as the crowds began to gather, word spreading rapidly beyond the streets of Dawn Park.

Hani bodyguard Sandile Sizani had been given the weekend off by the man he was to protect, and when he returned it felt as if he were lurching into his own grave. He threw his hands up in the air when he saw

Hani's body lying there, surrounded by blood. Then Sizani strode ferociously away and succumbed to the mayhem of sorrow, weeping openly in horror, regret and grief. He was desperate to get beyond the gaze of the murmuring, sobbing crowd, wiping his face with his T-shirt but unable to quell his tears.

Retha Harmse was already in the protection of the police, but it was impossible for her to let go of how Walus had approached Hani and fired several times. Wearing a favourite tracksuit for a day of harmonious disengagement with the world, Hani was unarmed. As he collapsed in the driveway, Walus walked right up to him and pulled the trigger again. Two rounds behind the ear. Pure execution.

'It takes on this presence,' Lerutla said, pointing towards an untidy veil of purple flowers rumpled at the foot of the trees at the edge of the paving. She took a breath. 'I think of it as the spirit of Hani protecting me because he was a soldier.'

When Walus came prowling on 10 April in the borrowed red Ford, few in the Dawn Park neighbourhood would have paid any attention to a young white man moving around their area. And he fitted the fringes. Perhaps it was there, on the periphery of everything that mattered – politics, relationships, fatherhood, social encounters – that he started to become enticed by the possibility Clive Derby-Lewis had mooted of creating enough anarchy to change the tide of history. Walus would no longer be a husk of a man if he killed Hani, the anti-Christ. On the contrary, he would surely be the ultimate hero of the right-wing Afrikaners' Third Freedom Struggle. He would be in the vanguard of their liberation as he steered order back on the path of white righteousness.

The new neighbours in Dawn Park wouldn't have thought about the meaning of his presence. They were already on edge, unsure of each other. When blacks like Hani, Sexwale, Grootboom and Lerutla had started moving in around the whites, the mood had become slightly unpredictable. When the Hanis moved to Dawn Park in 1992, the CP chief council whip and councillor for Dawn Park was a man called Andries du Toit. The *Sunday Star*'s Peter de Ionno reported the day after Hani's murder that Du Toit had said at the time of Hani's arrival in the suburb that 'there might be something drastic done to show him we don't want him here'.

Yet Hani had moved into the suburb precisely to live his life the way he felt it in his heart, without acrimony. His modest home was a gesture against contempt. At the time of Hani's assassination, whites were already leaving Dawn Park for other suburbs. Today, Ernest and Magda Smith and their children make up four of only a handful of whites remaining. 'I couldn't ask for better neighbours than I have now,' laughed Magda. 'When you're standing outside, your arm is constantly raised in greeting.'

On the day of the killing, Ernest Smith had just set up their TV reception at a campsite at Potchefstroom Dam. He switched it on, and saw someone standing on his front lawn. When they got home, 'it was almost like the Rand Show, the way the people packed the streets. I would struggle to get into my house.' The Smiths chipped in by making dozens of cups of coffee for the shocked mourners.

Ernest recalled how Hani would come jogging past their house at exactly 5.50am every morning. 'I knew who he was. He was very friendly. He'd always ask: "How are you doing?"' The Smiths may not have been typical of a young white Afrikaans couple of the time. Many like them would have secretly sided with the Ystergarde of the Afrikaner Weerstandsbeweging (AWB), who vowed to protect whites as enmity spiralled across the nation in the wake of Hani's death.

Hani told British journalist Peter Hitchens that he had moved his family to Dawn Park 'because his wife did not understand Johannesburg's rigid racial geography and bought the house by mistake'. But 'with genuine pleasure', he told Hitchens he believed he was on good terms with neighbours, and that it was reassuring to see his children going out on bike rides with white friends.

Yet, Hani was never without his bodyguards. They were like those in Lusaka in the late 1980s – all ex-combatants, highly trained guerrilla fighters, but not completely versed in guarding VIPs in an urban setting. Yet the men were the best the ANC could offer to protect its most prized leaders, as the state had refused to give any close cover. Pretoria's racist

## THE ASSASSINATION

politicians each had at least three security agents with them all the time. One man would be in front, the other behind, and another at their side. If an apartheid political figure had gone jogging daily – as Hani did – there would have been a bulletproof car cruising behind.

The ANC did its best for Hani. On a campaigning trip in the eastern Cape just three weeks before he was killed, Hani had at least six MK bodyguards. Two sat in the front of the car in which he rode, and four others were in surrounding cars. So the absence of bodyguards on the day of his death remains a painful mystery. Hani's Lusaka bodyguards are still pained about that absence – that Hani had to compromise his own safety because it bothered him that his guards hardly had time off. The most common version of events is that Hani wanted them to spend the Easter weekend with their loved ones. But, if this was indeed the case, many ANC members are still furious that the guards listened to Hani, as they should never have buckled to his dangerous demand. Their job was to remain at his side, no matter what.

Bantu Holomisa, who had provided men from his own security detail and from among his army officers to protect Hani just a year earlier, was still enraged when we interviewed him. He cannot accept that the ANC could have allowed a future leader to face such peril alone. He reminded us that the threat was great when Hani was exiled to Transkei after Pretoria retracted his temporary amnesty.

On that Saturday morning, Hani had been expecting to be joined by Peace Desk spokesperson Gungubele. The *Sunday Times* reported that they had had a telephone conversation the night before, in which Hani had told Gungubele that he was going to post money to one of his children in Cape Town the following day, and, after that, he would be taking Nomakhwezi to Spruitview to the hair salon she liked. In the afternoon, he planned to watch Bafana Bafana play Mauritius in a friendly. 'I told him I would be free to go with him because it would not be safe for him to go alone,' said Gungubele. 'He agreed. He promised to call again in the morning,' which Hani did. Within 20 minutes of their conversation, Hani was dead.

For Hani, the match would have been a time to relax. In a tribute for *Sunday Star*, written the day after the murder, Esther Waugh, political correspondent for *The Star*, described how Hani had been an avid Orlando Pirates fan and supporter of Bafana Bafana. 'He was looking forward to sitting in the stands again,' she wrote. 'He loved going to soccer. From the moment the whistle blew, he was transported out of the world of politics.'

\* \* \*

Although voters in the whites-only referendum in March 1992 had given De Klerk's government nearly 69 percent support for continuing negotiations, the ANC itself had withdrawn from CODESA in July that year in protest at state-sponsored conflict. A Record of Understanding signed that September re-established a relationship, but it was delicate.

In the hours after Hani died, FW de Klerk went onto the SABC's current affairs programme, *Agenda*, and spoke to Freek Robinson, an ambitious Afrikaans journalist. Feigning statesmanship, De Klerk said it had become necessary to offer reassurance to political leaders and he had given orders that greater protection should be offered to them. However, De Klerk looked weak, his position pointless, when the true leader of the people of South Africa, Mandela, went on air and called for calm and an honouring of Hani's memory.

In an obituary for Hani, published in the *Independent on Sunday* on 11 April 1993, British journalist John Carlin wrote:

If Mandela was the patriarch, the jailed Messiah, Hani was the man with whom activists identified on a more familiar level. He was the brother in arms, an idol among black youth, the symbol of armed resistance, before they even knew what he looked like. His charisma survived the legend.

Yet Mandela had to face recriminations almost immediately. SA Students' Congress regional political officer Palesa Motloung articulated the mood in the *Weekly Mail*: 'We had Boipatong and Mandela said we should be restrained in our response. We now have this and he will say we should be restrained. We are tired of being restrained.' ANC Youth League member Macbeth Ndaba threatened to tear up his ANC membership and take up arms if the ANC did not pull out of negotiations. 'We listen to our leaders when they say we must stop violence, but when we stop, the boers start to kill us,' another Youth League member told journalists Enoch Mthembu and Bafana Khumalo, as he wept. 'The war will only stop if open war is waged against the government.'

Police admitted they had refused an ANC request to give Hani police protection, on the grounds that it was impractical to offer protection to all political leaders. Then police commissioner Johan van der Merwe – in reference to the list found at Walus's flat – said police would offer protection to 'non-office-bearing politicians until the threat has been traced and removed'. Mandela said that in 1992 the ANC had asked the Minister of Law and Order, Hernus Kriel, to provide protection for Hani, but the government took no action. The ministry confirmed receipt of the request but said it had been unable to act as Hani did not occupy an official position.

In a 1994 symposium on 'What's left for the Left' for the periodical *Work in Progress*, Moeletsi Mbeki – brother of the former president, Thabo Mbeki – described how Hani's security had been tightened as the threats against his life increased towards the end. 'He had to spend more and more time hanging around the lobby on the ground floor [of ANC headquarters], presumably waiting for the all-clear to move out of the building.'

In his interview with American journalist Jerelyn Eddings three weeks before he was gunned down, Hani revealed he was tired and that death was on his mind. The interview appeared in the *Weekly Mail*'s edition of 16 April 1993; in it, Eddings wrote: 'His back was stiff after two hectic days of meetings and rallies in the towns and villages of the Transkei. His voice was hoarse. And his words were haunting.' Hani told Eddings:

I've never wanted to spare myself because I feel there are people who are no longer around who died for this struggle. What right do I have to hold back, to rest, to preserve my health, to have time with my family, when there are other people who are no longer alive – when they sacrificed what is precious: namely, life itself?

Jeremy Cronin, then a member of the SACP's Politburo, said shortly after Hani's death that Hani and his wife Limpho had selected a site for his grave in South Park Cemetery in Boksburg in the weeks before his murder.

* * *

This was all so different to Hani's mood upon his return from exile in 1990. Yet it was exactly at that time, the year he landed at Jan Smuts Airport after 30 years away, that the right wing had started plotting seriously. Clive Derby-Lewis was a confidant of the CP's leader, Dr Andries Treurnicht, and an elected member of the Hoofraad (National Council) of the CP, which consisted of 35 members representing the four provinces as well as CP members of parliament.

The party had showed open disgust with the NP's policy of reform of the late 1980s, and when De Klerk announced on February 2 1990 that the ANC, SACP and other liberation movements had been unbanned, this was regarded, if not as treason, then as the most provocative of betrayals.

The CP held a mass meeting at the Voortrekker Monument in Pretoria on 26 May 1990 with Treurnicht the key speaker. Both Walus and Derby-Lewis were in the enthusiastic audience listening to Treurnicht's message, which was crowded with the invective of a boere rebellion: the third freedom struggle had begun.

At subsequent CP events, it was insisted that the time had come to prepare for war. Whites should arm themselves against the ANC–SACP alliance. By the time the general congress of the CP was held at Kimberley in 1992, a mobilisation plan was being readied for the boer nation to fight for its freedom. And so began a series of rallies across the country.

Derby-Lewis would say this was a call to the trenches, and his belief was that the CP's own armed struggle had started then, in 1992. Bomb attacks were launched as the CP encouraged its membership to examine how to achieve freedom of its people, and on 26 March 1993 the party announced it would implement a full-scale mobilisation plan. It sowed fear amid the ignorance of its membership, repeating over and over again how the NP's negotiations would realise communist domination – a state that would leave the country in utter misery. Afrikaners, it contended, would lose their culture, while communists – led by Hani – would effectively eradicate their unique way of life.

For the CP, a future with Hani as a leader was anathema, and it was against this background that Derby-Lewis and Walus plotted Hani's assassination. Hani had raised the fury of the white right with threats to lift the suspension of the armed struggle should this become a last resort. He publicly and repeatedly invoked the ANC's right to act according to its own code of conduct and set of principles.

Treurnicht died soon after the assassination and was succeeded by the deputy leader Ferdi Hartzenberg, who appeared as a witness at the request of Derby-Lewis and Walus at their TRC amnesty hearings. While Walus and Derby-Lewis had hoped Hani's killing would further the right-wing cause, there was some uncertainty in right-wing ranks about the impact of the assassination. In an interview 15 years after Hani's death, the AWB's André Visagie laughed off the importance of the assassination, insisting instead that violence against whites had intensified to the point of genocide. AWB leader Eugene Terre'Blanche became feverish at the suggestion that Hani's murder played a role in shifting post-democracy politics. 'He was only one man. Just one. What the hell does that matter? So many whites have died.'

In the fragmented political space of the early 1990s, it was sometimes unclear who was the most reactionary among all the contrary forces. As recently as two weeks before Hani was murdered, three bold-faced criminals appearing in the Rand Supreme Court claimed that the bank robbery for which they had been charged had been masterminded by Hani and Sexwale. The men, who were also charged with murder, said that a portion of the stolen money had been handed over to Sexwale at ANC headquarters. Their ridiculous statements, redolent of disinformation, gave Hernus Kriel, apartheid's last Minister of Law and Order, the opportunity to accuse MK of involvement in crime.

Mysteriously, the men disappeared on the evening of the court appearance in which they had advanced their lie. Prison officials said they had hijacked the prison vehicle just after they arrived back at Diepkloof Prison, and reversed right out of the gates, which happened to be open.

Sexwale was never questioned, and, at the time of the criminals' original statements, Hani said: 'These so-called public servants, the police and the prosecutor, seem to be more intent on making up political propaganda than on investigating a serious crime.' Interestingly, Hani saw the chief accused, Zolomon Mqaqeni, as 'a pawn [used] to make a propaganda point'. After the men escaped, he said: 'I am frankly now worried for Mqaqeni's safety. In the past, fake prison escapes have been used to eliminate people.'

The SACP journal *Umsebenzi* reported in its first edition of 1993 that the Communist Party had requested that the Goldstone Commission examine the behaviour of the investigating officers in the case, as well as the circumstances of the escape – and any possible involvement by Kriel.

\* \* \*

Behind the scenes, just two weeks before he was gunned down, Hani was talking about the critical need for a conference of the left, to try to redefine the nature of socialism. He knew the only solution would be one that was nonracial. Moeletsi Mbeki, one of the people with whom he discussed this plan, said his belief was that Hani's election as general secretary of the SACP had offered him

> ... the first opportunity to construct his own vision as the top person.

As MK chief of staff, he had been third in command under the leadership of Tambo and Modise. Being in such a central position in the party opened up new areas of work.

Within days of his election, he was burrowing away with his characteristic energy and enthusiasm and, above all, his openness of mind and spirit. He was trying to make his mark on the SACP and South Africa as a socialist, not a military man.

Moeletsi Mbeki said Hani – who he described as 'a strategist for a socialist South Africa' – was 'emphatic' that he no longer saw the SACP as the vanguard party of the working class, with the right to define what was or was not true socialism. At the same time, he did not agree with those – like Thabo Mbeki – who were critical of the Communist Party, particularly after the fall of the Berlin Wall. That communism had failed in Europe did not have meaning within the South African context.

But he was equally forthright about COSATU. At the time, its leadership was vacillating between positions – trying to do deals with capitalists on macroeconomic issues and trying to secure a better life for the working class. 'Instead,' said Moeletsi Mbeki, 'he stressed the need for unions to fight for democracy at plant level. He said he got the impression that this aspect of working-class aspiration was being abandoned by the union movement in return for a search for deals with capital – something he did not think was feasible.' British journalist Carlin wrote that 'by the time of his death, [Hani's] political vision had mellowed into something more closely resembling [Labour Party leader] John Smith's than Fidel Castro's.'

And yet not everyone had the desire to listen properly to Hani. In his last major public speech, made on the weekend before he was killed, Hani spoke about the establishment of a peace corps of young men and women who could spend two years in crime prevention and clean-up operations, building tolerance. He envisaged a demilitarised society. 'It is imperative,' he said in that final speech, 'that the ANC and its allies become ever bolder and more creative in building a momentum for peace.'

In the *Weekly Mail* of 16 April 1993, journalists Enoch Mthembu and

Bafana Khumalo wrote about a ceremony to mourn Hani which had turned into an exercise of hate. Inkatha Freedom Party official Buel Kubheka and a Red Cross official almost lost their lives to a gang of about six young men, one of whom had an AK47, outside Sebokeng Stadium. Kubheka had been talking to a Peace Accord monitor, when the young man with the weapon started brandishing it.

'Seeing the potential for violence,' the journalists said, 'local ANC chairman LL Mbatha conducted Kubheka to a car and asked a nearby Red Cross official to escort her out of the area. As accusations were hurled at [her], the crowd grew.' The next thing Mthembu and Khumalo saw was the young gunman 'coolly' step forward. He was wearing a blue overall and a military-style khaki jacket with his face covered in a white scarf. Without blinking, he lifted his weapon and fired off a volley of shots at the swiftly departing cars. A bullet or two shattered the windscreen of the Red Cross vehicle, and a stampede was immediately set off as the young man in the scarf 'ambled across the street and disappeared into the maze of houses near the stadium'. Mthembu and Khumalo spoke to LL Mbatha afterwards. Shaken, he said 'there is nothing I can do to control these boys.'

There was such a critical need for young South Africans to feel free, to take on their liberation and exult it to the benefit of the nation. The solidarity that Hani's death could bring about was symbolic of this kind of unity. The sorrow was hard to take, but the bonds should have been unbreakable. ANC Youth League member Solly Nhanyane told the *Weekly Mail* outside Sebokeng Stadium that 'this thing is confusing me. Hani was talking peace. Those who talk about war are still alive. I thought negotiations were the only solution, but now I have changed my mind.'

It is worth remembering the stain of hate in order to understand the sacrifices, the agony of suppressing retaliation – the strain of allowing the normal course of justice, rather than violence, to punish a man like Walus, who dared to look straight at Limpho Hani at his trial, and tell her, 'take it cool, take it calmly'.

In that same final public speech, Hani had condemned the PAC for continuing its armed struggle and called for those who could not commit to the peace process to be isolated. 'The message is being sent to the white population that Chris Hani is the devil himself,' he told the *Sunday Times* shortly before he was assassinated:

The police see me as the brains and key strategist. I have given up trying to prove that I am campaigning for peace. These guys see me as someone who is bad news. I fear that there are people who have the capacity to eliminate me. I am frightened about what they are planning.

Hints at possible ANC involvement in Hani's assassination came the day after his death, based on propaganda put out by sources aimed at destabilising the movement in the weeks before his death. These 'hints' emanated out of claims that Hani had said that, after elections, he would set up 'an alternative socialist alliance', and that he was 'not prepared to serve in a government of national unity'.

Further allegations were that these 'statements' – which were immediately refuted not only by Hani but by the ANC itself – had alarmed 'ANC moderates', and it was said that these same 'moderates' had demanded to know the source of the interview in case there was a transcript they could access for 'internal reasons'. The conservative view was expressed by the UK's *Sunday Telegraph* in its Hani obituary, written by Peter Taylor. In it, Taylor accused Hani of 'organising torture against ANC dissidents' and said that he had led an 'insurrectionist faction of the ANC'.

This should not have mattered. Yet what was interesting was how important Hani's assassination was to the British and other international media. Although it is true that the world's journalists were already in South Africa to cover CODESA, the violence, and the struggle for power and democracy, Hani's murder made the front pages of the *Independent on Sunday*, *Observer*, *Sunday Telegraph* and *Guardian*, among others. Most papers immediately speculated that the assassination was an attempt to derail the negotiation process, and most carried fairly lengthy analytical obituaries, most sympathetic.

By the Monday after his murder, even international newspapers had started to speculate on a successor for Hani in the SACP, with *The Times* (of London) concerned that Hani's 'solid Xhosa rural base gave a quite unrivalled dimension to his popular appeal'. Within the ANC, most media identified only Thabo Mbeki and Cyril Ramaphosa as possible candidates to assume power after Mandela, the assumption being that Hani would have been that person had he not been killed. *The Times* stated clearly that neither Mbeki nor Ramaphosa 'has Hani's popular appeal …'

On Tuesday, 13 April, most reports covered the spike in violence, although newspapers also paid particular attention to a march by 6 000 people in Boksburg, which was peacefully dispersed after the crowd was addressed by ANC Youth League leader Peter Mokaba. The international press – especially The *Financial Times* – examined how carefully the ANC stressed nonracialism in every statement and every speech.

Meanwhile, the news was coming through about the source of the weapon used by Walus. While the doom of a right-wing conspiracy seemed inevitable, AWB leader Terre'blanche condemned the murder, and even suggested it may have emanated out of a 'retribution' group within his own resistance movement. *The Guardian* lashed out at Pretoria's security establishment, slating 'the almost unbelievable incompetence of the political masters in failing to facilitate security points to a command structure which can hardly be expected to effect the transformation expected of them'.

On Wednesday 14 April, Mandela's televised appeal for a peaceful day of mourning was carried everywhere. But again, conspiracy lurked: *The Independent*, in particular, carried a substantial report on claims by ANC officials that the regime's intelligence service had links to the assassination. It insisted that De Klerk's security force 'purge had not gone far enough'.

By the Thursday, the word 'riots' was being used to describe the violence that had indeed spilled over at certain venues where mourning services and people's memorials to Hani were hosted. The *Guardian* went as far as suggesting that there were 'alarming signs that the ANC was losing control of nationwide militancy'. Certainly, the booing of Mandela was regarded as significant, with *The Independent*, *Daily Telegraph* and *The Times* calling it 'almost embarrassing'.

On Friday 16 April, reports noted the death toll as well as the deployment of 3 000 additional troops. There were also cautious reports about the National Party government negotiator, Roelf Meyer, apparently having stated that he would like to 'speed up' the introduction of the Transitional Executive Council.

The headlines seldom took the veil off the private pain experienced by the SACP and ANC members who knew Hani best. Joe Slovo gave some insight into this to the *Sunday Star* as he sat behind Hani's desk at the Communist Party offices in Rissik Street, Johannesburg, on the day Hani died. 'His office is pleasant. Spartan,' wrote Peta Thornycroft and Newton Kanhema. 'A few pot plants, a bookcase with copies of Lenin's works, a couple of posters, a pen-and-ink drawing of workers and the struggle …' They said his desk was 'a humble size'. Hani's deep thoughts and worries about the SDUs were evident even on his desk, where he had scribbled notes about this on the Friday before he was killed. Slovo was weary when the journalists saw him that day. He sat heavily. 'He was a warm, warm man,' Slovo said, reflecting on the first time he met Hani, who was then 'thin, so young, so shy, never said a word'.

The current SACP leader, Blade Nzimande – who survived the horror unfolding in the Natal Midlands in the early 1990s under Hani's inspirational leadership – says the party will continue to demand an inquest into the assassination. It will always be an issue for the organisation.

Significant overtures have already been made to the party from the assassins, but it will not talk to them. And the convicted killers, Walus and Clive Derby-Lewis, refused to talk to us. Clive's wife Gaye Derby-Lewis snarled at requests for an interview: 'I have absolutely nothing to say to you. Sorry about that.'

A week before his assassination, during an interview with historian Luli Callinicos at the SACP headquarters, Hani spoke of the possibility of his impending death. This upset Callinicos. 'They know where you live. Why don't you move?' she asked him, shaken by the alacrity with which he had confided in her. 'Whatever happens, happens. I have really messed my family around so much. I owe them some stability,' replied Hani.

To Callinicos, this was all about the searing remorse he felt over the short time he had spent with his family, especially his two youngest daughters, whom he had hardly seen. Yet once they were finally living together as a family, boundaries remained on their most private space. Limpho Hani later related in a piece by Shirley Firth in *Business Day* how she knew never to cook for fewer than eight, and that her husband was only occasionally home by 10pm. Yet, they were somehow entwined, even if this made little sense to Limpho's detractors.

Hani's comrades still remark warmly on his kindness, of how he could never keep a jacket on his back and would often return with an empty wallet. People as influential as Bantu Holomisa, Ronnie Kasrils and Blade Nzimande still miss him. They experience the sting of his loss both politically and emotionally, as a leader and as a friend. They remain moved by his humility. On 11 April 1993, boarding a commercial flight back home to Umtata after travelling to Johannesburg with Mandela, Holomisa – who is notoriously unemotional – said he grieved in his own way. He said that when he was alone in his airline seat, the full weight of what had transpired overwhelmed him. 'I had never cried myself ... but then, I broke down. The ladies were bringing me tissues and I thought: "Who else are we going to trust?"'

When we interviewed him, Kasrils was struck by the poignancy of memory: 'His humanity always shone through. He was totally obsessed with Hamlet's wrestling over to do or not to do.' Hani would almost certainly have been moved by the next generation of ideologues like Buti Manamela and Castro Ngobese of the Young Communist League (YCL), who have stripped themselves of capitalist confections. The YCL launched the ambitious Million Signature campaign in favour of reopening the murder case, while the Be Like Chris campaign lionises an authentic hero.

## THE ASSASSINATION

Like many others, lawyer George Bizos believes Hani's death 'strengthened Mandela's hand to force them [the NP] to fix a date for the election. Mandela was kicking for touch.' Sixteen days after the assassination, FW de Klerk announced the election date – for a year later. This ushered in one of the bloodiest periods in the country's history. The country was rocked by nearly 40 right-wing bomb blasts in the space of eight months. However, Hani's decision to lay down arms was vindicated when millions cast their ballot in April 1994. Even the AWB shut down in fury at what it regarded as self-inflicted disappointment on the part of white voters. An era of racist terror, it was fervently hoped, had passed.

But it is precisely that terror that will surely remain with Limpho, wearing the pain of loss behind her dark glasses. But she gives nothing away. At the funeral service, while people paid their very private respects either at the stadium or watching it live on television all over the country, she stood tall. There was considerable violence outside, as the incensed and the enraged were unable to contain their rage at the damage done to the nation.

At the helm of the family cortege at South Park Cemetery in Boksburg, the blood red of Limpho Hani's hat was unmistakable against a black sea of mourners. Eight years later, another world of pain opened to her when Nomakhwezi died. The young woman's final resting place is an unmarked grave at her father's feet, a place of solace where widowbirds skitter and swoop in an anguished waltz along the gravestones. All those years ago, tens of thousands of grieving people had walked from as far away as Soweto, Katlehong and Germiston to pay final homage. It was bewilderingly emotional. Even police and uniformed MK cadres, there to protect the crowd, were brought to tears.

Every year, on the day of his death, songs are chanted at Hakea Crescent, and fragrant wreaths are laid. The last of the birds, preparing to make their passage north, cannot help but flock over the park nearby, their dances solitary, the veils of their tail feathers waving in the highveld winter.

CHAPTER 13

# ANNE DUTHIE

*Names of some of the parties cited here have been changed by agreement to protect those concerned.*

Chris Hani was married only once, to Limpho, but he had his fair share of lovers. Charm and revolutionary zeal played their part in his attraction for women. But throughout his trials, his glories, his moments of abandonment and elevation by the movement to which he devoted his life, there was one woman who would be a constant, a companion, a love in times of pain, a source of understanding when so few got close. Her name was Anne Duthie.

In the 28 years in which they knew each other, she gained privileged access to his thoughts, their relationship meandering through cavorting in a Lusaka hotel room, into the fear of a young man going to war, across a distance bridged by airmail letters, through their respective marriages, which were challenged by their bond. Their moments together may be mere footnotes to the grand history of the battle for the liberation of South Africa, but they also provide a commentary and reflection of what shaped Hani. Duthie loved him, always. He told her he loved her. So when they had their final reunion in London, not long before he was murdered, and after quite an absence from each other, it was harsh and it was unforgettable.

After a series of phone calls – having been introduced to Duthie by other exiles who shared her friendship with Hani, and who have remained intimates – we met her in London's Covent Garden, then moved to a basement flat in Maida Vale. We had hours of conversation. But some of the more difficult truths have had to be obscured to protect Duthie.

That final reunion took place at a gathering of British anti-apartheid activists at London's Alexandria Burns Hall. The crowd was starting to warm up. In front of them, behind the main table, was the man they had all come to see – Chris Hani. 'Viva, SACP! Viva!' Fists were thrust awkwardly into the air. 'Amandla!' Again, fists punched the air, this time with greater conviction. 'Awethu!'

On either side of Hani were other South African revolutionaries who had just landed in London after a successful political tour to Havana, Cuba, where they were guests of Fidel Castro. It was 14 February, but the awkward sentiment of Valentine's Day was not the point of this supper party, which instead honoured the poet Robert Burns. In the interests of accommodating Hani, whose diary had been crammed with appointments made by his private secretary, Esther Barsel, the Burns Night organisers had held off setting a date for it until Hani could join them. Tonight the group had gathered to praise a man who stood for a cause they had supported with cash, placards and public jubilation for at least two decades. Hani was a hero in this room. Wearing a freshly pressed suit and tie, he stood up, the brotherly embrace of his smile complete. But he was tired. The cross-continental solidarity trip was but one item on a ruthless calendar of campaigning. Still, London offered emotional respite for Hani.

He looked around at the delegation closest to him. Also seated at the table was Maria Flores, Cuba's ambassador in Britain. The applause was strong for her, but it pumped up as Hani introduced his South African comrades. The ANC's international department head, Essop Pahad, also a member of the Politburo of the SACP, was there. Seated with him was Mbhazima Shilowa – then still known as Sam – a well-built, convivial man, a prodigy within the burgeoning South African trade union movement and a member of the Central Committee of the SACP. The chair of the PWV region of the SACP, Gwede Mantashe, occupied a critical position in the handpicked group, as the tireless organiser of the powerful National Union of Mineworkers. Rising star Nozizwe Madlala had been plucked out of the war zone of the Natal Midlands, where she was a member of the Central Committee of the southern Natal region, to accompany the general secretary to Cuba. Keeping company with the South African comrades were British journalist Victoria Brittain, Scottish folk singer Arthur Johnstone and Brian Filling, the chairperson of the powerful Anti-Apartheid Movement. By the end of the night, £1700 was in the kitty, and the SACP leadership – which had not been in much of a position to fund-raise on this scale while its leadership was in exile – was overwhelmed. After the traditional toast to the immortal memory of Burns, and the formalities which closed events to the sound of a great roar of cheers and clapping, Hani reminded the audience: 'Amandla!' He waited for the response, and now they were ready: 'Awethu!'

During the speeches, Hani had laid out the hard truth about the violent political stasis that was unfolding in South Africa, despite the peace talk of the ANC. Anne Duthie realised that the way he delivered his messages could envelop a crowd, lifting them up and carrying them with him into the heart of his conviction. At the dinner there was a mix of old and new faces to London, all drawn together by their opposition to apartheid. Those who had travelled this road together quickly rekindled old friendships, excitedly sharing reminiscences. Hani was the centre of attention.

Earlier in the day he had been able to talk to Duthie on the phone. He had got in touch to tell her that he would be in London. Although there had been a hiatus of a few years, it was clear that he hadn't changed. The threats to his life, the draining political undercurrents within his own movement, the wave of voices clamouring for his attention, had not aged him. There was the captivating humour, the easy charm, the sharp, incisive mind. And when he spoke, the familiar closeness he exuded only with those he knew best emerged strongly. Hani confided in her about his life in South Africa. The unfolding political situation, with the negotiations on tenterhooks, was wearying and personally perilous to him. This made it a struggle to be as one with his wife Limpho and his daughters. Over the next few weeks he began to call Duthie more frequently. They were old friends and he needed her support and objectivity. He held nothing back.

They had met in Lusaka in the 1960s, a few weeks after she had arrived there as a teacher. For Duthie, from Pateley Bridge in North Yorkshire, the journey was a complete change. Only months before, she had become the first in her family to graduate from university. Durham University had offered her an opportunity to dream of experiences beyond the market town where she grew up, where the highest excitement was reserved for the farmers who gathered monthly for the big livestock auctions. Beyond the classroom, she immersed herself in student politics, quickly developing an affinity with the philosophy of the British Communist Party and its espousal of worker values. With no money to speak of in her family, and no experience, Duthie had applied for a teaching job in Zambia. The country had been independent for just over a year and sorely lacked educators. By 1965, it had fewer than 100 university graduates.

After a month at sea, and a five-day journey by train from Cape Town, she arrived at her destination – one of only two secondary schools for African girls in the country. Her colleagues at the school were diverse. Some were from England. Others were from the American Peace Corps. Still others came from South Africa, most of them willing exiles who could no longer bear life under the apartheid regime.

Thandiwe L was polite enough but kept her distance from others, making sure everybody knew she came from royalty back home. The Zambians – mostly small-town people who were often the first to reach the exalted position of teacher in their families – were beneath Thandiwe. Yet, where she sometimes tried to reach out to Duthie, their colleague Nombeko M did little to conceal her utter disdain for all things and anybody white. Anyone walking past her classroom would be treated to lessons about colonialism, oppression and treachery. The best way to deal with whites was to keep away from them. Throughout, the racial division among teachers continued by default, each greeting the other politely before taking their seats in the staff room.

The secondary school was a microcosm of what was happening throughout the fledgling democratic Zambia. The popular Edinburgh Hotel was now open to all races, for instance, but was still almost exclusively frequented by whites, wealth working as effectively as the British system of racial division that went before it. Some of the white teachers quickly fell into step with their local compatriots, adopting patriarchal manners in the way they treated black students. But Duthie did not succumb to this. She was becoming whole in her surroundings. She often found herself in an all-white crowd, whether going to the hotel for tea, the cinema, restaurants or gatherings at somebody's house. Yet she searched for other experiences.

The first time she saw Hani was at the school where she taught. He came around, dressed in a casual shirt and jeans, with an effervescent smile and jovial gait. He'd come to see Thandiwe and Nombeko, and was introduced to Duthie as Chris Nkosana, 'another exile'. The second time he came, there was more of a connection. 'He was obviously different to the Zambians,' Duthie tells us. 'He was much better educated, much more talkative, much more self-confident. You didn't feel there were any barriers there.' So, she was interested. What was life like in South Africa? What was the education like? What was it like to grow up there? 'I found him fascinating. First of all for his politics. We talked about politics a lot! We were on the same wavelength and he was able to explain the situation in South Africa very convincingly. For the first time it came truly alive for me. I was impressed by his great compassion and the fact that he showed no racial hatred. I admired him greatly for putting his life in danger by becoming an activist and I could see that although he was still young he had the potential to become a leader.'

Soon Hani was visiting her regularly, and spending weekends with her. On the first date, the two walked hand-in-hand, the glares of passersby following the couple strolling down the main road so nonchalantly. As they approached the ticket office at the cinema, both stood still, looking about them, waiting. She looked at him. He smiled his all-embracing smile. She smiled. Finally it made sense: he didn't have any money. When the second date came around, Hani's declaration of love was quickly repulsed. Young women learn soon enough that too many young men are more than willing to pronounce on their heart's desire simply to earn a night in a woman's arms. That was not Duthie's style.

Hani was sometimes accompanied by his large, jovial friend, John Dube, a member of the Zimbabwe African People's Union (ZAPU). The three occasionally made their way to the football stadium to watch a local derby match, Hani's animated antics matching those on the field.

The burgeoning relationship between Duthie and Hani faced opposition – insults from strangers as well as so-called friends. On the streets of Lusaka, it seemed they were the only mixed-race couple, so they experienced a hush of whispers, of pointing. She was beautiful, captivating, thoughtful. She had already attracted her fair share of men since arriving in Zambia and had left a boyfriend behind in England. But her friendship with Hani was gradually drifting into something else. 'It was a mixture of the exotic and the familiar,' she described.

Even on her meagre teacher's salary, Duthie could still manage to buy a secondhand Morris Minor, and was soon regularly making the arduous three-hour trip out of town to see Hani. Inevitably, her brakes would snap or some part other than the one that was fixed a week before would collapse, forcing her to hitchhike.

In the low-slung Sixties world of cosmopolitan Lusaka, race mattered somewhat less among the better-heeled, better-educated and better-travelled inhabitants, and in these circles Duthie and Hani could try to be themselves. He always sought out the South African exile families, who were inevitably ANC supporters. This was the normal life which meant so much, even if Hani had a slightly eccentric way of infiltrating their ranks.

One of Duthie's most vivid memories of him came during one of these visits, when he took a 12-year-old boy aside and showed him how to disassemble and put together an AK47. She was only half-playfully enraged.

This was just a boy. But, insisted Hani, when the boy went home to South Africa, he would be going home to a war and needed to be prepared. They argued about that, with Duthie rushing to the moral high ground, arguing that one could not hope to bring about change through violence. 'Initially I was quite prissy about it,' she admitted. 'When you live in England you live in something of a bubble and you can philosophise about pacifism and all of these things. I came to realise that the armed struggle in South Africa was on a higher level, and you start to weigh what is worse.'

Among his friends, Hani was renowned for his stories and non-stop jokes, which were often self-effacing and told to the great amusement of the company. As his girlfriend, Duthie was always the greatest beneficiary of this – by association, a part of the star of the show. Driving through the suburbs of Lusaka, spontaneously striking up freedom songs, Hani's arm around her shoulders, she was on a high. She was integral to the cause. She belonged and she loved him.

And then it came time to have the talk. Hani had made it clear that his loyalty was to the ANC. As a member of MK, he was not supposed to have serious relationships, much less think about marriage. This did not mean he did not love her. This did not mean he did not want her, did not crave a life with her. But both recognised that he was a soldier and that he could be killed at any time. Neither of them wanted Duthie to be a widow, struggling on her own to raise fatherless children. So they could not get married then. It was just not to be. But was it already too late? They both knew when her time would be up. Nothing had been left unsaid. As always, time revealed that it grasped the meaning of everything.

In a year, a lifetime had passed for Duthie. On the train back to South Africa, her thoughts brushed those memories of a lover passionately relating stories of great Xhosa kings and valiant battles fought, and of how the battle had not started with apartheid but long before that. Her eyes were truly wide-open now. On the train, she saw the whites-only carriages, she watched the way white people conveyed a subtext of control. 'It was on that personal level. It was shocking,' she said.

On the Union-Castle ship back to Southampton there was enough open sea and more than a flicker of belief. It was not long before the first blue airmail letter arrived from Hani. He updated her on happenings in Lusaka. Friends. Places. For weeks, then months, the postman never arrived soon enough, bringing bills but also bursts of glorious emotion.

Then came the day came when the postman delivered an innocuous-looking airmail letter. Eagerly, she pulled at the edges, careful not to tear it. She tried to read slowly, but her eyes raced ahead as her mind tried to reign them in. He was going to war. She had known this day would come. He was a revolutionary. A liberation fighter. A soldier. She wrote back. Be careful. Survive.

It was no minor affair. The British media first mentioned battles taking place between terrorists and Rhodesian troops in the vicinity of the Wankie Game Reserve. Then, it began to cover the campaign with regular reports. For months, there was nothing personal, nothing to reassure her, until finally another letter came from Hani. He and some comrades had crossed into Botswana and had been detained. He confessed his disappointment in the Botswana government for arresting them, but he was otherwise upbeat. He was alive!

He asked her to send books to help pass the time behind bars. She did whatever else she could, she participated in rallies, but few had the time to listen. When Hani was released from jail in Gaborone in 1969, he confided it all to her – what really happened in Wankie, the devastating rush of what it felt like to squeeze a trigger, the rapid examination of the desperate race to take another man's life in order to save your own.

She said she found difficulty equating the Hani she knew with the machismo of war. He never paraded that. It was not part of who he was. Inasmuch as he was driven to fight, quite literally, for liberation, it was not an individual craving. It was not a calling. His soul was more familiar in the way he revealed how, rifling through the clothing of a fallen RAR soldier, he had found a portrait of the man's family and felt a deep sadness. This had a profound effect on him. These were the patterns. Over time, so much more was unveiled, primarily pain.

With this rich emotional time, the openness of a space for them seemed deceptively vast, and was never enough. Meanwhile, the blue airmail letters continued to arrive, but it became more difficult. Then she waited for his reply to perhaps the most difficult letter she wrote. They had always been somewhat pragmatic about their relationship, and now that relationship was changing. Their closeness being real, Duthie understood that Hani was becoming ever more immersed in the liberation movement. At this moment, there in Lusaka, Hani had no promises to make that he could keep, even if he wanted to.

When she had returned to England, her boyfriend had still been there, and it had seemed natural to pick up where they had left off more than a year before. The love in Zambia was another life, another world – and now Harold Vale proposed marriage. So Duthie married Vale, and it was a good match. He was a political activist drawn to the Left who shared her beliefs and provided her with love and stability. But it became clear that, married or not, she remained Hani's friend, and he hers. In any case, Hani would not release his hold. For a while, his was a desperate search for her comfort.

At the time of the Memorandum in 1969, he was indeed falling apart, and Duthie seemed to be near enough, yet far enough away, to offer emotional stability without the complexity of proximity. Although Hani could not get to England, he wrote to her and even tried to telephone. Despite the obstacles, Hani spoke openly to Duthie about how it troubled him that, on their return from war and prison, the Luthuli Detachment had been all but ignored by the ANC leadership. There were no ceremonies and no medals, no special briefings. Were it not for the party held by Jack and Ray Simons, it was possible that no one among the top brass would have mentioned their return at all.

It was not arrogance that agitated Hani. He was a self-deprecating hero. But he was perplexed that instead of using the soldiers from Wankie to inspire the troops in the camps, the army of which he was a commissar had left them on the periphery. Unable to cope with the lack of response over an extended period, and then finding himself and other ex-combatants shut out, abused and threatened by some within the leadership after they penned the Memorandum, Hani was in a state of disappointment and anger. It was not surprising that he fell into a depression. When he was suspended from the ANC – some say expelled – he had no stomach left for the fight, so he exiled himself from Lusaka. He got on a bus and headed for the solitude of the Copper Belt.

Hani confessed to Duthie that he was miserable and in a state of distress. He said he was battling internally with what had happened and he was very hurt. 'The thing is, he was not a street fighter at all,' she said. 'His first impulse was to talk. He found the attacks on him formidable.'

That was the private backdrop, when he even wondered if he shouldn't leave the movement altogether, and return to law and the serenity of the silence of books. Publically, and in the face of the movement, he was in despair over having to appear unbending. His decision to leave for the Copper Belt could be misinterpreted, but he was no longer in a position to care about that. This revealed the extent of his torment. Duthie explained to us that Hani liked to be liked. He would blame himself if he felt that another person was not treating him correctly. The converse applied in his opinion of others. He would agitate if necessary, to see justice done for someone else.

She gave him the same advice as had friends like Archie Sibeko and James April, who travelled to the Copper Belt to see him there, and told him to talk it through. She said this was an impossibly deep devotion in his life. Too impossible to cut it off. His innate leadership as a compassionate individual would surely overreach the negativity to which he had been subjected.

At first, when his friends arrived, Hani was remote and determined. He insisted he would never go back, and it was not petulance. But after many conversations with his old comrades, he could make a certain sense of his life. It took time for him to recover, Duthie said, and the entire set of events left a wound that would be opened again. Slowly, life back in Lusaka improved for Hani. He was beginning to find himself drawn into the ranks of the strategists. He was able to talk more openly about Wankie, to a more receptive audience within the administration.

She found that while he moved around in her head between letters, she, too, had gradually become enmeshed in her life in England, in her marriage and her job. Her ideology was developing, and she was finding herself increasingly connected to the left-wing intellectual circles around London. Any desire for something else remained completely barred inside her. Her respect for Hani made her want to contribute somehow to the southern African struggles in some way. She wanted it to be a way that was personally sustainable, so that she could involve herself not out of obligation but because it had meaning. Years later, it did. When Hani finally got to London, Duthie was able to see him, but it was complicated. She was not an insider among the ANC and SACP exiles, and although on the surface they were polite, they expressed their disapproval to Hani.

He explained that he did not have to fall under their control, but that their reasons were probably understandable. Either they would have preferred him to be with someone known to the movement, if not endorsed by the movement, or they would have wanted him to be connected only to his comrades.

Someone like communist stalwart Ray Simons did not have a predictable approach to anything because her whole existence had been about revolution. Since she was a young teenager, a mere 13 or 14, she had been involved in rebellion, having suffered because of oppression as a child. Others knew her as a potent influence, but also as something of a conspiracy theorist. It would be more simple if Duthie began to accept her this way. While his respect for Simons remained true, Hani nevertheless exhibited an independent streak. He was not prepared to be told who his friends should be, and paid no attention to the advice he was given. And so it went on. They talked and wrote when it was possible, as friends. From time to time they would meet in London when Hani was on his way to the USSR, the GDR and other places. Then came the news.

Anne Duthie had lunch with an old friend around this time, a man they nicknamed ZZ, and she always gained pleasure from seeing him. But ZZ had an announcement. Hani had got married.

Like many people, then and now, ZZ had the sense that there was less to Hani's marriage than romance and desire, if indeed there were even those qualities of grace. Depending on who you speak to, there is a sense that the ANC leadership would sometimes instruct particular people to get married. Did that happen to Hani? Whatever the truth of the matter, his marriage marked another change in the relationship. Soon after finding out about Hani's wedding, Duthie became pregnant with her first child. A few years later came the second. Motherhood was loveliness, her career was going well. Her friendships with other like-minded people were growing. England was home again. But Hani was going through hell.

She woke up one morning to the news in the paper that the ANC flats in Maseru had been attacked by a crack squad of the regime's soldiers. Duthie felt cold. She was horrified. Although the contact with Hani had begun to wane as each came to terms with lives that, essentially, had little in common, they had still kept in touch when they could. Duthie used every channel available to her until she got hold of him by phone that day. It was beyond a relief to realise that not only was he uninjured in the Maseru attack, he had not been at the flats at all that day. She wanted to help. It disturbed her that his daughters were there when the assault happened, so she asked Hani what she could do.

He asked for something that was typical of his priorities: help with an education for his daughters. And so began an extended investment by Duthie in the people Hani loved the most, which continued even after he was killed. After the Maseru raid, she and Hani began to communicate again, even if neither spoke about the fundamental rift. They were again becoming close friends.

As Duthie's own consciousness developed, and she found herself more and more drawn into politics, she considered ways in which Hani could properly explore his interest in internationalism. He was a sophisticated African communist, who would tease about the weight of dialectical materialism on the tongue. He never lost his intellectual lure for her.

The 1980s were a time of true terror inside South Africa and within the exile communities. Even Duthie, far away in England, came up against that cold wall. Refusing to wallow in fear, Hani focused on why he was doing what he did. He spoke persistently about the poor. Rural communities were under siege, and it tortured him. He reiterated in many conversations his reasons for joining the ANC and MK in the first place, with his membership of the SACP increasingly important. Duthie, like others close to Hani, began to see this shift as the most critical in his life. As a communist, he wanted to recruit. It was the most normal thing to do.

She told us there was plenty of violence and rancour from which Hani purposely excluded her during the 1980s. He wasn't comfortable talking about the hardships of his experiences in the camps in Angola, and he would never – as a loyal member of Umkhonto we Sizwe – reveal details of internal strife where it was expected to remain confidential.

Still, she worried about Hani. He was under tremendous strain. He was carrying too much. The leadership was relying on him too much. Those aspects of political life within the ANC that he found disturbing, rumbled around in his head. He confided some of those things to Duthie. He said there were times when the ANC seemed unyielding. 'I felt he was becoming more and more uneasy. Every time something happened, like him moving offices or going away for a while, it seemed to be attached to something else that was threatening.'

The ANC was utterly under siege then, and there were those in the leadership, who were not as secure within themselves as Hani, who used their power and influence to hurt the movement and its cadres. For this, Hani had some regrets. His heightened political activity, and the pressure to intensify the armed struggle, were exacerbated by the personal danger he experienced. There had been attempts on his life, there were perpetual death threats. He worried about his family. He naturally feared for himself. Lesotho was neither a safe nor a happy place, and it was only when Hani was finally recalled to Lusaka that he began to be able to breathe properly again.

A hiatus followed in the early 1990s, and it made perfect sense. Hani had come home. He was back in South Africa after 30 years away, and it was probably the most wearying but fulfilling time of his life. Everyone sought his advice and counsel. He wanted to stretch his way into as many homes of ordinary people as possible, to give his condolences to the families of dead cadres, to pay tribute to the contributions of others. He would confide in Duthie about how this was opening up his life. He was even thinking about how this could give him another experience outside the ANC.

It was tough to see how the pressures were affecting him, particularly the way the government was presenting him as a bogeyman. He couldn't get over that. It was that kind of thing, all this disinformation, that worried him so much.

On one occasion, not long before he died, bank robbers claimed he had put them up to their robbery, and he was so worried about what this was doing to his reputation among those people he cared about. He phoned me to reassure me that he was not involved, but of course I would never have believed anything else.

Every time he rang he told her he was concerned for his safety; he thought he might die, that he might be killed. It was tough to take. She wished desperately that he could feel free, even if only for a few days.

Duthie had a sense that Hani was more concerned about prospects for the SACP, where he felt so comfortable and so true to himself. So she thought that the interest he had in internationalism could be challenged by meetings with senior leaders in the Labour Party in Britain, particularly with leader John Smith. She got a friend of a friend to set up a meeting for Hani. But it was not meant to be. The news of Hani's assassination came like a bombshell and Duthie was plunged into a deep grief that was all the more difficult to bear because it could not be shared with those closest to her.

# POSTSCRIPT

Clive and Gaye Derby-Lewis were sitting in their family room, watching the 6pm news when they suddenly heard 'a lot' of car doors slamming outside. 'I thought, that is strange,' the former Conservative Party MP said. 'The neighbours must be having a party. What in fact happened was I got a terrible shock,' he told the Truth and Reconciliation Commission at the end of 1997. 'When they told me they were going to arrest me, I went white but I didn't faint.' After Derby-Lewis asked for some sugar water, South African Police investigator Captain Nic Deetlefs took him by the arm. 'He [told me], "look, you better lie down on the couch for a minute."' It was the beginning of the end for the mastermind of Chris Hani's violent death.

More than 15 years have passed since the trial and sentencing of Clive Derby-Lewis and Janusz Walus. The two were sentenced to death on 15 October 1993 in the Rand Supreme Court by Judge CF Eloff. The ANC opposed the death penalty and De Klerk had suspended it, so the sentences were commuted to life imprisonment. Yet in October 2008, after a month of mystery around Derby-Lewis's parole application, legal matters surrounding him became as tortuously coiled as a double helix. Or perhaps it was opportunism, wrapped in an enigma, that took advantage of a department that didn't seem to know its acts from its elbow.

Derby-Lewis was insistent that he was entitled to parole, even if the fight would be long and hard, ending up in the Constitutional Court. However the killer seemed to have grasped the wrong end of the stick. The nation was outraged when it filtered into public consciousness that Derby-Lewis had already been eligible for parole for more than a year. Limpho Hani, in turn, was furious when she received an e-mail from the Remission and Review Board of the Department of Correctional Services asking her to make representation to the Parole Board to be considered when Derby-Lewis's case was reviewed. The message read:

Morning mam.

The Minister of Correctional Services instructed the Chairperson of the Parole Board Pretoria to request if you or your family would like to make a representation. Alternatively you may attend the Parole Board session to provide verbal inputs. You will be given 14 days to respond to this request. If possible please provide us only with a postal address to send you a registered communication inviting you to participate in this process.

Yet, however tragic, these were almost small matters compared to what became Derby-Lewis's fiercest fight: against an Act of Parliament.

The core of his argument was simple, but inexplicably clouded over as a haunted month passed for both sides. Advocate Nkopane Thaanyane – who represented the Hani family and who filed their motion for intervention as co-respondents in the case – explained it: the 72-year-old Derby-Lewis was sentenced before the Correctional Services Act 111 of 1998 came into force. The Act provides for those sentenced to life imprisonment to be paroled or released upon 15 years, after the age of 65. His sentence had been handed down when the old Correctional Services Act 8 of 1959 was still in effect, and that law required those locked up for life to have been inside for 20 years before parole could be granted. There was nothing else to it. Derby Lewis just did not qualify. But his lawyer

Marius Coertze – who had been acting *pro bono* for Derby-Lewis since the middle of 2008, after his client apparently gave up on his previous attorneys, De Klerk & Marais – was adamant that there was more to it than that. Coertze alluded to political considerations, and resolved to argue the case all the way to the Constitutional Court. Derby-Lewis somehow believed the new Act was designed to discriminate against him, although even the most dispassionate observer would have considered such belief absurd.

He said he was over the required age of 65, that he had behaved himself behind bars for 15 years and that the parole board – on the basis of a report from the Case Management Committee of the Department of Correctional Services – had recommended his release in August 2007. Derby-Lewis's understanding was that the decision was supposed to have been implemented by 15 October 2008, 15 years after he was sentenced. When nothing seemed to be happening, he got anxious. Then came the saga of the e-mail to Hani's widow. But before the Constitutional Court heard any arguments, the Mystery of the Missing File, the Act that Wasn't and the Hearing that Started Too Early had to be solved.

What happened to the Case Management Committee's report on Derby-Lewis, which must have been handed to the Parole Board 15 months before he should have been considered? It was gone, 'dumped in file 13,' quipped Coertze. Neither Thaanyane nor Advocate BR Tokota – for the Minister of Correctional Services – knew where it was. But a couple of days after that discomforting news, Coertze said the file had apparently been found at the State Attorney's office and that he had requested it. It would become part of court papers, he said, but still, Thaanyane did not know of its whereabouts.

The Mystery of the Act that Wasn't coughed up two seemingly contradictory issues. Since Derby-Lewis had been sentenced under the old Act, which allowed for parole to be considered only after 20 years for lifers, why was he considered a year before he was due? And, if the Parole Board thought he should be considered upon 15 years, why did it allow him to appear before it after only 14 years inside? In 2007, any consideration – even made on the basis of bizarre ignorance – was too early.

Small wonder the Hani family applied to be a co-respondent in Derby-Lewis's urgent application for release. The Hani motion was filed by Advocate Thaanyane on a Monday afternoon. On the Tuesday morning, not long before Judge Ferdi Preller walked into Court 6A, a motion for intervention had been filed by Advocate Marumo Moerane on behalf of the National Council for Correctional Services for the council to be added as another co-respondent.

Advocate BR Tokota appeared on behalf of the minister. According to Tokota, the postponement that Preller granted was partly influenced by the fact that Derby-Lewis's lawyer had not yet filed a supplement to his papers, so there was no affidavit from their side yet. Thaanyane, who had filed an affidavit, explained what was in the Hani family application:

> First, it is based on the fact that in terms of the Correctional Services Act of 1998, in terms of which Derby-Lewis is applying for parole, the family must be informed that the Parole Board is considering releasing a prisoner on parole. The Hani family [also] believes that in terms of the Act, a requirement for release on parole is that a record of the trial must be placed before the Parole Board. The board must know what the judge's comments were as those will be informative in terms of whether this person must be released or not.
>
> The Hani family is of the view the record shows Derby-Lewis did not show any remorse during the trial and that must weigh against him.

An irritated Judge Preller, under the impression he would be considering the matter then and there, said he wasn't sure what the intervention of the Hani family had to do with it. 'This is between Mr Derby-Lewis and the state,' he said, which was strange, considering that the principle of restorative justice certainly applied. The new Act insisted upon it.

The confusion was heightened by Coertze outside court. His view was the state may suggest Derby-Lewis did not qualify for parole because the 'six years' in which he was on Death Row 'would not be counted'. The inference was the state would say the killer had thus only been behind bars since his sentence was commuted to life in 1995. This would have been shocking – if it had been true. And it was difficult to tell whether Coertze, evidently a jocular personality, was trying to be funny or not. But since Derby-Lewis was sentenced in 1993, there could be no question of 'six years' anyway. A senior judge, speaking off the record, laughed when asked to comment: 'They've got it all wrong. They're clutching at straws which don't exist.'

Derby-Lewis was clutching only at his own hands when he was spotted clambering noisily in his leg irons up a flight of stairs at the Pretoria High Court in the company of Pretoria Central prison warders. Coertze said he was there because he had been scheduled to appear before the court, under the impression proceedings would go ahead.

'This was no ordinary murder,' said Thaanyane. 'If we are going to release such people, we've got to be sure they will not be able to carry out those activities again. This is as important to the Hani family as to the nation.'

There was certainly political embarrassment for Ngconde Balfour, the Correctional Services Minister, throughout this saga. When the e-mail from Balfour's office reached Limpho Hani, the pain of Hani's assassination was as immediate as ever. His murder still hurt. Many believed that, had he not been shot dead on that quiet Easter Saturday morning, none of the enmity that had been evident in the ANC over the year before, as Mbeki and Zuma fought for power at the critical Polokwane conference in December 2007, would have happened. Hani, said so many, would have been the man in charge.

But Walus and Derby-Lewis had put paid to that vision. The pair were deemed to have been such liars by the Truth and Reconciliation Commission that it turned down their request for amnesty. Yet the correctional supervision and parole board at Pretoria Central Prison recommended Derby-Lewis be set free.

And had it not been for the intervention of Tozama Mqobi, the regional commissioner of correctional services, the killer might indeed have walked through the gates of Pretoria Central – and gone home. The request from Mqobi's office came more than a month after the recommendation had been made by the parole board. He insisted the family be involved, and soon it was all but over for Derby-Lewis.

Balfour immediately distanced himself from the e-mail and said it had been sent by 'a junior official', ostensibly in his name. He apologised 'to the Hani family, the SACP, the whole alliance and the people of South Africa for the inappropriate handling of the issue', and said he had not been aware that parole was being considered.

The SACP called the parole board's recommendation an act of 'extreme provocation'. Limpho Hani said it was 'quite obvious' what her response would be, but insisted that she would not react 'to a casual e-mail – this must be done with decency'.

Shortly before his death, Hani said: 'I have given up trying to prove that I am campaigning for peace. These guys see me as someone who is bad news. I fear that there are people who have the capacity to eliminate me. I am frightened about what they are planning.' At last, it was Derby-Lewis and Walus who had something to fear. The reaction to Derby-Lewis's proposed parole exposed the wound that will not heal.

# EPILOGUE 2023

You can't put away the pain of such a murder. It's a bloodied baton passed from the hands of one generation to the next.

It's been 30 years now, but it takes about two minutes to do the Walk of Remembrance near Chris Hani's gravesite in Germiston, Gauteng. The explanatory plaque describes the monument as in the form of a circle, to symbolise unity, equality and inclusion. There are a further five circles inside it 'to represent the ... decades of the life he shared so selflessly'.

You can stroll around it, but be careful. If you can't put away the pain, the site will showcase the anger. It languishes unfinished, like Chris Hani's ideals. And the ignominy that led to his death – represented by white supremacy and capital – has proved to be the country's undoing.

We wrote this epilogue near the end of 2022 as the ANC shuddered towards its 55th national conference and the Constitutional Court set aside the government's earlier rejection of Janusz Walus's application for parole. There was a heatwave during load shedding and the feeling on the streets had moved beyond mistrust into antagonism due to the impacts of landlessness, soaring unemployment,[1] food insecurity, unsafe schools, broken hospitals, gender-based violence, corrupt officials and violent crime.

A disgrace.

The richest one percent – who held a staggering 41 percent of South Africa's wealth – were still mostly white, mostly men and all capitalists. To enter that realm, you needed a net worth of at least R4.2 million, although most members of this group averaged around R22 million.[2]

The rest, the 99 percent, still consisted of people who were not adequately protected, did not own the means of production, had not been given back the land, were not guaranteed a roof over their heads and might not bother to vote in the 2024 election if they were under the age of 25.

This was what happened after Hani's ideas were shut down in 1993. To paraphrase his warning as he saw what was unfolding: 'Be wary of making only a neo-colonial shift.' As we know, 30 years later, the socialism he refused to give up – as the freedom South Africans most needed – was not even seriously considered by the power brokers in his movement. The SACP, which he was rapidly expanding to mobilise the masses, was kept small and controlled after he died.

It is only over the past five or six years that the party has begun to edge its way out of an alliance with the ANC, which has also restrained the independent power of the trade unions. Both could conceivably contest the 2024 election without the ANC, although each would need a stronger parliamentary partner to propel its ambitions forward under the current constitutional democracy set-up. And that 'stronger partner' would have to be willing to engage with Hani's vision, because the capitalist system entrenched after democracy has no intention of serving the people who were made to believe they 'won' in 1994.

'We didn't win' was another warning Hani issued during his tireless tours around the country and abroad to secure backing for 'a strong organisation' from mid-1990 after he returned home from exile. He conceded to supporters that 'there was no other life for us except the African National Congress', but it was not the ANC alone that defined the way forward. He urged: 'Let us build our party.'

'Let us make it a strong organisation, because it is the alliance of the ANC and the party which makes this army into what it is.' That party was the SACP, which later sat back as leaders of the former liberation movement did deals with apartheid's invested capital and new donors, which sold out the liberation.

If Hani's words – 'We didn't win' – had been given support by the ANC, it would of course have had to take on board the message of continued struggle. Instead, it twisted Hani's words and agreed at CODESA to the sunset clause and a government of national unity, which would avoid a winner-takes-all situation.

That 'coalition' – the ANC's original post-democratic political method, which the party is now replicating throughout the cities and provinces of this country – endorsed an economic status quo that protected elites. Over the past 15 years, since we started researching this biography, the elites and their funders have determined how far the intervention of the state will go. The state's hand is slipping ever more off the levers of power, as if to prove that investors are the answer to all our problems.

This was what Hani dreaded, the self-fulfilling prophecy – the 'neo-colonial shift' – that great African and development intellectuals had long identified as a mistake. Hani knew South Africa, as in 'the people', would never be free unless 'the tyranny of the market' was rolled back. Instead, it rolled forward relentlessly.

Those who have seen Hani's grave in Thomas Titus Nkobi Cemetery[3] and Winnie Madikizela-Mandela's grave in the private Fourways Memorial Park, about a half an hour's drive away, will have noticed that the sites reveal two Johannesburgs, two South Africas and two responses to protecting our titans. These dichotomies reflect life in this country.

The names of Hani and Madikizela-Mandela would forever be linked if there were lists of revolutionary war heroes. As comrades who didn't fit the appeasement of white supremacy and finance capital that defined the early 1990s, they stoked such levels of fear that both were obvious targets for elimination.

Madikizela-Mandela's family were, however, able to control how she was memorialised, because everybody knew that the ANC was not always on her side. That very public contestation and rift went on for some time.

But the ANC controlled how Hani was remembered, because it claimed him as its own when he died, and his family supported that. It is only in recent years that others have tried, with some success, to wrest him from the movement's hegemony.

By not introducing him to every South African child as a hero whose values should represent their own, by not incorporating his ideas into any policy that could be implemented and by not invoking a militancy for social change that would drive it forward in his name, the ANC ensured that he stayed dead.

Today, energy and courage are needed to reinvigorate his name.

\* \* \*

'The first time I heard about Chris, I was in high school. There was this guy who was recruiting for MK in my neighbourhood at the time. And so he used to teach about not your ordinary ANC. He used to talk about what was happening in MK. He used to talk about Chris.'

South Africa's most important newspaper editor, S'thembiso Msomi, catches himself in a fond memory, relatable to those who were old enough at the time. 'Because I had seen pictures of Joe Slovo, I also assumed that Chris was a white man because Hani wasn't a [common] kind of surname. Also, in government there was a guy called Chris Heunis, so I got a bit confused.

'But this MK guy would talk about Chris, and he would talk about this leader, this charismatic leader, and everything he said about him was actually true.'

Msomi – whose newspaper carried the first pictures of Hani dead in his driveway in April 1993 – is moved because the 30 years since Hani was cut down also define his passage. The *Sunday Times* editor is a highly regarded student of the liberation movements whose early years as a young activist were shaped in part by his exposure to Hani.

Msomi makes a valuable distinction: 'You know that people talk about leaders, like, I used to talk about JZ [Jacob Zuma] where I came from [in KwaZulu-Natal], because it was the area, and when he came out,[4] I found him very boring at the time. But Chris wasn't that way.

'He was the person that this guy was talking about, the military leader that he was.'

Msomi's description helps us to refine the responsibility of writing an epilogue for this updated edition of Hani's biography in the 30th anniversary year of his death. This is appropriate: Hani was a military leader first and foremost, and everything else stemmed from that.

An epilogue should be the work of leaders of the generation most afflicted by his assassination – those who were then the youth, who should by now have been living in a country with a proud history, instead of contemplating perennial 'what if' questions: what would South Africa have been like if Hani had lived?

Msomi and the commander-in-chief of the Economic Freedom Fighters (EFF), Julius Malema, are exceptional leaders. We drew them in here to find out what they had learnt from Hani, and how we could retain him as a nexus and a guide. Like us, Msomi and Malema were relieved about a few things when we approached them to look at these important ideas. These things were, however, not about the acceleration of people's power. Rather, they were simple historical facts.

At the time of writing, Chief Justice Raymond Zondo said in a unanimous judgement from the Constitutional Court that Walus was eligible for parole because denying his release would infringe on the Bill of Rights that people like Hani had fought for.

This was met by an outcry, not least from Hani's wife, Limpho, who said the decision was 'diabolical'.

'I have never seen something like this in my life,' she told News24 immediately after the court's decision in November 2022. 'If my husband was not killed, we would have never had elections. Mandela, after my husband was murdered, said to [FW] de Klerk for us to stop this, give us an election date. That is why Zondo and his friends today are sitting in this court.'

Public animosity and opposition from successive ANC ministers of justice, the Hani family and the SACP had prevented Walus from getting parole for more than a decade, with his most recent application rejected in February 2022. He had then approached the Constitutional Court.

'The now 68-year-old Walus ... said his time behind bars had led to him having interactions with black people. This ... had given him a better understanding of them,'[5] wrote Naledi Shange in 2021.

'If I do not succeed with this application,' Walus wrote in his court papers, 'it appears that I will be incarcerated forever, which is an unjust, inhumane and cruel punishment ... I have had lots of interaction with many different persons of different races in prison, and I have come to realise that apartheid was wrong and that all persons are born equal.'

His petition to the Constitutional Court came 'in the hope that it [would] find that the Supreme Court of Appeal was wrong in dismissing his leave to appeal against a ruling delivered by the high court in Pretoria [in 2020], where he was again denied parole'.

Advocate Muzi Sikhakhane, representing the SACP and Limpho Hani had argued that the nature of the crime committed by Walus was not 'merely the murder of an individual'. It was the murder of a democratic dream': 'It's a murder of a country, of a society and its democratic dream and it's a murder of a family, not just Mr Hani's.'[6]

'Mr Walus is not entitled to parole. No one is entitled to parole. People are entitled to be considered for parole.'[7]

On 29 November 2022, two days before his scheduled release, Walus was stabbed close to the heart by another prisoner while in the dinner queue. When we went to print, the killer was still under medical care. Conspiracies were everywhere, again. In the same week, Hani's memorial at his grave site was vandalised.

The other convicted assassin, 'rabid racist'[8] Clive Derby-Lewis, was dead. He had spent more than 20 years behind bars before he was granted medical parole in 2015. He died a year later of lung cancer.

It's worth recalling that when Derby-Lewis committed his crimes, he was not only a member of the President's Council, which was instituted in 1980 to recommend a constitutional blueprint to the apartheid government, but also a vice president of the Western Goals Institute, a well-funded London-based anti-communist 'think tank'. That connection helped motivate Malema's belief that Hani's death was 'calculated' beyond 'racism and hatred'.

Our view as writers remained that, if there was more to Hani's assassination than existed in the judgment against Derby-Lewis and Walus in 1993, the truth would emerge no matter how long it took. And over the 13 years since we wrote this book, we have heard many theories about what 'really' took place, some so incendiary that, if true, they could burn down the ANC's house of cards.

The thing was, we hadn't embarked on an investigation into Hani's death. This biography sought a wider understanding of his life, and so it was reassuring for us, when we set out to write this epilogue, that a few of Hani's comrades who were with him in the USSR, Tanzania, Zambia, Zimbabwe, Botswana and the guerrilla camps of sub-Saharan Africa were still alive to keep the MK commander's morality fierce and factual.

The Walk of Remembrance seeks to portray Hani as a jovial, delightful man whose radiance held the world in its thrall, but this was not entirely accurate. Hani's comrades would confirm that he was a fighter who had no patience with traitors; his personal warmth did not undermine his militancy.

We recall *Vice* writer Edward Ongweso Jr's scathing criticism in 2014 of the whitewashing of Martin Luther King, Jr: 'Every year, the third Monday of January is set aside to honor the memory ... [and] to celebrate this unforgettable man and his legacy ... but which legacy?[9]

'Are we to celebrate the image of a loved-by-all preacher whose struggle for human dignity was limited to one year of his life – 1963 – when he gave his "I Have A Dream" speech and showed his dedication to non-violence through protests and boycotts throughout the South?

'Or are we to celebrate the real Martin Luther King, Jr: an anti-war, anti-capitalist activist who called for direct action as much as non-violence, democratic socialism as much as equality, and black identity as much as integration?

'The first Martin Luther King is a fairy tale, a convenient story which avoids the hard truth of Martin's harsh but lucid critiques of American society. The second MLK is too easily forgotten, as is the case with all true visionaries, and to ignore his analysis is to deny Martin Luther King himself a voice and place a shoddy mannequin in his stead.

'We cannot tell ourselves this day is set aside for King when there is a systematic refusal to acknowledge his core beliefs.'

It is disconcerting to see the Walk of Remembrance's reductive portrayal of Hani. He had such a short time back home before he was killed that, surely, few outside his family and his comrades in exile could have said they really knew him. But what we all know is that he went to war against the apartheid regime intentionally, not as a last resort. We know he spent 20 years leading other soldiers with the intention to go to war.

Surely he would not have compromised his intention to bring about revolution in South Africa, or have tolerated an economic system that went only halfway, or part-way, to ending poverty and empowering the poor and working class, as we have seen happen. And so, any attempt to memorialise the life of Hani – even a monument – should incorporate his menace to private ownership and profiteering as much as it recognises that he was an obstacle to white power.

Mavuso Msimang, the respected former Home Affairs director-general who went on to co-found the African Parks Network, was a member of the ANC NEC in 2022. He knew Hani from the 1960s onwards and can account for his principles.

A member of the high command of MK and its chief communicator, Msimang served with Hani at the ANC's first military base in Kongwa, Tanzania, after their training in the USSR. They shared the discontent of seeing soldiers from FRELIMO, the MPLA and SWAPO leaving the camp to fight for the liberation of their countries from colonialism while MK stayed behind. Hani was driven to a level of rebelliousness that the ANC leadership struggled to control as time dragged on, and the movement's concern about deploying fighters to face the apartheid regime on the ground could not, in the end, prevent the Wankie campaign. Hani was single-minded about taking command on the battlefield.

As described in this book, the Luthuli Detachment's infiltration of then Rhodesia in 1967 was both brave and foolhardy, and Msimang testifies to the strength of the personalities who carried it out. Hani was a fighter through and through, and the 'radicalism' he expressed in the Memorandum, penned in anger after the Wankie debacle, was indeed addressed at the ANC's conference in Morogoro, Tanzania, in 1969.

Msimang was present at those momentous events and witnessed a Hani who wouldn't stand down easily. He saw no purpose in waiting to mobilise troops for the perfect moment to go to war against the regime. There was no 'perfect moment'. When Msimang looks back, in 2022, it's at an outspoken, fearless, determined comrade.

But that wasn't the whole story of the Morogoro Conference. Hani was still young, and he and the ANC had a long way to go together, as Msimang tells it. The Hani he knew in 1969 and the Hani encountered by Msomi, as a student activist in the early 1990s, describe the evolution of a revolutionary.

Msomi and Malema draw inspiration from that evolution. And it was also a comfort in compiling this epilogue – the idea that a store of memories of Hani's life can still be opened and keep revealing more of the truth.

Some believe Malema has the drive to be the president of the country in the 2030s, to lead the 'army' that Hani saw as the people on the move. When we spoke to Malema for this epilogue, he had indeed had enough of consolation prizes. He was working actively to unite 'leftist forces' in the way Hani would have wanted.

Like Msomi, Malema was conscientised by Hani when he was younger, and has spent much of his life strategising how to honour his hero. He is now moving on how to deliver, through revisionist politics, the South Africa that Hani had envisaged. At the age of 41, Malema has time and bodyguards, and he fears fokol.

On the day we interviewed him, Malema was on a reconfigured political track. He sat up straighter in his chair when he started talking about how Hani's dream was cultivated in him, from the age of nine, in Masakaneng, Seshego, Limpopo: 'We grew up knowing about our leaders [but] we were not exposed to their faces. We were not exposed to newspapers or television. We only had access to speeches that are given live in meetings, and we only had access to radio, to a particular extent.

'So when the death of Chris was announced, somehow an impression was created that it is going to be a turning point, that we're going to be called to war because one of the greatest leaders of the revolution has been killed, and therefore we need to ready ourselves. We waited for that call.' But it did not come.

He now wants to be the one to issue the call.

In a show of power, the EFF held a protest which shut down the N1 North highway near Johannesburg on the day Walus was to be released.

\* \* \*

Hani's Transkei family wanted his remains to be interred in lower Sabalele, where his parents were buried in the wild grass near the family home. They didn't want him left in Johannesburg, but his remains stayed at Thomas Titus Nkobi Cemetery (then still known as South Park Cemetery). The shambolic state of his grave reflected what had been lost when the ANC turned its back on the future it had promised.

Once a year, the gravesite is cleaned up, the grass is mowed and the shabby containers on either side of his headstone are jammed with flowers as earnest admirers and family members engage in sombre pageantry with grifters and crooks bearing bouquets.

It felt certain that, in 2023, observers would again remark on how this only happened once a year, and so the circle goes round and round until the politics of the new eventually wipes out even the memory that is made.

This is why there is a renewed urgency about presenting Hani as much as possible, as often as possible, on as many stages as possible, with no holds barred. Hani should be remembered for how he lived, and for his ethics.

'What I thought was important about [Hani] at the time,' says Msomi, 'was the fact that he tended not to talk [in the same way as] the leaders who came out of prison and came back from exile. They mostly spoke politics, pure politics. [Hani] spoke politics and linked it to civic issues, linked it to housing, linked it to health, linked it to issues around poverty.

'He was one of the earliest ANC leaders talking about free education.

'To me, he's someone who wasn't just thinking that apartheid is about to end and that's the end of the struggle. And I suspect that in the SACP, he was one of the people who insisted on this thing of it being "a breakthrough", rather than freedom.

'When you got to '94, the ANC's Mayibuye had "Free at Last", and the SACP was talking about a "breakthrough", which was the idea that "now we have political power, what are we going to do with it?" [The SACP was saying] this is an important milestone, but we are still going somewhere, whereas the ANC ... seemed to be saying, "We have arrived."

'I think the important thing about him, for me, was that even back in the early 1990s, he was already thinking about post the elections. He was the one leader who was already talking about what needs to happen ... the role of the civil society, the role of trade unions. His decision that, instead of positioning himself to go into government, he was ... going to the SACP and, from there, to work with unions and other civil society groups.

'For me, [it] suggested someone [for whom] the struggle still continued.'

For the ANC, however, it was as if the movement dropped anchor when Hani was killed, and it has never pulled it up. Malema takes this disillusionment a step further.

'The disappointment starts from 1994, where you say revolution took place and we took power, but those who were in power literally lost nothing. How can the revolution take place and then the oppressor loses nothing, yet the oppressed claim to have emerged victorious, because there is nothing to show that indeed there was a revolution in 1994?'

Like Hani did in the Memorandum, Malema names names. He dubs Cyril Ramaphosa an 'arriviste', created by capital to service its post-apartheid ambitions – a significant aspect of these being to ensure that the ANC's leaders were compliant from the late 1980s onwards.

'The killing of Chris was not an act of hatred or racism,' Malema says. 'It was a calculated move to get rid of a leader they feared because they could not corrupt [him]. When [representatives of white corporates] went to negotiate with the ANC in the late 1980s ... [they] identified Thabo Mbeki as one of those people they can work with – such an "intelligent person" – and Chris was already identified as a problem.'

Malema takes it back to Morogoro and even earlier, saying, 'instead of honouring what [Chris had] complained about ... and what he complained about throughout – that we need to go back home and fight and take over and deliver to our people – we have become the most corrupt state.

When we signed off on this chapter, Ramaphosa was facing a political crisis after a damning report into a 2020 robbery at his game farm.

'Chris, every platform he took, was the rejection of corruption – that we must not be co-opted by corporate South Africa and become corrupt and turn against our people. [That's why] the apartheid regime and the Americans and the British feared Hani more than anyone.'

Malema talks about the ANC's first conference after 1990, 'where Hani was going to contest Thabo Mbeki and ... [it was] demonstrated that Chris was going to win ... When the elders and those who had contact with the outside spies and handlers realised that Chris is going to emerge, they then introduced Walter Sisulu to be the deputy president of the ANC.

'But there was still some sense of discipline at the time, where the young will not contest the old. So that's how Chris withdrew, as a disciplined member, and Thabo Mbeki did the same as a disciplined member. From there, they knew that Walter was too old and ordinarily will not succeed Nelson Mandela, so this battle will never be resolved.

'Whatever you do, the next conference was the winner of this contestation.

'What do we do? We have to get rid of this guy, because this guy is going to turn South Africa into a socialist state. So they killed Chris.'

\* \* \*

Plumes of smoke from informal settlements twist morbidly in the distance above Hani's memorial. This is just as it was when he was being buried – only then the smoke was from fury as ordinary people lit fires, burned tyres and threatened to overthrow the system right away, without mercy.

Thirty years on, the smoke signals the harms that have continued through the democratic period in poor communities denied access to even an unstable energy grid and socialised into violent interactions to gain any sort of power.

The monuments at the ends of the Walk of Remembrance today deny what Hani saw coming.

In 2012, South African socialist Bobby Wilcox, a teacher who spent seven years on Robben Island as a member of the progressive African People's Democratic Union of South Africa, wrote a classic analysis of 'how the ANC has become notorious for its culture of self-enrichment and corruption': 'The petty bourgeois leadership … in order to promote its class interests, reached accommodation with the representatives of the bourgeois, the leadership of the National Party and formed a "government of national unity" with them.'[10]

'On assuming power, the ANC proceeded to reward Nelson Mandela, Walter Sisulu and its other leaders, who had served long terms of imprisonment under the regime, by sanctioning their unprecedented enrichment. Nobody, least of all the now critical liberals, questioned where this money came from and what its purpose was.

'Then, the salaries of politicians and high-ranking personnel in government offices were dramatically increased, besides the grand salary allocations for those in the employ of [the] ANC itself. This was ostensibly to reward Blacks with the kind of standard of living that they were previously denied. Suddenly, it became highly profitable to be a politician, particularly an ANC politician.'

There was not much more to it than that, on the surface. But South Africans striving to be part of a different society looked back at their first encounters with Hani, and how these shaped their beliefs.

Malema's recollection of how Hani's death was marked in his community, and how he took the moment as a summons to action, is anecdotal. But because he memorably raised it in court in 2011, when AfriForum first charged him with hate speech for singing 'Dubul' ibhunu' (Shoot the Boer), South Africans came to link Hani and the fiery young Malema in their memory.

Malema tells us: 'When the day came for his funeral, we joined everybody else who was going there. I was too young and I was not allowed to come to the funeral because we were travelling almost four hours from Polokwane to Johannesburg, so I insisted. I tried.

'There were taxis which were hired together with buses. I tried to get into a taxi, and I was discovered. Then I was removed from a taxi and told to go home. But the reason I didn't go home is because we were told there are trains, there's going to be a train that will take us from there. So I knew the controller of the train and somehow I managed to manoeuvre myself into the train.

'The story of the train fell off, and buses came. When the buses arrived, and nobody has been assigned to be in charge of this or that bus, I immediately went into a bus and sat under the seat. And then we travelled. Halfway through, we stopped at a garage to go and get food, and that's when they discovered I was there, and started assigning each other that I need to be looked after.'

After a night vigil in which the young Malema was given the responsibility of keeping a fire going outside the stadium, he was gripped by the anticipation of what would surely follow.

When Peter Mokaba – the first president of a united ANC Youth League in 1991 – stepped up to address the crowds, 'We thought he is going to speak, and we're looking forward that Peter is the one who is going to give the order.'

But 'he shouted [for a] few seconds, then he sat down, saying the "president general" is the one who's going to speak, and then President Mandela spoke, as you know, and ... we were all left disappointed that there was no war declared.

'Later we came to appreciate the wisdom of the leadership at the time, because when you now look at the strength of MK, its capacity to engage the apartheid regime, how it was structured, you realise that it couldn't have declared any war and win it, because we literally weren't ready ... but that's how we get to connect with the spirit of Chris.

'Young as we were, the determination, the anger, the frustration of those thousands and thousands of our people there is what kept us going [to believe that] one day we will get our freedom.'

Msomi's first encounter is also anecdotal, but he saw Hani in the flesh – and such was the light that switched on that he still feels the excitement today. Hani was at the time under severe pressure. He had taken refuge in the Transkei after returning to South Africa in April 1990 under a provisional amnesty order issued by FW de Klerk after the unbanning of the ANC in February. Msomi was among the students at UNITRA [University of Transkei, today Walter Sisulu University] who were addressed by Hani at that time.

Hani had stayed with Madikizela-Mandela in Soweto for a short while after he came home, but when his 'amnesty' was revoked – the apartheid regime said it had 'expired' – he had to move to his 'homeland', where he fell under the protection of Major General Bantu Holomisa.

'We were relaunching COSAS [Congress of South African Students], and he arrived to address the students. He was just as charismatic [as we had been led to believe],' says Msomi. 'He didn't come with a speech like Mandela. Mandela came in and read a whole speech about the struggle of students from 1976 up until 1980-something.

'Chris just spoke about the issues that were [then] confronting schoolkids and what needed to be done going forward. He spoke about what people's education would look like – or what it should look like – post-apartheid.'

Msomi recalls how he had also attended a meeting at the University of Durban-Westville – an epicentre of struggle politics – when the ANC NEC took the decision to suspend the armed struggle in August 1990.

'This was the weekend. There's a gathering of a few MK people who had returned and others who were working in the underground, SDUs and so on. And then Chris talks about the NEC decision and he defends it.

'He says, "Personally, I disagree with this, but these are the reasons this was taken." And he defended every point, which I thought was quite fascinating because, now looking at it, leaders generally think about their own popularity and so they would try and distance themselves from things. But he would say, "I was not convinced by 1, 2, 3 but this is why the NEC took this decision and so we all have to fall into line.

'Because of that, a lot of people were more accepting of the decision to suspend the armed struggle, at least where I was, than there had been before, when the decision was announced, [when] people had said that it was a sell-out position.

'So when it was Chris talking about it, it had a lot of impact.'

Malema joined the struggle without having met Hani, in the belief that 'at some point we're going to join MK, we're going to leave and we'll be under the command of people like Chris and Joe Modise, many other people that the MK people sang about.'

'We were being prepared psychologically, young as we were. In those trainings, for us it was preliminary trainings to prepare us to the actual training. So I grew up wanting to be a soldier – not just a soldier, but the revolutionary soldier that belongs to the revolutionary people's army aligned to the ANC.

'Leaders did not want to lower the guard, despite the fact that there was [the] release of Elias Motsoaledi. There was [the] release of Walter Sisulu before Nelson Mandela, because of age and all of that.

'As they kept on releasing our leaders, I think the leadership thought they were bluffing and therefore we should not lower the guard. We should prepare them when they're young so that when that time comes, they're ready to engage in a war.'

Those were populist positions then, but can the capacity for change, of the kind Hani inspired in young people like Msomi and Malema in the 1990s, be reactivated today? Socialist reconstruction movements took place in Czechoslovakia, Hungary, Chile and Portugal in the second half of the 20th century, of course, and since then there's been the Bolivarian Revolution in Venezuela, Buen Vivir in Ecuador and other 'pink tide' movements in Latin America.

Malema believes it is possible, but it must be propelled by true confidence in the ideology: 'Chris was such a good orator who, in his speeches, simplified Marxism and make it part of who we are and what we want to become. He always understood that to throw phrases and jargons at people that are being agitated and mobilised behind the revolution will not serve any purpose.

'So you will have Chris, you will have Winnie, you will have Peter, you will have Tony Yengeni and them as agitators and good orators of the movement, but everybody knew that Chris was one of the best intellectuals produced by our movement, because the ability of a revolutionary intellectual is to simplify complex concepts of Marxism, Lenin and them, and he would do that with ease.

'That's why, when he passed on, despite the fact that we never had any physical contact with him, we connected with him because he spoke our language.

'We had a distortion of socialism through Bantu education. It was so vulgarised that none of us wanted it – that when you park your car, someone is going to come and take your car and move. Someone can just come and sleep in your house, and all manner of things.

'But through Chris and them, we came to understand that, actually, socialism means that the landless must have the land, the people must control the means of production, and that which constitutes the core of the economy should be controlled by the state.

'Private ownership will be allowed under a socialist state except on strategic sectors of the economy. For instance, you can't privatise, as we speak now, Eskom, which is the most strategic asset.

'Now they make it so dysfunctional so that they say, no, there's someone who's coming to rescue us. And that's how capitalism works: it first makes it look like it is failed, so that when they say, no, there is a person who is coming to rescue, everybody just say, maybe that is the solution.'

Msomi returns to how Hani had 'the ability to work in different terrains of struggle – which is something that I don't think is true of every leader in South Africa'. That ability would have kept people focused on what they needed to do as a collective, to transform South Africa, instead of being distracted by party-based politics directed by capital.

'When you look at him – Fort Hare, Cape Town, student, youth organisations, goes into exile, is in the army, at different levels, comes back but is able to connect. He is one of the people who started the units that used to talk to trade unions in the 1970s. He understood what the workers' struggles are.

'When he went to a place to speak, he connected with people. In Durban, during the political violence, he was not like Jeff [Radebe], who tried to discourage violence but showed no appreciation for why the violence was taking place.

'Hani will talk about how to protect communities and then talk about the need to enter into peace agreements with other oppressed communities – without rejecting the community for whatever they were doing at that time.'

Msomi is more ambivalent about whether there is sufficient unity and understanding of purpose among the progressive forces now. 'I always think about #FeesMustFall,' he says. 'It was a challenge to the thinking about where the struggle was going, but the working-class leadership wasn't there. [It] wasn't provided by anyone because they just didn't know how to respond to those students who were again linking the two issues of class and race in a more creative way than the ANC had done before. So they didn't know how to react to that.

'They didn't take opportunities that came with that movement. Actually, they just took leaders into their organisation and that was it.'

That doesn't mean Msomi does not believe it could happen.

'I do think that we are likely, as the ANC collapses, to see a realignment of left organisations. The question is whether they will then be able to attract the population, or not. The thing is, with [us South Africans] it seems to me that ideology is not the most important thing.

'It's the [political parties] that had an element of race in them that actually attracted people's attention. So the issue is: in a post-apartheid [society], is that still the truth or not?'

Malema's antagonists insist he is obsessed with race and would wish to exclude white people from any future narrative, and the 'Dubul' ibhunu' matter – which resurfaced again in 2020, with AfriForum again taking Malema to court – is a satisfying example for them.

The EFF leader is unperturbed with what he says are 'smears', just as Hani was.

'When we were 11, 12 and now we were training public speaking, we used to stand next to a wall and speak alone, and you ought to imagine there's so many people listening to you and some trying to disrupt you, some distracting you from the message.

'Do not leave what becomes the central message of what you want to give these people. What's important is by the time you leave, you can say so many things, but there ought to be a central message that must be delivered, and it must be delivered in such way that our people appreciate and take heed of that message, and they can repeat it everywhere.

'Ordinarily, when we come back from rallies, like churches, you are asked, "Which verse did the pastor read today?" to demonstrate you're from church. So the same thing with rallies. Who spoke and what did he say?

'You can't just say, "He spoke very well", like they used to do in [the] IFP when Mr Buthelezi will address them throughout in English and they say, "The child of the king has spoken." But what did he say? They don't know because he spoke in English.

'[Like Chris] we must always speak one message through many voices, and that's part of what we were able to take from those things.'

Today, the ANC calls this 'leftist', as does Malema, whose party probably does have the 'capacity' to mobilise forces on the ground in some areas. But to mobilise in the numbers one sees in Iran, Hong Kong and even the United States during the #BlackLivesMatter rallies in 2020 would take a full social agreement that has not yet been forged in South Africa.

Hani could have done that, and in this respect Malema acknowledges the difference between himself and Hani. Malema is not a giant. He sees that his apparent 'flip-flopping' needs to be contained and honed, constantly, into a single message. He realises that his stature – in terms of corruption, morality and example – is far from unassailable.

Hani could get through to millions of people rather quickly because there was trust and integrity. Malema has to continue working on these, even if he has the ability to persuade around common concerns.

'Today, we are bombarded with the story that Eskom is costing the state billions,' he says. 'It's not making profit and all of that. But Chris's teachings taught us that its purpose [anyway] is not to make profit. It's an intervention in this country [for the good of the people]. However, it must raise sufficient money to run itself so that it doesn't cost the taxpayer. So we appreciated that.

'When we grew up now into causes, we attended congresses of NUM [National Union of Mineworkers], Communist Party and the likes, and we loved the NUM congresses more because they were more political, and they were more theoretical, and Marxism and Leninism were deeply discussed by mineworkers who worked underground, who actually appreciated and understood Marxism and Leninism better than teachers.

'So if you attend a SADTU [South African Democratic Teachers' Union] conference and you attend a NUM conference, the theoretical, ideological engagement are more exciting out of those of underground mineworkers than of teachers who, some of them, did not even have an idea what we're talking about – partly because they heard throughout when they're growing up that this socialism is bad, because that's what the capitalist education system taught.

'But Chris made it simple for us to understand that, actually, this is what we're looking for.'

Msomi agrees. 'Chris had a different idea to what these guys [the current ANC] are doing here. I may be wrong here. But I think Hani's significance was his ability to link the national struggle against oppression, against apartheid, to the class struggle [without suggesting] that one is over the other.

'If you listened to Chris, the ANC leader, he spoke like an ANC leader. But if you listened to Chris the communist, he spoke like a communist. So in his mind the link between the two was genuine, and therefore he never said the one precedes the other, which is something I think the current leadership is grappling with.

'In COSATU now, I think the current that is becoming stronger is one that says, "Why are we bothering to be in an alliance with our supposed class enemies? Why don't we just form or work towards a working class, an independent working-class formation that has no alliances with other people and we fight for socialism?" which will win them a lot of support from other smaller, left-leaning organisations.

'The question is whether that will make them connect with communities, because, to use an SACP formulation, possibly the dominant conflict in South Africa remains race, although the fundamental one is class. So, then, most people get attracted by identity politics rather than class politics.

'Now, when you are saying we de-emphasise the identity politics to focus on class, it seems to me that you attract a lot of people in the academic space and leaders of unions, but you don't attract the general population.

'Chris seemed to work in both spaces and therefore win over people from both sides, whereas the conservative leaders in COSATU and the SACP, and even in the ANC who are on the left, are stuck in the "We have to defend the National Democratic Revolution", to a point where you even abandon workers today.

'[The youth] see that the problem has always been that ... the ANC is a leader, yet the ANC does not want to take us where we want because we want to fight capitalism. I think that's where the contradiction is, and I don't think there is a leader like Chris right now who's able to articulate the link between the two in a way that is convincing.'

\* \* \*

The problem in 2022 is also those grifters and crooks who place bouquets on Hani's grave every April. They take advantage of the confusing propaganda put out by the ANC to justify its right to win elections.

The Hani monument in the cemetery is reached by a circular set of steps. The accompanying plaque says that the steps are designed to 'encourage interaction, illustrating [Hani's] warm personality, hospitality and philosophy of sharing', the purpose being to 'beam outwards to symbolize the ripple effect that Chris had on the lives of millions'.

It's misleading. Hani never sought the idolatry that was given to a Mandela or a Gandhi. He did not espouse 'hospitality', and his warmth wasn't shared with everybody but with his comrades, the people who would benefit under a socialist mantle, and with allies of that philosophy. At a banquet held in East London in 2006 to mark the 13th anniversary of Hani's death, then deputy president Phumzile Mlambo-Ngcuka quoted 'Hani's neighbour in Zambia': 'If that man was weather, it would always be sunny. He doesn't change. He's always the same, friendly, smiling, full of humour and caring. I think Kaunda must make him a Cabinet minister so that he doesn't go back to South Africa.'[11] The 'ripple effect' would feel real were it not that Hani is so selectively celebrated.

Yes, water and electricity have been provided to millions of people who did not have those essential services under apartheid. Yes, there are tarred roads in places where that was not the case before. Yes, the laws have changed to create an impression of universal suffrage, and we're always reminded that 'the whole world' admires our Constitution.

But Hani got under the skin of his leadership in the 1960s because he wasn't willing to be pushed aside by what had already been done, and by promises. Like Madikizela-Mandela, he was far too passionate, even reckless, to be pacified.

'They said [when we were kids], "We're going to live like white people" – that our places will have tar roads, our places would have clean running water, electricity, we'll have proper houses that look like white people's houses,' says Malema. 'We were told these are the sorts of things that are going to happen to us.'

'What even attracted us to the revolution was that the kind of education we [were told we] would receive will be such that it will give us opportunities, not only in South Africa but all over the world. And we've all said we want this.'

In general, what the youth, ordinary villagers – anyone with a stake – should be able to acquire, what they need from the state, has been rendered beyond the means of government. Too expensive. Too much to ask.

To that end, the people's desires have been made laughable by the educated, capitalist class who laager not around their backgrounds but around the accumulation of wealth.

'Where Hani comes from, the rural poor, issues around the fight against poverty would have found resonance,' says Msomi. 'Most of the people who were being recruited, especially from Fort Hare [in the 1960s], came from relatively well-to-do families. They were middle-class people. He wasn't. He would have been a peasant in another country.

'He also gets recruited into the SACP by Govan Mbeki. That man was a radical. South Africa would have been completely different if that man was Mandela. He had his own radical ideas of what needed to be done, and I think that would have influenced Chris in a way.

'Chris also had a lot of friends from beyond just the ANC and the SACP. I think he got influences from the PAC, the Non-European Unity Movement in Cape Town, which I think an ANC member in Natal or Transvaal would not have been exposed to, because if you look at what was happening in the western Cape, I mean the ideological debates there were more vibrant than in these other areas, than in Natal and Transvaal.

'The key ideology was simply African nationalism, pure and conservative. So Chris, being that creative leader, knew the importance of theory and practice.

'With communists, they tend to be very rigid, and they go according to dogma. And even when I try to look at his writings, I think that in the past, the SACP would not have elected this guy as the general secretary because he didn't write a lot. He didn't write the formulaic stuff. When he did, it was just speeches, or he was doing propaganda, but he was a man of action.

'From those experiences, he could formulate ideas, which is why they then end up with the Memorandum, which is what they have seen when they tried to come back into the country. So I think that influenced him.

'Compare him to people like [Thabo Mbeki], who would be more at a theoretical level and not involved in day-to-day struggles and therefore not in touch. They see these things as a science … [but] Chris was more in touch with what was happening on the ground, the killings of people and how vicious the system had become in terms of repression.'

Hani set the bar high.

Malema says, 'without any fear of contradiction', that when he and fellow EFF leaders Sindiso Magaqa and Floyd Shivambu were expelled from the ANC in 2012, 'we were pursuing what Chris had actually taught us'.

'In 2011, when we took the resolutions we took in the ANC Youth League conference – very leftist, very radical – we were accused [for instance] that our nationalisation resolutions are about bailing out mines.

'I mean, Jeremy Cronin[12] used to say we are "bought" by these mining companies – and some of them, I was hearing their names for the first time – and that [the mines] were actually … bankrupt [and] they wanted the government to buy them out. And that's not what we're talking about. We were talking about what Chris spoke about before, [in this case] nationalisation.

'After every conference – a lot of people don't know this – I go home and I sit alone. I remain alone after conference … to make reflections of what transpired. So as I was sitting alone in 2011, Tony Yengeni knocks at my door and says, "I'm here to see you." I welcome him, and he says, "They're either going to expel you or they're going to kill you."

'I said, "Why?" He said the resolutions you have taken [are] exactly what led to the killing of Chris Hani. This mining intelligence is the best. Way better than the state intelligence. Two things are going to happen to you. They're going to expel you from the ANC or they're going to kill you for those resolutions you have taken.

'It didn't take three months. [Afrikaner billionaire] Johann Rupert spoke for the first time publicly on politics on South Africa and said the ANC Youth League is like an irritating mosquito which needs a Doom [insecticide]. And Gwede [Mantashe, the then ANC secretary-general] became that Doom that killed this irritating mosquito called the ANC Youth League.

'For what? For repeating what Morogoro said, what Chris said, what all other leaders who came before us [said], what the 1949 Programme of Action of the ANC Youth League spoke about. So we were released because we were saying to the leadership: let's go back to the basics, because we are moving away.'

Malema says the EFF was formed to create 'an alternative platform for that struggle to be continued, because if there is no left party that is strong [enough] to pull the ANC to the left, the ANC was unapologetically moving to the extreme right, and even though, following the EFF formation, the ANC went to the 2017 conference in Nasrec and took the same resolutions as the EFF, [it] elected wrong leadership which did not implement those resolutions'.

Malema sees the party as such a home for Hani's ideas, that even 'that tendency' in the ANC, once pushed, could move back in the right direction either to reorient their own movement or to join his.

Was there discussion about Hani when Malema was still in the ANC? Was Hani alive in the ANC corridors when he was there, or was Hani behind a screen? Did he even exist in discourse?

'No, no, no, no,' says Malema. 'They had abandoned him completely – and, even now, Chris is not part of the core thinking that constitutes what we call the "leadership of the ANC".

'We lived Chris because we lived with his people. We lived with Peter. We lived with Tony. We lived with Holomisa. We lived with Winnie. And in their articulation, they repeatedly said, "Chris said this," seeking to remind us of what Chris Hani represented and why we should not move away from all those ideas.

'I mean, for obvious reasons, I think, President Mbeki would have ordinarily had problems with Chris and feel threatened by Chris, and that speaking about Chris under his leadership would ordinarily suggest you are challenging him.

'Wittingly or unwittingly, he would have [perhaps wished] his name away.'

Malema and Msomi both point to unresolved historical conflicts between Mbeki and Hani as significant when they reconsider the past 30 years. Msomi characterises these conflicts as 'rivalry, and because [older ANC leaders] took [each] under their wing, that "thing" was always there'.

He believes it intensified early on when 'Chris and his comrades made a mistake by naming names when they wrote the Memorandum': 'I think Thabo Mbeki would carry a grudge – if you know that, in that Memorandum, this is what they said about you as an individual. [And then] people like Joe Slovo … identified Chris as the alternative [to him].'

But he also considers their similarities, which were remarkable, and highlights a prophecy, if you like, that Mbeki made in 1994. It shakes us because it seems to have been forgotten, in the way South Africa tends to forget more than to remember: 'Four months after the elections, Mbeki writes "Unmandated Reflections",[13] which looks forward to what will happen – that a left-leaning party will emerge from within the ANC and accuse it of selling out. He too was thinking beyond where we are, and that's what made [Hani and Mbeki] brilliant in that sense.'

Malema would say that this 'left-leaning party' is the EFF, and reassert how it intends to bring the ANC 'back to its roots' after 2024, but with the EFF in control, operating under a proxy mandate from Hani. Mbeki would be unlikely to respond positively to such an eventuality.

But Msomi and Malema are affected by how Hani set an example of how to respond to changing political circumstances – through consistency. In our opinion, Malema would do well to promote consistency and staying true to your positions, if he has the political sincerity to emulate Hani.

'Chris is probably the only one of the prominent ANC leaders, black ANC leaders who were very prominent in the SACP, who did not quietly resign in 1991,' Msomi reminds us. 'Like the Zumas, the Thabos, others used the justification that, because we are in negotiations, we don't want the Afrikaners to think that everyone they are negotiating with is a communist, so we will let our membership lapse.

'Chris didn't.

'You'd look at senior members of the SACP like Josiah Jele, who let his membership lapse. They all left. Chris [instead] decided to stay and build an organisation that, when you look at it globally, was supposed to perish because all communist parties were collapsing all over the world.

'So he must have had some idea in his mind that "this is what we are going to do, going forward: build a new front using the SACP to just push forward with the struggle". The others were just "Now we are in the stage where it is ours to govern."'

Malema has a singular frustration with the scant attention that has been paid in the former liberation movement to the scale of that mentality: 'Chris was one of those big giants that should have been celebrated at the same level as Nelson Mandela and the same level as OR Tambo. Chris was not just an ordinary person. He was a thinker, he was a commissar, and to be a commissar, it was the highest level.

'I mean, we've seen with the years since I left, I don't know what inspires that, but you have some years dedicated to certain individuals by the ANC, but there's never been a year that is dedicated to Chris. Because to say that this is the year of Chris Hani, then you have to go back to that political morality of Chris and ensure that the things that Chris stood for are actually implemented.

'Today, [the ANC has the] OR Tambo political school, internally. What is there today, internally, that is actually dedicated to the memory of Chris Hani so that his political morality characterises what [the ANC is] today?'

Winnie Madikizela-Mandela once said that South Africans 'worshipped Chris Hani'. Could it be that the ANC's failure to embrace Hani unconditionally over the past three decades has made it less contentious for Malema and others on the left – who equally 'worship' Hani – to claim Hani as their own?

'In 2022, on his birthday, the EFF did a Hani lecture, and when they saw us doing a Hani lecture, they [the ANC] were quickly rushing to do the same thing because they need someone to remind them of who they are. They've actually forgotten,' says Malema.

'We took a conscious decision that we need to revive Chris's memory – the same way we are doing with Winnie Mandela – because, if we were not there, they would have just buried her name and destroyed it not for anyone to remember it.

'Chris is at the level of Che Guevara, the way Che is being celebrated all over the world. That's how Chris should be celebrated – here, in the continent and the diaspora, because that was our African Che Guevara. We saw that opportunity and we said, in the EFF, we make acknowledgements, that we're not the ones who started the revolution.

'There were people who came before us and we must never pretend that we're the ones who started the revolution. And the only way to honour these people is to make sure that we consistently remind our people of who these people are: Robert Sobukwe, Steve Biko, Chris Hani, Anton Lembede, AP Mda and many others.

'It's always important that we remind society of who we are and what these people represented.

'Self-criticism, Chris teaches us that – and Lenin and Marx teaches us that. We ought to be critical of ourselves. We must self-criticise, and if we get a genuine criticism coming from genuine people, it will always be well-received.

'When we had completed school with matric and our people said, "The last person to lead us with no tertiary education is Zuma – you must go to school," we responded to the call because it's a constructive engagement.'

\* \* \*

Mavuso Msimang was in the news in October 2022 when he 'took a swipe at Cyril Ramaphosa, saying his five years at the helm of the governing party [had] been dismal'.[14] TimesLive reported Msimang saying that 'the

ANC was facing a crisis of existence because of [the] poor leadership "it has absorbed into its ranks"'.

The article reported that he had told SABC News: 'The bar is very low when you get people who have been implicated in very serious issues and scandals wanting to run for president', and that the ANC's approach to dealing with corruption within the party was 'a betrayal to voters'.

Msimang acknowledged to us that neither Hani nor the ANC leadership were blameless in the anger that accompanied discussion of the Memorandum in 1969, but that Hani had ultimately deferred to the leadership. This was not acquiescence. Hani was not yet ready to vie for power of any kind. Over time, and with experience, he would try to earn it.

It appears that the current ANC leadership doesn't share that point of view. Malema goes further. His antipathy for Ramaphosa was always wide-ranging, but he harbours a dislike for Mandela's submission and surrender too.

He circles back to the assassination. We remark on how, in the weeks before he was murdered, Hani was talking about 'the system' wanting to kill him. What was 'the system'?

'It's the [forces of capital] that owned and established, firstly, the South African economy, and, secondly, the political system of South Africa,' says Malema. 'When they [the white South African business contingent] left into Lusaka [to meet with the ANC in exile in the mid-1980s], they made it very clear to the ANC: the National Party's going to unban you, you're going to take over power, and we continue business as usual.

'And Chris was not about that. [He said] it can't be about business as usual. So Chris was a threat to the Oppenheimer family. Chris was a threat to the ... Rupert family – all these families that owned South Africa.

'They didn't like Chris, because they didn't have access to Chris. They had infiltrated Nelson Mandela through Cyril Ramaphosa.

'Cyril Ramaphosa goes to the university, comes back, works for the Oppenheimers in their legal department and then forms a union for the underground workers, and he has never been underground himself, because they have sponsored him to form a union that will be a sweetheart union to the Oppenheimers, who are the monopolies in the minerals complex.

'Now, Chris says no, we can't have that. We can't have one family, and few families, dominating a strategic sector. So, boom, they form COSATU.

'Ramaphosa is there. Mandela's reception committee is formed. Ramaphosa is there. An arriviste of note, he is the one that goes and briefs Mandela on what's going to happen when [he] gets out of prison – this is what we're going to do, this is what is going to happen. When he finishes that, he doesn't only do that.

'Mandela comes back. He stays briefly in Soweto. [Ramaphosa] takes Mandela from Soweto to stay in the same house – not in the same complex, in the same house – with the Menell family.

'Mandela wakes up in the morning with a gown. They pass each other on the corridors with the Menell family. They eat breakfast together. Menell's child, when Mandela passes on, says, "Hey, we used to see famous people, rich people, at home through this guy."

'Why? Cyril took Mandela to his adopted family because the Menells adopted Cyril as their child and looked after him. That's why Mandela wanted Cyril, when Chris died, wanted Cyril to be deputy president, and he wanted to make it sound political – that we can't have Xhosas in one office of the presidency.

'What type of politics are those? We can have Xhosas in the whole political leadership – as long as they have got the correct politics. So what's wrong with that?

'So he thought he was being reasonable, but the reality was that he was pursuing a capitalist agenda that wants to capture and continue to capture the economy of South Africa.

'Chris – they couldn't do that with him.

'President Mbeki and many of them, when they came back to South Africa, they stayed in the flats in Hillbrow when Hillbrow was still the best of the best. Where did they get the money to afford the flats in Hillbrow when they just returned from exile?

'When they went to stay in Hillbrow, Chris Hani left to stay in Orange

Farm. He didn't stay with them in Hillbrow. Winnie Mandela remained in Soweto. She didn't come and join them in Hillbrow. But they are all revolutionaries?

'They had this access which Chris refused and said, "When we're in a struggle, we're in a struggle against these people." Today, we must be friends with them and protect that which they stole from us?

'I'm not part of that.

'So that's why Chris was killed, because he refused to be part of this nonsense that hijacked the ANC.'

When the CODESA negotiations were under way in 1992, and the ANC and the National Party were effectively agreeing to perpetuate the dominance of a capitalist system that protected white interests, Hani walked out of the talks.

At a press conference in Washington, DC, in April 1991,[15] he said, 'I was in the forefront of the MK soldiers, I was one of the first soldiers to cross the Zambezi River [into Wankie], I saw the blood of our people flowing like a river. They didn't die fighting for freedom of movement, but died fighting for the land.

'So therefore, I cannot let their blood go in vain by signing this document. I will not sign until you return our land.'

\* \* \*

In this 30th anniversary of Hani's death, it's not only monuments to Hani, or presidents who are unable to enact the simple duty of telling the truth, that fail to show the militant leader to the people. It is also our neglect to use our capacity as South Africans to make sure we comprehend the arguments Hani made, such that we can decide a fair future.

Not far from the Thomas Titus Nkobi Cemetery is Hani's old house in Hakea Crescent, Dawn Park, where he was shot dead by Janusz Walus on 11 April 1993. It's supposed to be a museum. In fact, it also has a plaque – this one saying it was opened in 2021. But it's not open yet. It's not quite finished, although the budget for it was set at several million rands.[16]

The house is all but empty. It has some rudimentary exhibits, mostly blown-up photographs, waiting to be seen one day. Our footsteps clatter lightly on a conventional white-tiled floor, and the small kitchen – seen from the lounge – would be familiar to anyone who knows middle-class South African suburbia.

There's nothing special about it, yet it feels stifling as you go through the front door. Many conversations took place here that could have laid out an alternative path for South Africa. We're not privy to those.

Hani had got used to would-be assassins hunting him down. He must have known that, at some point, one would succeed. But how could he ensure that even if they killed the man, as with Guevara, his ideas would live on?

'All the left forces have to be united,' says Malema. 'They must be consolidated. They must be united, because the capitalist forces are united and they are very clear on their agenda – and that agenda is to suppress any alternative system to capitalism. So the Communist Party was failed by Blade [Nzimande], who failed to take it from where Chris left it, because Chris had wanted to make this a mass party, where we conscientise society of what are these alternatives – more than taking power.

'We ought to first conscientise society as the vanguard party of the working class, but they've failed in doing that, and kept the party very small, and became very small, and the only time we got to hear that the party's big is when they tell us the numbers, but those numbers are never translated into any things or [any] programme by the Communist Party.

'The Red October programme [is what] sought to galvanise the masses around the ideological perspective of the Communist Party.

'So I [have been] very happy to see Vavi ... and NUMSA [talking again]. They need to resolve their differences. SAFTU. COSATU. SACP. EFF. The PAC. They need to consolidate, including the ANC. It needs to come back to its original ideological perspective so that we deliver that which our leaders died for, because if we're going to fail to deliver what they died for, they would have died in vain.

'That left movement is very important. Chris was very unapologetic when it came to making the left movement a mass movement, and that agenda was abandoned when the leadership of the party got consumed by positions of government and abandoned their leftist revolutionary duty of mobilising on the ground.

'We look crazy – that we have these crazy ideas, [as if] we didn't inherit them from revolutionaries.'

But in this 30th year after Hani was murdered, how does the left remain committed to its 'revolutionary duty' without financial support?

'Well, I deliberately refuse to meet rich people,' says Malema, 'because I come from a very poor background and I still have behind me a lot of poor aunties, uncles, relatives, cousins and all that. A day doesn't go by [for me] without a relative or some black fellows saying, I need food – even if you send me just R1 000. I need a house. My child has been expelled from school and all manner of things. All those troubles are occupying our minds, and a person comes and says, here's the money. Once you take that money, the language changes.'

Malema says he was even 'offered R50 million, when we started the EFF, to walk away from politics'. He notes how Hani handled such situations: 'You want to meet Chris? Here, come. Here are the ANC offices. Here are the Communist Party offices. Let's meet here. What are the issues? That's how it was with him.

'[The advice is to] avoid secret meetings with rich people. They thrive through buying people, and we are worse, because we've got too many problems.'

There were benefactors who shared Hani's socialist vision. At that April 1991 press conference, he told journalists how sponsorship of his American tour came through 'a coalition of groups in the US', including *People's Weekly World*, the 'paper of the American Communist Party'.

'When we were invited, of course we jumped in accepting it, because this enabled us … to inform the American people.'[17]

Malema also believes in allegiances with a like-minded cohort, but investment in parties like his is scarce, across the board. They may be 'descendants of Hani', as Malema calls them, but they don't yet have a leader who has the bearing, weight and promise of being able to manage a country's deeper expectations from the grassroots, as Hani did. That does not mean it could not happen.

Msomi is a proponent of stability. 'A lot of people on the left tended to make it look like, really, the struggle is against capitalism – [in the past] it just so happens that South Africa has apartheid, so we are more socialist than nationalists. Chris somehow had a way of balancing the two.'

But Hani is gone, and there is no balance. To be frank, we're in a mess on this 30th anniversary as we again mark the death of what Muzi Sikhakhane said, in his responding papers to Walus, was a 'democratic dream'. We can go around in circles, as at the dishevelled monument to Hani, but unless we pick up that bloodied baton, we'll never truly know what he wanted.

As authors, we can only say, *a luta continua*, and aim to keep this book alive with ideas. Let us all add to this epilogue as time goes on.

But we won't drop this maxim: long live, Chris Hani. Long live.

APPENDIX I

# THE ANC'S PRESS RELEASE UPON THE ASSASSINATION OF COMRADE CHRIS HANI, 10 APRIL 1993

At around 10.00 hours on Saturday 10th April 1993, Comrade Martin Tembisile (Chris) Hani, General-Secretary of the South African Communist Party, Member of the National Executive Committee of the African National Congress and former Chief of Staff of Umkhonto we Sizwe, was shot and killed outside his home in Dawn Park.

The assassination of Comrade Chris Hani comes at a time when the hopes of millions of South Africans for peace and tranquillity have been raised by the re-commencement of multiparty negotiations. Comrade Chris Hani himself has in past weeks been at the forefront of a nationwide campaign calling for peace. As recently as the night of Thursday 8th April he participated in an SABC broadcast around the theme of peace.

Because of Comrade Chris Hani's commitment to the struggle for liberation and his record of implacable resistance to racism, he has for decades been the object of assassination plots hatched by the agents of the apartheid regime.

Two weeks ago a new and more sinister page was turned in efforts to destroy him when a criminal on trial for bank robbery tried to implicate him. His accuser inexplicably escaped from police custody on that very evening.

The ANC has no doubt that those responsible for Comrade Chris Hani's murder will be found amongst the elements who have for so long sought his demise by fair means or foul. We appeal to all our supporters to remain calm and not permit themselves to be provoked by those intent on wrecking the peace process.

The ANC dips its banners in respectful homage to Comrade Chris Hani, a man who has dedicated his entire adult life to the struggle for democracy and freedom in South Africa. He served both the ANC and the SACP with distinction, great courage and an unswerving loyalty. Comrade Chris is survived by his wife, Limpho, and his three daughters.

The leadership of the ANC will issue a more considered statement later today when the facts surrounding this heinous crime are clearer.

Issued by the Department of Information and Publicity

APPENDIX II

# STATEMENT FROM THE SACP, PRESENTED BY CHRIS HANI TO THE CONVENTION FOR A DEMOCRATIC SOUTH AFRICA (CODESA) AT THE WORLD TRADE CENTRE, 20 DECEMBER 1991

The South African Communist Party enters the Convention for a Democratic South Africa with a total commitment to ensuring that the process succeeds. The oppressed and working people long for peace. They long for an end to the violence. They long for their freedom that has so long been denied.

The SACP, in alliance with the ANC and COSATU, has grasped the first opportunity that has arisen – as a result of our struggles to secure a negotiated settlement of the apartheid conflict. The CODESA process is a victory for our people! We believe that it is our responsibility as a vanguard organisation of the working class, together with our allies, to pursue this process with the utmost vigour.

But we need to make clear that we are not mesmerised by the word 'process'. We want it to succeed and get on track and remain on track. But that is not our only preoccupation. We are in this process because we want it to lead to a democratic result. We are in this process because there are a majority of South Africans who do not have a say in the rules governing their own lives. We are in this process because there are millions of South Africans who need a new government that will listen to their needs.

We want this process to succeed because without a new constitution there can be no peace. Peace must be based on a secure foundation, on a lasting constitution enjoying overwhelming support of the majority of our people.

Such a new constitution must also provide the framework within which this society can be transformed from a paradise for a small minority and misery for most others, to one where all enjoy peace and social justice.

These are our broad goals, but how do we proceed from here? We believe, with the ANC, that it is essential that this meeting emerges with decisions that are enforceable, that we are all bound by these decisions.

Without wanting to be unduly provocative, it must be clear to all with open minds that no reasonable person can justify a government elected by 5 percent of South Africa's adult population, holding a veto over the decisions of these proceedings. All decisions carried through a process of sufficient consensus must be implemented.

But what are the decisions that we would like to see emerge from CODESA I?

In the first place, we in the SACP reiterate our belief that it is not possible to pursue the process of negotiations successfully unless a climate of free political activity exists. This demands the immediate and unconditional release of all political prisoners, return of exiles, repeal of all repressive legislation, an end to the violence, and freedom of all to pursue their political activities without harassment.

We are especially concerned at this time with the failure of the government to implement its undertakings under the Groote Schuur and Pretoria Minutes by continuing to hold as prisoners, including on death row, people who are being punished because of their actions against apartheid.

We insist that these people be released – not after further representation or consideration by some or other intricate bureaucratic process or the presentation of new facts. We demand that these people be released now. The government can do this without any further formalities. We are saying that they must be free to spend their first Christmas for many, many years with their families.

When we call for free political activity we do so in the context of a climate of violence that we know has persisted for many years, particularly in Natal, the Transvaal

## APPENDIX II

and the western Cape. But it is found throughout the country. Not only is this causing havoc to community life, but it obviously makes a mockery of any attempt to organise politically. This freedom of political activity is obviously also impeded by continued evidence of government funding of organisations that it favours. We need to know the truth, and there is no doubt that the truth is only emerging gradually under pressure and that the scale of government financing of organisations to which it feels well disposed is much greater than previously admitted. This must end.

We believe that the present government has shown its unwillingness or incapacity to tackle these issues. That is why we demand the immediate installation of an Interim Government of National Unity to oversee the process of transition towards a democratic constitution. The longer the installation of such an Interim Government is delayed the longer we allow the violence to continue, the more we endanger not only lives at the present moment, but we also build into our culture a sense of the normality of such violence.

We want to reiterate that one of the prime tasks of such an Interim Government is to oversee elections for a Constituent Assembly – the body that we see as best suited for drawing up a new constitution. We see this as the most democratic and inclusive way of making the new constitution, enabling our people to make their impact on their own future. That is how the new democratic, nonracial, nonsexist constitution must be made.

There is no reason why this process should be drawn out. We believe that the parties should commit themselves to ensuring that the establishment of an Interim Government and elections for a Constituent Assembly should be completed within 18 months.

The SACP is determined that this process should lead to a functioning multiparty democracy with regular elections. That is why the SACP commits itself to abide by the results of any such elections, independently verified as free and fair. We call upon the South African government to make a similar commitment. We cannot have any party to negotiations setting itself up with a form of veto right over democratic decisions. It is important to note that while this Convention primarily addresses itself to constitutional questions, it takes place amidst a social and economic crisis of unprecedented proportions. The level of unemployment and the scale of poverty is a source of great alarm to us. The economic policies pursued by successive apartheid regimes have resulted in a distorted and stagnant economy.

We need a democratically elected government in place as soon as possible, a government with a mandate to deal with the social and economic issues that are fundamental to any real transformation. Of all sectors of our society, it is the black working people who have suffered most from the racism and exploitation. It is above all their aspirations that will have to be addressed. We are participating in this process, in the first place, to articulate their needs. We are also concerned that women be able to occupy their rightful place as equals at every level of society in any new democratic order. We in the SACP do not hide our belief that political freedom without social reconstruction will be meaningless. There needs to be a new growth path which creates wealth more efficiently than the present economic policies, but also ensures that such wealth is used to better the lives not only of a few, but of all.

For the peace process to succeed demands from all who are committed to democracy, the greatest possible unity. I want to say to organisations which have not traditionally formed part of the ANC–SACP–COSATU alliance or even the mass democratic movement that this is not the time to emphasise our differences. It is our job to build on the highest level of unity we can develop to take ourselves forward, not to narrow sectarian goals but the broad democratic system that is in all of our interests.

To those who are not part of this process either through withdrawing or failing to join, we make a special appeal. Let us turn CODESA into a truly patriotic contribution, the remaking of our beloved country into one to which we will all feel an abiding loyalty. Let this be the work of all of us, no matter what our differences may be. Let us put aside these differences and concentrate on what unites us and ensure that that unity results in a product that is truly enduring.

At the same time, this is a period where all of us must exercise the maximum degree of responsibility. It is not helpful for any of us to raise the spectre of civil war. Anyone with knowledge of what has happened in Angola and Mozambique must know that words like 'civil war' should not be lightly bandied about; let us rather redouble our efforts to bury any possibility of such a fate enveloping us.

Let me conclude by expressing the wish of the SACP that this Convention should

## APPENDIX II

succeed in laying the basis for peace in our country, a process that will unlock the talents of all South Africans in building a new nation, which will secure the health, happiness and wellbeing of all our people.

APPENDIX III

# MEMORANDUM (1969)

The ANC in exile is in a deep crisis as a result of which a rot has set in. From informal discussions with the revolutionary members of MK we have inferred that they have lost all confidence in the ANC leadership abroad. This they say openly and in fact show it. Such a situation is very serious and in fact a revolutionary movement has to sit down and analyse such a prevailing state of affairs. The situation is further aggravated by the fact that accredited members of the organisation are no longer consulted or no longer participate in policy-making decisions of the organisation – there have been two or three conferences when the leaders met and did not consult or inform the membership of the resolutions. The inference is that we are no longer considered members of the ANC. As the leading revolutionary core of the organisation, it is imperative for members of MK to participate in all matters affecting the revolutionary struggle in South Africa. We raise the above points so as to arrest the present trend.

We, as genuine revolutionaries, are moved by the frightening depths reached by the rot in the ANC and the disintegration of MK accompanying this rot and manifesting itself in the following way:

1. The ANC leadership in exile has created a machinery which has become an end

## APPENDIX III

unto itself. It is completely divorced from the situation in South Africa. It is not in a position to give an account of the functioning branches inside the country. There has never been an attempt to send the leadership inside the country since the Rivonia arrests. There has been an over-concentration of people in offices – this has become a fully fledged activity in itself, for e.g., you get a Director of Youth who maintains no liaison with the home front. There are other departments, such as the Treasury Department which is to all intents and purposes catering for activities outside, and whose functioning is only limited and known only to a few individuals; the Department of the Secretary-General, which has not furnished any reports on political activities in the various regions of the country; the Department of Publicity, which is giving out propaganda geared only to external consumption. The quality of information is not revolutionary and is out of step with the existing political situation inside the country. Its material hardly gives a deep analysis of the prevalent situation inside. We strongly feel time has come that the department should make every effort to reach the masses of our people by seeing to it that more and more of its revolutionary propaganda is written in the languages of our people.

2. We are perturbed by the careerism of the ANC leadership abroad who have, in every sense, become professional politicians rather than professional revolutionaries. We have been forced to draw the conclusion that the payment of salaries to people working in offices is very detrimental to the revolutionary outlook of those who receive such monies. It is without doubt that such payments corrupt cadres at any level and have the effect of making people perform their duties or fill offices because of money inducement rather than dedication to the cause – they become in effect merely salaried employees of the movement. It is high time that all members and cadres of the ANC, be they in MK or not, should receive equal treatment and be judged only on the basis of their dedication and sacrifices to the cause we serve. The principle of thorough selection of cadres should be on the basis of merit and such selection should never be delegated to an individual – this will prevent individuals owing allegiance to those who appoint them rather than to the revolution.

3. The leadership of the ANC abroad must be committed to a resolution and programme of going home to lead the struggle there, which resolution and programme

must be seen to be implemented. Presently there is a leadership vacuum at home as all the leaders are either locked up in Vorster's prisons or are in exile. This has deprived the SA masses of leadership, which is so vital at this crucial moment of our revolution. A situation where our people, because of this vacuum, will be deceived by opportunists of all shades is strongly developing. We feel that the number of leaders attending international conferences and other globe-trotting activities should be cut down to a reasonable few and the remainder should work around the clock working on the home front.

4. There are certain symptoms which are very disturbing and dispiriting to genuine revolutionaries. These comprise the opening of mysterious business enterprises which to our knowledge have never been discussed by the membership of the organisation. For instance, in Lusaka a furniture industry is being run by the ANC. In Livingstone a bone factory, whose original purpose was to provide cover for underground work in Botswana, is now being used as a purely commercial undertaking. As a result of these enterprises more and more MK men are being diverted to them. And some of the people in charge of these enterprises are dubious characters with shady political backgrounds. We are therefore compelled to conclude that there is no serious drive to return home and carry on the struggle. This is disturbing because the very comrade, Thabo More, who is supposed to be planning, directing and leading the struggle in South Africa is fully involved in these enterprises. Now he has assumed complete responsibility for the running of these enterprises in collaboration with others and it is extremely doubtful that with his attention so divided he can do justice to the armed struggle in South Africa which should be his primary and absolute concern. The leadership of the ANC can't but be blamed for this state of affairs.

5. An equally disturbing situation is that MK is being run independently of the Political Organisation. The Political Leadership Abroad is not aware of the activities and the plans of MK. We therefore infer that MK is separate from the ANC; that there is conflict between the ANC and MK; that the ANC has lost control over MK; that there is no coordination between the ANC and the MK. All this has brought about a situation where MK is run single-handed by the Commander-in-Chief, who appoints and dismisses arbitrarily – as a result there is a tendency among members of

## APPENDIX III

the Headquarters to owe allegiance to the individual who appoints and dismisses them and it takes a genuine revolutionary to challenge him. We are compelled to blame the National Executive for this anomalous situation.

6. The Security Department is internally directed. It is doing nothing against the enemy. It has achieved nothing of military importance. The failure of this so-called Security Department has been shown by its inability to furnish the organisation with the fate of our most dedicated comrades in Zimbabwe. Or how is it possible that so many comrades have been able to desert so successfully? In the prosecution of its internally directed activities the Security Department has become notorious. Those who serve in it have the central task of suppressing and persecuting genuinely dedicated cadres of MK who have nothing to lose by participating in the struggle except their chains!

There is no Security Department in our organisation. For instance, the arrest of Msomi and Matthews was inevitable as the fact of their presence in South Africa was common knowledge; as well as of comrades bound for home. This situation is tantamount of betrayal of comrades.

In Morogoro, Joseph Cotton, Shadrack Tladi and Boy Otto are openly flirting with the Peace Corps, an internationally known CIA front, a counter-revolutionary and espionage organisation. The first two handle vital information as they are connected with the radio transmission service relaying organisational material. Boy Otto is moving between Zambia and Tanzania transporting MK personnel and war material. Most disturbing is that a comrade raised this matter with the Secretary-General and Chief of Security of the ANC, Duma Nokwe, who agreed that the matter of the above comrades flirting with the Peace Corps was true and that it should be furnished in writing, but no action was taken. This is very disturbing and discouraging to serious revolutionaries who know fully well that these three comrades are close to the leading figures of the ANC and MK. For instance, Joseph Cotton is the son of Moses Kotane the Treasurer-General of the ANC and General Secretary of the SACP. Shadrack Tladi is a relative of Thabo More, who is the C-in-C of MK and member of the National Executive of the ANC Abroad. This has made us and many other comrades conclude that there is nepotism in the ANC. An equally perturbing fact is that Mrs V Nokwe, the wife of the Secretary-General and Chief of Security of the ANC,

Comrade D Nokwe, is presently working for Amiran Israel, an internationally known Israeli intelligence organisation operating under the cover of an import–export firm. This Amiran Israel is a coordinating centre for Israeli intelligence services (Shin Bet) in southern Africa, central Africa including Congo–Brazzaville and Congo–Kinshasa. Israel is a nest of imperialism which is actively sabotaging the National Liberation. Presently it has colonised parts of Arab territories and is maintaining close links with the most reactionary and fascist governments, such as South Africa and the revanchist Federal Republic of Germany. We demand an explanation for this anomalous situation and we demand that she should cut links with this counter-revolutionary organisation forthwith and should there be any other links with Israel, the ANC should sever them in the interests of our revolution.

7. The tragedy of the Zimbabwe campaigns is the fact that we have been unable to analyse our operations so as to be able to assess and draw lessons that would make it possible for us to formulate a correct strategy and tactics vis-à-vis the enemy.

8. It is a cause for serious concern that comrades who have come back from the battlefront have not been accorded a comradely reception and the fact that there has been no reappraisal of their combat experience. We are shocked by the criminal neglect of our most dedicated comrades, who have either fallen in battle, sentenced to death or serving long-term imprisonment in Zimbabwe. These men are heroes who have performed their revolutionary tasks gallantly without flinching. How can we possibly keep quiet about these valorous sons of South Africa? Is this not an indication of callousness and irresponsibility on the part of the leadership? The behaviour of the Secretary-General and Chief of Security of the ANC D Nokwe and his attitude towards Comrade J Mlenze, when we petitioned for a meeting, disturbed us greatly. For him to have said he did not know, did not recognise Mlenze is a height of indifference and cynicism and we are really very worried about it. Here is a comrade from the battlefront, a commander of a unit, and a Security Chief of a vital region, namely Transkei, accorded this type of snub.

9. We are perturbed by the fact that certain members of the MK are receiving payments from the External Mission, e.g. the C-in-C and the CPO who as a matter of fact

APPENDIX III

are getting allowances and the fact the C-in-C has a posh and militarily irrelevant car at his disposal. The fact that these soldiers are paid has a very demoralising effect on the other revolutionaries.

10. Individual leaders keep cars and run them and this coupled with the fact that they receive salaries, alias allowances, is in every way building them up as a middle class in our revolutionary organisation and in MK.

11. A strange and alarming trend is developing whereby secret trials and secret executions have been carried out. We are not against the execution and liquidation of traitors but we are against this veil of secrecy. We are having in mind the trials of Zola Zembe, Wellington Mbata, Phalanyane and Bopela. It is a shame that we should have been witnesses to the emergence of extremely reactionary methods of punishment in MK. There have been instances when offenders in MK have been dumped in dugouts filled with several drums of water without blankets or any other protective material for periods of up to about 22 days. The cases in point are those of Daphne Zwane, Tallman Ndlovu, Bob Zulu, Erends and Joseph Ndlovu. This type of punishment, among others, is, from any angle, criminal and inhuman, and must have been designed to break the physical and moral integrity of victims.

12. The ANC is the vanguard of the revolutionary struggle in South Africa and it is strange that its leaders have not been obliged to take the MK oath. We strongly feel that there is no difference between the leaders of the ANC and men of MK who are obliged to take the oath, for such an oath might have dealt with J Radebe's desertion and will definitely deal with any other leader harbouring right-wing designs of sabotaging our revolution.

13. The development of the revolution has necessitated a renewal and rejuvenation of those who are leading it. We must guard against the fossilisation of the leadership as this is likely to hinder the progressive development of our revolution. There has been a tendency to appoint people to the National Executive outside. We would like to know what is the yardstick for these appointments. After proper consultation with all the members of the ANC a method should be found of changing leadership

and the fact that there have been no conferences involving all our members at home should not be used as an excuse for not renewing the leadership. We should not depend on mandates given at national conferences 10 or more years ago. We have been forced to conclude that a few individuals are monopolising posts in the organisation. This has brought about a situation where members of the Planning Council are also members of the National Executive.

14. It is very alarming that double standards as regards to health of the members of the organisation are maintained. Whenever leaders are sick arrangements are made for them to receive excellent medical attention without delay but this sort of concern is hardly shown to the rank and file of the movement. We maintain that all of us are important in so far as the revolution is concerned and should thus be accorded the same treatment.

15. We consider the youth in MK as the most revolutionary. We strongly feel that we should be consulted on matters affecting the youth. For instance we must be informed about the revolutionary international youth gatherings and we should be given priority in the sending of delegates. The farce of the Bulgaria ANC Youth delegation should never be repeated and those responsible should acknowledge the mistake they made. The youth of South Africa is not located in London or in any European capital. We therefore take particular exception to the appointment of certain students as leaders of the ANC Youth. Thabo Mbeki who went to London on a scholarship sponsored by NUSAS is leader of a bogus ANC Youth Organisation.

We are convinced that the ANC leadership in exile is according better treatment and attention to the students. This attitude and practice has had a disastrous effect of diverting many would-be revolutionaries into the academic field. We feel that it is high time that the MK personnel which is in fact the core of our revolution should be given the best treatment by virtue of having volunteered with their lives to give the supreme sacrifice for the revolution.

Another disturbing symptom is the glaring practice of nepotism where the leadership uses its positions to promote their kith and kin and put them in positions where they will not be in any physical confrontation with the enemy. The sending of virtually all the sons of the leaders to universities in Europe is a sign that these

## APPENDIX III

people are being groomed for leadership positions after the MK cadres have overthrown the fascists. We have no doubt that these people will wait in Europe and will just come home when everything has been made secure and comfortable for them playing the typical role of the Bandas and others. As opposed to the treatment of the students, we find complete indifference and apathy to the heroes and martyrs of our revolution who have fallen both in South Africa and Zimbabwe. We have in mind the gallant sons of our country, who without doubt lay their lives in the struggle against imperialism. These include among many Patric Mosedi, one-time President of the ANCYL and former treason trialist; Benson Ntsele, the tireless Commissar; the young cream of our country Sparks Moloi, Chris Mampuru, James Masimini and Andries Motsepe. We have not forgotten those who have defiantly and stubbornly refused to be frightened by the hangman's noose in Rhodesia following the heroic example set by our murdered martyrs Vuyisile Mini, Zinakile Mkhaba, Diliza Khayingo, W Bongco and others. These comrades are the dedicated Alfred Mninzi, known to many of us as James Hermanus; Tamane, known as Zami, the son of that great revolutionary and women's leader Dora Tamane; the young Rhodes Msuthu Ngamlana, known to us as Charles Mhambi; and Tula Bophela.

16. We call for a full definition of the ANC–ZAPU alliance, its form and content. We demand that a serious and genuine effort should be made toward the intensification of ways and means of going home. This should be one actively involving the most dedicated members of MK and it should be on the basis of a correct strategy.

In conclusion, all these problems must be resolved by a conference between the ANC leadership and members of MK, and not just handpicked individuals.

signatories:

APPENDIX IV

# UMKHONTO WE SIZWE MILITARY CODE (ABRIDGED)

This document was released at the ANC National Consultative Conference at Kabwe in June 1985.

## Preamble
Recognising that our army, Umkhonto we Sizwe, must define its aims and objects in clear and precise terms, and that the rights and duties of each member should be likewise defined without ambiguity, the Politico-Military Council, acting on behalf of the African National Congress of South Africa, has adopted and hereby decrees this code for the guidance of members in cell positions.

## 1. Umkhonto we Sizwe – a People's Army
The ANC and its allies created Umkhonto as a new and indispensable weapon in the struggle for people's power. Unlike the armed forces of the racist regime of South Africa, which we have vowed to crush and annihilate, and unlike all other armies of imperialism, Umkhonto we Sizwe is a People's Army organised and dedicated to waging a people's war for the liberation of our country.

Umkhonto is an army of volunteers. It consists of volunteers drawn from the revolutionary sections of our people. By joining Umkhonto, combatants commit themselves to the solemn and noble duty of serving our suffering and dispossessed people in the struggle that will continue for each and all of us until victory or death. In the words of our founding Manifesto, published on the historic day of 16th December 1961: 'Umkhonto we Sizwe will be at the front line of the people's defence. It will be the fighting arm of the people against the racist government and its policies of racial oppression. It will be the striking force of the people for liberty, for rights and for their final liberation.'

The founding Manifesto of Umkhonto we Sizwe is our definitive declaration of intent, and an essential guide to the reasons for the creation and aims of this, the People's Army. We append the Manifesto to this Code, to be studied and understood by every Umkhonto combatant. It was no coincidence that MK's first operations were launched on December 16, Dingane's Day. Umkhonto will carry on the warrior traditions of our people under the conditions of modern guerrilla warfare. Those who join Umkhonto we Sizwe, the People's Army, perform a sacred duty to our people, our nation and the South African Revolution. When we have liberated our country, Umkhonto will constitute the basis of the defence forces of our country and the Revolution, and will serve as an instrument of social progress. An Umkhonto combatant has the opportunity to serve in the forefront of the liberation struggle, to meet the enemy and engage him with modern weapons, to become a steeled revolutionary who at all times is determined to serve and protect the people and his fellow comrades-in-arms.

We look back with great pride to the period of militant non-violent struggle waged by the ANC. During this period our people learnt through their own experience that they could not satisfy their aspirations except by means of armed struggle arising out of our mass political activity and culminating in a revolutionary seizure of power. When time was ripe for violent forms of struggle, our people understood and supported the decision to take up arms. They clearly understood as long ago as December 1961, that our Movement had exhausted all peaceful avenues, and that the oppressor had imposed on us a war situation. The alternative to armed struggle was submission. As the Umkhonto Manifesto declared: 'The People's patience is not endless. The time comes in the life of any nation when there remains only two choices – submit or fight. That time has now come in South Africa. We shall not submit and we have no choice but to hit back by all means within our power in defence of our people, our future and our freedom.'

## 2. Political and Military Struggle

Umkhonto we Sizwe is the fighting arm of the ANC and its allies. Our armed struggle is a continuation of our political struggle by means that include armed force. The political leadership has primacy over the military. Our military line derives from our political line. Every commander, commissar, instructor and combatant must therefore be clearly acquainted with the policy with regard to all combat tasks and missions. All of us must know clearly who the enemy is, and for what we are fighting. Thus MK cadres are not only military units, they are also organisers of our people. That is the major distinction between our people's revolutionary army and the army and wholly militarised authoritarian armed forces of the racists, imperialists and reactionary regimes. Umkhonto cadres, with arms in hand, are political activists and leaders, as well as warriors. This combination of political and military functions is characteristic of all popular, revolutionary armies, especially in the phase of guerrilla warfare.

## 3. People's War

Umkhonto is a people's army fighting a people's war. We fight to liberate our oppressed and exploited people. We fight for their interests. Umkhonto has no mercenaries, no paid soldiers or conscripted troops. It consists of the sons and daughters of the most oppressed, the most exploited sections of our people. For these reasons we claim with pride and truth: Umkhonto is the Spear of the Nation.

We fight a people's war, not by armed struggle alone, but first and above all by political education, leadership and mobilisation. It is a people's war because the struggle is to win the active support and participation of all who resist oppression, discrimination, poverty and injustice.

The people support their army by providing it with recruits – their sons and daughters – food, shelter, and information about the enemy. The people open the way for our guerrillas and make the enemy's path hard. Everyone can become a freedom fighter. The struggle has many fronts and is not confined to trained soldiers alone. The ANC mobilises the people in support of the revolution through skillful combination of all forms of struggle: violent and non-violent, legal and illegal, strikes and demonstrations, boycotts and non-collaboration, propaganda, education and sabotage. A people's war is fought by the people with arms and all other forms and methods of struggle. Without the organised support of the people, armed struggle is in danger of being isolated and strangled. The enemy attempts to isolated us by launching campaigns to win the 'hearts and minds' of the people – of our people, the oppressed and suffering workers and peasants. To defeat the enemy, we must involve the entire people in the National Democratic Revolution.

The enemy controls the state, its armed forces, police and courts. But he does not command the hearts and minds of the people. They are with us in a just war for national liberation. Their support is our chief weapon. What gives the guerrilla his advantage is his political superiority and people's support. As pointed out in Operation Mayibuye (1963) the most important guarantee of victory is 'the support of the people who in certain situations are better protection than mountains and forests'.

### 4. Our People's Army

Umkhonto we Sizwe fights to liberate our people from racial discrimination, national oppression and exploitation.

The common enemy is the racist minority which identifies with and gives aid to the National Party regime, the creator and driving force of apartheid.

Our programme is the Freedom Charter; it defines the goals of all democrats regardless of colour, race or creed.

The interests of the people and the demands of the revolution are inseparable and the main concern of the people's army.

Our MK Manifesto declares that the army includes in its ranks South Africans of all races. But the overwhelming majority are members of the most oppressed and exploited people. By this dedication and commitment and training, they represent the vanguard of our people. In Umkhonto language, the army is the Spear of the Nation.

### 5. Umkhonto insists on a high standard of selfless devotion to the revolution on the part of all its members. They are required at all times to:
- behave correctly to the people;
- respect their persons and property;

- refrain from molesting or interfering with their legitimate activities;
- assist them to solve their problems and where possible give material aid in their labour; and
- demonstrate high moral qualities in word and deed.

## 6. Revolutionary Discipline and Consciousness

To defeat the enemy in combat, our soldiers must be disciplined, trained to obey commands promptly, and ready to spring into battle immediately when ordered. Vigilance, alertness and readiness to engage the enemy at a moment's notice are qualities that can develop only out of discipline, proper training and political consciousness. Bourgeois and reactionary armies, like the army forces of the racists, instil a mechanical and robot-like obedience in their units. The people's army has a different conception of discipline and loyalty. Umkhonto soldiers are volunteers, willing and trained to carry out orders in the knowledge that instant obedience is the only way to safeguard life, both of the individual and his comrades-in-arms, and to protect the people he serves.

Umkhonto soldiers pledge themselves to safeguard the revolution at all times regardless of personal hardships, suffering and danger. A soldier who breaks discipline, disobeys commands or by improper conduct betrays the high moral standards of our army will be punished. Such punishment is necessary to maintain the qualities expected of a people's army. Every attempt is made to correct bad behaviour and rehabilitate members who violate the army's code. But punishment is severe in cases of serious crimes, treachery and criminal neglect endangering the safety of others and the security of the army.

Our procedure and rules are well defined, precise and to the point. Military orders are issued with a definite purpose and must be obeyed. It is the duty and responsibility of every soldier to know and understand the army's code of conduct, to recognise his military commanders, to be clear about his own duties, and to carry out orders immediately and without question. Orders must be obeyed cheerfully, promptly and exactly. A soldier who does not understand an order has a right to have it explained. He must know when to raise problems, to whom he must report, and how to obtain clarification. He must not, in any circumstances, refuse to obey a command or argue over the execution of an order.

## APPENDIX IV

Outright disobedience and failure to obey an order promptly may have serious consequences. A soldier who thinks that he has been given a wrong order must obey it first and if need be complain afterwards to his commander. Our commanding officers, commissars, instructors and others who are entrusted with responsibility to lead must be above reproach. They are to be a shining example of modesty, sound moral behaviour, correct attitudes towards all members, respectful and helpful to every member of the army, regardless of his position. Commanders and Political Commissars occupy a central role in Umkhonto. Without them disorder can result. They are the principal target of the enemy and must be given maximum protection. Umkhonto is engaged in guerrilla warfare, against a powerful and remorseless enemy which resorts to torture, banditry and terrorism.

During the stage of guerrilla warfare, great initiative and resourcefulness are required of every combatant. Under such conditions, formalities such as the courtesy of saluting commanders are reduced to a minimum, while discipline and vigilance are maintained at the highest levels.

In our external training bases, however, we have conditions and facilities similar to those of a regular army. Here we insist on full military procedures, including the practice of saluting commanding personnel; higher ranks; parades; roll calls; and fall-ins. These are necessary for the orderly camp life and discipline and co-operation among guerrillas in combat zones.

The inner forms of discipline, arising from political maturity and consciousness of our struggle, are far more important and enduring than a discipline enforced from above. But a proud bearing, alertness and quick response to commands, a smart uniform, and respect of leadership, commanders and commissars are the hallmarks of a good soldier who is proud of his platoon, detachment and army.

With the triumph of our revolution, Umkhonto will be the official army of our country, the true shield of our nation, defending the people against external aggression and internal counter-revolution. To prepare ourselves for these noble tasks, we must live up to the army's code of conduct in all respects and at all times during the present phase of our struggle.

# NOTES ON SOURCES

All interviews conducted with sources were done in person, with the exception of the interview with Ruth Mompati, which was done by telephone. Much of the oral testimony we have used for this book was thus firsthand. We had email and telephone exchanges with, among others, Joyce Leeson and Anne Duthie, although we also met Duthie in London. Requests for interviews with Thabo Mbeki and Jacob Zuma were heard but went unanswered. Lawyers for Clive Derby-Lewis and Janusz Walus approached their clients, who would not agree to see us.

## CHAPTER 1: THE ROOTS OF A MAN

The Hani quote on page 6, referring to returning to Sabalele, is to be found on page 117 of Charles Villa-Vicencio's *The Spirit of Hope: Conversations on Politics, Religion and Values* (Skotaville, 1991).

The reference to Hani's early education, on page 13, is contained in an unpublished interview with Hani conducted by Luli Callinicos in 1993. See detail of this in the notes on the next chapter.

References to growing up in Sabelele and Hani's move from the church to the SACP – both on pages 14–15 – are also from the Villa-Vicencio book (pp 118 and 119).

NOTES

## CHAPTER 2: FORT HARE

The results of the election in Sabalele are available on the Independent Electoral Commission's website (www.elections.org.za).

Many of the descriptions of Lovedale are to be found among Phyllis Naidoo's papers at the University of KwaZulu-Natal. We used testimony received in interviews, and found it corroborated in sources such as Mark Gevisser's *Thabo Mbeki: The Dream Deferred* (Jonathan Ball, 2007) and Luli Callinicos's *Oliver Tambo: Beyond the Engeli Mountains* (David Philip, 2004).

The dialogue with Hani, from an extensive interview conducted by Callinicos with him just weeks before he was killed, is extraordinary. Hani's openness to revealing some of his most private thoughts was invaluable. We are grateful to Callinicos, not only for giving us sight of the interview, but for her assistance in general.

Equally, Gevisser's biography of Thabo Mbeki was critical to an understanding of the times and the characters who circulated around Hani.

The documents cited, such as Hani's school reports and letters to the Department of Education, are to be found at the ANC archive at Fort Hare, and also among Phyllis Naidoo's collection, which is a trove of papers, letters, interviews, contextual documents and newspaper clippings.

The quotes from Govan Mbeki appear in different places, but in this chapter we used *Workers' World* magazine on www.workers.org. The interview with Mbeki was conducted by Key Martin and Johnnie Stevens for the documentary *Chris Hani Viva*, in which they discuss Hani as a student, an activist and then an ANC leader.

The quotation from Hani regarding 'necessary violence' comes from an interview in the *Road Ahead Perspective* (1990), found among Phyllis Naidoo's papers.

## CHAPTER 3: FLIGHT INTO EXILE

The reference to Elias Motsoaledi on page 43 can be found on page 124 of *The Road to Democracy. Volume 1 (1960–1970)*, produced by the South African Democracy Education Trust (SADET) (Mutloatse Arts Heritage Trust, 2008).

The story of the Mamre farm is based on discussions with Archie Sibeko and Albie Sachs, and is also covered in *The Road to Democracy. Volume 1 (1960–1970)*.

The reference to Jean-Paul Sartre's *The Wall* is in Naidoo's collection.

The reference to Looksmart Ngudle and Govan Mbeki is referred to by Mbeki in *Workers' World* (see previous chapter notes), in his letters from Robben Island, and in 'The Search for Looksmart', a series of articles by Shaun Smillie and Neo Ntsoma that appeared in Independent Newspapers titles, including *The Star*, in June 2007.

## CHAPTER 4: THE USSR

The reference on page 61 about Lawrence Phokanoka being recruited by Hani features in an interview with Phokanoka in *The Road to Democracy. Volume 1 (1960–1970)*, page 417.

References on page 61 to Hani's impressions of the USSR are drawn from the unpublished interview with Callinicos and an interview with Wolfie Kodesh, which was held at the University of the Western Cape–Robben Island Mayibuye Centre for History and Culture in South Africa, Oral History of Exiles Project. Kodesh's interview was conducted on 1 April 1993.

Simon Senna's journey to the USSR, which is described on page 62, is to be found in an interview published in *The Road to Democracy. Volume 1 (1960–1970)*, page 428.

Radilori Moumakwe's journey to the USSR, which is described on pages 62–63, is to be found in an interview in *The Road to Democracy. Volume 1 (1960–1970)*, pages 326 and 327.

On page 64, the reference to the opening of a training centre in the Crimea is from Vladimir Shubin's *ANC: A View from Moscow* (2nd edition, Jacana, 2008).

NOTES

On page 65, the reference to women running at the sight of black soldiers is from from an interview with Justice Mpanza, conducted by Naidoo and included in her papers.

Also on pages 65–66, Hani's comments about life in the USSR are from the unpublished interview with Callinicos.

## CHAPTER 5: KONGWA

Reference on page 78 to covert meetings convened along tribal lines is to be found in *Umkhonto we Sizwe: Fighting for a divided people* by Thula Bopela and Daluxolo Luthuli (Galago, 2005), page 47.

The reference to stealing trucks, on page 77, comes from an interview with Justice Mpanza in *The Road to Democracy. Volume 1 (1960–1970)*, page 342.

Hani's reference on page 79, about the passage to Zambia, is found in the Kodesh interview.

## CHAPTER 6: WANKIE

The reference to the secret meeting, on page 86, is from a paper written by Amos Ngwenya, former ZAPU member of the Central Committee, among Naidoo's papers.

The reference on page 88 to the joint high command comes from *The People's Voice*, 23–29 September 1990.

Tambo's reference, on page 89, to the Wankie campaign as a 'heroic failure' comes from 'Victory or Death', a statement he made on 16 December 1986, on the occasion of the 25th anniversary of MK.

The Joe Slovo reference on page 116 is from 'The Green Book', published in *From Protest to Challenge: A Documentary History of African Politics in South Africa 1882–1990. Volume 5: Nadir and Resurgence, 1964–1979* by Thomas G Karis and Gail M Gerhart (Unisa Press, 1997).

The reference to the 'Ho Chi Minh bridge' on page 92 is taken from Hani's own testimony about Wankie, published in the souvenir edition of *Dawn*, 1986.

Hani's remarks on page 94 are taken from an interview in *Mayibuye*, 1993.

Hani's remarks about meeting Tambo, on pages 94–95, are from the Callinicos interview.

The reference to ZIPRA's Dumiso Dabengwa, also on page 95, is to be found in *The People's Voice* article cited above.

The remarks about Ruth Mompati on page 97 come from the interview with her in *The Road to Democracy. Volume 1 (1960–1970)*, page 307.

The reference to Point Lolo, to be found on page 98, comes from an article headlined 'Zambezi took a share' by RMT Ngungwana, among Naidoo's papers.

The Phokanoka reference on page 99 is from *The Road to Democracy. Volume 1 (1960–1970)*, page 421.

The descriptions of the Wankie battle on pages 100–101 come from an interview with Hani published in *City Press* on 25 April 1993, under the headline, 'A great MK cadre, a great MK victory'.

The reference to Major-General Ron Reid-Daly on page 103 comes from different sources, including Raymond Suttner's *The ANC Underground in South Africa* (Jacana, 2008) and the SADET Oral History Project documents compiled by Rendani Moses Ralinala, Jabulani Sithole, Gregory Houston and Bernard Magubane. They, in turn, also drew on *Dawn's* Souvenir Issue on the 25th Anniversary of MK in which the Battle of Nyatuwe was described.

The references to the ill-fated campaigns led by Josiah Jele and others, before Wankie, to reinfiltrate South Africa via Botswana and Mozambique, come mostly from the SADET Oral History Project, in particular the research on the Wankie and Sipolilo Campaigns. The Jele aspect of this story emerged from an interview with Jele conducted telephonically by Gregory Houston and Bernard Magubane in June 2003, Pretoria.

Other texts which proved invaluable to us for an understanding of Wankie, included *Mayibuye* Special Issue No 11, 1981, 'The Year of the Youth'; Karis and Gerhart's *Nadir and Resurgence 1964–1979* (see details above); and testimony from TT Nkobi in his article 'Crossing the Zambezi' in *Dawn's* Souvenir Issue, 1986, found among Naidoo's papers.

NOTES

## CHAPTER 7: THE MEMORANDUM

Hani's comments on the Wankie campaign, to be found on pages 107–108, are from the interview with Kodesh.

On page 109, Hani's comments on jail in Botswana are also to be found in the Kodesh interview.

Hani's remark that 'we blew our tops', to be found on page 114, is included in the interview with Callinicos.

On page 114, the reference to a second Memorandum is from a paper by Hugh MacMillan: 'After Wankie: The Hani Memorandum and its repercussions at Morogoro and on the ANC in Zambia, 1968 to 1971' was presented at a workshop on liberation struggles in southern Africa, New Perspectives Centre for African Studies, University of Cape Town, September 2008.

Hani's comments on Kaunda meeting Vorster, to be found on page 119, are from the Callinicos interview.

Hani's remarks about the 'painful' experience of being expelled, to be found on page 120, were made in the Kodesh interview.

Hani's remarks about the 'continuation of the struggle', to be found on page 121, come from the interview in the *Road Ahead Perspective* (1990), cited above.

The reference to the 1977 assassination of Leonard Nkosi is based on interviews with a number of MK cadres, and the ANC's second submission to the TRC.

Hani's comments on being unselfish, also to be found on page 121, are also from Kodesh.

The reference on page 123 to 'The Enemy Hidden Under the Same Colour' is originally to be found in *The African Communist*, Second Quarter, 1976.

The quote from Tambo, on page 124, is taken from his closing address at the Morogoro Conference.

Hani's comments on a guerrilla army, to be found on page 125, are from the interview with Kodesh.

## CHAPTER 8: LESOTHO

On page 126, Hani's story of arriving at the ticket office in Zeerust comes from Villa-Vicencio, page 122.

On page 133, the reference to Hani and Moloi being suspected of funnelling money to the banned BCP comes from Shubin, page 162.

Lennox Lagu's intervention, described on page 133, is from SADET's *The Road to Democracy in South Africa. Volume 2, 1970-1980* (Unisa Press, 2006), page 423.

Tambo's quote on page 134 comes from Luli Callinicos's *Oliver Tambo: Beyond the Engeli Mountains* (cited above); page 7's reference to 1976 being the watershed comes from the unpublished interview with Callinicos.

On page 135, Hani's quotes come from the same interview with Callinicos.

On page 147, Hani speaking about forgiveness is from Villa-Vicencio, page 126.

Also on page 147 the first reference to the Maseru raid is from Phyllis Naidoo's *Le Rona Re Batho: An Account of the 1982 Maseru Massacre*.

The account relating to the actual planning and execution of the Maseru raid, on page 148 and after, comes from Peter Stiff's *A Silent War: South African Recce Operations 1969–1994* (Galago, 2002), pp 412-26.

## CHAPTER 9: KABWE

References are generally cited within the text. Other sources used include: the political report of the National Executive Committee to the National Consultative Conference, June 1985, presented by the president of the ANC, Oliver Tambo; *Mayibuye* No 5/6, 1985, 'Year of the Cadre'; the message to the ANC conference sent by Nelson Mandela on behalf of Pollsmoor and Robben Island prisons, from Naidoo's papers; the interview in the *Road Ahead Perspective* (1990), also among Naidoo's papers; documents of the Second National Consultative Conference of the African National Congress, Zambia, 16-23 June 1985, at the University of the Witwatersrand from the Karis/Gerhart catalogue (as cited above).

## CHAPTER 10: ANGOLA

References are generally cited within the text. Other sources that gave valuable insight into the events, and substantiated testimony, included: Peter Stiff's *The Silent War* (cited above); *Umkhonto we Sizwe: Fighting for a divided people* (full details above); James Sanders's *Apartheid's Friends: The Rise and Fall of South Africa's Secret Service* (John Murray, 2006); *Challenge: Southern Africa within the African Revolutionary Context*, edited by Al J Venter (Ashanti Publishing, 1989); articles published under the cover headline 'Hope in Africa' in *Time* magazine, 4 October 1976 – 'A Dr K offer they could not refuse', and 'Anguish in the heart of whiteness'.

Jacques Pauw's *Into the Heart of Darkness: The Story of Apartheid's Killers* (Jonathan Ball, 1997) is cited in the text.

Phyllis Naidoo drew up extensive timelines for the SADF's incursions into southern Africa. These were also used in this chapter.

The Umkhonto we Sizwe testimony to the Truth and Reconciliation Commission, both the original and the revised versions, were used extensively for understanding, quotes and references. These are most easily available on www.info.gov.za. Equally, the ANC's own testimony to the TRC was used for this purpose.

The message from José Eduardo dos Santos to Dr Javier Perez de Cuellar, on page 173, was published in *The Times* (London) on 24 November 1984.

The reference to Operation Lebanta on page 176, comes from www.allafrica.com/stories/200404190944.html, with reference to Peter Stiff.

The remarks made by Oliver Tambo at Joe Gqabi's funeral, on pages 176–177, are most easily found at www.anc.org.za/ancdocs/speeches/1980s/sp810809.html

The reports of the Stuart Commission, the Skweyiya Commission and the Motsuenyane Commission are downloadable at www.anc.org.za/ancdocs/

## CHAPTER 11: COMING HOME

On page 213, Hani's references to the armed struggle come from an interview for United Action for a Democratic South Africa done on 21 January 1990.

The account of the Bisho Massacre was a first-hand account by Busisiwe Dingaan Stofile narrated to Phyllis Naidoo.

Hani's time in Transkei and his reference to intimidation tactics are from an interview that originally appeared in *The Guardian* on 21 August 1990, by Patrick Laurence.

Quotes by Hani on pages 219–220 are from a supplement to the *Financial Mail* published on 28 September 1990.

## CHAPTER 12: THE ASSASSINATION

References are generally cited within the text.

The summary of the appeal of Clive Derby-Lewis and Janusz Walus, including comments, inferences and information used in this chapter, can be downloaded on www.saflii.org/za/cases/ZASCA/1994/189.html

The lines from Nomakhwezi Hani's poetry were taken from reports of her funeral at St Francis Catholic Church in Reiger Park, Boksburg, which was attended by dignitaries including Jacob Zuma, Aziz Pahad, Joe Modise and Blade Nzimande. The SAPA news agency disseminated this information on 17 March 2001.

The application by Derby-Lewis and Walus to the amnesty committee of the TRC, which we have also cited and interpreted from in this chapter, is most easily found at www.justice.gov.za/trc/media/1998/

The radio and television reports cited are in the SABC audio and video archive, which we accessed at length.

The reference to Peace Desk spokesperson Mondli Gungubele appeared in the *Sunday Times* on 11 April 1993.

Esther Waugh's tribute to Hani appeared in the *Sunday Star* of 11 April 1993. Other articles by Waugh appeared in *The Star* in the week of 12 April 1993, and were included in Naidoo's collection and *The Star*'s archive.

Excerpts from conversations with Tadeusz and Wanda Walus come from

NOTES

the Peter Malherbe interviews in the *Sunday Times* of 18 April 1993.
The reference to alleged bank robbers claiming Tokyo Sexwale and Hani had been involved in their heist, comes from the April 1993 issue of the ANC's journal, *Mayibuye*.

## EPILOGUE 2023

1 'South Africa Unemployment Rate', Trading Economics, July 2022, https://tradingeconomics.com/south-africa/unemployment-rate.
2 Staff Writer, 'How much money you need to be in the richest 1% in South Africa – and how you compare to others', BusinessTech, 5 January 2022, https://businesstech.co.za/news/wealth/548810/how-much-money-you-need-to-be-in-the-richest-1-in-south-africa-and-how-you-compare-to-others/.
3 The South Park Cemetery, to which we referred in the first edition of this book, was renamed Thomas Titus Nkobi Memorial Park by the Ekurhuleni Metro Municipality in 2010. Nkobi was a Zimbabwean-born ANC leader and lifelong anti-apartheid activist who was the party's Treasurer-General and an ANC MP at the time of his death in September 1994.
4 Zuma, the ANC's then Intelligence chief, was the first NEC member to arrive at the then Jan Smuts International Airport, off a flight from Lusaka, in March 1990. Zuma arrived as a 'scout' to see what the response would really be like before Hani and others flew home a few weeks later.
5 Naledi Shange, 'I'm sorry I killed Hani. I now reject apartheid and have gone back to my Catholic roots', TimesLive, 7 December 2021, https://www.timeslive.co.za/news/south-africa/2021-12-07-im-sorry-i-killed-hani-i-now-reject-apartheid-and-have-gone-back-to-my-catholic-roots-says-janusz-walus/.
6 Kaylynn Palm, 'Concourt reserves judgment in Janusz Walus parole bid', EWN, 22 February 2022, https://ewn.co.za/2022/02/22/concourt-reserves-judgment-in-janusz-walus-parole-bid.
7 Jeanette Chabalala, 'Janusz Walus not entitled to be released on parole, lawyer tells ConCourt', News24, 22 February 2022, https://www.news24.

com/news24/southafrica/news/janusz-walus-not-entitled-to-be-released-on-parole-lawyer-tells-concourt-20220222.
8 John Carlin, 'Hani suspect a key figure of far right', *The Independent*, 18 April 1993, https://www.independent.co.uk/news/world/hani-suspect-a-key-figure-of-far-right-former-south-african-conservative-mp-arrested-in-anc-murder-inquiry-is-president-of-controversial-londonbased-thinktank-1456153.html.
9 Edward Ongweso, Jr, 'The Second Assassination of Martin Luther King Jr: White-washing a Legacy of Dissent', genius.com, 20 January 2014, https://genius.com/Edward-ongweso-jr-the-second-assassination-of-martin-luther-king-whitewashing-a-legacy-of-dissent-annotated.
10 Bobby Wilcox, 'The corruption of the ANC', Socialist Resistance, 11 August 2012, https://socialistresistance.org/the-corruption-of-the-anc/3801.
11 'P Mlambo-Ngcuka: Anniversary of death of Chris Hani', address delivered by the Deputy President, Ms Phumzile Mlambo-Ngcuka, at a banquet to honour the 13th anniversary of the death of Chris Thembisile Hani, Regent Hall, East London 8 April 2006, https://www.gov.za/p-mlambo-ngcuka-anniversary-death-chris-hani.
12 Cronin, a member of the SACP and a former member of the ANC NEC, was Deputy Minister of Public Works at the time.
13 The *Mail & Guardian*'s editorial on 25 October 2006 offered clarification on this point: 'In 1994, Mbeki, then ANC deputy president, authored an internal party document titled "From Resistance to Reconstruction: Tasks of the ANC in the New Epoch of the Democratic Transformation – Unmandated Reflections". Mbeki said "forces" would try to "destroy the ANC from within …".' In 2006, 'debates and power struggles [raged] in the ANC and the alliance structures in an atmosphere of suspicion, fear and treachery'. *Mail & Guardian*, 25 October 2006, 'Do not look where you fell, but where you slipped', https://mg.co.za/article/2006-10-25-do-not-look-where-you-fell-but-slipped/.
14 Unathi Nkanjeni, 'The bar is very low – what ANC veteran Mavuso Msimang thinks of party presidency battles', TimesLive, 17 October 2022, https://www.timeslive.co.za/politics/2022-10-17-the-bar-is-very-

low-what-anc-veteran-mavuso-msimang-thinks-of-party-presidency-battles/.

15 Press conference, National Press Club, Washington, DC, 24 April 1991, broadcast on C-Span II, htttps://blf.org.za/2019/07/.

16 The *Boksburg Advertiser*, which has covered the issue more than any other media, wrote in December 2020, 'The project to convert the house into a museum will cost about R50-million', https://boksburgadvertiser.co.za/401263/chris-hani-museum-expected-to-open-next-year/.

17 Press conference, National Press Club, Washington, DC, 24 April 1991.

# INDEX

**A**
African National Congress (ANC) ix, x-xi, 16, 21, 23, 28, 29, 36, 37, 41, 42, 43, 45-46, 49-50, 58, 68, 69-70, 73-74, 75, 76-77, 80, 84, 85, 86, 88, 89, 93, 106, 112, 114, 116-118, 120, 122, 123, 128-129, 132, 133, 134-135, 136, 137, 140-142, 147, 150, 156-157, 158, 159, 160, 161, 162, 164-165, 167-169, 172, 178, 179-183, 186, 191, 200-201, 209-210, 211, 213-214, 217, 220, 222, 223-225, 226, 227, 227-229, 249, 263, 264, 266, 271, 273, 331-332, 333, 334, 338-345
Afrikaner Weerstandsbeweging (AWB) 262, 267, 272, 275
Alexander, Ray 35, 42
Amin, Idi 203
Amnesty International 183
ANC Youth League (ANCYL) 24, 33, 112, 270, 272
April, James 42, 99, 104, 120, 121, 285
Azanian People's Liberation Army (APLA) 86

**B**
Balfour, Ngconde 294, 295
Barsel, Esther 277
Basotho Congress Party (BCP) 128, 133, 134
Basotho National Party (BNP) 128
Basotholand People's Party 86
Battersby, John 152, 153
Benyon, Jack 32, 33
Biko, Steve Bantu 135
Bizos, George 240, 246, 275
Black Consciousness Movement (BCM) 107, 134, 135, 136, 137
Bonga, Thami 122
Bopape, Stanza 177
Boraine, Alex 156
Botha, Pik 201, 221, 253
Botha, PW 152, 158, 166, 170-171, 175, 227
Botha, Simon 195
Brezhnev, Leonid 61
Brittain, Victoria 278
Brynard, Karen 253
Bunting, Brian 42
Buqa, Charles 43
Buthelezi, Mangosuthu 33, 159

**C**
Callinicos, Luli 13, 30, 71, 89, 131, 136, 273-274

# INDEX

Carlin, John 264, 269
Castro, Fidel 173, 232, 269, 277
Central Intelligence Organisation (CIO) 96
Chikerema, James 88, 101
Chiliza, Tsitsi 177-178
Chortley, Keith 244-245
Clark, Edwin 258
Clinton, Bill 161, 244
Coertze, Marius 292, 293-294
Coetzee, Colonel Eben 144
Coetzee, Dirk 146
Coloured People's Organisation 47
Communist Party of South Africa 36
Congress of South African Trade Unions (COSATU) 10, 24, 84, 200, 228, 269, 333, 336
Congress of the People xi, 16
Conservative Party (CP) 226, 227, 232, 240, 253, 256, 266-267, 290
Convention for a Democratic South Africa (CODESA) 226, 264, 273, 333, 334
Cotton, Joseph 111, 310
Crocker, Chester 159
Cronin, Jeremy 266

D
Dabengwa, Dumisa 95, 98
Dadoo, Yusuf 75, 116
Darroll, Keith 246
De Bruin, Sergeant Karel 144, 145
De Klerk, Frederik Willem (FW) x, 187, 191, 207, 210, 211, 218, 223, 226-227, 230, 232, 264, 266, 272, 275, 290
De Kock, Eugene 177
De Vos, Hennie 247
Democratic Alliance 21
Derby-Lewis, Clive 231, 236-237, 240, 243, 245-248, 251, 252, 254-256, 257, 258, 259, 261, 266, 267, 273, 290, 291-295
Derby-Lewis, Gaye 236, 237, 239, 240, 245, 247, 248, 251, 253, 254-256, 257, 258, 273, 290
Dhlakama, Afonso 171
Dikeledi, Paul 177
Dingaan-Stofile, Bususiwe 229-230

Dlodlo, Theophilus 177
Dos Santos, José Eduardo 159, 173, 201
Douglas Commission 187
Du Bois, WEB 134
Du Plessis, Tim 253
Du Rant, Elizabeth 246
Du Rant, Lionel 246, 258
Du Toit, Andries 261-262
Duarte, Jessie 6, 217
Dube, John 88, 99, 103, 106, 108, 281
Duma, Edgar 77
Dumagude, Diliza 196
Duthie, Anne 276-289
Dyasop, Luthando Nicholas 201

E
Ebrahim, Ebrahim Ismail 153
Eddings, Jerelyn 232, 265-266
Ellis, Stephen 187
Eloff, Judge CF 290

F
Fanon, Frantz 134
February, Basil 81, 96, 97, 112, 117, 124
Filling, Brian 278
First, Ruth 28, 175
Firth, Shirley 274
Fourie, Johan 259
Frente de Libertação de Moçambique (FRELIMO) 75, 76, 86, 92, 94, 172, 178, 192

G
Gagarin, Boston 98
Gevisser, Mark 33, 210
Giap, General Vo Nguyen 141
Goldberg, Denis 37, 43, 44, 51, 245
Goldberg, Esmé 51
Goldstone, Richard 230, 253, 268
Gottschalk, Bernard 50
Gqabi, Joe 28, 149, 175-176
Gqozo, Oupa 229, 230
Graeff, Peter 14
Grimbeek, Anton 254
Grootboom, Noxolo 242, 261
Group of Eight 121-124
Guevara, Che 44

Gumede, William Mervyn 155
Gungubele, Mondli 260, 263
Gwala, Harry 216

H
Haneae, Andile 205-206, 208
Hani, Aluta 7, 9, 12, 18, 19
Hani, Christopher Nkosana 2, 3, 25
Hani, Cleopatra Thunyiswa (Cleo) 7-8, 9, 12, 13, 17, 18-19, 20, 21
Hani, Gilbert 1, 4, 5, 15, 30, 31, 33, 38, 41-42, 129-130, 250
Hani, Limpho 7, 10, 12, 17, 80, 126, 131, 142-143, 144, 145, 148, 150-151, 205-206, 260, 266, 270, 274, 275, 276, 279, 291, 294, 295
Hani, Lindiwe 10, 12, 205, 241, 243
Hani, Martin Tembisile ('Chris') ix, x, xi, 2, 3, 235
   ANC 29, 31, 45-46, 49-50, 132, 136-137, 140, 142, 147, 154, 160, 161, 191, 223-225, 249, 273, 288, 331-332
   Angola 171, 179, 182, 183-187, 188, 197, 199, 202-203,
   Anne Duthie 276-289
   armed struggle 36-37, 38, 50, 70, 71, 108, 125, 135, 136, 152-153, 157, 165-166, 173-174, 210, 212, 213, 217, 271, 288
   assassination attempts 143, 144-146, 148-149, 231, 232, 251, 287
   assassination x, 23, 208, 231, 236-238, 240-243, 244-245, 248, 249-252, 256, 259, 260-264, 265-266, 267, 268, 271-273, 275, 289, 290, 295, 331-332
   bodyguards 8, 143, 144, 200, 201-208, 209, 234-235, 251, 254, 260-261, 262-263
   Cape Town 30, 40-41, 42, 47-49, 50
   childhood 4, 5-6, 11, 12, 30, 74, 198
   Ciskei march 227-230
   clandestine work 23, 35, 45-46, 47, 127, 131-133, 136-140, 172, 214
   Communism 15, 31, 35, 36, 61, 74, 75, 155-156, 187, 269, 277, 287
   *Dawn* 70, 74
   early education 5, 13, 14, 17, 25
   exile 5, 40, 50-53, 56, 58

family life 2, 4-5, 142-143, 144, 147, 234, 262, 274, 279
football 263-264, 281
Fort Hare 33-35, 38
friendships 8, 207, 274, 281, 282
guerrilla warfare 92, 94
ideology 31, 35, 61, 65-66, 81, 155, 156, 219, 234, 268-269
influence of religion 14-16, 33, 81
jailed in Botswana 79, 104-105, 106-110, 113, 283
Kongwa 69, 70, 71-72, 74, 75-76, 77, 78, 79
legacy 23-24, 233, 294
Lesotho 19, 124, 126-127, 129-133, 134, 136-140, 141, 142-151, 210
Lobatse conference 49, 50, 70
love of reading 70-71, 80, 81-82, 108-109, 110
Lovedale College 25-27, 28, 29, 30, 32-33
Lusaka 78-79, 86, 87-88, 94-95, 96, 113, 125, 147, 172, 178, 197, 205-208, 212, 279, 280-282, 285-286
Lusaka Manifesto 118-119
Luthuli Detachment 89, 93, 98, 100-101, 103-105
marriage 126, 276, 286-287
Memorandum 77, 110-113, 114-116, 117, 119-120, 124-125, 184, 185, 284, 285, 338-345
MK 36-37, 38, 43, 61, 69, 70, 76, 78-79, 84, 87, 112, 132, 141, 147, 153, 157, 159, 160, 165-166, 171, 172, 178-179, 183-187, 191-193, 197, 200, 201-205, 212, 213, 214, 219, 260, 269
Morogoro conference 115, 116, 119-120
negotiations 154, 155, 156, 213, 217, 226, 234, 257-258, 333-337
policing and security 218, 219-220, 225-226, 232, 267-268, 269
recruitment and training 136-138, 141, 213
release of prisoners 223
return from exile 6, 7, 21, 207, 209-211, 214, 266, 288-289
running 19, 72, 113, 143, 202, 205, 216, 235, 262

SACP 29, 37, 61, 74-75, 137, 155-156, 160, 161, 215-216, 226, 234, 255, 269, 273, 277, 278, 333-337
suspension 120, 285
Tanzania 68-79, 126, 200
teaching 74, 233
trains in East Germany 127
trains in the USSR 34, 59-67, 235
Uganda 201, 203, 204-205
Umtata 208, 218, 221-222
Wankie campaign 80-81, 88, 89-90, 92-101, 103-105, 106-108, 113-114, 192, 283, 285-286
Winnie Mandela 214-215
Hani, Mary 1, 2, 4, 5, 15, 18, 25, 38, 206, 250
Hani, Mbuyiselo Victor 2, 3, 19, 22, 25, 250
Hani, Milton 42
Hani, Neo 12, 143, 145-146, 150, 205
Hani, Nolusapho 1, 2, 9, 16-17, 19, 21, 22, 250
Hani, Nomakhwezi 12, 145, 205, 239, 240-241, 242-243, 250-251, 263, 275
Harmse, Retha 237-238, 242, 261
Hartzenberg, Ferdi 267
Hitchens, Peter 262
Ho Chi Minh 92
Hodgson, Jack 43
Holmes, Mike 254
Holomisa, Bantu 21, 204-205, 208, 212, 218, 221-222, 228, 249, 263, 274
Huna, Bernard 45

I
Inkatha Freedom Party (IFP) 159, 225, 226, 270
Institute for Democratic Alternatives in South Africa (IDASA) 156
Ismail, Aboobaker 156-157

J
Jele, Josiah 78, 92, 136
Johnson, Shaun 221
Jonathan, Leabua 128, 133-134
Jordan, Pallo 8, 23, 154, 207, 249

K
Kanhema, Newton 273

Kasrils, Ronnie 127, 153, 192, 218, 227, 229, 230, 274
Kaunda, Kenneth 55, 73, 87, 118, 161, 172
Keitsing, Fish 49, 53
Kekana, Simon 29
Kemp, Arthur 254-256, 257, 258
Kgosana, Philip 41
Khama, Sir Seretse 108
Khan, Sam 48
Khumalo, Bafana 265, 270
Kodesh, Wolfie 43, 109, 119, 125, 131, 184, 185-186, 187
Kondile, Sizwe 146, 175
Kondleka, Mzwakhe 43
Kotane, Moses, 64, 66, 88, 111, 341
Kriel, Hernus 265, 268
Krushchev, Nikita 60-61
Kubheka, Buel 270
Kubukeli, Pumlani 201

L
La Guma, Jimmy 35
Lagu, Lennox 69, 78, 133, 193-194, 196
Leeson, Joyce 84
Lembede, Anton 33
Lerutla, Racheal 245, 259-260, 261
Lesotho Liberation Army (LLA) 128, 145
Loots, Hermanus 154, 180, 186, 187-188
Losa, Elijah 43, 45
Lumumba, Patrice 32
Luthuli, Albert 32, 36, 93

M
Maake, Cassius 140, 153, 177, 189
Mabandla, Brigitte 182
Mabhida, Moses 69, 73, 90, 160
Mabitse, Edwin 195
Mabizela, Stanley 200
Mabula, Lefty 87
Macau, Patrick 177
Machel, Samora, 76, 161, 172, 192
Madlala, Nozizwe 278
Mafikeng, Elizabeth 42, 129
Mafolo, Jabu 195
Magubane, Ben 79-80, 81, 101-102, 110, 205
Maharaj, Mac 145, 154, 218, 253
Mahlangu, Solomon 149, 172

Makalima, Mac 33
Makiwane, Ambrose 69, 78, 121, 123
Makiwane, Tennyson 78, 90, 121, 123, 124
Malan, DF 16
Malan, Magnus 222
Maledza, Zaba 195
Malherbe, Brigadier Frans 244, 258, 259
Malherbe, Peter 251
Mali, Thami 197-199
Malindi, Zola 45
Manamela, Buti 274
Mandela, Nelson Rohlihlala 6-7, 33, 36, 43, 93, 102, 118, 161, 183, 211, 212, 217, 218, 221, 224, 235, 238, 248-250, 253-254, 264, 265, 272, 273, 275
Mandela, Winnie 214-215, 249
Manga, Amrit 236, 259
Mantashe, Gwede 278
Manuel, Trevor 223
Maphatsoe, Emmanuel 201-205
Maphoto, Ike 72-73
Marcus, Gill 245, 260
Marks, JB 69, 73, 74, 75, 88, 90
Masekela, Barbara 80
Masekela, Hugh 4
Maseko, Vuyisile 196
Masemula, Sam, 54, 55, 56
Masire, Quett 33
Masondo, Andrew 190
Mass Democratic Movement (MDM) 137, 161, 221
Matanzima, Kaiser 33, 42, 46, 124, 130, 221
Mathe, Soyisile 196
Mathebula, Sipho 195
Matlou, Jonas 115, 121
Matokoane, Pule 205, 206-207, 208
Matshaya, Mfanelo 201
Matthews, Joe 90
Mbali, Jackson 74
Mbeki, Govan 27, 28, 29, 33, 35, 42, 50, 58, 210, 249
Mbeki, Moeletsi 23, 265, 268-269
Mbeki, Thabo ix, x, xi, 22, 23, 33, 70, 77-78, 112, 140, 154-155, 156, 160, 161, 186-187, 210, 224, 265, 269, 272, 294, 344
Mbele, George 121
Mbokodo 90, 113, 179, 183, 186, 195, 196, 199

Mbongwa, Sibusiso Sihle 164-165
McBride, Robert 226
Meyer, Roelf 273
Mhlongo, Kate 195
Mini, Vuyisile 112
Miyela, Philemon 77
MK Military Veterans Association (MKMVA) 24
Modise, Joe 51, 53-54, 62, 69, 78, 97, 111, 112, 115, 140, 160, 165, 190, 199, 269
Moerane, Marumo 293
Mokaba, Peter 272
Mokhehle, Ntsu 133-134
Mokoena, Julius 195
Moloi, Lehlohonolo Lambert 129, 132, 133, 138, 139, 147
Molotsi, Zakes 223
Mompati, Ruth 97, 108
More, Thabo 341
Morena, Kgotso 195, 196
Morodi, Graham 94
Moroka, Sidwell 195
Moshoeshoe I 128
Moshoeshoe II 128, 149
Motau, Sello 153
Motaung, Grace 195
Motloung, Palesa 264-265
Motsepe, Andries 98-99
Motsoaledi, Elias 43
Motswane, Eizabeth 247, 258
Motumi, Tsepo 225
Motwa, Bongani 195
Moumakwe, Radilori 62-63
Movimento Popular de Libertação de Angola (MPLA) 75, 86, 94, 178
Mpanza, Justice 77
Mpetha, Oscar 42
Mphahlele, Zeke 79
Mqobi, Tozama 294-295
Mqota, Themba 121
Mqotsi, Livingstone 109-110, 111, 112, 113, 115, 139
Msimang, Mavuso 76
Mswati III 249
Mthembu, Enoch 265, 269, 270
Mthembu, Patrick 52, 53
Mthembu, Sipho 115

# INDEX

Mthintso, Thenjiwe 136, 204
Mti, Linda 130, 135-136
Mtshali, Eric 80, 87
Mugabe, Robert 33, 86, 176
Mxenge, Griffiths 135, 175
Mxenge, Victoria 177
Mxwaku, Mjojo 97, 100
Mzamane, Mbulelo 80, 130-131
Mzamane, Nthoana 80
Mzima, Jabu 177
Mzima, Petrus 177
Mzonke, Faldon 47, 48

N
Naidoo, Phyllis 8, 30, 32, 34, 146, 148, 156, 174, 210
NAT *see* Mbokodo
National Party (NP) 28, 152, 157, 158, 171, 222, 224, 225, 226-227, 232, 266, 267, 275
National Union of South African Students (NUSAS) 112, 313
Ndaba, Macbeth 265
Ndlovu, Gasson 96-97
Ndzamela, Ndibulele 201
Neto, Agostinho 159, 172, 173
Ngakane, Pascal 122
Ngobese, Castro 274
Ngudle, Looksmart 43, 45, 51, 58
Nhanyane, Solly 270
Nhlanhla, Joe 260
Njamela, Felinyaniso 43
Nkadimeng, John 153
Nkadimeng, Vernon 177
Nkobi, Thomas 10, 79, 80, 88, 90, 115, 136
Nkomo, Joshua 86
Nkosi, Leonard 121
Nokwe, Duma 111, 114, 115, 341-342
Nondala, Marwanqana 5, 249-250
Nontshatsha, Mncedi 43
Nqini, Zola 147, 149, 175
Nxumalo, Henry 28
Nyanda, Siphiwe 153, 260
Nyanda, Zweli 177
Nyembe, Dorothy 123
Nyerere, Julius 68, 69, 73, 74, 76, 172
Nyimbana, Alban 5, 13, 14, 198

Nzimande, Blade 10, 215, 273, 274
Nzo, Alfred 75, 90, 123, 136 149, 200

O
Organisation of African Unity (OAU) 61, 62, 71, 104, 108, 118, 220
Owen, Ken 253

P
Pahad, Aziz 180
Pahad, Essop 277
Pan Africanist Congress (PAC) 21, 29-30, 41, 80, 86, 96, 115, 123, 133, 134, 211, 226, 270-271
Pather, Dennis 210
Perez de Cuellar, Dr Javier 173
Phokanoka, Lawrence 61, 99
Phungulwa, Sipho 200-201
Piliso, Mzwai 90, 113, 115, 179, 190
Poqo 86, 96
Preller, Judge Ferdi 293
Prinsloo, Hendrik 143, 144, 145
Progressive Federal Party 156

Q
Qolombeni, Mahelele 5, 13
Qumbela, Mountain 43

R
Ralebitso, Matumo 149
Ramaphosa, Cyril 249, 272
Ramatolo, Ernest 144, 145
Ras, Maria 239, 251-252
Reagan, Ronald 159, 161
Reid-Daly, Major-General Ron 103
Relly, Gavin 154
Resha, Robert 90, 122
Resistência Nacional Moçambicana (RENAMO) 162, 171
Rhodesian African Rifles (RAR) 89, 101, 103
Ribeiro, Fabian 177
Ribeiro, Florence 177
Robinson, Freek 264
Rudolph, Piet 'Skiet' 245

## S

Sachs, Albie 43, 44, 50, 70, 102-103, 150, 151, 177, 199
Sartre, Jean-Paul 44, 58
Savimbi, Jonas 171
Schoon, Katryn 177
Sechaba, Tsepo 187
Sekamane, Limpho *see* Hani, Limpho
Sekamane, Ntathi 10
Sekamane, Nthoana 131
Sekamane, Tjaoaone 131
Sekhukhune, William 31
Selassie, Haile 61-62
Selous Scouts 103, 197
Senghor Léopold 134
Senna, Simon 51, 62
September, Dulcie 177
Setlapelo, OK 122
Sexwale, Lesetja 147
Sexwale, Tokyo 10, 147, 214, 230, 243, 244, 260, 261, 268
Shangase, Nomava 182
Shilowa, Sam (Mbhazima) 260, 277-278
Shope, Mark 53, 55, 66, 189
Shubin, Vladimir 92, 128
Sibeko, Archie 41, 45, 46, 47, 48, 49, 50, 51, 52-53, 57, 58, 66, 83-85, 86-88, 285
Sibeko, Solly 194-195
Sigxashe, Sizakele 180
Simelane, David 124
Simons, Jack 42, 79-80, 81, 110, 114, 125, 189, 284
Simons, Ray 115, 125, 284, 286
Sisulu, Walter x, 33, 52, 210, 221, 224, 245
Sisulu, Zwelakhe 52
Sixishe, Daniel 134
Sizani, Sandile 260
Skinner, James 56, 57
Skweyiya Commission 182-183, 186
Skweyiya, L 182
Skweyiya, Zola 45, 56
Slabbert, Frederik van Zyl 156, 212
Slovo, Joe 64, 69, 91, 116, 117, 127, 132, 140, 153, 160, 161, 216, 249, 253, 254, 273
Smith, Ernest 262
Smith, Gavin 246
Smith, Ian 93
Smith, John 269, 289
Smith, Magda 238, 262
Sobukwe, Robert 29, 33, 41
Society of Young Africa (SOYA) 29
South African Communist Party (SACP) ix, 5, 10, 24, 29, 35, 37, 42, 50, 64, 74-75, 90-91, 121, 122, 123-124, 125, 128-129, 137, 154-155, 160, 161, 200, 211, 215-216, 226, 227, 234, 266, 268, 273, 277-278, 295, 333-337
South African Congress of Trade Unions (SACTU) 42, 47, 141, 177
South African Institute for Race Relations 164
South African Students Congress (SASCO) 24
South African Students Organisation (SASO) 107
South West Africa People's Organisation (SWAPO) 75, 76, 86, 172, 174
Soze, Bogart 153
Strachan, Harold 43
Stuart Commission 180-182, 184, 186, 192, 194, 195, 196
Stuart, James *see* Loots, Hermanus

## T

Tambo, Adelaide 245
Tambo, Oliver (OR) x, 33, 37, 58, 68, 69, 73, 75, 79, 80, 83-84, 87, 88, 93-95, 97, 98, 101, 102, 108, 109, 114, 115, 123, 124, 133, 134-135, 136, 150, 154, 157, 158, 159, 164, 167-169, 174-175, 176, 178, 188, 192, 210, 211, 224, 225, 245, 249, 252, 269
Tanganyika African National Union (TANU) 68
Tarshish, Jack 50-51
Taylor, Gene 246
Taylor, Peter 271
Terre'Blanche, Eugene 267, 272
Thaanyane, Nkopane 291, 292, 293, 294
Thema, Moss 195
Thornycroft, Peta 273
Thunyiswa, Judy 5, 17, 18, 19
Tladi, Shadrack 111, 310
Tokota, BR 292, 293

# INDEX

Treurnicht, Dr Andries 266, 267
Truth and Reconciliation Commission (TRC) 143, 145, 146, 157, 163, 174, 175, 179, 185, 186-187, 200, 201, 215, 238, 240, 243, 246, 248, 258, 267, 290
Tshali, Lennox 153
Tshwete, Steve 8, 207, 227
Turok, Ben 43
Tyeku, James 47, 48

## U

Umkhonto we Sizwe (MK) ix, 5, 36, 37, 43, 51, 58, 62, 64, 65, 66, 68, 69, 70, 72, 75-76, 78, 84, 87-88, 89, 90, 91, 92-93, 93, 94, 95, 96, 97, 98, 103, 106, 112, 132, 141, 147, 150, 153, 160-161, 162, 163, 165, 166, 168, 171, 172, 177, 178-183, 184, 185, 188-191, 191-196, 197-198, 201-205, 212, 214, 218, 221, 222, 260, 346-352
UN High Commissioner for Refugees 136
UNITA 171, 172-173, 184-185, 189, 192, 202
United Democratic Front (UDF) 223
United Democratic Movement 21
United National Independence Party (UNIP) 55, 56, 57
Unity Movement 29, 80

## V

Van der Merwe, Johan 265
Van Rensburg, General Nic 146
Van Wyk, Spyker 47
Van Zyl, MC 254
Vavi, Zwelinzima 10, 24, 84
Venter, Faan 246, 247-248, 258
Venter, Maureen 248
Verwoerd, HF 27, 36, 93

Viktor, Colonel JJ (Johan) 144
Viljoen, General Constand 149
Villa-Vicencio, Charles 6, 14, 15, 155, 182, 185, 187
Visagie, Andre 267
Vorster, John 93, 118, 133-134, 170

## W

Walus, Janusz x, 231, 232, 234, 235, 236-239, 241-242, 243-244, 247, 248, 251-253, 254, 256, 257, 258, 259, 261, 265, 266, 267, 270, 272, 273, 290, 294, 295
Walus, Tadeusz 239, 251
Walus, Wanda 239, 251
Watson, Ronnie 260
Waugh, Esther 264
Webster, David 177
Williams, Teddy 185
Wina, Sikota 56, 57

## Y

Young Communist League (YCL) 24, 274

## Z

Zembe, Zola 343
Zimbabwe African National Liberation Army (ZANLA) 96
Zimbabwe African National Union (ZANU) 76, 86
Zimbabwe African People's Union (ZAPU) 76, 79, 84, 85, 88, 92, 93, 96, 281
Zimbabwe People's Revolutionary Army (ZIPRA) 84, 95, 96, 97, 98, 103, 106
Zulu, Thami 199
Zuma, Jacob ix, 150, 153, 294

www.ingramcontent.com/pod-product-compliance
Lightning Source LLC
Chambersburg PA
CBHW070958160426
43193CB00012B/1821